T0399602

SCIENCE AND VISUAL CULTURE IN GREAT BRITAIN IN THE LONG NINETEENTH CENTURY

Science and Visual Culture in Great Britain in the Long Nineteenth Century

General Editor: Barbara Larson

Volume I
Zoology
Edited by Diana Donald

Volume II
Marine Life
Edited by Kathleen Davidson

Volume III
Physics
Edited by Iwan Morus

Volume IV
Evolutionism
Edited by Jonathan Smith and Barbara Larson

Volume V
The Natural Science Museum
Edited by Kathleen Davidson

Volume VI
Health and the Body
Edited by Fay Brauer

SCIENCE AND VISUAL CULTURE IN GREAT BRITAIN IN THE LONG NINETEENTH CENTURY

General Editor: Barbara Larson

Edited by Diana Donald

Volume I
Zoology

LONDON AND NEW YORK

First published 2025
by Routledge
4 Park Square, Milton Park, Abingdon, Oxon OX14 4RN

and by Routledge
605 Third Avenue, New York, NY 10158

Routledge is an imprint of the Taylor & Francis Group, an informa business

British Library Cataloguing-in-Publication Data
A catalogue record for this book is available from the British Library

Library of Congress Cataloging-in-Publication Data
Names: Donald, Diana, editor.
Title: Zoology / edited by Diana Donald.
Description: Abingdon, Oxon ; New York, NY : Routledge, 2024. | Series: Science and visual culture in Great Britain in the long nineteenth century ; Volume 1. | Includes bibliographical references and index.
Identifiers: LCCN 2024018490 (print) | LCCN 2024018491 (ebook) | ISBN 9780367620776 (v. 1 hardback) | ISBN 9781003107835 (v. 1 ebook)
Subjects: LCSH: Zoology—Great Britain—History—19th century. | Art—Great Britain—History—19th century. | Art and society—Great Britain—History—19th century.
Classification: LCC QL21.G7 Z66 2024 (print) | LCC QL21.G7 (ebook) | DDC 591.941—dc23/eng/20240506
LC record available at https://lccn.loc.gov/2024018490
LC ebook record available at https://lccn.loc.gov/2024018491

ISBN: 978-0-367-62077-6 hbk (vol I)
ISBN: 978-1-003-10783-5 ebk (vol I)

DOI: 10.4324/9781003107835

Typeset in Times New Roman
by Apex CoVantage, LLC

CONTENTS

VOLUME I ZOOLOGY

PART IV
Natural Science and the Lay Public: Education, Museology, Spectacle, Entertainment 515

ACKNOWLEDGEMENTS

I am most grateful to the series editor, Barbara Larson, and to Routledge's Simon Alexander for their patient guidance throughout the development of the project, and to Barbara for her constructive and judicious editing of the text. Christopher Christie, June Holmes, Conor Jameson, and Catherine Sidwell have also given me valued help in various ways. Trevor Donald has been, as always, a kind and encouraging advisor.

James Wilson's letter to Thomas Bewick (Chapter 6) is published by permission of Tyne and Wear Archives and Museums.

Passages from John Hancock's manuscript correspondence in the Hancock Archive, Newcastle (Chapters 16, 33.1, and 71) are published courtesy of the Natural History Society of Northumbria Archive, Great North Museum: Hancock, Newcastle upon Tyne.

The letters from the 4th Earl of Aberdeen to Edwin Landseer (Chapter 36) are published with the permission of the Marquess of Aberdeen and of the Victoria and Albert Museum.

Friedrich Keyl's manuscript notes on his conversations with Edwin Landseer (Chapter 42) are in the Royal Archives at Windsor Castle: RA VIC/ADDX14. They are published in this work by the permission of His Majesty King Charles III.

A letter from Briton Riviere to Elinor Mary Bonham-Carter in the Darwin Correspondence archive, DCP-LETT-7833 (Chapter 52) is included here by permission of Cambridge University Press.

INTRODUCTION

In Victorian times, it was customary for the president of the Royal Academy to invite the leaders of the scientific world to a grand banquet that celebrated the opening of the Academy's annual art exhibition. In 1877, it was the turn of the leading botanist Joseph Hooker – Charles Darwin's closest friend and now president of the Royal Society – to respond to the Academy's 'toast of Science':

> Dr. Hooker . . . happily performed what at first sight would seem a hard task under the circumstances. Dr. Hooker showed that the incongruity between art and science was only apparent; that art lends valuable aid to science, and that all true art must really be based on scientific principles; and that moreover the two have this in common, that success is unattainable in neither unless by close observation, enthusiasm, and the skilful exercise of the imagination.[1]

Thomas Huxley, lecturing 'On Science and Art in Relation to Education' in 1882, agreed with Hooker. Learning to draw developed one's powers of accurate observation, while study of great art provided the scientist with an intellectual and imaginative stimulus. As a morphologist, Huxley took 'a thorough aesthetic pleasure' in 'tracing out the unity in variety of the infinitely diversified structures of animals and plants' – 'That is where the province of art overlays and embraces the province of intellect'.[2]

The nineteenth century was indeed a period when the interplay between natural science, especially zoology, and visual culture was very marked, with knowledge and inspiration flowing in both directions. As the texts chosen for this collection of sources will show, naturalists needed artists to illustrate their books, bringing into play the 'close observation' and accuracy of depiction mentioned by Hooker. Through 'skilful exercise of the imagination', artists could also align with natural scientists in evoking the life of animals in the wild; in fact, the notion of 'survival of the fittest' in a hostile environment was vividly pictured by painters and illustrators some decades before the publication of Darwin's *On the Origin of Species*. From the 1870s onwards, the analysis of nature's beauties of colour and form and theories about their causation preoccupied entomologists and ornithologists, and these qualities were of equal interest to philosophical writers on art. Many of the latter came to believe that animals themselves had an aesthetic sense, transmitted through evolution to humankind. Thus, education of the public in the new scientific ideas – an urgent undertaking in the later nineteenth century – could draw on a wealth of visual material that represented animals as creatures with active minds, dynamic energy, varied beauties, and infinitely subtle adaptations to their environment.

THE VICTORIAN TASTE FOR ZOOLOGY AND ZOOMORPHISM

The Victorians did not assimilate zoology only from the pages of books. They chose to create a domestic ambience that was strikingly – almost obsessively – filled with animals and their material remains, or with representations of them in pictures by Landseer and other contemporary artists. Leaving aside live dogs and cats, caged birds, and drawing-room aquaria, there was a fashion for collecting specimens of seashells, insects, birds' eggs, and other natural curiosities, to be displayed in cabinets. The upper classes would often ornament their country houses and hunting lodges with sporting trophies such as the heads of stags or of tropical animals. Even objects of use were sometimes made of animal parts: the famous taxidermist Rowland Ward supplied 'Wardian Furniture' in the form of 'Zoological lamps' supported by stuffed tropical birds or monkeys, a liqueur stand made from an elephant's foot, and a 'grizzly bear holding a tray in its paws and utilised as a "dumb waiter"'.[3] The dress and ornamental objects belonging to wealthy people also made lavish use of tropical birds' feathers, beetle wing cases, hides, tortoiseshell, sealskin, and ivory, as well as a variety of furs.[4] In the popular journals that often lay on these people's tables, the latest arrivals at the London Zoo and the latest pictures of animal life in the wild were featured as large wood engravings: these were sometimes pull-out supplements intended for scrapbooks, albums, or framing. Zoological reality shaded into fantasy: John Tenniel's illustrations to Lewis Carroll's *Alice* books, with their alarming Jabberwock monster, revivified dodo and eccentric talking beasts, shared their idiom with the zoomorphic cartoons in *Punch*. There statesman William Gladstone might be caricatured by Linley Sambourne as Sir Edwin Landseer's famous heroic rutting stag in his painting *Monarch of the Glen* (1851), and Sambourne's 'feathered ladies', slaves to a cruel fashion, were transmuted into human-bird hybrids.[5] Yet British artists seldom went beyond satire or children's fiction to create fantasy worlds inhabited by strange half-human beasts and birds, such as one finds in the paintings of Odilon Redon, Arnold Böcklin, Max Klinger, and Alfred Kubin during this period.[6]

The obsession with all things zoological was, at one level, simply a response to the enormous influx of actual live animals and animal specimens resulting from the growth of the British Empire. The politician and naturalist Sir John Lubbock, who was president of the British Association for the Advancement of Science in 1881, reminded those attending its annual gathering that a dramatic expansion of zoological knowledge had taken place since the Association's foundation fifty years ago. Darwin's ideas had transformed scientific thinking, and the actual materials for research had grown massively over the same period, in such a way as to invalidate earlier works on natural history:

> As regards descriptive biology, by far the greater number of species now recorded have been named and described within the last half-century, and it is not too much to say that not a day passes without adding new species to our lists. A comparison, for instance, of the edition of Cuvier's 'Règne Animal,' published in 1828,[7] as compared with the present state of our knowledge, is most striking.
>
> Dr. Günther has been good enough to make a calculation for me. The numbers, of course, are only approximate, but it appears that while the total number of animals described up to 1831 was not more than 70,000, the number now is at least 320,000.
>
> Lastly, to show how large a field still remains for exploration, I may add that Mr. Waterhouse assumes that our Museums contain not fewer than 12,000 species of insects which have not yet been described, while our collections do not probably contain anything like one-half of those actually in existence. Further than this, the anatomy and habits even of those which have been described offer an inexhaustible field for research, and it is not going too far to say that there is not a single species which would not amply repay the devotion of a lifetime.[8]

THE HUNTING CULT AND CONCEPTS OF THE NATURAL ORDER

This glut of specimens, certain of which swamped the museums and often defeated the best efforts of cataloguers, was the product of uncontrolled hunting and collecting activities in Britain's territories across the world. Some specimens were the products of expeditions undertaken by professional collectors, who might be working to order for clients in the home country, or they were the stock-in-trade of dealers in ivory or furs. Others again were the spoils of hunting safaris, financed and led by British army officers, wealthy aristocrats, or adventurous mavericks. Such 'sportsmen', armed with powerful guns, were prodigal in the shedding of blood and indiscriminate in the species they hunted and killed, preferring those that could be found in previously untouched and therefore seductive virgin territories.[9] Explorer William Charles Baldwin, whose account of his *African Hunting* was published in 1863, recorded that he and three others in his party shot in one year (1860) near the Zambesi sixty-one elephants, twenty-three rhinoceroses, eleven giraffes, thirty buffalos, twenty-one elands, eighteen impala, twenty-five springboks, twelve wildebeests, and seventy-one quaggas (a species which is now extinct), beside many other creatures. There was also a very high level of mortality among the dogs, horses, and oxen that serviced such safaris and fell victim to disease, predation, thirst, and exhaustion. Baldwin himself was puzzled by the strength of the urge to hunt and kill relentlessly, whatever the costs and dangers to life. 'I only know this, there is a secret feeling of inward satisfaction at having conquered, that is almost worth the risk to be run'.[10]

The elation produced by the consciousness of conquest went much beyond big game hunting: it conditioned the whole mentality of the Victorians, which was founded on belief in a natural hierarchy with humans as the supreme species. Once, in the era of natural theology, nature had been conceived as a divinely composed harmony of lifeforms, for which human beings had a duty of stewardship. Though the whole natural world had fallen from grace through man's original sin, it would ultimately be redeemed, and the lion would lie down with the lamb. In the imperial age, this wishful view of nature – already challenged in the eighteenth century by religious sceptics like the philosopher David Hume – gave way to a much harsher interpretation of the natural order. 'The earth should be a reflection of Heaven – and Heaven is an Empire', wrote historian Winwood Reade[11] – a point developed by the sportsman John Madden in his book on *The Wilderness and Its Tenants* (1897) as a justification for his own actions:

> Some forms of animated Nature are created strong, and others weak and timid; and the law of force appears to govern throughout the whole range of the animal, and even the vegetable kingdom. Every form of life is found engaged in waging a continual warfare with everything around it, wherein the iron necessities arising out of the fierce struggle for existence render each class pitiless in its dealings with the rest; and so the weak go down before the strong, and life flourishes upon the destruction of other forms of living creatures . . . 'the hunting instinct' has descended among the whole animal creation, as part and parcel of their nature, and in this the *genus homo* is necessarily included. This makes good our contention respecting the 'sporting tastes' in human nature, which are therefore by no means to be lightly decried on the grounds of being demoralizing and unnatural; for, in fact, man was created a hunting animal, and still is, and will always continue to be one of the beasts of prey; however much doctrinaires may desire to gloss over the fact, he is the most destructive of all such creatures. See how whole races of valuable, beautiful, and harmless birds and animals have been exterminated by him![12]

Though few Victorians would have ventured to dismiss theological notions so brutally and explicitly, a pleasure in mastery and a sense of entitlement conditioned all their interactions with the natural world, not just big game hunting. The ruthless appropriation of animal products such as sealskin and tropical bird feathers, causing physical and mental suffering to the creatures involved, as well as the depletion of many species, aroused little protest until the last two decades of the century. Rare visitant birds sighted in Britain were shot, and their nests raided for eggs – on behalf of collectors who often included Anglican clergymen and the local squirearchy. Artists, too, often presented the natural world as a battleground in which survival depended on ferocious trials of strength and on narrow escapes from disasters of fire, storm, and flood. Madden's reference to the 'fierce struggle for existence' gave this trait a Darwinian frame of reference, but in fact animal painters from the first decades of the nineteenth century onwards presented nature as a scene of flux and conflict – struggles arising from sexual rivalry or predation, but also struggles against hostile conditions. Nature itself could become an enemy, condemning weaklings to destruction, a phenomenon which in artistic imagery could be invested with infinite pathos, in a manner quite different from eighteenth-century scenes of the wild.

Thus, the more thoughtful writers projected onto the animal world a kind of fatalism arising from their own loss of belief in a benign power presiding over human destiny. In the words of the novelist and science writer Grant Allen in *Physiological Aesthetics* (1877),

> During the present century the desire for this melancholy tone in art has steadily increased, and the reason why is clear. Man stands to-day, as he never stood before, face to face with the naked realities of nature. Solitary in a boundless universe, alone on a little isthmus of historic time . . . he finds himself awe-struck and ignorant, ready to fall prostrate before the terrible forces of nature, which work out unswerved their fatal will in apparent disregard of his happiness or misery, of his prayers or imprecations.[13]

In this view of things, humans were not, as once thought, beings with a unique spiritual destiny, but fellow-sufferers with all the other living species in a hostile world. John Stuart Mill, writing in the 1850s before the publication of *On the Origin of Species*, likewise thought that the traditional wisdom of 'following nature' did not stand up to philosophical or moral scrutiny.

> If a tenth part of the pains which have been expended in finding benevolent adaptations in all nature, had been employed in collecting evidence to blacken the character of the Creator, what scope for comment would not have been found in the entire existence of the lower animals, divided, with scarcely an exception, into devourers and devoured, and a prey to a thousand ills from which they are denied the faculties for protecting themselves![14]

Mill's analysis of the system of nature did not differ greatly from that of Winwood Reade or Madden, but his conviction that it was cruel and malign – something that humans should resist rather than imitate – sets him apart from proponents of the hunting culture borne of imperialism. For Mill, humans should be considered not as the natural killers of 'lower' species, but as the unique possessors of moral faculties that should set them *against* the cruelties endemic to the wild.[15]

NATURE REAPPRAISED: A NEW SPIRIT OF REVERENCE AND DELIGHT

The culture of hunting, and the dark view of the natural order in which it was embedded, did not pass unchallenged. John Ruskin, the most influential writer on aesthetics in the mid-century, viewed animals as autonomous beings to be loved and revered for their beauty, not 'mastered' or murdered by humans. In *Modern Painters* he wrote in the spirit of Coleridge's *Ancient Mariner* and Wordsworth's *Hartleap Well* to castigate

> those accursed sports in which man makes of himself, cat, tiger, serpent, chætodon, and alligator in one; and gathers into one continuance of cruelty, for his amusement, all the devices that brutes sparingly and at intervals use against each other for their necessities.[16]

And in *The Elements of Drawing* Ruskin noted that the depiction of animals was a lesson in nature's beauties of contour and colour, requiring humility, '*innocence of the eye*', 'refinement of perception . . . delicacy of drawing and subtlety of sight', all contributing to 'the vital and joyful study of natural history'.[17] These were to be representations of animals as observed in their natural surroundings, not as stricken in the hunt, dissected in a laboratory, or hung in a game larder. 'Delicate' and 'vital' are words which constantly recur in Ruskin's thoughts on the art of depicting animals, and colour was of critical importance: infinitely subtle, fugitive, and changeable. In Ruskin's view, birds themselves possessed an aesthetic sense, although they might exercise it unconsciously. He noted in his lecture 'The Eagle's Nest' (1872) that a bullfinch's nest shown to him by the ornithologist John Gould was intricately, even artistically constructed: 'becoming, decorous, harmonious, satisfying', and a lesson in taste to human beings.[18] It followed that there could be no objections or difficulties; in fact, there was an enrichment when architects took nature as their pattern in decorative designs. As Ruskin explained to would-be artists in his mid-century lecture series 'The Two Paths', the creation of such ornament involved sensibility which a mere naturalist might not possess.

> He may, perhaps, if he be an amiable naturalist, take delight in having living creatures round him; – still, the major part of his work is, or has been, in counting feathers, separating fibres, and analyzing structures. But *your* work is always with the living creature; the thing you have to get at in him is his life, and ways of going about things. It does not matter to you how many cells there are in his bones, or how many filaments in his feathers; what you want is his moral character and way of behaving himself. . . You must get the storm spirit into your eagles, and the lordliness into your lions, and the tripping fear into your fawns; and in order to do this, you must be in continual sympathy with every fawn

> of them; and be hand-in-glove with all the lions, and hand-in-claw with all the hawks.[19]

Animal painting of the high Victorian era, together with the illustrations in popular zoologies like those authored by Revd John George Wood, did arguably aim at this kind of lively characterisation of its subjects. Each wild species was presented in a tableau, within a landscape setting that was meant to evoke its natural habitat, but violence was nearly always implicit, either between predatory animals and their prey or between an unseen human hunter placed in the position of the viewer, and this temptingly displayed quarry. The animals were *objectified* for the delectation of the human viewer, not treated with the kind of fellow-feeling and 'continual sympathy' that was Ruskin's ideal. These elaborate, stagey compositions, often in the form of coloured lithographs or wood engravings, declined in popularity in the last two decades of the century, as did dramatised taxidermy. This change in taste was partly due to the new availability of photographs of wildlife, and later of cinematography. However, at a deeper level, it signalled the advent of a new attitude to nature itself: less proprietorial, less violent, but instead imbued with a sense of the autonomy and dynamism that truly characterised animals' lives in the wild. One encounters it in the writings of the novelist and naturalist W.H. Hudson and in his comments on styles of wildlife illustration. While admiring the skills of established illustrators, Hudson deplored the heaviness of the pictorial conventions that still imprisoned the images of birds in conventional ornithological works. Writing to an artist friend, he complained that 'Thorburn has got into a groove, a manner, and is going the way of all these natural history illustrators – Wolf, Keulemans, and the rest. They all get hard – their plumage is made of zinc and painted over'.[20] Such images could not convey the 'sublimity' of a large airborne flock of birds – the 'sudden revelation of wild life in its nobler aspect – of its glorious freedom and power and majesty'.[21] The illustrations in his own publications were often sketchy, open-ended vignettes rather than framed pictures.[22] Their model was not Thorburn or Keulemans, but rather the Japanese ink sketches and woodcuts that captivated Hudson's generation of nature lovers. The Japanese artists' impressions of birds in flight, flocking, or alighting; their exuberant running horses; and their mythic dragon-like creatures all seemed to possess a freedom and autonomy that made viewers aware for the first time of the anthropocentrism endemic to traditional European depictions of animals, and thus opened the way to the greater freedom of animal art in the twentieth century.

The primary sources that I have chosen to illuminate the interplay between zoology and visual culture in nineteenth-century Britain present four broad themes, sketched out earlier in this Introduction. Part I exemplifies the very diverse means by which scientific data could be brought into the visual sphere and communicated through imagery – ranging from engraved zoological illustrations to taxidermy, microscopy, and photography. Part II presents the drama of imagined scenes of animal life in the wild, centring on the work of Landseer. It reveals the sense of crisis or tragedy that arose from a growing conviction that the workings of nature involve a ruthless battle for survival. It seemed that, in a hostile and godless world, the human race could no longer be considered as wholly distinct from other species in either its moral status or its psychology, and this was a realisation that both prompted and problematised representations of animal mentality. Part III illustrates, in apparent contrast, the aestheticisation of nature, which became an important aspect of campaigns for animal protection. Here too, however, the traditional values of natural theology inherited from earlier centuries came into conflict with Darwinian science: for Darwin and his disciples, colour and beauty in nature were aspects of survival of the fittest, not gifts from God. Part IV is about the varied means by which knowledge of zoology was communicated visually to the public at large, whether through museums, zoos, aquaria, dramatic spectacles such as dioramas, popular illustrated publications, or various kinds of teaching and lecturing that involved the projection of visual images. Education could not be divorced from entertainment, a realisation which entailed much creative thinking about effective means of instruction of the public at large.

Indeed, the overall relationship between zoology and visual culture in the Victorian era is characterised by its diversity, with no hard and fast distinctions between professionals and amateurs in their fields of knowledge or methods of research. I have tried to convey this richness of resources in my choice of texts, which range from the erudite to the popular, making full use of the resources of the online Biodiversity Heritage Library, as well as of manuscript sources. All these writings were based on a conviction that artistic imagery could enhance understanding of the natural world: there was as yet no sign of C.P. Snow's 'two cultures', supposedly dividing scientists from devotees of the visual arts and literature.[23] Happily, twenty-first-century thinking has confirmed the Victorian view that there is immense value in cultural exchanges and alliances between them.

Thus, the compilation of this collection of extracts from nineteenth-century sources has been a journey of discovery, and the extraordinary richness of the material has made the final selection of texts very difficult. I hope the book will suggest many fresh lines of interdisciplinary research for other scholars to develop.

Endnotes

1 'Notes', *Nature*, 16 (10 May 1877), p. 31. Hooker was himself an accomplished and sensitive draughtsman in his watercolours of landscapes and plant life.

2 'Address to members of the Liverpool Institution', in Thomas H. Huxley, *Science & Education: Essays* (London: Macmillan, 1895), pp. 160–88, on p. 177. Huxley also stressed his aesthetic sensibilities in 'Science and Morals', a lecture of 1886, included in his *Evolution & Ethics and Other Essays* (London: Macmillan, 1894), pp. 117–46, on pp. 123–4.

3 Rowland Ward, *A Naturalist's Life Study in the Art of Taxidermy* (London: Rowland Ward, 1913), pp. 48, 51–5, 57–60. See also Chapter 35 of this volume.

4 Helen Louise Cowie, *Victims of Fashion: Animal Commodities in Victorian Britain* (Cambridge and New York: Cambridge University Press, 2022).

5 Linley Sambourne, 'Punch's Essence of Parliament', *Punch* (31 July 1880), p. 46; Sambourne, 'I would I were a bird', *Punch* (23 April 1870), p. 167 and 'A bird of

prey', *Punch* (14 May 1892), p. 231. The bird cartoons are reproduced in Diana Donald, *Women Against Cruelty: Protection of Animals in Nineteenth-century Britain*, 2nd edn. (Manchester: Manchester University Press, 2021), p. 264.

6 David Bindman, 'Mankind after Darwin and nineteenth-century art', in Diana Donald and Jane Munro (eds.), *Endless Forms: Charles Darwin, Natural Science and the Visual Arts* (New Haven, CT, and London: Yale University Press, 2009), pp. 143–65.

7 Georges Cuvier's *Le règne animal distribué d'après son organisation: pour servir de base à l'histoire naturelle des animaux et d'introduction à l'anatomie comparée* (Paris: Déterville, 1817) appeared in numerous editions and translations, as a pioneering work on zoology and comparative anatomy.

8 'Address by Sir John Lubbock', *Report of the Fifty-first Meeting of the British Association for the Advancement of Science, held at York in August and September 1881* (London: John Murray, 1882), pp. 1–51, on pp. 8–9. The address was separately reprinted in Lubbock's *Fifty Years of Science* (London: Macmillan, 1882).

9 The best account of hunting in the colonies is given by John M. MacKenzie, in *The Empire of Nature: Hunting, Conservation and British Imperialism* (Manchester and New York: Manchester University Press, 1988, 2017).

10 William Charles Baldwin, *African Hunting from Natal to the Zambesi . . . From 1852 to 1860* (London: Richard Bentley, 1863), pp. 426, 443.

11 William Winwood Reade, *Savage Africa: Being the Narrative of a Tour in Equatorial, South-Western, and North-Western Africa*, 2nd edn. (London: Smith, Elder, 1864), p. 31.

12 John Madden, *The Wilderness and Its Tenants: A Series of Geographical and Other Essays Illustrative of Life in a Wild Country*, 3 vols. (London: Simpkin, Marshall, Hamilton, Kent, 1897), vol. 3, pp. 176–7.

13 Grant Allen, *Physiological Œsthetics* (London: Henry S. King, 1877), p. 277.

14 John Stuart Mill, 'Nature', in his *Nature, the Utility of Religion and Theism*, 2nd edn., published posthumously by Mill's stepdaughter Helen Taylor (London: Longmans, Green, Reader, and Dyer, 1874), p. 58.

15 This train of thought was inherited by Thomas Hardy and expressed in poems like 'In a wood', no. 40 in *Wessex Poems*. The trees battle blindly but ferociously for survival, and Hardy, dismayed, turns to his fellow humans to find the 'life loyalties' of which other species are incapable.

16 *The Works of John Ruskin*, eds. E.T. Cook and Alexander Wedderburn, 38 vols. (London: George Allen, 1903–12), vol. 4, p. 149. The chætodon is a fish.

17 *Works of Ruskin*, vol. 15, p. 27, note.

18 *Works of Ruskin*, vol. 22, pp. 157–9.

19 *Works of Ruskin*, vol. 16, pp. 367–8.

20 Manuscript letter from Hudson to the artist and illustrator Emma Hubbard, a close friend, 17 March 1899: Manchester Central Library, 34 GB 127, D32. Hudson here refers to the work of Archibald Thorburn, Joseph Wolf, and John Gerrard Keulemans.

21 W.H. Hudson, *Adventures Among Birds* (London and Toronto: J.M. Dent & Sons and New York: E.P. Dutton, 1923), p. 41. The essays therein were based on previously published articles.

22 See, for example, the '15 drawings by A.D. McCormick', which illustrated Hudson's *Lost British Birds*, a pamphlet published for the Society for the Protection of Birds in 1894.

23 C.P. Snow in *The Two Cultures and the Scientific Revolution* (1959) deplored the 'polar' gulf of mutual incomprehension that allegedly existed between scientists and literary scholars in his day. He accused the cultural elite of a disdain for scientific knowledge.

BIBLIOGRAPHY

PRIMARY SOURCES: ARCHIVAL

The granting of permission to publish some of the archival sources is noted in the Acknowledgements.

W.H. Hudson papers in Manchester Central Library (see Introduction).

Thomas Bewick papers in Tyne & Wear Archives, Discovery Museum, Newcastle upon Tyne (see Chapter 6).

John Hancock correspondence, Natural History Society of Northumbria Archive, Great North Museum, Hancock, Newcastle upon Tyne (see Chapters 16, 33.1, and 71). Typed transcriptions of all the letters to and from Hancock in this Archive were made by the late Ann Stephenson. (Those quoted here have been checked for accuracy by the present writer.)

Edwin Landseer correspondence, National Art Library, Victoria & Albert Museum, London (see Chapter 36).

Friedrich Keyl papers in the Royal Archives, Windsor (see Chapter 42).

Archive of the Royal Society for the Protection of Birds, The Lodge, Sandy (see Chapter 69).

Archive of the School Nature Study Union, Brotherton Library, University of Leeds (see Chapter 80).

PRIMARY SOURCES: PUBLICATIONS

Allen, G., *Physiological Aesthetics* (London: Henry S. King & Co., 1877).

———, *The Colour-sense: Its Origin and Development. An Essay in Comparative Psychology* (London: Trübner & Co., 1879).

Anon., 'Mr. Gould's collection of humming-birds at the Zoological Society's Gardens, Regent's Park', *Illustrated London News*, 18 (31 May 1851), p. 480.

———, 'Mr. Gould's collection of humming-birds in the Zoological Gardens, Regent's Park', *Illustrated London News*, 20 (12 June 1852), p. 457.

———, 'The Brighton Aquarium', *Illustrated London News*, 61 (10 August 1872), pp. 121, 123.

———, 'A new animal painter: Richard Friese', *The Art Journal*, 48 (June 1886), pp. 161–4.

Argyll, 8th Duke of, [G.J.D. Campbell], *The Reign of Law* (London: Alexander Strahan, 1867).

Audubon, J.J., *The Birds of America*, 'double elephant folio' plates (London: Robert Havell, 1827–38).

——— and W. MacGillivray, *Ornithological Biography, or an Account of the Habits of the Birds of the United States of America* (Edinburgh: Adam & Charles Black, 1831–9).

Baldwin, W.C., *African Hunting from Natal to the Zambesi . . . From 1852 to 1860* (London: Richard Bentley, 1863).

Beddard, F.E., *Animal Coloration: An Account of the Principal Facts and Theories relating to the Colours and Markings of Animals*, 2nd ed. (London: Swan Sonnenschein and New York: Macmillan, 1895).

Bell, T., *A History of British Quadrupeds*, 2nd ed. (London: Van Voorst, 1874).

Bewick, T., *A General History of Quadrupeds* (Newcastle upon Tyne: S. Hodgson, R. Beilby, T. Bewick, 1790).

———, *History of British Birds*, vol. 1, *Land Birds* (Newcastle upon Tyne: Beilby & Bewick, 1797).

———, *History of British Birds*, vol. 2, *Water Birds* (Newcastle upon Tyne: Bewick, 1804).

———, *My Life*, ed. I. Bain (London: Folio Society, 1981).

Browne, M., *Artistic and Scientific Taxidermy and Modelling: A Manual of Instruction in the Methods of Preserving and Reproducing the Correct Form of all Natural Objects* (London: Adam and Charles Black, and New York: Macmillan, 1896).

Chambers, R., *Vestiges of the Natural History of Creation, and Other Evolutionary Writings*, ed. J.A. Secord (Chicago and London: University of Chicago Press, 1994).

Crane, W., and L.F. Day, 'The living interest in ornament', in *Moot Points: Friendly Disputes on Art and Industry between Walter Crane and Lewis F. Day* (London: B.T. Batsford, 1903), pp. 86–94.

Cuvier, G., *Le règne animal distribué d'après son organisation: pour server de base à l'histoire naturelle des animaux et d'introduction à l'anatomie comparée* (Paris: Déterville, 1817).

Darwin, F. (ed.), *The Life and Letters of Charles Darwin*, 3 vols. (London: John Murray, 1888).

———, and A.C. Seward (eds.), *More Letters of Charles Darwin*, 2 vols. (London: John Murray, 1903).

Dickens, C., 'The tresses of the day star', *Household Words*, 3:65 (21 June 1851).

Dixon, C., *Rural Bird Life, being Essays on Ornithology* (London: Longmans, Green, 1880).

Drayson, Capt. A.W., *Sporting Scenes amongst the Kaffirs of South Africa, illustrated by Harrison Weir, from designs by the author* (London: G. Routledge, 1858).

Dresser, H.E., *A History of the Birds of Europe*, 9 vols. (London: The author, 1871–96).

Fothergill, C., *An Essay on the Philosophy, Study, and Use of Natural History* (London: White, Cochrane, 1813).

Gosse, P.H., *The Aquarium: An Unveiling of the Wonders of the Deep Sea* (London: J. Van Voorst, 1854).

———, *A Manual of Marine Zoology for the British Isles* (London: J. Van Voorst, 1855).

———, *Tenby: A Seaside Holiday* (London: J. Van Voorst, 1856).

———, *Actinologia Britannica: A History of the British Sea-anemones and Corals* (London: J. Van Voorst, 1860).

Gould, J., *The Birds of Europe*, 5 vols. (London: the Author, 1837).

———, *The Birds of Australia*, 7 vols. (London: the Author, [1840]–1848).
———, *A Monograph of the Trochilidæ, or Family of Humming-birds*, 5 vols. (London: the Author, 1849–61).
———, *A Monograph of the Ramphastidæ, or Family of Toucans*, 2nd ed. (London: the Author, [1852]–1854).
———, *The Birds of Great Britain*, 5 vols. (London: the Author, 1873).
Greenwood, T., *Museums and Art Galleries* (London: Simpkin, Marshall, 1888).
Hancock, J., *A Catalogue of the Birds of Northumberland and Durham* (*Natural History Transactions of Northumberland and Durham*, VI, 1873) (London: Williams and Norgate, 1874).
Harris, Captain W.C., *The Wild Sports of Southern Africa; Being the Narrative of a Hunting Expedition* (London: John Murray, 1839).
Hewitson, W.C., *Coloured Illustrations of the Eggs of British Birds*, 2 vols. (London: John Van Voorst, 1846).
Hudson, W.H., *Lost British Birds*, leaflet no. 14 (Society for the Protection of Birds, 1894).
———, *Osprey; Or Egrets and Aigrettes* (Society for the Protection of Birds, 1896).
———, *Adventures Among Birds* (London and Toronto: J.M. Dent & Sons, and New York: E.P. Dutton, 1923).
Huxley, T.H., *Science & Education: Essays* (London: Macmillan, 1895).
Johns, C.A., *British Birds in Their Haunts* (London: Society for Promoting Christian Knowledge, 1862).
Kearton, R., *Birds' Nests, Eggs and Egg-Collecting* (London: Cassell, 1896).
Kirby, Revd W., *Monographia Apum Angliæ; . . . with Descriptions and Observations* (Ipswich: the Author, 1802).
———, *On the Power, Wisdom, and Goodness of God as Manifested in the Creation of Animals and in Their History, Habits, and Instincts* (London: William Pickering, 1835).
Leighton, J., *On Japanese Art: A Discourse delivered at the Royal Institution of Great Britain, May 1, 1863* (privately printed, 1863).
Levick, G.M., *A Gun for a Fountain Pen: Antarctic Journal, November 1910 – January 1912* (Perth: Freemantle Press, 2013).
Lilford, T.L. (Baron Powys), *Coloured Figures of the Birds of the British Islands*, 7 vols. (London: R.H. Porter, 1885–97).
Lubbock, Sir J., *Fifty Years of Science* (London: Macmillan, 1882).
Lydekker, R. (ed.), *The Royal Natural History*, 6 vols. (London: Frederick Warne, 1894–5).
———, *Sir William Flower* (London: J.M. Dent and New York: E.P. Dutton, 1906).
MacGillivray, W., *A History of British Birds, Indigenous and Migratory*, 5 vols. (London: Scott, Webster and Geary, later London: William S. Orr, 1837–52).
Madden, J., *The Wilderness and Its Tenants: A Series of Geographical and Other Essays Illustrative of Life in a Wild Country*, 3 vols. (London: Simpkin, Marshall, Hamilton, Kent, 1897).
Manson, J.A., *Sir Edwin Landseer, R.A.* (London: Walter Scott Publishing and New York: Charles Scribner's Sons, 1902).
Mill, J.S., *Nature, the Utility of Religion and Theism*, 2nd ed. (London: Longmans, Green, Reader, and Dyer, 1874).
Morris, Revd F.O., *A History of British Butterflies* (London: Groombridge & Sons,1853).
———, *A Natural History of British Moths* (London: Henry Edward Knox, 1871).
Muybridge, E., *Animal in Motion: An Electro-Photographic Investigation of Consecutive Phases of Animal Progressive Movements* (London: Chapman and Hall, 1902).

Newton, A., 'Ornithology', article in the *Encyclopædia Britannica*, 9th ed., 1884.
Phillips, S., ed. F.K.J. Shenton, *Guide to the Crystal Palace and Its Park and Gardens* (Sydenham: Crystal Palace Library, 1860).
Ponting, H., *The Great White South, or With Scott in the Antarctic* (London: Duckworth, 1923).
Reade, W.W., *Savage Africa: Being the Narrative of a Tour in Equatorial, South-Western, and North-Western Africa*, 2nd ed. (London: Smith, Elder, 1864).
Robinson, P., *Birds of the Wave and Woodland* (London: Isbister, 1894).
Romanes, G.J., *Darwin and After Darwin: An Exposition of the Darwinian Theory and a Discussion of Post-Darwinian Questions* (London: Longmans, Green, 1892).
Ruskin, J., *The Works of John Ruskin*, ed. E.T. Cook and A. Wedderburn, 39 vols. (London: George Allen, 1903–12).
Saunders, H., *An Illustrated Manual of British Birds* (London: Gurney and Jackson, 1889).
Savigny, J.-C., *Mémoires sur les Animaux sans Vertèbres* (Paris: Gabriel Dufour, 1816).
Shaw, G., *General Zoology, or Systematic Natural History*, 14 vols. (London: G. Kearsley,1800–1826).
Spencer, H., *Essays: Scientific, Political & Speculative*, 3 vols. (London and Edinburgh: Williams and Norgate, 1891).
Stillman, J.D.B., *The Horse in Motion as Shown by Instantaneous Photography* (Boston: Osgood, 1882).
Swainson, W., *Zoological Illustrations, or Original Figures and Descriptions of New, Rare, or Interesting Animals, selected chiefly from the Classes of Ornithology, Entomology, and Conchology*, 3 vols. (London: Baldwin, Cradock, and Joy, and W. Wood, 1820–3).
Syme, P., *Werner's Nomenclature of Colours . . . Arranged so as to Render it Highly Useful to the Arts and Sciences*, 1814 (Edinburgh: William Blackwood, and London: T. Cadell, 1821).
Taylor, J.E., *The Aquarium: Its Inhabitants, Structure and Management* (London: Hardwicke & Bogue, 1876).
Vernon, H.M. and K.D.E., *A History of the Oxford Museum* (Oxford: Clarendon Press, 1909).
Wallace, A.R., *The Malay Archipelago*, 2 vols. (London: Macmillan, 1869).
———, *Darwinism: An Exposition of the Theory of Natural Selection with Some of Its Applications* (London: Macmillan, 1889).
Waterton, C., *Wanderings in South America, the North-West of the United States, and the Antilles, in the Years 1812, 1816, 1820, & 1824, with Original Instructions for the Perfect Preservation of Birds, &c., for Cabinets of Natural History*, 2nd ed. (London: B. Fellowes, 1828).
Wilson, A., *American Ornithology; Or, The Natural History of the Birds of the United States: Illustrated with Plates, Engraved and Colored from Original Drawings Taken from Nature*, 9 vols (Philadelphia: Bradford & Inskeep, 1808–14).
Wolf, J., and P.L. Sclater, *Zoological Sketches*, 2 vols. (London: Henry Graves, 1861–7).
Wood, Revd J.G., *The Illustrated Natural History*, 2 vols. (London: Routledge, Warne and Routledge, 1862).
———, *Homes without Hands: Being a Description of the Habitations of Animals, Classed According to Their Principle of Construction* (London: Longmans, Green, 1865).
Yarrell, W., *A History of British Birds* (London: John van Voorst, 1839).

SECONDARY SOURCES

Allen, D.E., *The Naturalist in Britain: A Social History* (Harmondsworth: Penguin Books, 1978).

Altick, R.D., *The Shows of London* (Cambridge, MA, and London: Belknap Press of Harvard University Press, 1978).

Amato, S., *Beastly Possessions: Animals in Victorian Consumer Culture* (Toronto: University of Toronto Press, 2015).

Baigrie, B.S. (ed.), *Picturing Knowledge: Historical and Philosophical Problems Concerning the Use of Art in Science* (Toronto, Buffalo, London: University of Toronto Press, 1996).

Bain, I., *Thomas Bewick Vignettes* (London: Scolar Press, 1979).

———, *The Watercolours and Drawings of Thomas Bewick and His Workshop Apprentices*, 2 vols. (London: Gordon Fraser, 1981).

Baker, C., *The Monarch of the Glen: Landseer* (Edinburgh: National Galleries of Scotland, 2017).

Barlow, P., and C. Trodd, *Governing Cultures: Art Institutions in Victorian London* (Aldershot: Ashgate, 2000).

Belknap, G., 'Illustrating Natural History: Images, Periodicals, and the Making of Nineteenth-Century Scientific Communities', *British Journal for the History of Science*, 51:3 (Sept. 2018), pp. 395–422.

———, 'The Evolution of Scientific Illustration', *Nature*, 575 (7 Nov. 2019), pp. 25–8.

Berkowitz, C., and B. Lightman (eds.), *Science Museums in Transition: Cultures of Display in Nineteenth-Century Britain and America* (Pittsburgh, PA: University of Pittsburgh Press, 2017).

Blau, E., *Ruskinian Gothic: The Architecture of Deane and Woodward. 1845–1861* (Princeton, NJ: Princeton University Press, 1992).

Blunt, W., *The Ark in the Park: The Zoo in the Nineteenth Century* (London: Book Club Associates, 1976).

Boase, T., *Mrs Pankhurst's Purple Feather: Fashion, Fury and Feminism – Women's Fight for Change* (London: Aurum Press, 2018).

Braga, A.V., 'Microorganisms, Microscopes, and Victorian Design Theories', *British Art Studies*, 21 (30 Nov. 2021).

Brookman, P. (ed.), *Helios: Eadweard Muybridge in a Time of Change* (Washington, DC: Steidl and Corcoran Gallery of Art, 2010).

Browne, J., *Charles Darwin: Voyaging* (London: Pimlico, 1995)

———, *Charles Darwin; The Power of Place* (London: Jonathan Cape, 2002).

Bullen, J.B., 'Alfred Waterhouse's Romanesque "Temple of Nature": The Natural History Museum, London', *Architectural History*, 49 (2006), pp. 257–85.

Burkhardt, F., and J.A. Secord (eds.), *The Correspondence of Charles Darwin*, 30 vols. (Cambridge: Cambridge University Press, 1985–2023).

Chansigaud, V., 'Scientific Illustrators' in B. Lightman (ed.), *A Companion to the History of Science* (Chichester: Wiley Blackwell, 2016), pp. 111–25.

Cowie, H.L., *Exhibiting Animals in Nineteenth-Century Britain: Empathy, Education, Entertainment* (Basingstoke, UK: Palgrave Macmillan, 2014).

———, *Victims of Fashion: Animal Commodities in Victorian Britain* (Cambridge and New York: Cambridge University Press, 2022).

Curry, H., N. Jardine, J. Secord, and E.C. Spary (eds.), *Worlds of Natural History* (Cambridge: Cambridge University Press, 2018).

Daston, L., and P. Galison, *Objectivity* (New York: Zone Books, 2010).

Davis, L.S., *A Polar Affair: Antarctica's Forgotten Hero and the Secret Love Lives of the Penguins* (New York and London: Pegasus Books, 2019).

Desmond, A., and J. Moore, *Darwin* (London: Michael Joseph, 1991).

Desmond, R., *Great Natural History Books and Their Creators* (London: The British Library and New Castle, DE: Oak Knoll Press, 2003).

Donald, D., 'Pangs Watched in Perpetuity: Sir Edwin Landseer's Pictures of Dying Deer and the Ethos of Victorian Sportsmanship', in The Animal Studies Group, *Killing Animals* (Urbana and Chicago: University of Illinois Press, 2006), pp. 50–68.

———, *Picturing Animals in Britain 1750–1850* (New Haven, CT, and London: Yale University Press, 2007).

———, and J. Munro (eds.), *Endless Forms: Charles Darwin, Natural Science and the Visual Arts* (New Haven, CT, and London: Yale University Press, 2009).

———, 'The Arctic Fantasies of Edwin Landseer and Briton Riviere: Polar Bears, Wilderness and Notions of the Sublime' (online Tate Research Publications, 'The Art of the Sublime', 2013).

———, *The Art of Thomas Bewick* (London: Reaktion Books, 2013).

———, *Women Against Cruelty: Protection of Animals in Nineteenth-century Britain*, 2nd ed. (Manchester: Manchester University Press, 2021).

Doughty, R.W., *Feather Fashions and Bird Preservation: A Study in Nature Protection* (Berkeley, CA, London: University of California Press, 1975).

Fyfe, A., and B. Lightman (eds.), *Science in the Marketplace: Nineteenth-Century Sites and Experiences* (Chicago: University of Chicago Press, 2007).

Girouard, M., *Alfred Waterhouse and the Natural History Museum, London* (New Haven, CT, and London: Yale University Press, 1981).

Hamlett, J., and J-M. Strange, *Pet Revolution. Animals and the Making of Modern British Life* (London: Reaktion Books, 2023).

Hill, K., *Women and Museums, 1850–1914: Modernity and the Gendering of Knowledge* (Manchester: Manchester University Press, 2016).

Hoage, R.J., and W.A. Deiss (eds.), *New Worlds, New Animals: From Menagerie to Zoological Park in the Nineteenth Century* (Baltimore: Johns Hopkins University Press, 1996).

Holmes, J., *Temple of Science: The Pre-Raphaelites and Oxford University Museum of Natural History* (Oxford: Bodleian Library and Oxford University Museum of Natural History, 2020).

Ito, T., *London Zoo and the Victorians, 1828–1859* (London: The Royal Historical Society and the Boydell Press, 2014).

Jackson, C.E., *Bird Etchings: The Illustrators and Their Books, 1655–1855* (Ithaca, NY: Cornell University Press, 1985).

———, 'The Painting of Hand-Coloured Zoological Illustrations' and 'The Materials and Methods of Hand-Colouring Zoological Illustrations', *Archives of Natural History*, 38:1 (2011), pp. 36–64.

———, *Menageries in Britain, 1100–2000* (London: Ray Society, 2014).

———, 'The Ward Family of Taxidermists', *Archives of Natural History*, 45:1 (April 2018), pp. 1–13.

———, *A Newsworthy Naturalist: The Life of William Yarrell* (Oxford: John Beaufoy Publishing, 2022).

Jameson, C.M., *Finding W.H. Hudson: The Writer Who Came to Britain to Save the Birds* (London: Pelagic Publishing, 2023).
Jardine, B., 'Made Real: Artifice and Accuracy in Nineteenth-Century Scientific Illustration', *Science Museum Group Journal*, 2 (Autumn 2014), unpaginated.
———, 'Microscopes' in B. Lightman (ed.), *A Companion to the History of Science* (Chichester: Wiley Blackwell, 2016), pp. 515–29.
Jardine, N., J. Secord, and E.C. Spary (eds.), *Cultures of Natural History* (Cambridge: Cambridge University Press, 1996).
Kean, H., and P. Howell (eds.), *The Routledge Companion to Animal-Human History* (London and New York: Routledge, 2019).
Kete, K. (ed.), *A Cultural History of Animals in the Age of Empire* (Oxford and New York: Berg, 2007).
Kohn, D. (ed.), *The Darwinian Heritage* (Princeton NJ: Princeton University Press, 1985).
Kort, P., and M. Hollein (eds.), *Darwin: Art and the Search for Origins* (Frankfurt: Schirn Kunsthalle and Wienand Verlag, 2009).
Larson, B., and F. Brauer (eds.), *The Art of Evolution: Darwin, Darwinisms, and Visual Culture* (Hanover, NH, and London: Dartmouth College Press and University Press of New England, 2009).
———, and S. Flach (eds.), *Darwin and Theories of Aesthetics and Cultural History* (Farnham: Ashgate, 2013).
Lightman, B. (ed.), *Victorian Science in Context* (Chicago and London: University of Chicago Press, 1997).
———, *Victorian Popularizers of Science: Designing Nature for New Audiences* (Chicago: Chicago University Press, 2007).
———, (ed.), *A Companion to the History of Science* (Chichester: Wiley Blackwell, 2016).
———, and B. Zon (eds.), *Evolution and Victorian Culture* (Cambridge: Cambridge University Press, 2014).
Livingstone, K., *C.F.A. Voysey, Arts and Crafts Designer* (London: V & A Publishing, 2016).
MacKenzie, J.M., *The Empire of Nature: Hunting, Conservation and British Imperialism* (Manchester and New York: Manchester University Press, 1988, 2017).
Marshall, N.R. (ed.), *Victorian Science and Imagery: Representation & Knowledge in Nineteenth-Century Visual Culture* (Pittsburgh, PA: University of Pittsburgh Press, 2021).
Merrill, L., *The Romance of Victorian Natural History* (Oxford and New York: Oxford University Press, 1989).
Miller, C.G., and M. Lowe, 'The Natural History Museum Blaschka Collections', *Historical Biology*, 20:1 (Feb. 2008), pp. 51–62.
Mitchell, W.R., *Watch the Birdie: The Life and Times of Richard and Cherry Kearton, Pioneers of Nature Photography* (Settle, UK: Castleberg, 2001).
Morris, P.A., *Rowland Ward: Taxidermist to the World* (London: MPM Publishing, 2003).
———, *A History of Taxidermy: Art, Science and Bad Taste* (Ascot, UK: MPM Publishing, 2010).
Munro, J., '"More like a Work of Art than of Nature:" Darwin, Beauty and Sexual Selection', in D. Donald and J. Munro (eds.), *Endless Forms: Charles Darwin, Natural Science and the Visual Arts* (New Haven, CT, and London: Yale University Press, 2009), pp. 253–91.
Ormond, R., *Sir Edwin Landseer* (Philadelphia Museum of Art and Tate Gallery, London, 1982).

———, *The Monarch of the Glen: Landseer in the Highlands* (Edinburgh: National Galleries of Scotland, 2005).
Otis, L. (ed.), *Literature and Science in the Nineteenth Century: An Anthology* (Oxford: Oxford University Press, 2002).
Prodger, P., 'Illustration as Strategy in Charles Darwin's "The Expression of the Emotions in Man and Animals"', in T. Lenoir (ed.), *Inscribing Science: Scientific Texts and the Materiality of Communication* (Stanford, CA: Stanford University Press, 1998).
Ralph, R., *William MacGillivray: Creatures of Air, Land and Sea* (London: Merrell Holberton and the Natural History Museum, 1999).
Ritvo, H., 'Learning from Animals: Natural History for Children in the Eighteenth and Nineteenth Centuries', *Children's Literature*, 13 (1985), pp. 72–93.
———, *The Animal Estate: The English and Other Creatures in the Victorian Age* (Cambridge, MA: Harvard University Press, 1987).
———, 'The Order of Nature: Constructing the Collections of Victorian Zoos', in R.J. Hoage and William A. Deiss (eds.), *New Worlds, New Animals. From Menagerie to Zoological Park in the Nineteenth Century* (Baltimore and London: Johns Hopkins University Press, 1996), pp. 43–50.
———, *The Platypus and the Mermaid, and Other Figments of the Classifying Imagination* (Cambridge, MA: Harvard University Press, 1997).
———, *Noble Cows and Hybrid Zebras: Essays on Animals and History* (Charlottesville: University of Virginia Press, 2010).
Roberts, J.L., *Transporting Visions: The Movement of Images in Early Modern America* (Berkeley: University of California Press, 2014).
Rothfels, N., *Savages and Beasts: The Birth of the Modern Zoo* (Baltimore and London: Johns Hopkins University Press, 2002).
———, (ed.), *Representing Animals* (Bloomington and Indianapolis: Indiana University Press, 2002).
Roy, M., C. Sharp Jones, and C. Tipp, *Animals: Art, Science & Sound* (London: British Library, 2023).
Samstag, T., *For Love of Birds: The Story of the Royal Society for the Protection of Birds, 1889–1988* (Sandy, UK: the RSPB, 1988).
Schulze-Hagen, K., and A. Geuss (eds.), *Joseph Wolf (1820–1899) Tiermaler/Animal Painter* (Marburg an der Lahn, Germany: Basilisken Presse, 2000).
Secord, J.A., *Victorian Sensation: The Extraordinary Publication, Reception, and Secret Authorship of 'Vestiges of the Natural History of Creation'* (Chicago and London: University of Chicago Press, 2000).
———, 'Monsters at the Crystal Palace', in S. de Chadarevian and N. Hopwood (eds.), *Models: The Third Dimension of Science* (Stanford, CA: Stanford University Press, 2004), pp. 138–69.
———, *Visions of Science: Books and Readers at the Dawn of the Victorian Age* (Chicago: University of Chicago Press, 2015).
———, See also under Burkhardt, F., *The Correspondence of Charles Darwin* (joint editor).
Siegel, J. (ed.), *The Emergence of the Modern Museum: An Anthology of Nineteenth-Century Sources* (Oxford and New York: Oxford University Press, 2008).
Smith, J., *Charles Darwin and Victorian Visual Culture* (Cambridge: Cambridge University Press, 2006).

———, 'Evolutionary Aesthetics and Victorian Visual Culture', in D. Donald and J. Munro (eds.), *Endless Forms: Charles Darwin, Natural Science and the Visual Arts* (New Haven, CT, and London: Yale University Press, 2009), pp. 237–51.

Stearn, W.T., *The Natural History Museum at South Kensington: A History of the Museum, 1753–1980* (London: Natural History Museum, 1998).

Strathie, A., *Herbert Ponting: Scott's Antarctic Photographer and Pioneer Filmmaker* (Cheltenham, UK: History Press, 2021).

Tattersfield, N., *Thomas Bewick. The Complete Illustrative Work*, 3 vols. (London: The British Library and The Bibliographical Society, and New Castle, DE: Oak Knoll Press, 2011).

Thwaite, A., *Glimpses of the Wonderful. The Life of Philip Henry Gosse 1810–1888* (London: Faber and Faber, 2002).

Tomalin, R., *W.H. Hudson: A Biography* (London: Faber and Faber, 1982).

Tree, I., *The Bird Man: The Extraordinary Story of John Gould* (London: Barrie & Jenkins, 1991).

Tucker, J., *Nature Exposed: Photography as Eyewitness in Victorian Science* (Baltimore: Johns Hopkins University Press, 2005).

Uglow, J., *Nature's Engraver, A Life of Thomas Bewick* (London: Faber and Faber, 2006).

Velten, H., *Beastly London: A History of Animals in the City* (London: Reaktion Books, 2013).

Whittington-Egan, R., *The Natural History Man: A Life of the Reverend J.G. Wood* (Great Malvern: Cappella Archive, 2014).

Wonders, K., *Habitat Dioramas: Illusions of Wilderness in Museums of Natural History*, PhD thesis, Uppsala University, 1993 (*Acta Universitatis Upsaliensis Figura Nova Series 25*).

Wylie, C.D., 'Teaching Nature Study on the Blackboard in Late Nineteenth- and Early Twentieth-Century England', *Archives of Natural History*, 39:1 (April 2012), pp. 59–76.

Yanni, C., *Nature's Museums: Victorian Science and the Architecture of Display* (Baltimore: Johns Hopkins University Press, 1999).

FIGURES

CHRONOLOGY OF RELEVANT EVENTS IN NINETEENTH-CENTURY BRITAIN

1798 Publication of Thomas Robert Malthus's *An Essay on the Principle of Population*. Malthus argued that populations of humans and animals tend to increase beyond the capacity of the available food supply to maintain them, unless their numbers are controlled. His ideas influenced natural scientists as well as economists through the nineteenth century.

1802 Publication of William Paley's *Natural Theology: Or, Evidences of the Existence and Attributes of the Deity, Collected from the Appearances of Nature*. This interpretation of nature as a revelation of the designing hand and 'benevolence' of God had a wide influence. Darwin mused on but later rejected Paley's arguments.

1809 Publication of Jean-Baptiste Lamarck's *Philosophie zoologique, ou exposition des considérations relative à l'histoire des animaux*. Lamarck presented a theory of evolution based on the notion that animals develop certain more advanced features through adaptation to their environment and that these acquired traits are heritable.

1822 Gideon Mantell and Mary Ann Mantell discovered the teeth of a dinosaur, the Iguanadon, in Sussex, at a time of major advances in palaeontology, which called into question the permanence and fixity of species.

1824 Founding of the [Royal] Society for the Prevention of Cruelty to Animals, the first such organisation in the world.

1826 Founding of the Zoological Society of London. Its gardens and growing menagerie were opened to Fellows of the Society and their guests in 1828, and the public gradually gained entry without needing guest status. Admission was fully open to the public from 1847 onwards.

1830 Publication of Volume 1 of Charles Lyell's three-volume *Principles of Geology*, which presented the theory of 'uniformitarianism': landforms had been gradually shaped by slow natural processes, not by catastrophic upheavals like those described in the Old Testament. Lyell's interpretation of the earth's history influenced the development of Darwin's evolutionary theories.

1831 Founding of the British Association for the Advancement of Science. It held annual meetings in different cities for the presentation of scientific papers and for debates, which were widely reported in the press. Women gained admission to its sessions.

1831–6 Charles Darwin was on the *Beagle* voyage round the world, an experience which helped to shape his scientific knowledge, theories, and insights.

1837 Queen Victoria's accession to the throne. She reigned over the British Empire until 1901.

1841 William Henry Fox Talbot patented the 'calotype' process. It produced photographic negatives from which an indefinite number of positive prints could be taken, facilitating the rise of commercial photography.

1844 Robert Chambers's *Vestiges of the Natural History of Creation* was published anonymously. He suggested that evolution had occurred through transmutation of life forms. The scandal that the book caused on religious grounds deterred Darwin from publishing his own evolutionary theories until 1859.

1845 The Museums Act empowered borough councils to fund the establishment of local museums through a levy on the rates.

1851 The Great Exhibition of the Industry of All Nations took place in London in Paxton's Crystal Palace. It was the first such international exhibition, displaying the manufactures and artefacts of countries from across the world.

1854 The Crystal Palace, which had been rebuilt in an enlarged form at Sydenham in South London, was opened to the public, featuring reconstructions of ancient buildings and cultures as well as zoological and ethnic exhibits and contemporary art works. In the grounds there were life-size models of dinosaurs.

1858 Papers by Darwin and by Alfred Russel Wallace, both independently outlining the theory of natural selection, were read out by Joseph Hooker and Charles Lyell at a historic Linnaean Society meeting in London.

1859 Publication of Darwin's *On the Origin of Species by Means of Natural Selection*, causing a furor in the scientific world and beyond.

1860 The famous debate at Oxford about Darwin's theories, with their implications for human evolution. Thomas Huxley and Joseph Hooker defended Darwin's ideas against the ridicule and hostility of the Bishop of Oxford, Samuel Wilberforce.

1862 The International Exhibition was held in London, a world's fair that especially highlighted the achievements of the British Empire. It included new technology, manufactures, and art works, including Japanese artefacts.

1862 Publication of Darwin's *On the Various Contrivances by which British and Foreign Orchids are Fertilised by Insects*.

1866 Ernst Haeckel's *Generelle Morphologie der Organismen*, followed in 1868 by his *Natürliche Schöpfungsgeschichte*, introduced Darwin's ideas to Germany but included many new theories – for example, that the development of embryos recapitulated the evolutionary process.

1869 Publication of Alfred Russel Wallace's *The Malay Archipelago*, a major contribution to the development of biogeography.

1870 William Forster persuaded Parliament to pass the Elementary Education Act, through which local school boards were established, with the authority to set up schools in areas where they were needed. Further laws on schooling followed over the next decade, widening the provisions of the 1870 Act.

1871 Publication of Darwin's *The Descent of Man, and Selection in Relation to Sex*.

1872 Publication of Darwin's *The Expression of the Emotions in Man and Animals*.

1873 The opening of Anton Dohrn's Stazione Zoologica in Naples, supported by Darwin, promoted international research in marine biology.

1879 Founding of the Museums Association, which fostered discussions of the principles and practices of curatorship across a wide range of institutions.

1881 Opening of the new Natural History Museum designed by Alfred Waterhouse in South Kensington. William Henry Flower became its superintendent in 1884, succeeding Richard Owen, and fostered more adventurous approaches to display of the collections.

1885 Founding of the Selborne Society, dedicated to nature conservation.

1889 Founding of the [Royal] Society for the Protection of Birds by a group of women. Emily Williamson, Eliza Phillips, and Margaretta Lemon played leading roles, together with William Henry Hudson.

1891 Founding of the Humanitarian League by Henry Salt and Alice Drakoules. One of its leading aims was the promotion of better treatment of animals.

1895 Auguste and Louis Lumière presented moving pictures to audiences through their Cinématographe, leading to the beginnings of commercial cinema. Several natural history films were produced in the early 1900s.

SILENT CORRECTIONS

Chapter 3: James Sowerby identified Sir Isaac Newton as sir Isaac Newton in *A New Elucidation of Colours*.
Chapter 5: *catalogue raisonné* is misspelt *Raisonnéé*.
Chapter 6: In his letter to Thomas Bewick, James Wilson misspells Sivright as Sivwright throughout.
Chapter 10: Pritchard misspells chrysalis as crysalis.
Chapter 19: Alfred Palmer misspells Daniel Giraud Elliot as Daniel Giraud Elliott throughout.
Chapter 20: The anonymous journalist, writing of a lecture by Muybridge, misspells zoöpraxiscope as zoepracticoscope.
Chapter 21: W. P. Adams misspells Meissonier as Meissonnier.
Chapter 32: The anonymous reviewer of natural history exhibits at the Great Exhibition refers to John Hancock as Mr. Handcock.
Chapter 36.2: Otterhound is spelled as Otter-hound.
Chapter 41: The reviewer of a Landseer retrospective refers to fellow animal painter Briton Riviere as Mr. Rivière.
Chapter 43.1: The reviewer of Wolf's *The Life and Habits of Wild Animals* identifies D. G. Elliot as D. C. Elliot.
Chapter 53: *Chums* magazine identifies Riviere as Rivière throughout.
Chapter 55: Meandering was spelled meandring.
Chapter 70: Marks also spells Riviere as Rivière.
Chapter 77: The Edgeworths spell scissors as scissars.
Chapter 81: Samuel Highley misspells diagrammatic as diagramatic.
Chapter 82: aerie is spelled aeiry.
Chapter 89: visitor is spelled visiter.
Chapter 93.2: The reviewer identifies J. G. Wood as J.T. Wood.
Chapter 94: Revd John George Wood spells Dullness as Dulness (an old alternative spelling) in his 1887 article 'The Dulness of Museums' for *Nineteenth Century*.

Part I

VISUALISATION AND IMAGE-MAKING IN THE SERVICE OF SCIENCE

INTRODUCTION

In the history of the natural sciences, visual imagery has always been an indispensable accompaniment to verbal description. The general appearance of an animal, its proportions and peculiar features, are far more easily grasped through a visual image than through a text. In fact, communicable knowledge of its colours, so difficult to define in words, has, until the twentieth century, practically depended on hand-painted samples, like those provided in *Werner's Nomenclature of Colours*.[1] Clearly, illustrators needed a substantial knowledge of zoology in order to record with precision the definitive features of a specimen, representing it from the most revealing and significant angle of vision. They often had to contend with the difficulties of working from defective, ill-mounted, or faded specimens, or they might be re-working earlier images, which required all their own scientific expertise to amend. Sometimes, indeed, artists compiled and published works of natural history with plates on their own initiative, often featuring previously unknown species.[2]

Lorraine Daston and Peter Galison have advanced our understanding of the conceptual difficulties inherent in such imagery, as scientific illustration evolved over the eighteenth and nineteenth centuries through interactions between scientists and the artists they employed. There were difficulties in discriminating between typical and accidental features occurring in samples of a species, and of then choosing between an ideal image and an 'objective' rendering of a particular specimen. The two-dimensional image on the page was, moreover, always conditioned by preconception, technical limitations, and representational conventions.[3] Yet the practice of this difficult art – falling as it did between the hallowed fields of scientific enquiry and 'fine' art – usually enjoyed little respect or status. The Cambridge zoologist Professor Alfred Newton, in his article on 'Ornithology' in the *Encyclopædia Britannica*, certainly appreciated the importance of illustrations in bird books of the past and commented on them frequently as either an asset or a drawback in the use of various works. However, he did not discuss scientific illustration as an art form or a discipline in its own right, with its own history.[4]

DOI: 10.4324/9781003107835-1

In comparison with the theoretical knowledge and questing intellectualism of the scientist, the drawing of specimens could seem to be merely a technical skill; and in comparison with the high ideals of academic painting, focussing on epic subjects drawn from the Bible and history, it could be written off as narrow and trivial. Sir Joshua Reynolds, in his lectures to the students of the Royal Academy in the 1770s–80s, exhorted them to seek grand and uplifting human themes and to generalise forms in the interests of universality, emphasising tone rather than local colour: for 'it is certain, that a nice discrimination of minute circumstances, and a punctilious delineation of them, whatever excellence it may have, (and I do not mean to detract from it,) never did confer on the Artist the character of Genius'.[5] Illustrating the minutiae of nature's infinitely varied productions required scientific knowledge, powers of observation, and finesse, together with the ability to draw a *reverse* image of the specimen in question,[6] but it did not, supposedly, appeal to the intellect or imagination of any great artist. It was generally considered to be an occupation for illustrators of the second rank, who must always take directions from their learned employers.

One example of this kind of unequal working relationship between author and illustrator is on record because of the eminence of the scientist concerned: Charles Darwin. According to his son Francis, Darwin 'took much interest in the illustrations of his books', being anxious, or over-anxious, that they should support his arguments and help to convince the reader.[7] His volumes on the *Cirripedia* (barnacles) posed particular difficulties for the artists he employed – members of the Sowerby family – due to the peculiarity of these animals' distinguishing features as viewed through a microscope, and Darwin's stress on minute exactness in the representation of particular specimens – a good example of the new stress on 'objectivity'.[8] As he explained in a letter, everything depended on an accurate registration of 'lines of growth'.[9] The chosen artist in this case, James de Carle Sowerby, had to submit a preliminary drawing of each specimen to Darwin, based on an initial rough sketch by Darwin himself, indicating the desired viewpoint. Once Sowerby's drawing had been approved, he engraved it on a copper plate, alongside related species. His arrangements were carefully designed, with an eye to both scientific cogency and pleasing visual effect on the page. However, Darwin had often, in the interim, sent additional specimens to be fitted in on the same plate, or he had obtained a better specimen of a particular kind and requested Sowerby to erase his existing representation and substitute a new one. Such alterations were a tricky business when creating an intaglio engraving on copper.[10] Yet Darwin was continually urging greater speed, as collectors who had loaned specimens demanded their return: 'All this is very disagreeable to me & I do earnestly hope that you will endeavour to make more progress'.[11] It was not the first time that he had become exasperated with the artists who worked for him: in December 1837 he had confided to his friend and coadjutor Leonard Jenyns that those entrusted with the task of illustrating the *Beagle* voyage specimens were causing him endless trouble. With a nod to Voltaire, he joked that 'There will be no comfort in such undertakings, without a law is passed to empower naturalists every now and then to hang an artist for an example'.[12]

Darwin's expressions of frustration did not, understandably, acknowledge the expanding scope of zoological imagery in the 1820s and 1830s, which was one aspect of the growing interest in natural science – and of the wealthy public's pleasure in beautiful illustrations. Visual conventions originating in the old traditions of natural theology coalesced with the aesthetic tastes of bibliophiles. The magnificent bird drawings of Audubon, etched and hand-coloured as a 'double elephant folio' in the London workshop of Robert Havell, opened the eyes of British artists to the pictorial richness and dramatic power which zoological illustration could attain. At the same period the wood engraver Thomas Bewick produced books in which birds, while generally drawn from dead specimens, seemed to be brought back to life and restored to their natural habitats. His delicate vignettes depicting the various species gave glimpses of landscapes or watery settings, quite different in effect from the conventionalised tree stumps on which birds were perched in earlier ornithological works (see Chapters 5 and 6).

Audubon and Bewick stood at the head of two distinct but complementary genres in nineteenth-century natural history publishing. The scale and ambition of Audubon's images helped to inspire the many folios of illustrations of birds and the rarer species of mammals published during the century, which were aimed at wealthy book collectors, amateur naturalists, and art lovers. Works of this kind were generally issued in parts over a period of time and were sent out loose so that buyers could arrange them according to taste in their favoured taxonomic systems. However, the expense involved in drawing, engraving, printing, and hand-colouring the plates caused many projects to founder after a few instalments, especially if the number of subscribers declined. For more modest publications, Bewick's integration of text and wood-engraved vignettes on the page presented an important model – made possible by the fact that engraving on a wooden block is a relief medium that can be printed in one operation with the letterpress of the text and is very durable, allowing many reprints. This genre was developed in a classic work, William Yarrell's authoritative *History of British Birds*, which went through numerous editions,[13] and in the many popular illustrated books on animals produced for the Victorian middle-class public, which were often issued in monthly sections. Long after natural theology had ceased to be credible to scientists, the beauties of colour, form, and composition which it had inspired in zoological illustrations were retained by publishers on account of their visual appeal to potential buyers: an example is Frank E. Beddard's *Animal Coloration*, published as late as 1892, with its pretty vignettes of wildlife in natural surroundings.[14] Only when outdoor photography of birds and their nests was introduced into book illustrations during the 1890s did readers become conscious, through contrast, of the pictorial conventions to which they had long been accustomed.

The Victorian era was a time when growing interest in the natural world found expression in many visual and material forms beyond book illustration. One was the practice of making collections of animal specimens, which ranged from rich collectors' acquisitions of tropical insects to schoolboys' caches of British birds' eggs, plundered from the nests. In both cases, the specimens' aesthetic appeal could be as important to their possessor as the rarity or completeness of the collection. The improvement and diversification of taxidermy was another response to public interest in the natural world, and the development of dioramas or habitat groups of stuffed specimens was an attempt to simulate visually the conditions of nature itself. At the same time, the exploration of nature's minutiae became possible within the home through the manufacture of affordable microscopes, by means of which the behaviour of live creatures could be watched and even drawn. All these developments signalled the public's quest for knowledge, stimulated by the immense development of scientific theory and researches on the workings of the natural world. Gradually, nature was understood to involve constant movement and change – dynamic fluctuations and interactions that only a direct recording process could hope to capture. The development of outdoor photography, chrono-photography and eventually moving film was a response to this realisation, and the elaborate pictorial tableaux of animals represented in the plates of older natural history books correspondingly went out of favour. All these trends are exemplified in subsequent parts of this volume.

Notes

1 Patrick Syme, *Werner's Nomenclature of Colours . . . Arranged so as to Render it Highly Useful to the Arts and Sciences,* 1814, 2nd ed. (Edinburgh: William Blackwood and London: T. Cadell, 1821). This featured samples of colours, all delicately graded and nuanced. They were given names and referred to examples of their occurrence in animals, plants, and minerals. This work was widely used by natural scientists – Darwin had a copy on the *Beagle* voyage. However, the fact that each copy was hand-painted (colour printing was at that time incapable of producing the necessary range of tints with accuracy) limited its circulation.

2 There are many examples of this in the eighteenth century – for example, the ornithological works produced by Eleazar Albin, George Edwards, and James Bolton. John James Audubon's initiation of the *Birds of America* in the 1820s was, however, a project unique in its scope and ambition.

3 Lorraine Daston and Peter Galison, *Objectivity* (New York: Zone Books, 2010). Boris Jardine, 'Made Real: Artifice and Accuracy in Nineteenth-Century Scientific Illustration', *Science Museum Group Journal* 2 (Autumn 2014), n.p.

4 Alfred Newton, 'Ornithology', in *Encyclopaedia Britannica*, 9th ed., 1884. Reprinted by permission 'for private circulation' by the author, as an undated pamphlet.

5 *Sir Joshua Reynolds, Discourses on Art,* ed. Robert R. Wark (New Haven, CT, and London: Yale University Press, 1975), Discourse XI, 1782, pp. 191–204, on p. 192.

6 The specimen that served as a model had to be drawn and engraved in a mirror image, because this image would be reversed back again when an impression was taken from the plate or block. The printed image would then correspond to the direction of the original specimen. This was especially important when drawing, for example, the whorls of a shell. Cf. Warren D. Allmon, 'The Evolution of Accuracy in Natural History Illustration: Reversal of Printed Illustrations of Snails and Crabs in Pre-Linnaean Works Suggests Indifference to Morphological Detail', *Archives of Natural History*, 34:1 (2007), pp. 174–91.

7 *The Life and Letters of Charles Darwin*, ed. Francis Darwin, 3 vols. (London: John Murray, 1888), vol. 1, p. 156.

8 Jonathan Smith, *Charles Darwin and Victorian Visual Culture* (Cambridge: Cambridge University Press, 2006), ch. 2, 'Darwin's Barnacles', pp. 44–68. Members of the Sowerby family dynasty acquired considerable knowledge of natural science, as well as proficiency in drawing and engraving (see Chapters 3 and 4 in the present volume).

9 Darwin to James Scott Bowerbank of the Palaeontographical Society, 8 March 1850, Darwin Correspondence Project, letter no. 1310, at https://darwinproject.ac.uk/letter?docID=letters/DCP-LETT-1310.xml, and Darwin to James de Carle Sowerby, 13 April 1850, Darwin Correspondence Project, letter no. 1336, at https://darwinproject.ac.uk/letter?docID=letters/DCP-LETT-1336.xml [both accessed 14 November 2023].

10 Darwin's choice of line engraving on metal, an intaglio process, for the plates in the *Cirripedes* was unusual in the mid-nineteenth century: by then it had largely been superseded by the more convenient and durable media of wood engraving and lithography. However, Darwin prized the very fine linear detail that intaglio engraving provided. He had come to dislike lithography (which had been used for the plates in his *Zoology of the Voyage of HMS Beagle*) for its 'muzziness . . . a style of art . . . which in my opinion has been highly injurious to Nat. History – I do not care for artistic effect, but only for hard rigid accuracy'. Letter no. 1336 as cited in n. 9.

11 Darwin to James de Carle Sowerby, 12 or 19 August 1850, Darwin Correspondence Project, Letter no. 1346, at https://darwinproject.ac.uk/letter?docID=letters/DCP-LETT-1346.xml [accessed 14 November 2023].

12 Darwin to Leonard Jenyns, 3 December 1837, Darwin Correspondence Project, Letter no. 391, at https://darwinproject.ac.uk/letter?docID=letters/DCP=LETT-391.xml [accessed 14 November 2023].

13 William Yarrell, *A History of British Birds* (London: John van Voorst, 1839). Further editions of this work followed in 1843, 1845, 1856, and an edition revised by Professor Alfred Newton from 1874 to 1885.

14 Frank Evers Beddard, *Animal Coloration: An Account of the Principal Facts and Theories Relating to the Colours and Markings of Animals*, 1892, 2nd ed. (London: Swan Sonnenschein and New York: Macmillan, 1895).

Editorial Headnote

1. Thomas Martyn, *A Short Account Of The Nature, Principle, And Progress Of A Private Establishment* (1789)

This *Account*, which was intended to recommend Martyn's books to potential patrons, was originally inserted in his *The Universal Conchologist, Exhibiting the Figure of every known Shell accurately drawn, and painted after Nature, with a New Systematic Arrangement by the Author* ('Sold at his House', 4 vols, 1784). Martyn, himself a natural history painter, explains that this kind of illustration was little esteemed, and hence its practitioners were often poorly trained and badly paid – despite the growing importance of studies in natural science. He therefore decided to recruit ten underprivileged but gifted boys to learn the art of illustration under his guidance, and he was gratified that their drawings for *The Universal Conchologist* were praised by his distinguished, high-ranking patrons for their perfectionism.[1] Martyn explains that the quality of the boys' work improved so much through understanding and practice, that he decided to discard their first delineations of the various subjects: they were now able to produce much better ones for publication. This move was facilitated by the fact that the whole production of his great *Conchology* took place in-house: the original drawings, the etchings and engravings based on these drawings, and the printing and hand-colouring of each plate, were all consistent in style and quality. Accuracy in representing the various specimens was to be complemented by 'good taste', so that scientific illustration might gain admission to 'the circle of the polite arts'.[2]

Editorial Endnotes

1 Martyn printed several commendatory letters from grandees who had been sent early copies of the work on shells. In "Letter 1', dated 18 August 1787 (p. 36), Ignatius Baron Born assured him that it 'surpasses every thing that ever has been, or ever will be produced in the same kind. Natural history would make a rapid progress, if we could have paintings of all the organized bodies in nature executed with equal accuracy and fidelity. It is evident that the author joins to a very extraordinary degree of talent in his own art, the most profound knowledge of natural history, and especially of those bodies of which he treats'.

2 Christine E. Jackson, 'The Painting of Hand-Coloured Zoological Illustrations', *Archives of Natural History* 38:1 (2011), pp. 36–53, on p. 44. See also her article 'The Materials and Methods of Hand-Colouring Zoological Illustrations' in the same issue of *Archives of Natural History*, pp. 53–64.

1

A SHORT ACCOUNT OF A PRIVATE ESTABLISHMENT, INSTITUTED FOR THE PURPOSE OF INSTRUCTING YOUTH IN THE ART OF ILLUSTRATING, AND PAINTING, SUBJECTS IN NATURAL HISTORY

Thomas Martyn

Source: Thomas Martyn, *A Short Account of the Nature, Principle, and Progress, of a Private Establishment, Instituted for the Purpose of Instructing Youth in the Art of illustrating, and painting, Subjects in Natural History; by the Author, Thomas Martyn, At his House, N°16, Great Marlborough-Street* (London, 1789), pp. 26–32.

It is now upwards of seven years since the author first commenced the design of attempting a new work on Shells . . . In the prosecution of this design many and great difficulties necessarily presented themselves. To execute a work perfectly original in its kind, where the highest and most finished style of painting was intended particularly to characterise the performance, was an undertaking attended with obstacles of no common magnitude: for to have effected this purpose in the ordinary way, by employing those who might be found capable of executing the work according to the author's ideas, would eventually have been attended with an expense so great, as in its necessary consequences would more than have trebled the price of each volume.

One very essential cause of this aggravation of expense is, that there are few artists (we may indeed say none) who peculiarly devote the application of their talents to this particular branch of the art. Of the miniature painters who excel, it can never be worth the while, without a very liberal compensation, to interrupt their exertions in their own proper line, and to transfer their time and skill to other subjects, which they are in the habit of considering as of an inferior class[1] . . . In this distress the author conceived the project of endeavouring to accomplish his design by means as simple as they were new: he had to find for the execution of his purpose such hands as, possessing abilities adequate to the end, could not, from their situations in life, be more profitably employed in other occupations.

DOI: 10.4324/9781003107835-2

The labour of boys he knew is always cheaper than that of men: and he concluded, that where nature had plentifully sown the seeds of genius for any particular pursuit, very little art would be requisite to cherish and rear the plant to maturity.

There was also another recommendation, which powerful operated upon his mind. He thought it probable that in the productions of boys, all of whom had received their first rudiments of good taste from the same common preceptor, and who should execute whatever they did under his immediate inspection and controul, there would generally be found that uniformity and equality of style, conception, and execution, which it would be vain to require from a variety of independent artists, who may have been bred in very dissimilar schools, and over whom little authority could be exercised.

Impressed with this idea, his attention was now directed to discover, and instruct a number of young persons, who, born of good but humble parents, could not from their own means aspire to the cultivation of any liberal art; at the same time that they gave indications of natural talents for drawing and design, and of minds influenced by a decided preference for those pleasing and elegant studies . . . with their joint efforts in the space of two years such advances were made in the work as enabled the author to shew various specimens of their performances to several persons of distinguished rank, and acknowledged judges of the subject. – The flattering encomiums which they bestowed, and (what was the most convincing proof of their sincerity) the great number of orders which he received for the work itself, amply demonstrated the success of his plan . . . upwards of 70 copies of two volumes of the work were finished, containing nearly 6000 duplicate paintings of Shells.

By the variety of experiments necessarily made to complete this number of copies, the pupils had very greatly improved in their style of painting the various objects; and every day afforded new lights for the better understanding of the principles of the art itself, and for the more perfect execution of its several subordinate branches. It now appeared, that a very great progress had been made towards that degree of pre-eminence which the author had continually wished to attain; for by comparing the bulk of the work then finished with the latest specimens produced, the more early performances appeared so very inferior to the later, as at once to determine the author totally to reject the whole of the copies, the plates from which they were worked, and even the paintings from which those plates were engraved; consequently the whole was again begun to be pursued anew through all its parts in that improved style of execution, which was ultimately to determine the fate and reputation of the work. These sacrifices, so heavy in themselves, yet so necessary to give to the present publication all its possible perfection, were still encreased by other similar and concurrent circumstances; as it has been deemed requisite, in a variety of instances, to make six or ten duplicate paintings of some of the more difficult subjects that have occurred, before one could be obtained which the author judged sufficiently accurate to adopt for an original . . . In the work on English insects, particularly, very great expense, as well as disappointment, was incurred through the obstinacy or carelessness of the artist employed to etch the figures; who was too vain of his own judgment, or too frugal of his labour, to follow with due accuracy the drawings prepared for him: this rendered his whole performance, which he had twice attempted, altogether unserviceable, and gave occasion to introduce this additional branch of business into the academy. Since this occurrence, the art of etching has by some of his pupils been assiduously cultivated; and the author presumes, that *The English Entomologist*; *The Work on Spiders*; and the etchings of several views of different islands in the South Seas, together with a variety of other performances which already have or soon will be published, afford pleasing and satisfactory testimonies of their merits in that department.

Having so long laboured with patience and perseverance in this arduous enterprise, and having sunk in it no inconsiderable share of a private competence, the author has at length the singular gratification of seeing his most sanguine expectations realised by the event; and an animating prospect now begins to open upon him, that his academy will continue to rise in the estimation of mankind by the production of works still more important to the illustration of the different kingdoms of nature, and by giving that extension to the circle of the polite arts, which it is hoped will redound to the credit and honour of the country where this establishment has been first formed.

Editorial Endnote

1 Martyn is referring here to painters of miniature portraits, often mounted in lockets, watchcases, etc.

Editorial Headnote

2. Thomas Martyn, *The English Entomologist* (1792)

This book on beetles was published by Martyn in 1792 and dedicated to Charles IV, King of Spain – an indication of the international nature of his clientele. Martyn's preface explains his approach to illustration, expanding the information given in his earlier book on shells. He indicates the difficulties he experienced in reconciling the demands of scientific accuracy – representing each insect at life size, and in its correct taxonomic grouping – with patrons' expectation that each plate would be a thing of beauty. The fastidiously engraved and hand-coloured plates, with drawings of the various insects (often tiny species) arranged in symmetrical patterns on the page, do in fact reconcile scientific ordering with aesthetic appeal or 'show'. They probably echo the effect of the tastefully mounted specimens in collectors' cabinets.

2

THE ENGLISH ENTOMOLOGIST, EXHIBITING ALL THE COLEOPTEROUS INSECTS FOUND IN ENGLAND

Thomas Martyn

Source: Thomas Martyn, *The English Entomologist, Exhibiting all the Coleopterous Insects found in England: Including upwards of 500 different Species, The Figures of which have never before been given to the Public: The Whole Accurately drawn & painted after Nature. Arranged and named according to the Linnean System* (published by the author, 1792), pp. 2–6.

A good system being obtained,[1] the aid of the draughtsman and painter, are necessary auxiliaries to delineate the delicate figure, varied colours, the peculiar attitudes, and beautiful outline of nature: but more especially to pourtray, with minute accuracy, the essential characters which mark the several orders, and again divide their respective genera. A work that possesses these advantages, that has also good materials to show the merit of the execution, and is directed by a taste competent to dispose the objects with a pleasing effect; must have a decided superiority over every other performance of the kind, and be received with universal approbation.

How far we have succeeded in this attempt at superiority, we cannot presume to determine; but thus much with truth may be said, that no labour or cost has been spared to render this Publication as correct and beautiful, as the subject is interesting.

The Public are already acquainted, that the Author, at a very great expence, has established an Academy of Youths, whose principal requisite for their introduction is the possessing a natural Genius for Drawing and Painting, to be cultivated and exerted under his immediate and sole direction. From this institution two productions have already issued: the former work, on the Non-descript Shells of the South Seas; and the present, on the Coleopterous Insects of England. These publications, even if the Author should be ultimately prevented from completing those designs which he is still prosecuting, have at least a tendency, and will, it is hoped, be found to contribute not a little to the bringing into one view, faithful and elegant representations of that infinite variety of shells now distributed in many celebrated cabinets of Europe; to the illustration of all those beautiful and

DOI: 10.4324/9781003107835-3

curious species of insects found in England, of which the greater part are either non-descripts, or their figures hitherto unpublished; and lastly, and principally, to the founding an Academy of Painters of Natural History, working on principles which give a transparency, with richness of colours, and a facility of execution, that are entirely new; and altogether (it is presumed) redounding to national credit and honour.[2]

The present volume, therefore, and the subsequent ones which are to appear,[3] have, in the Author's mind, been long intended in the present form to be laid before the Public, and to accomplish this purpose in its fullest extent, every endeavour has been exerted for several years past, to assemble as far as possible all the necessary objects: the representations of the whole, with a very few exceptions, being drawn immediately from those insects which are contained in the Author's cabinet.

And here it will be necessary to mention, that all imaginable care has been taken, not to admit the figure of any one insect into this work, where the least doubt remained of its being a native of this country. Respecting the classification, the Author has exerted his utmost endeavours by a minute investigation of each object (as far at least as his poor abilities would allow), to place each individual in the respective order and genus to which its figure, and peculiar characteristics entitled it, as laid down in the Linnean System. At the same time, the Entomologist is acquainted, that to preserve a general uniformity in the disposition of the figures, no particular regard has been paid to place together those subdivisions or sections of genera, as defined in the illustrations at large; but where an essential difference was observed in the sexes, or a striking variety in the same species, strict attention was then had to show that variety, and also to give both male and female in the same plate. Peculiar care has also been had, that each figure shall be as near as possible in size to the particular insect which it represents; a method which the Author is aware, will with some persons affect the apparent value of the work: he has however little doubt but judges, and real lovers of this science, will applaud the sacrifice here made of show, to the more essential requisites due to accuracy, to truth, and to nature; to accomplish which, is well known to be far more difficult, than to present unnatural and magnified objects.

Editorial Endnotes

1 By 'system' Martyn means taxonomic arrangement and nomenclature, in this case based on those devised by Linnaeus.

2 No such academy materialised: the workshop system continued with specialisation in skilled roles; sometimes the colouring of prints was carried out in separate premises by outworkers.

3 The work on insects does not seem to have proceeded beyond this first volume.

Editorial Headnote

3. James Sowerby, *A New Elucidation of Colours* (1809)

James Sowerby trained as an artist at the Royal Academy, but he also acquired substantial knowledge of natural sciences, becoming an extremely fine illustrator of animal and plant specimens. Writing in the first decade of the nineteenth century, he confronted the difficulty that would also be experienced by his successors: to find a means of recording and naming colours consistently, for naturalists to reference when describing new or little-known species. The colours in nature were largely undefined: they were nuanced and variable according to light conditions or angle of vision, and they were often fugitive or subject to change, as were the pigments used to paint and record them. Like Werner in his famous *Nomenclature of Colours*, Sowerby nevertheless tried to find stable reference points in nature for the definition and exemplification of colours.[1]

Editorial Endnote

1 *Werner's Nomenclature* is discussed in the introduction to Part I of the present volume.

3

A NEW ELUCIDATION OF COLOURS, ORIGINAL PRISMATIC, AND MATERIAL

James Sowerby

Source: James Sowerby, *A New Elucidation of Colours, Original Prismatic, and Material; Showing Their Concordance in Three Primitives, Yellow, Red, and Blue; and the Means of Producing, Measuring, and Mixing Them: With Some Observations on the Accuracy of Sir Isaac Newton* (London: printed by Richard Taylor & Co., 1809), Introduction pp. 5–6, and p. 41.

[pp. 5–6]

That philosophers and artists have long wished for some never-fading colours to fix their ideas and universalize them, is in every age amply verified; and as coloured substances, like all other sublunary things, are liable to a certain decay, so it has been but weakly attempted lately; besides, the difficulty of finding a means of agreement in the modifying and arranging them has been a desideratum, as late works have abundantly shown . . . The use of a true original for colours, and a regularity of arrangement, is almost infinite; for to the artist in any line it will be a solid satisfaction to know when he treads on a sure foundation, laid by unerring Nature. The mineralogist, the botanist and the zoologist may in future agree in their descriptions and ideas, so as to identify them to all parts of the world, and the remotest ages . . . Yellow, red, and blue, I presume, therefore, will more properly form the remainder of the seven prismatic tints, than either two or more of the seven will form a single primary colour. I would not have insisted so much on this subject, but that the present improving state of natural science seems to demand a concordance of the primitives of prismatic tints and substantial colours, which appear so much to depend on each other; and it has been understood by many, from the time of Sir Isaac Newton, that the prismatic tints may be imitated by what I would consider as simple primitives, viz. yellow, red, and blue.[1]

[p. 41]

Colours are identically the same on any substance however reflected, whether mineral, as from earthy or metallic ones; vegetable, as from flowers or fruit; or animal, as from hair, feathers, &c. . . . I once thought of making more references to the three primitive colours in minerals, vegetables, and animals: however, as minerals are chiefly used, so they come of course in their places as material

DOI: 10.4324/9781003107835-4

colours.[2] Vegetables in Great Britain have good yellows, as most Ranunculuses[3]; perfect blues are more scarce, and perfect reds also. I cannot find that we can refer to any British insect for yellow, red, or blue. The Rev. W. Kirby, author of the Monographia Apum Angliæ, was so good as to point out some parts of insects, including some foreign ones, that would identify these colours very well, when the specimens are perfect; but perhaps it might be aggravating to make these references, as something might be wrong.[4] Birds and quadrupeds have the local colours in parts occasionally very brilliant. The scarlet Ibis is universally allowed to be so; and D. Turner, Esq. in his *Fuci*, considers red as between crimson and scarlet; which seems to me to be perfectly correct.[5]

Editorial Endnotes

1 Sowerby means that red, yellow, and blue, as primitive or primary colours, cannot (unlike orange, green, and purple) be formed by a mixture of tints. The nature of colours and human ocular perceptions of them were to be widely discussed in the nineteenth century.
2 Sowerby seems to mean that natural minerals were often used in paints, as was indicated in the names given to the latter.
3 'Ranunculuses' are plants of the buttercup family.
4 The Revd William Kirby, a leading entomologist, was the author of *Monographia Apum Angliae* (1802), a work on British bees. Kirby's *Introduction to Entomology* (1818) figures as Chapter 55 in the present volume.
5 Dawson Turner, *Fuci; Or, Coloured Figures and Descriptions of the Plants Referred by Botanists to the Genus Fucus*, 4 vols. (London: John and Arthur Arch, 1808–19), a work on seaweeds.

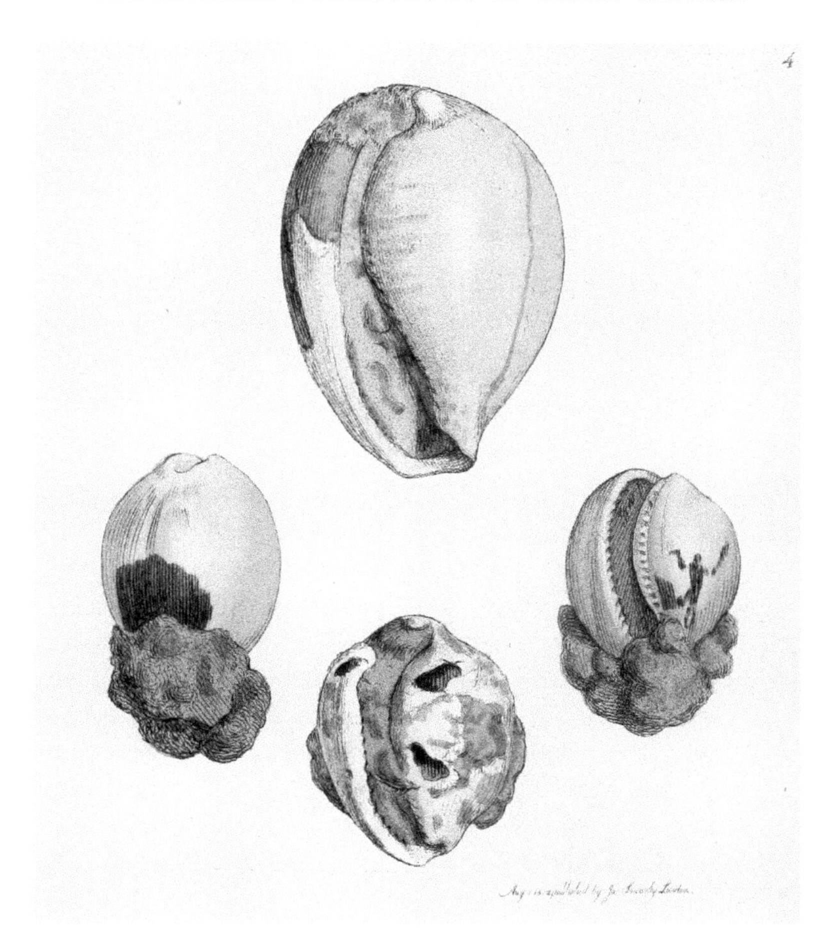

Figure 1 James Sowerby, *The Mineral Conchology of Great Britain*, (London: printed by Benjamin Meredith for the author, 1812), plate IV, 'Cypræa oviformis', engraving and watercolour. (Biodiversity Heritage Library)

Editorial Headnote

4. James Sowerby, *The Mineral Conchology Of Great Britain* (1812)

The plates of James Sowerby's *Mineral Conchology* have varying dates and were probably first issued as separate sheets. There were eventually seven volumes to the *Conchology*. This first volume was published in 1812, and Sowerby added volumes 2–4 between 1818 and 1823, the work being subsequently 'continued' by his sons and completed as late as 1846. In the early 1800s, extensive excavations for engineering projects, mining, quarrying, etc. brought many previously unknown kinds of fossil shells to light. Sowerby collected, borrowed, or was given a great number of them, his benefactors including the palaeontologist Gideon Mantell and the geologist William Smith. Such specimens were a vital tool in the expansion of scientific knowledge, despite their damaged state and the loss of their geological context. As his son James de Carle Sowerby would later explain, 'examination of the structure of the earth's crust' had hardly begun in the early 1800s, but the illustrations in the *Mineral Conchology*, with identifying names attached to them, had an abiding value as points of reference in geological research.[1] The text of Sowerby's book is essentially a commentary on the plates (on facing pages), where he attempted to convey in two dimensions the peculiarities of shape in his specimens. He considered that the shells, though long hidden in the earth, reflected divinity in their beauties of form and colour. His delicate drawings of them, rendered as intaglio prints (line engraving and etching) with hand-colouring, were a labour of love – he delighted in their wavy striations, spirals, and patterning, and arranged them harmoniously on the page (see Figure 1). Even the chemical changes that had occurred over time were often treated as providential enhancements of their beauties. However, Sowerby also discussed the affinities between fossil shells and some extant or 'recent' species – a worrying phenomenon for believers in natural theology, as it pointed to the extinction or evolution of some life forms over the millennia.

Editorial Endnote

1 James de Carle Sowerby, *Systematical, Stratigraphical and Alphabetical Indexes to the First Six Volumes of the Mineral Conchology of Great Britain* (London: the Author, 1835), n.p. In 'Preface to the Indexes', Sowerby's son explained the need to systematise the *Mineral Conchology* in the light of more advanced knowledge, and to 'crave consideration for errors towards those who alike were more conversant with the pencil than the pen, and who have sacrificed much towards the advancement of their favourite sciences'.

4

THE MINERAL CONCHOLOGY OF GREAT BRITAIN

James Sowerby

Source: James Sowerby, *Mineral Conchology*, pp. vi–vii. *The Mineral Conchology of Great Britain; with Coloured Figures and Descriptions of those Remains of Testaceous Animals or Shells, which have been preserved at various times and depths in the earth*, 7 vols (London: printed by Benjamin Meredith . . . and sold by the Author, J. Sowerby, 1812), vol. 1, pp. vi–vii, 17–18, 57, 74.

[pp. vi–vii]

The remains of Shells are sometimes so well preserved that many recent ones are not equal to them, either in preservation or beauty, and it often happens that the peculiar nature of their situation preserves them in a manner that excels all our art in representation. The pearly lustre is, in some, even superior to that of the most recent Shells, and the changes into Carbonate of Lime with the crystallized structure, into Flint, Calcedony, &c. are generally such as to excite our admiration; every minutia being so well cast as to preserve the most attenuated striæ or elaborate markings; and even the polish and colour are often admirably retained, and additional splendour gained under ground, by means of Sulphuret of Iron, giving a metallic lustre which equals, if it does not surpass every thing else . . . The description will say in general what change a specimen may have undergone, and the figures will be done in such a way as to help the description as much as may be, with the shining pearly stony or metallic brilliancy. Many species of one genus may be included in a plate, as it might be thought insignificant to figure a single small Shell alone. I have long since possessed a tolerable collection of British Fossil Shells. To the addition of a fine series from Highgate, by favour of my indefatigable friend B.G. Snow, Esq. may be attributed my more particular attention to this branch of Natural History.[1] I here beg leave to thank him and other kind friends for the many specimens received, and hope the present undertaking will meet their approbation.

[pp. 17–18]

CYPRÆA oviformis . . . The shell is most gibbous[2] at about one-third of its length downwards, then tapering to a short beak, which forms a broadish canal; the aperture vertical, narrowest where the body of the shell is most gibbous, and much widest towards the beak, dentated on both sides. The whole shell smooth and shining, with the striæ of growth generally delicately marked in elegant

DOI: 10.4324/9781003107835-5

curves round the beak; there are some longitudinal angles, scarcely perceptible, surrounding the most swelling parts; colour pale brown buff. It does not appear that this shell was known any where before the opening of the hill at Highgate, not even in Hampshire. Some specimens are so well preserved as to retain entire the external shining porcelain coat, which is so admirable in some recent shells of this Genus, but not the transparent epidermis, although it looks almost as if it were in some of these preserved specimens; this china-like polished surface seems to prevent parasitical shells or animals from adhering to it. This coat is often more beautiful in consequence of external marks, but the present species is sufficiently preserved to show if there had been any. The upper shell has a little remains of the shining outside, the upper part is a little broken, the lower part or beak is very entire, and shows some of the teeth . . . It is to be observed that accidently the plate of these shells has been reversed in the engraving, bringing the mouths to the left instead of the right side.[3]

[p. 57]

VENUS lineolata . . . Length about one inch and three quarters, width about two inches and and half; the beak is rather prominent, and the thickness of the shell not remarkable; the cicatrix is cordate, but not well defined.

This is the Venus from Blackdown, near Collumpton in Devonshire, spoken of by Mr. Parkinson, and which I had much wished to see, and my wishes were soon gratified, for almost the same day a parcel arrived from Miss Hill, with this extraordinary specimen, which, notwithstanding the great change that has taken place in its substance which is now siliceous approaching to Agate or Calcedony, has the elegant zigzag lines yet distinct.[4] It adheres by its inside to agglutinated sand so strongly, that I could not attempt to get at the hinge without danger of spoiling it; I therefore have placed with it a shell which shows the hinge, and from the outward contour appears to be of the same genus. The numerous greenish black particles of Chlorite in this sand characterize the stratum.

This shell does not agree with Linnæus's description of Venus castrensis.

[p. 74]

EMARGINULA reticulata . . . It is remarkable that this shell is so strictly concordant in every character with the recent Patella fissura of Linn. [Linnaeus] that it cannot be separated as a distinct species, a circumstance that may be adduced to strengthen the idea of a learned gentleman and friend of mine, that many recent shells may be the same species as the deeper or older fossils, but are more or less degenerated, or have from various causes even assumed such new characters as not to be identified, being more different than mules. The little we know of this subject at present, makes it difficult to comprehend the wisdom displayed on the globe, but as the field is open, and the enquiry began, I hope it will be improved, as I have no doubt of Almighty indulgence, since these relicts are so miraculously preserved, not only for our times, but for ages yet to come, especially as improvement in this science has of late years been very rapid.

Editorial Endnotes

1 The excavations for a cutting on the road to Highgate, north of London, had exposed a large number of fossils embedded in the soil.
2 'Gibbous' means rounded out, protuberant.
3 The drawing engraved on a copper plate is reversed in the process of printing. Sowerby or an assistant must have been absentminded when engraving this specimen in the same direction as the model. See Part 1 Introduction, note 6.
4 Sowerby often mentions the names of women like Miss Hill who were themselves expert shell-collectors and who assisted him by sending specimens and information. Shell-collecting, like botany, was considered a suitable branch of natural history for ladies to take up, as it involved no cruelties, like the shooting of birds. The further reference is to James Parkinson's *Organic Remains of a Former World. An Examination of the Mineralized Remains of the Vegetables and Animals of the Antediluvian World; Generally Termed Extraneous Fossils*, 3 vols. (London: Sherwood, Neely and Jones, 1811), vol. 3, p. 187.

Editorial Headnote

5. Anon., '*The History of British Birds . . .* By T. Bewick', Review in *Annals of Philosophy* (1822)

The *History* in question was a new, expanded edition, published in 1821, of an already famous work by the Newcastle wood engraver and author Thomas Bewick.[1] According to this reviewer, it contained 'no less than *thirty-eight* cuts of birds not before figured by Mr Bewick' (p. 294), meriting a fresh appraisal of his achievements. Bewick's *History of British Birds* had appeared in two volumes: volume 1 on land birds was first published in 1797 and volume 2 on water birds in 1804.[2] Both were immediately successful in their combination of fine wood engravings of bird species and country scenes set into the text pages, and there were numerous subsequent editions with many variations and additions.

Editorial Endnotes

1 There is an extensive literature on Bewick. See especially Iain Bain, *The Watercolours and Drawings of Thomas Bewick*, 2 vols. (London: Gordon Fraser, 1981); Bain (ed.), Thomas Bewick, *My Life* (London: Folio Society, 1981); Jenny Uglow, *Nature's Engraver, A Life of Thomas Bewick* (London: Faber and Faber, 2006); Nigel Tattersfield, *Thomas Bewick. The Complete Illustrative Work*, 3 vols. (London: The British Library and The Bibliographic Society, and New Castle, DE: Oak Knoll Press, 2011); Diana Donald, *The Art of Thomas Bewick* (London: Reaktion Books, 2013). However, this article in *Annals of Philosophy* has not previously received attention.

2 Full bibliographical information is provided in Tattersfield, *Thomas Bewick*, vol. 2, pp. 35–6.

5

'THE HISTORY OF BRITISH BIRDS . . . BY T. BEWICK', REVIEW

Anon., Annals of Philosophy

Source: Anon. ['H'], review, '*The History of British Birds* . . . by T. Bewick', *Annals of Philosophy*, new series, 4:4 (October 1822), pp. 294–308.

It would be foreign to our present purpose to give any analysis of the principal work, public opinion having long since decided on its merits. But as an opportunity has never occurred of particularly adverting to it, we would here desire to express the gratification which repeated perusals of that instructive and entertaining production have afforded us. Its original pretensions, it is well known, were of the most unassuming kind. The 'History of Quadrupeds,' to which it was a sort of sequel, was intended as a succedaneum for the book of 300 animals.[1] That paltry collection, however it might please the eye of childhood, was justly deemed an appendage fit for the nursery only. An elementary treatise which, while it inculcated a better taste and more correct knowledge, should by its amusing form imperceptibly win the minds of our youth to the study of natural history, was a desideratum. These objects, however, are so much better set forth by the author himself in his preface to the second volume of the present work, that, although it be stepping a little out of our way, we cannot help recurring to it. The passage to which we are about to quote contains a fair specimen of his general style, sentiments, and manner. 'The great work,' he says, 'of forming the man cannot be begun too early. Among the many approved branches of instruction Natural History holds a distinguished rank. To enlarge on the advantages which are derivable from a knowledge of the creation, is surely not necessary; to become initiated into this knowledge, is to become enamoured of its charms; to attain the object in view requires but little previous study or labour; the road which leads to it soon becomes strewed with flowers, and ceases to fatigue: a flow is given to the imagination which banishes early prejudices and expands the ideas; and an endless fund of the most rational entertainment is spread out, which captivates the attention and exalts the mind. For the attainment of this science in any of its various departments, the foundation may be laid insensibly in youth, whereon a goodly superstructure of useful knowledge can easily be raised at a more advanced period. In whatever way indeed the varied objects of this beautiful world are viewed, they

DOI: 10.4324/9781003107835-6

are readily understood by the contemplative mind; for they are found alike to be the visible words of God. Could mankind be prevailed upon to read a few lessons from the great book of nature, so amply spread out before them, they would clearly see the hand of Providence in every page.'[2]

'In ideas congenial with these, originated the first incitements which drew forth the histories of quadrupeds and British birds. From these humble attempts – for every attempt to depicture nature must fall short of the original – it is hoped that some useful instruction may be gathered, and at the same time a stimulus excited to further enquiry. To the rising generation these efforts to instruct and please are principally directed, and are set forth with an ardent wish that they may be found to deserve the notice of youth, and contribute to amuse and to inform them. May the reader, impressed with sentiments of humanity, on viewing the portraits, spare and protect the originals, and when these books shall become obsolete, or be lost in the revolution of time, may some other more able naturalist arise equally inclined to produce better to supply their place.'

Writing like this, it must be acknowledged, harmonizes admirably with the author's design, and is well calculated to promote the end at which he aims. His work, though in the first instance directed to the rising generation, has not been unproductive of advantage even to the initiated. In fact, it has been gradually becoming a book of authority and reference to the naturalists of every country. This character it owes scarcely less to the mass of select and valuable matter accumulated by its industrious author, than to his long established celebrity as a painter and engraver. It is true, there does not appear in it much display of that elaborate systematic research which some other works can boast, but the information contained in it is not on that account the less ample, precise, and authentic.

It is not our business to enter into the history of that beautiful and useful art which it was reserved for our able countryman to revive, and in reviving (dare we say?) to perfect.[3] A few particulars, however, relating to it, we may notice, for the sake of correcting some misconceptions which strangely enough prevail even to the present time.

It has, for example, been repeatedly alleged, and is perhaps very generally credited, that wood is better adapted than copper to the pourtraying of animated nature. Whereas, the fact is quite the reverse. The superiority of copper is notorious, so far as regards softness of outline, delicacy and minuteness of execution, truth and fineness of ultimate effect . . . We have investigated this subject with some attention, and our conviction is that had Mr. B. practised copper engraving, he could with equal ease have excelled in it. Nay he might have surpassed even his present reputation on wood[4] . . .

Wood, however, has some compensating advantages of which it would seem he thought proper to avail himself. Possessing every suitable requisite for beauty, accuracy and effect, (at least in Mr. Bewick's hands,) it is also more *durable*, paradoxical though that may sound . . . It results from these circumstances that the expense of publication and the cost to purchasers are prevented from exceeding the bounds of moderation. Thus one of the primary objects of the work, that of combining pleasing and useful instruction with economy, is effectually accomplished . . . These results, according to our judgment, fully warrant the opinion, that in truth and vigour of conception, boldness of outline, justness of proportion, fidelity and minuteness of delineation, adherence to physiognomy, attitude, character, manner, in short, in all that constitutes 'nature's copy,' Mr. Bewick has in his own particular province never been approached . . . We well know the difficulty in a provincial town of procuring good specimens, and we would heartily forgive him any reluctance he might feel to compromise his reputation by engraving from bad ones. The possessors of rare British birds do not seem to be yet thoroughly aware of the advantage they deny themselves of having their specimens imperishably preserved by *fac similes* from the graver of Mr. Bewick.[5]

The birds are arranged somewhat promiscuously in the Supplement. We must content ourselves with presenting little more than a sort of *Catalogue Raisonné*, interspersed with such notices as do not appear in the text, but which may not be wholly uninteresting[6] . . .

Strix Bubo – *Lin.* Le Duc ou Grand Duc – Buf. Eagle Owl, or great Eared Owl. – The most sage and dignified, if not the largest of the owl tribe, justifying by its sedate and thoughtful look the conceit of the ancients, which made it symbolical of wisdom. The cut affords a striking instance of the success of wood engraving in conveying all the difficulties of indistinctly variegated plumage. In the body of the work, we would particularly point out the white owl (*S. Flammea*), the long eared owl, bittern, night jar, tame duck, woodcock, and starling, as splendid examples of the same kind . . .

Strix Scops – *Lin.* Scops ou petit Duc – Buf. Little Horned Owl. – The engraving art scarcely furnishes any thing to surpass the softness and delicacy of touch displayed by Mr. Bewick in the plumage of this, the most diminutive of the owl kind. Indeed, we may remark that in the representation of plumage, he stands unrivalled. Artists in general content themselves with giving a rough resemblage of plumage. Mr. Bewick gives each particular feather, or at least all the important classes of feathers, as they are to be seen on the body of the bird . . .

Larus Fuscus – *Lin.* Goéland a manteau gris brun – Buf. Herring Gull . . . we notice it here for the purpose of remarking that the portrait now given of it, will, we have little doubt, be allowed by every attentive observer to be admirable. The artist has, with his usual intuitive and felicitous tact, seized on the leading peculiarities in the character and manner of this bird, – particularly its eager watchfulness, readiness to take flight, and give warning to all in its neighbourhood of approaching danger . . .

Scolopax Canescens – *Lin.* (Gmel.) Cinereous godwit. This bird terminates the supplement. Mr. B. closes his description of it with some remarks on the confusion which prevails regarding the scolopax and tringa genera. The fluctuation of plumage, reserved habits, and near affinities of these numerous and ill-defined tribes will long oppose obstacles to the settlement of their respective claims. Nor will the absence of all precision in the language of colour, be one of the least obstacles to such settlement. Writers on natural history have, indeed, denied themselves a powerful auxiliary in so long hesitating to adopt Werner's Nomenclature of Colours, or some other constructed on a similar basis. We must give full credit to Mr. B. for the disinterestedness of his wishes on this point (excepting so far as he has to depend on the information of others), for no one stands less in need of colour to render his figures recognizable.[7]

Editorial Endnotes

1 The reviewer here suggests that Bewick's *A General History of Quadrupeds* of 1790 was originally intended as a high-quality book for children – a replacement for Thomas Boreman's wholly unscientific but often reprinted *Description of Three Hundred Animals* (see chapter 77 in the present volume, n. 1).

2 On Bewick's belief in natural theology: Donald, *The Art of Thomas Bewick*, pp. 49–50, 85–8.

3 Bewick was credited with reviving, or developing, the art of high-quality wood engraving. By working on the polished end grain (i.e., a cross-section) of dense boxwood, he was able to achieve fine detail that would have been impossible when working on a plank of pear wood, etc., such as was used for cheap popular woodcuts.

4 The writer distinguishes between the nature of wood engraving, in which the lines to be inked and printed are in relief, and the nature of copper engraving and etching, which are intaglio media. For the significance of this distinction in scientific illustration, see the Introduction to Part I of the present volume.

5 Bewick did, in fact, receive many specimens of freshly killed birds from which to draw his illustrations, as well as using museum collections.

6 In these entries, 'Lin' indicates Linnaeus's *Systema Naturae* and 'Buf' the comte de Buffon's *Histoire naturelle*. 'Gmel' is Johann Friedrich Gmelin, who edited a posthumous edition of Linnaeus's work.

7 For Werner's *Nomenclature of Colours*, see the Introduction to Part I of the present volume.

Editorial Headnote

6. Letter From James Wilson to Thomas Bewick (1828)

The Scottish zoologist James Wilson authored two works, which represent the two main types of early nineteenth-century publishing on natural history. *Illustrations of Zoology* (c. 1827–31) was an ambitious folio, with engraved and etched plates (hand-coloured in some copies) based on drawings by Wilson himself or by other artists (see Chapter 7 and Figure 2). The models for the drawings were either captive living animals or stuffed specimens – the latter mainly located in Professor Robert Jameson's Edinburgh University museum: these were collections that Wilson himself had helped to assemble. The subjects were apparently chosen for their availability and their visual appeal rather than for scientific coherence, and the engravings were issued sporadically with accompanying letterpress texts. Like many such projects, the *Illustrations* was discontinued after a few issues, mainly due to the expense of producing the plates. Wilson's *Introduction to the Natural History of the Animal Kingdom* was, in contrast, a modest octavo publication, intended to cover more systematically, and more economically, the whole range of zoology in four volumes. However, this project, too, seems to have foundered. Its illustrations, being wood engravings, were intended to be set into the text pages. In this connection, Wilson wrote to Thomas Bewick in September 1828, to request the use of some of his woodblocks with engravings of birds. Wilson noted that Bewick replied on 4 October, but the latter died a few days later. The letter provides interesting evidence of the respect which Bewick enjoyed among authors and print collectors; it was quite exceptional for an illustrator or engraver of that time. Wilson's request also throws light on the concept of such popular zoologies, blending scientific information with visual appeal, a genre that would grow exponentially during the Victorian era.

6

LETTER TO THOMAS BEWICK, 13 SEPTEMBER 1828

James Wilson

Source: James Wilson, letter to Thomas Bewick, 13 September 1828, Tyne & Wear Archives, Newcastle upon Tyne; Thomas Bewick and Company, engravers, papers.

Woodville, Canaan, Edinburgh, Sepr. 13th 1828

Dear Sir,

I use the freedom to address you on the subject of a few Wood Cuts of Birds which I had lately the pleasure of seeing for the first time in the Valuable Library of my friend Mr Sivright of Meggetland.[1] I need scarcely trouble you by expressing here, what I have on several occasions more publicly expressed elsewhere, my high admiration of your unrivalled efforts as a Natural History Engraver. I would as soon with the french Critic exclaim 'I very much approve Shakespeare'.

I have been for about a year and a half engaged among other things in publishing a Work under the title of 'Illustrations of Zoology' consisting of figures drawn and coloured from Nature – In addition to these I am about to undertake a Work in 4 Vols 8vo, in which it will be my object to give a popular as well as accurate view of the principal facts in the different branches of the modern science of Zoology, an 'Introduction to the Nat. Histy. of the Animal Kingdom'. My Publisher Mr Blackwood is anxious to have the thing done in all respects in the best style and it will add to the success of the Work if it can be made ornamental as well as useful. Whether I can make it the latter or not remains to be tried. It is certain that you can make it the former.

In Mr Sivright's Collection above alluded to there is a Vol. containing your Land birds, but without the letter Press.[2] In addition to the ~~common~~ British species, I observed the Bearded Vulture, the Serpent Eater and several other foreign species, done with your usual accuracy and elegance, and in the preface it is intimated that these latter formed part of a general Work on Birds which you had it at one time in view to execute.[3] It is in regard to the Blocks of these foreign species that I now trouble you. They would exactly suit the Work which I have in view, and I shall have great pleasure in hearing how many of them are at your disposal, and on what terms it wd be agreeable to you to part with them, or to permit their

DOI: 10.4324/9781003107835-7

being used for the Work in question. Mr Blackwood has authorised me to write to you on the subject and in reply you can address yourself either to him or me. Allow me to express the sincere respect with which I remain

Your obliged & faithful James Wilson

Editorial Endnotes

1 Thomas Sivright of Meggetland near Edinburgh was a Scottish landowner and collector of art works.

2 Bewick sometimes issued fine impressions of his wood engravings from *British Birds* separately, without the letterpress, for the benefit of print collectors. Nigel Tattersfield, *Thomas Bewick: The Complete Illustrative Work*, 3 vols. (London: The British Library and The Bibliographic Society, and New Castle, DE: Oak Knoll Press, 2011), vol. 2, p. 49.

3 Bewick had originally intended to publish a book on the birds of the world, to match the scope of his *Quadrupeds*. However, as he became aware of the great numbers of species that were then being newly identified, he realised that this project was far too ambitious. He therefore decided to work on British birds alone, and the wood blocks he had already engraved with representations of non-British species were laid aside, though they were occasionally used to create single prints for collectors. Diana Donald, *The Art of Thomas Bewick* (London: Reaktion Books, 2013), p. 62.

Figure 2 James Wilson, *Illustrations of Zoology*, (Edinburgh & London: Blackwood and Cadell, 1828), no. III, plate of 'The Jaguar, or American Panther', from a drawing by Alexander Mosses; engraved and etched by W.H. Lizars, Edinburgh. (British Library)

Editorial Headnote

7. Christopher North [John Wilson], 'Wilson's Illustrations of Zoology', *Blackwood's Edinburgh Magazine* (1828)

John Wilson, who as a journalist took the pseudonym Christopher North, was the brother of James, author of *Illustrations of Zoology*. James Wilson's publisher for *Illustrations of Zoology* (see Chapter 6, Headnote), William Blackwood, also produced *Blackwood's Edinburgh Magazine*, and the main writer for the latter was John Wilson. Hence, it is not surprising that the journal published John Wilson's eighteen-page review of his brother's *Illustrations of Zoology*, even though the latter work was incomplete. This review essay is discursive and strangely fluctuating in its themes and judgements, reflecting the unsettled state of attitudes to the natural world at the time. It begins with high-minded reflections on the uplifting effect of studying God's perfect creation 'under awe of its Maker' and ends with a eulogy of Bewick's wood engravings. Yet, in between, a more sensual and violent view of nature's operations emerges, more akin to that expressed in romantic poetry and in the early works of Landseer, which date from the same period.

7

'WILSON'S ILLUSTRATIONS OF ZOOLOGY', REVIEW

'Christopher North' [John Wilson]

Source: Christopher North [John Wilson], 'Wilson's Illustrations of Zoology,' *Blackwood's Edinburgh Magazine*, 23:140 (June 1828), pp. 856–73.

[p. 859]

In speaking of the effect of such studies on the temper of the mind, in tranquillizing it, we cannot help noticing the natural calmness, independent of those other affections which attend such studies, arising out of the very nature of the objects themselves, about which the naturalist is occupied . . . all calm in their uniform tenor. Shall he be the only restless and perturbed being, when everything else is full of tranquillity – of silence? Advert, too, for a moment, to the occupation of him who watches, in nature, the courses of animated life. Looking at all the living beings in nature – in their happy play – in their busy occupations, – to see young things rejoicing in life – to see mothers nursing their young – to see insects, or beasts, or birds, concurring in mutual assistance or defence, as if they had contrivance and thought – to see life like the life – feelings like the heart – and something even of a faint and dim resemblance of the intelligence of man![1] . . .

[p. 865]

In Number III we have the Jaguar, or American Panther,[2] in his spotted beauty, recumbent beneath a cliff, – manifestly purring to himself as he eyes his fast-approaching prey, – while you see his tail marked with irregular black spots, and its lower part encircled by three sable rings, of which the last is terminal, curling in cruel delight, and his velvet paws unsheathing a little their crooked daggers – the most important claws in his will. What whiskers! What upper and lower lips! A pretty little pond close at hand in which to wash off the blood. He has probably just been lapping – but still his throat, and palate, and tongue, and jaws, are athirst – for water is to him 'wersh and unslockening,'[3] and he is slightly panting in the lust of blood. What a fine formidable yellow fellow he is, lying in burnished

DOI: 10.4324/9781003107835-8

brightness upon the dim desert sand! 'Tis a fair creature. You know now what Wordsworth had in his eye, when he said of the seducer of poor Ruth, –

> 'The Panther in the wilderness
> Was not more fair than he!'[4]

Yet he has not so much the look of a seducer, as of a ravisher. The two characters, however, are kindred – cognate – and in those paws a maiden, who had been wandering by herself into the woods, would be soon made to feel the meaning of gentle violence. How he would dandle the kid! With what gloating eyes would he suck her blood – nuzzling with that snokey nose of his in about the joining of her small neck with her full-formed breast – the fair jugular about to spout redness – the white collar-bone to be crunched into gore by one grinding tusk! Lord preserve us, he is playing with the Indian maid like a cat with a mouse – now suffering her to drag her wounded length in among some bushes, now gently and tenderly, so as not to hurt her – not even a hair on her head – drawing her towards him, first with one sheathed paw, and then with another, as if wiling her, in her reluctant bashfulness, into the warmth of his soft breast – and it is soft – soft as the down of the swan . . .

[pp. 870–3]

. . . Yet bright bird as is the Scarlet Ibis, there are other birds as bright as he, which ought to be a lesson to each gentleman of genius and lady of beauty not to hold up their heads so very high as if they opined themselves respectively to be the only Apollo and the only Venus in the universe. Such successful rival to the Scarlet Ibis, in plumage we mean, is the Quetzal, or Golden Trogon, burning on Plate VII. No. II.; and it is proof of the power of the paper it illumines, that the glory does not set it on fire. He ought to be painted on asbestos. Head, neck, breast, back, scapulars, wing, and tail-coverts, all of the richest golden green, with vivid reflections of blue and yellow – primary and secondary wing-feathers, very dark mulberry-brown, approaching to black – and so forth. But the two central upper coverts of the tail are of extraordinary length and brilliancy. His tail is many times the length of his body, 'and trailing clouds of glory, does he come,' brightening along the dark woods . . .'[5]

It is indeed this judicious combination of the picturesque and the zoological which forms one of the great charms of this work; and we know nothing more likely to raise the character of natural history amongst us than the amalgamation of its peculiar doctrines, with perceptions and associations, if not of a higher and more important order, at least of a kind more widely participated in and enjoyed. We confess it has always appeared to us, that the study of Zoology was of all others the most varied and delightful, both for young and old. This, however, is not felt as it should be in this country, although as far as we are competent to scan the signs of the times, a great change is now effecting on the subject in the public mind. The great evil seems to be, that few very influential members of society care a straw about the matter; and as there is a fashion in everything, so the stream of that fickle feeling has hitherto flowed in a different current, if not in a contrary direction, to that which favours the pursuit of the most diversified of the natural sciences . . .

Yet naturalists, and none more than those of our own country, almost always write well. The reason is simple – they love all they write on, and hence their spirit shines through their pages . . . Then, who ever read, without the most exquisite delight, White's History of Selborne? It is indeed a Sabbath Book, worthy a whole library of sermons, nine-tenths of the Bampton Lectures included; and will make a Deist of an Atheist, of a Deist a Christian.[6] Even Doctors Latham and Shaw write far better than ordinary men on ordinary subjects, although the former is too dry, and the latter too diffusive; and although they both smell rather too much of cabinets of curiosities, and stuffed collections, and mummified museums, and not sufficiently strongly of marshes, bogs, fens, meadows, ploughed fields, old leas, groves, woods, and forests – the schools of philosophy in almost all its departments – the great wide church-establishment of nature, from which there are in truth no dissenters, no sectarians, as long as its worship is felt to be the worship of the Living and True God.[7] Have we forgotten, in our hurried and imperfect enumeration of wise Worthies, have we forgotten,

'The Genius that dwells on the banks of the Tyne,'[8]

the Matchless, the Inimitable Bewick? No. His books lie in our parlour, bedroom, dining-room, drawing-room, study table, and are never out of place or time. Happy old man! The delight of childhood, manhood, decaying age! – A moral in every tail-piece – a sermon in every vignette. Not as if from one fountain flows the stream of his inspired spirit, gurgling from the Crawley Spring so many thousand gallons of the element every minute, and feeding but one city, our own Edinburgh. But it rather oozes out from unnumbered springs. Here from one scarcely perceptible but in the vivid green of the lonesome sward, from which it trickles away into a little mountain rill – here leaping into sudden life, as from the rock – here bubbling from a silver pool, overshadowed by a birch-tree – here like a well asleep in a moss-grown cell, built by some thoughtful recluse in the old monastic day, with a few words from Scripture, or some rude engraving, religious as Scripture, OMNE BONUM DESUPER – OPERA DEI MIRIFICA; and imbibed in gratitude by the way-worn traveller – soldier or soldier's widow returning from the wars; and hoping, from the mercy of Him who tells the earth to gush forth its blessings to the lips of poverty, dusty and sore athirst, some quiet nook for a nest to the wing-wearied bird, before it flees away and is at rest![9] . . .

Once more, then, we bid our present amiable and enlightened naturalist[10] farewell. None who purchase the numbers of his 'Illustrations' will repent their bargain. They will add to the knowledge of the scientific, in brown study, and in green grove. They will please all those who prefer being taught something of natural history by lessons given in a popular style, and look beautiful, as they are turned over, on a show-table, of the circular oak-tree-root, and claws withdrawn from touching the feet of the admiring group, by boys and virgins. There is much here to delight alike the learned and unlearned.

The accuracy of Mr Wilson's observations, minute and intense, has, for a good many years, given him high rank in the science – and his genius, though in such Illustrations those qualities have had no very frequent opportunities of being displayed, is, however, known to be distinguished by powers of comprehensiveness and generalization, fitting him for great achievements. He is an admirable drawer – and paints to very life. Bewick's Birds are not more characteristically set before us – nor in natural ease and variety of attitude – and we cannot pay him a higher compliment – does he appear to us to be inferior to Audubon. It is true, however, that his Illustrations embrace comparatively but few subjects – whereas Audubon, a man of wonderful genius, and destined, ere long, to be illustrious – has painted, it may almost be said, the whole American forest.[11]

Editorial Endnotes

1 William Paley in his widely read *Natural Theology* (1802, and many later editions), in the section titled 'Of the Goodness of the Deity', enthused over the happiness and tranquillity of animals in a state of nature, setting a pattern for later writers.

2 The animal was drawn by Alexander Mosses 'from a very beautiful Jaguar from Paraguay, which was some time ago alive in Liverpool' (p. 867). The drawing belonged to Dr Traill, who lent it to Wilson for engraving by Lizars (see Figure 2). Wilson's accompanying text drew on Humboldt's descriptions of the cunning and ferocity of jaguars in the wild, as he had observed and recorded them in his *Personal Narrative of Travels to the Equinoctial Regions*, 2nd ed. (1825).

3 Insipid and unrefreshing (Scottish).

4 A loose quotation from Wordsworth's poem 'Ruth' (1800), about a girl seduced and later abandoned by a semi-savage American youth who had 'roamed about, with vagrant bands/Of Indians in the West'. The Scottish colloquial adjective 'snokey' in the following paragraph is similarly suggestive of lustful intimacy: a *Dictionary of the Vulgar Tongue* published in 1811 includes 'snoach', meaning to snuffle.

5 The phrase 'burnished brightness' recalls William Blake's 'burning bright' description of 'The Tyger' in *Songs of Experience* (1794). Such phrases heighten Wilson's evocation of the sexual violence of the beast, which is hardly justified by Mosses's tame depiction of an actual jaguar. There is also a loose quotation from Wordsworth's poem 'Ode: Intimation of Immortality from Recollections of Early Childhood' (1807). 'Trailing' is here made to refer literally to the bird's long tail.

6 Revd Gilbert White's *The Natural History and Antiquities of Selborne* (1789) was already a classic and seemed to epitomise the reverent fascination with the workings of nature characteristic of natural theology. A 'Sabbath Book' was any pious and improving work reserved for reading on Sundays. The Bampton lectures at the University of Oxford were on theological subjects.

7 Wilson refers to two multi-volume works: John Latham's *A General Synopsis of Birds* (1781–5) and George Shaw's *General Zoology, or Systematic Natural History* (1800–26).

8 A reference to the opening lines of Wordsworth's poem 'The Two Thieves' (1800): 'O now that the genius of Bewick were mine,/And the skill which he learned on the banks of the Tyne'.

9 Wilson is referring to the many tailpiece designs by Bewick which showed thirsty travellers, thankful to find a fresh spring by the roadside. In one of them a rock is engraved

with this Latin quotation, which can be translated: 'Every good thing is from above – the wonderful works of God'.

10 He means James Wilson.

11 The great *Birds of America*, a 'double-elephant folio' with hand-coloured engravings taken from John James Audubon's drawings, was produced by Robert Havell and his London workshop and began to appear in 1827–8, putting Wilson's enterprise in the shade.

Editorial Headnote

8. Captain Thomas Brown, *The Taxdermist's Manual* (1833)

Thomas Brown, who was Scottish born, had an army career and then turned to authorship of works on natural history, especially on conchology and entomology; he became curator of the Manchester Museum in 1840. In this *Manual* he attempted to raise the status of taxidermy to that of an art and a science, and he criticised the crude 'stuffing' of specimens by untrained artisans. In support of his arguments, he quotes at length the advice given by Charles Waterton – the eccentric landowner, traveller, and naturalist – on the knowledge and imagination which good taxidermy requires.

8

'INTRODUCTION', *THE TAXIDERMIST'S MANUAL*

Captain Thomas Brown

Source: Captain Thomas Brown, *The Taxidermist's Manual: or the Art of Collecting, Preparing and Preserving Objects of Natural History. For the Use of Travellers, Conservators of Museums, and Private Collectors* (Glasgow: Archibald Fullerton, 1833), 'Introduction', pp. 1–6.

The advantages to be derived from a collection of objects of Natural History, are too apparent to require any illustration; and their beauty and variety of their forms have, in a preserved state, ever attracted the admiration of mankind, as being next in point of interest to the living animals. Although good drawings and engravings will give us a perfect knowledge of the general appearance of animals, still they are deficient in many particulars; for by them we cannot be made acquainted with the texture of the skin, nor the structure of the hair or feathers.

The naturalist, on all occasions, prefers a reference to the stuffed animal to that of a pictorial representation, as by this means he is enabled to trace, compare, and decide, on the creature in its several characters and relations.

In museums and cabinets are brought together natural objects of all kinds, from the most extreme points of the globe; and presented in a form that enables us, as it were, to look upon the mighty field of nature at one view; with the additional advantage of having the various Classes and Genera placed in systematic order, to investigate which, in their native wilds, would be the business of several lifetimes. Besides, we can here contemplate, without dread, the most destructive and furious quadrupeds, and the most noxious reptiles. Here we can muse upon and study the animals which have created in us the highest of sentiments while reading the tale of the traveller, or the singularity of organization, pointed out by the naturalist . . .

Although considerable advances have been made of late years in the art of Taxidermy, it is still far from perfection. This is to be attributed, in a great measure, to the education of the persons who practise this art; for among all I have met with employed in the preservation of animals, none have had the advantage of anatomical study, which is quite indispensable to the perfection of stuffing. One or two individuals, it is true, have attended to the structure of the skeleton of Man, and a few of the more common animals, but this is far from the information which they ought to possess; for nothing short of a general and extensive knowledge of

DOI: 10.4324/9781003107835-9

comparative anatomy can qualify them sufficiently for an art which is so comprehensive and varied in its application.

These observations are particularly applicable to Quadrupeds and Reptiles, for what are even the best stuffed specimens of the first museums in the world compared to the living subject? Nothing better than deformed and glaringly artificial productions, devoid of all the grace and beautifully turned points of living nature. A knowledge of drawing and modelling are also indispensable qualifications, to enable the stuffer to place his subject in a position both natural and striking. It is the too frequent practice for the stuffer to set about preserving the animal without having determined in what attitude he is to place it, so that it will appear to most advantage, and be in character with the ordinary habits of the creature. This he leaves to the last efforts of finishing his work, and, consequently, its proportions and character are likely to be devoid of all appearance of animation.

The first thing, therefore, to be attended to in all great national natural history establishments, is to choose young persons who are yet in their boyhood, to be instructed in this art, most important to science.[1] Their studies should be commenced by deep attention to drawing, modelling, anatomy, and chemistry, while they, at the same time, proceed with the practical part of their art. Every opportunity of examining the habits and actions of the living subject should be embraced, and its attitudes and general aspect carefully noted. Without strict attention to these points, so manifestly obvious, the art of preserving animals *never will* attain that degree of perfection which its importance demands. On the other hand, if this art is pursued in the manner here recommended, artists may be produced who will fulfil the objects of their profession with honour to themselves and advantage to their country. Would any person expect to arrive at eminence as a sculptor if he were unacquainted with the established preliminaries of his art, namely, drawing and anatomy? The thing is so self-evident, that I am only surprised it has not long ago been acted upon. Upwards of twelve years have elapsed since I pointed out these facts to the Professor of Natural History in the University of Edinburgh, but things continue as they were before that time.[2]

Although these observations apply with their full force to the preservation of the MAMMALIA, or Quadrupeds, they are equally applicable to Birds and Fishes. It is quite true that defects in ill-stuffed birds are not so obvious as in quadrupeds, because the feathers assist in a great measure to conceal such deformities; and in fishes, imperfections are also less observable, owing to the smooth and unmarked appearance of their external surface, from the circumstance of their bones being principally small towards their outside, and the larger bones being deeply concealed under the muscles.

I am happy to find that the ingenious Mr Waterton agrees with me on this important subject.[3] 'Were you,' says he, 'to pay as much attention to birds as the sculptor does to the human frame, you would immediately see, on entering a museum, that the specimens are not well done.'

'This remark will not be thought severe, when you reflect, that that which was once alive, has probably been stretched, stuffed, stiffened, and wired, by the hand of a common clown.[4] Consider, likewise, how the plumage must have been disordered by too much stretching or drying, and, perhaps, sullied, or at least deranged, by the pressure of a coarse and heavy hand, – plumage which, ere life had fled within it, was accustomed to be touched by nothing rougher than the dew of heaven, and the pure and gentle breath of air . . . But if you wish to excel in the art, if you wish to be in Ornithology, what Angelo was in sculpture,[5] you must apply to profound study and your own genius to assist you. And these may be called the scientific requisites.'

'You must have a complete knowledge of Ornithological anatomy. You must pay close attention to the form and attitude of the bird, and know exactly the proportion each curve or extension, or contraction, or expansion of any particular part bears to the rest of the body. In a word, you must possess Promethean boldness, and bring down fire and animation as it were, into your preserved specimen.'

'Repair to the haunts of birds on plains and mountains, forests, swamps, and lakes, and give up your time to examine the economy of the different orders of birds.'

'Then you will place your Eagle, in attitude commanding, the same as Nelson stood in, in the day of battle, on the Victory's quarter deck.[6] Your Pie[7] will seem crafty, and just ready to take flight, as though fearful of being surprised in some mischievous plunder. Your Sparrow will retain its wonted pertness, by means of placing his tail a little elevated, and giving a moderate arch to the neck. Your Vulture will show his sluggish habits by having his body nearly parallel to the earth; his wings somewhat drooping, and their extremities under the tail instead of above it, – expressive of ignoble indolence.'

'Your Dove will be in artless, fearless innocence, looking mildly at you, with its neck not too much stretched, as if uneasy in its situation, or drawn too close into the shoulders, like one wishing to avoid discovery; but in moderate, perpendicular length, supporting the head horizontally, which will set off the breast to the best advantage.'

To the traveller who wanders in search of knowledge, but without the means of conveying skins of quadrupeds or birds, we would say a word or two. When he has killed and examined an animal or bird, which appears new to him, after having noted down all its characters, he ought to attempt a drawing of the object, as the next best substitute for the skin.

The indefatigable Wilson, whose unbounded zeal led him to explore the mighty wilds of America, in search of information regarding the feathered tribes, but who, without either money or patronage, could not transport their skins across these nearly boundless wildernesses, was compelled to adopt these, the only means he had, and to delineate their forms and features, in their native colours, as faithfully as he could, as records at least of their existence.[8]

Audubon adopted this method. He pinned the bird to a tree in some natural position, held out by wires, &c., then made a drawing while the animal was yet warm. By this means he could imitate those beautiful tints which are alone to be found in living nature; and the forms being still those of the real subject, were likely to surpass those of stuffed specimens.[9]

Editorial Endnotes

1 There is a parallel here with Thomas Martyn's enlistment of gifted boys to learn the art of zoological illustration under his tutelage (see Chapter 1 of this volume).
2 Presumably Professor Robert Jameson is indicated.
3 Smith here gives a long quotation from Charles Waterton's entertaining *Wanderings in South America, the North-West of the United States, and the Antilles, in the Years 1812, &c, for Cabinets of Natural History*, 2nd ed. (London: B. Fellowes [successor to Mr. Mawman], 1828), pp. 321–3. A few minor slips in Brown's transcription of Waterton have been silently corrected.
4 A 'clown' then meant an ignorant rustic.
5 The Italian Renaissance artist Michelangelo was considered supreme in the sculpting of the naked human body.
6 Admiral Horatio Nelson was celebrated for his commanding role at the Battle of Trafalgar in 1801, during which he was fatally wounded.
7 'Pie' is the magpie.
8 Alexander Wilson was the author of *American Ornithology; Or, The Natural History of the Birds of the United States: Illustrated with Plates, Engraved and Colored from Original Drawings taken from Nature*, 9 vols. (Philadelphia: Bradford and Inskeep, 1808–14).
9 Audubon explained this practice to members of the Wernerian Society, Edinburgh, at a meeting of the Society on 16 December 1826, but he there specified a board rather than a tree trunk: *Memoirs of the Wernerian Natural History Society, for the Years 1826–31*, VI (Edinburgh: Adam Black and London: Rees, Orme, Brown and Green, 1832), p. 562.

Editorial Headnote

9. William Swainson, *A Preliminary Discourse on the Study of Natural History*, [1834]

Here the naturalist and zoological illustrator William Swainson – a prolific author – discusses extensively the relationship between text and image in works on natural history. At the conceptual level, he made an evaluative distinction between them: science was a collaborative field of study in which knowledge was transmitted and augmented over the generations, while illustration was a mere skill which had to be acquired from scratch by each practitioner. Moreover, progressive science, as the direct study of God's perfect creation, could never be outshone by the products of mutable artistic taste. At the same time, Swainson recognised that a corpus of good zoological illustrations had immense value and a long afterlife, even when the accompanying text was amateurish or had become outdated. The production of coloured plates for natural history publications involved considerable expenditure, but Swainson thought that the government had a duty to finance them, because visuality was often essential to cognition and to the registration and transmission of knowledge.

9

A PRELIMINARY DISCOURSE ON THE STUDY OF NATURAL HISTORY

William Swainson

Source: William Swainson, *A Preliminary Discourse on the Study of Natural History*, no. 53 in the series *The Cabinet Cyclopædia*, conducted by Revd Dionysius Lardner (London: Longman, Rees, Orme, Brown, Green, & Longman and John Taylor, undated [1834]), pp. 41–2, 98–101, 402.

[pp. 41–2]

A splendid addition was made to illustrated entomology in 1746, by the coloured figures of Rœsel[1]; and here also we may notice the valuable collection of figures by our countryman Edwards; whose works, although terminated at a time when most writers arranged their materials according to the Linnæan method, were commenced in 1743, and belong to the illustrative, more than to the scientific class, of zoological publications.[2] Edwards was the friend of Sir Hans Sloane, and for many years filled the office of librarian to the College of Physicians.[3] He has no pretensions to scientific talent, or to original research; yet it is an extraordinary fact, that, destitute of such qualifications, his works are assuredly the most valuable, on general ornithology, that have ever appeared in England. This arose from his being the first who figured and described a vast number of birds, then new to naturalists, who consequently refer to him as the original authority for all such species. The figures of Edwards were copied and recopied by nearly all succeeding writers, up to the year 1820, when we ventured, in the *Zoological Illustrations*, to introduce a new style of delineation; and to substitute original figures for those that were then copied into nearly all the popular compilations[4] . . .

[pp. 98–101]

The mutability proverbially belonging to human learning, has been indiscriminately applied both to arts and sciences; whereas it is by no means equally shared between both, nor is it so universal as some would lead us to imagine. Art more correctly implies physical dexterity: science, on the contrary, is purely intellectual. The first cannot exist in any eminent degree without the second; but science requires not the auxiliary help of her sister. The one is transient, and, however great, dies with its possessor. The painter cannot bequeath to his disciple that skill which it has cost him his life to attain; the poet cannot infuse his 'unutterable thoughts' into another before his death; nor can the musician, while he transfers his instrument, delegate also the pathos or the dexterity which gave it utterance. The degree of perfection to which each of these artists has attained, dies with its possessor; and those who succeed him have to begin, themselves, at the foot of the ladder, and not from that height which their predecessors had reached. Hence it is, and the inference is remarkable, that in those pursuits which more immediately regard art, mankind has but little, if at all, advanced, during many centuries. Nay, it may be said rather to have retrograded; else we should not consider those productions of antiquity which time has spared to us, as fit models for our present imitation.[5] That science, on the other hand, participates in this mutability, no one would think of denying; but that it is not equally affected with art is very manifest. Before the invention of printing, indeed, there was good reason to apprehend, that the world might lose the knowledge acquired by its sages: but the discovery of that noble art has given the true philosopher a channel of permanent communication, with succeeding ages; he can bequeath to posterity, in a compendious form, those truths which have resulted from a life of study; and he can enable those, who wish to tread the path which he is quitting, to start from the point at which his enquiries terminated: so far as his discoveries extend, and so far as his deductions therefrom are sound, so far are his works imperishable, because they relate to things which are, in this world at least, unchanging. Had the ancients busied themselves with the study of comparative anatomy, and bestowed upon the construction of the common animals of their country, one half of the attention and talent that was lavished upon other studies, their writings in natural history would be just as valuable now, as they would have been then; and the works of Pliny, instead of being a tissue of fables and absurdities, would have held the same rank with us as those of a Savigny or a Cuvier.[6] Mutability in science only belongs to *error:* for truth, no less than nature, is unchanging; whereas mutability, on the contrary, is a necessary accompaniment of art, and is interwoven with its very excellence.

There is an inexpressible satisfaction, an intellectual delight, in the pursuit of truth, which few but the philosopher can fully understand. This luxury of the soul, as it may well be termed, belongs more especially to the pursuit of natural science; particularly to those branches which are usually termed demonstrative. The man who studies the forms of nature, has before him, so far as those forms are concerned, models of perfection. He has no need to suspect that others exist, in distant countries, more perfect of their kind, than those before him, and which he should previously see and study. He has not to consult popular taste, ephemeral fashion, or arbitrary opinion, on the value or importance of his pursuits. He has before him *truth:* his sole business is to analyse all the parts and all the bearings of that truth, and make them known to the world.[7] The models and materials of his study are divine; and how much they exceed those of any human artist, will be manifested by a blade of grass, compared with which the most exquisite carvings in stone or ivory sink into insignificance. The calculations of the astronomer, and the results of the chemist, are productive of much the same feelings. Truth indeed is but seldom attained, yet with superior minds this very difficulty serves but to increase the ardour of its pursuit.

Another advantage, almost exclusively belonging to the natural sciences, is this, that they carry the mind from the thing made, to Him who made it. If we contemplate a beautiful painting or an intricate piece of mechanism, we naturally are led to admire the artist who produced them, to regard his superiority with respect, and to enquire who and what he is. We mention his name with honour, and take every fitting opportunity of extolling his talents. If such are the effects of contemplating human excellency, how much stronger will be the same train of thought and of feeling in the breast of every good man, when he looks into the wonders of the natural world, and thinks upon the surprising phenomena which it exhibits!

[p. 402]

The importance of the class of publications we are now speaking of, not only to the advancement, but to the right understanding of science, cannot be questioned.[8] Words, however many, or however well selected, cannot picture to the eye the forms of things. And, next to the examination of the real object, an advantage seldom to be obtained, its correct representation is the most to be desired. Without the aid of accurate figures, natural history, in all its branches, would be involved in doubt and complexity, from the poverty of language to express the innumerable forms, and modifications of those forms, in the objects upon which it treats. So much more easy is it to impress a definitive image upon the mind through the medium of the eye, than the ear, that a rough outline, a small woodcut occupying but a square inch, will accomplish this object better than a whole page of the most elaborate description. In proportion to the complication of the object we wish to make known, so is the necessity increased for calling in the aid of the graphic art. It is, therefore, absolutely essential that such works should abound in every department of zoology, because the objects to be made known by such means pour in upon us from all parts of the world, while the difficulty of discriminating them, by mere words, is proportionably increased.

Editorial Endnotes

1 August Johann Roesel von Rosenhof, *Der Insecten Belustigung* (1740), a collection of engravings of insects. Roesel was a German eighteenth-century miniaturist and naturalist who produced entomological works with his own fine-coloured illustrations.

2 George Edwards was the author of *A Natural History of Uncommon Birds* (1743–51) and of *Gleanings of Natural History: Exhibiting figures of quadrupeds, birds, insects, plants &c.* (1758–64).

3 The physician Sir Hans Sloane left his extensive collections of natural specimens to the British Museum. Most were later transferred to the Natural History Museum in South Kensington.

4 Swainson, *Zoological Illustrations, or Original Figures and Descriptions of New, Rare, or Interesting Animals, selected chiefly from the Classes of Ornithology, Entomology, and Conchology*, 3 vols. (London: Baldwin, Cradock, and Joy, 1820–1), vol. 1. In the preface to this first volume, Swainson explained that he wished to discourage 'the publication of distorted figures copied from old authors, by accustoming the public eye to original designs and correct representations of natural objects' (p. iii). Swainson's birds are still conventionally perched on a segment of tree trunk or on a twig, against a blank background, but there are no out-of-scale decorative accessories like those which

featured in Edwards's designs. Swainson's birds are also more accurately depicted than those of Edwards, being based on studies from life.

5 Swainson is thinking of the general admiration for ancient Greek and Roman sculptures, which art students were encouraged to study.

6 Pliny the Elder's *Natural History* was written in c.77CE. Jules-César Savigny, *Mémoires sur les Animaux sans Vertèbres* [invertebrates], 1816. Georges Cuvier, *Le Règne Animal*, 1817, with numerous subsequent editions.

7 There is a sad irony in Swainson's confidence that unchallengeable scientific 'truths' may be established by studying 'the forms of nature'. His 'quinarian' theories (shared with William Sharp Macleay and others) about the relationships between life forms were widely attacked and later dismissed. Aaron Novick, 'On the Origins of the Quinarian System of Classification', *Journal of the History of Biology,* 49:1 (2016), pp. 95–133.

8 Swainson is thinking here of publications containing large coloured plates, which were an especially important adjunct in the case of unfamiliar species. In point of fact, the government did sometimes award grants to underwrite the huge costs of such illustrations, for example, in the case of Darwin's *Zoology of the Voyage of the H.M.S. Beagle* volumes.

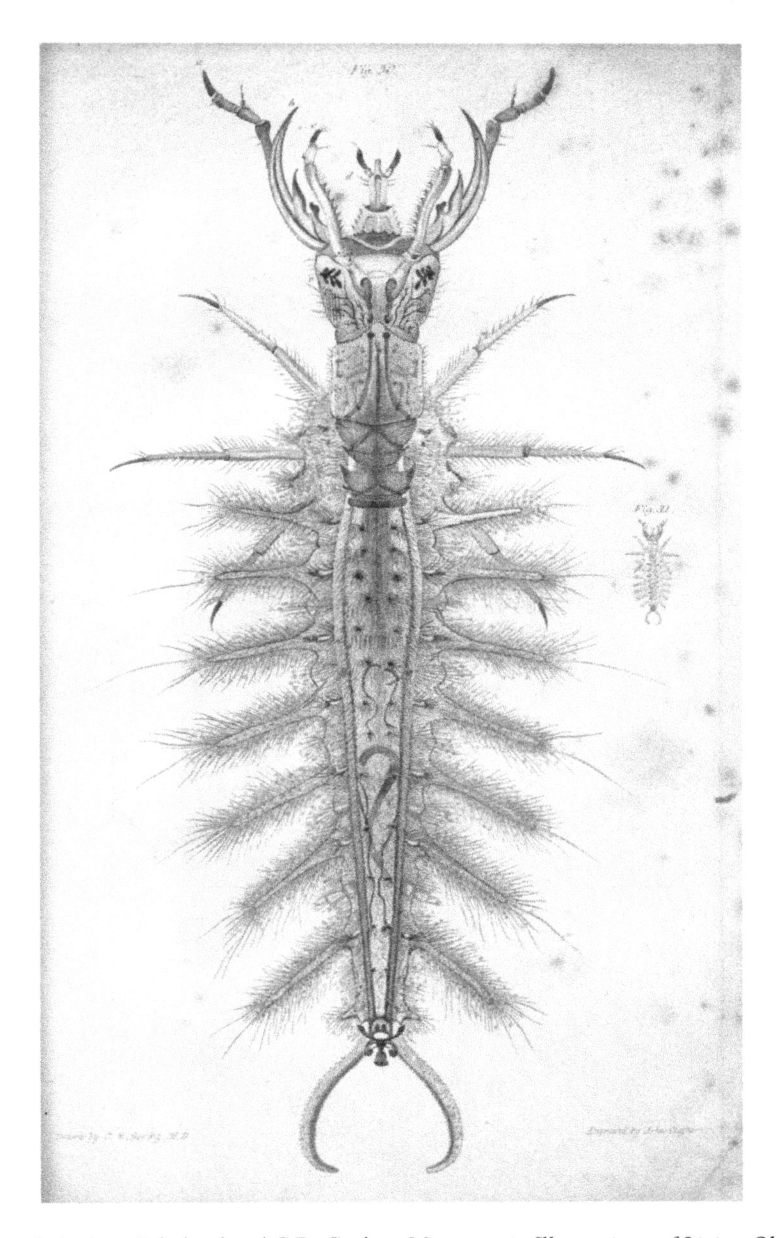

Figure 3 Andrew Pritchard and C.R. Goring, *Microscopic Illustrations of Living Objects* (London: Whittaker, 1840), fig. 30, 'Larva of British Hydrophilus', 'kept . . . without food, in order to render its interior organization more clear'; engraving, hand-coloured in some copies, from a drawing by Goring. (Biodiversity Heritage Library)

Editorial Headnote

10. Andrew Pritchard and C. R. Goring, *Microscopic Illustrations of Living Objects* (1840)

The mid-nineteenth century was a time of significant development in the design and commercial manufacture of microscopes, of varying degrees of sophistication.[1] Andrew Pritchard enthuses over the capacity of his achromatic and compound microscopes to reveal the intricate structures of living insects and aquatic organisms through all their metamorphoses – the marvels of God's creation. 'Surely, then, as works of art merely, instruments which can effect so much as this are justly entitled to a due share of consideration even from the most refined and polished minds' (p. 25). The living images produced by the microscope could even be 'represented on a screen, and dilated to the extent of about two feet in length' for the pleasure and instruction of a discriminating audience, who could watch the minute creatures preying upon one another (pp. 32, 61). Engraved illustrations, based on drawings from life, were also an important feature of such books (see Figure 3). However, attempts to draw and thus record live specimens as they were seen through the microscope involved all kinds of practical difficulties, which Pritchard's co-author Charles Goring, himself an innovator in microscopic techniques, explained to the reader (pp. 233–7).[2] Pritchard's *Microscopic Illustrations of Living Objects* was originally published in 1830, and there were many variant editions.

Editorial Endnotes

1 Compound microscopes have two lenses to increase magnification. An achromatic microscope has a complex lens shaped in a manner that eliminates the distortion of colours caused by their varying refractions, bringing red and blue wavelengths to the same focus.

2 Charles Goring was a leading figure in the development of more powerful and accurate microscopic lenses. See Boris Jardine, 'Microscopes', in Bernard Lightman (ed.), *A Companion to the History of Science* (Chichester: Wiley Blackwell, 2016), pp. 515–25, on p. 525.

10

MICROSCOPIC ILLUSTRATIONS OF LIVING OBJECTS

Andrew Pritchard and C.R. Goring

Source: Andrew Pritchard and C.R. Goring, *Microscopic Illustrations of Living Objects, Their Natural History, &c. &c. with Researches Concerning the Most Eligible Methods of Constructing Microscopes, and Instructions for Using them by C.R. Goring*, new ed. (London: Whittaker, 1840), pp. 233–7.

If any portrait painter had to execute a likeness of some person afflicted with chorea,[1] who could not be prevailed upon to be quiet for more than half a minute together, who was perpetually jigging about the apartment, and exhibiting his tail instead of his head, &c., &c., I think he would be compelled to admit that he had undertaken a task which would at least require time and patience for its completion; but if, in addition, the said person was to be removed to a distance, so that the artist could only see him with a powerful telescope, and had to follow his motions as well as he could, and be content to catch a glimpse of him crossing his field of view now and then, according to the humour and good pleasure of the said individual, I think the worthy limner would begin to think that after all there was *some* difficulty to contend with.

Now this case I conceive to be an exact parallel to that of drawing living objects with a microscope.

Their incorrigible restlessness so baulks and baffles the artist, that he is frequently compelled to lay down his pencil to regain his lost temper, and fresh courage to proceed: in many cases his best resource is to study the object *till he has got all its features by heart* – then to set them down on paper – study again, and gradually correct them: by the time he has made half a dozen rough sketches he will get pretty near the truth: he may then commence a regular drawing. I can safely say that I have drawn many of my objects *five or six times over* before I could arrive at my portraiture. I have heard a great deal about shutting one's eyes after having made an observation, and *drawing from the impression left on the retina*. This, I suspect, is better in theory than in practice, and it is evident that, unless the object is *stationary*, the last impression must be so confounded with the preceding ones that no distinct image can be left.

But it will probably be asked, why I did not kill my object before I drew it, instead of giving myself all this unnecessary trouble? I answer, that I never could make a

DOI: 10.4324/9781003107835-11

drawing to my mind from a dead aquatic larva or insect. Such is the extreme delicacy of their organs, and so rapid their decomposition in water, that long before a drawing can be executed, the main and capital parts of the internal, and even external structure, in most subjects, will become confused and unintelligible. If they are removed out of the water, a still greater change is effected by their drying: their colours vanish, and their whole appearance is totally changed; to say nothing of the fact, that a dead aquatic insect so loses the peculiar distinctive character derived from its favourite attitude and position, that though the component parts might, in some instances, be correctly given, the *tout ensemble* would be scarcely recognized . . . I also made various attempts to confine them in a narrow compass, so as to prevent much latitude of motion; but was compelled to desist from the project, finding that they got into constrained and unnatural positions, and injured themselves by struggling . . .

I suspect that other individuals have met with the same obstacles as myself in making drawings of living microscopic objects; for I think it may be affirmed, without any illiberality, that, with very few exceptions, those of my predecessors are proportionally more rude and incorrect than those of any other subjects of natural history whatever; their various lineaments and features being frequently false, and exaggerated to a degree amounting to caricature; nevertheless, they have been handed down from one bookmaker to another, ever since the days of Swammerdam,[2] as if they needed no improvement whatever. I have made my drawings at that period of the growth of the larva or chrysalis in which I thought it made *the best and most interesting object*, and that they vary greatly in their appearance, according to the degree of maturity to which they have arrived. There are also many varieties, very closely resembling each other, which it is not very easy to particularize; but I am quite confident, that when the genuine object is procured, in the state in which I drew it, the correctness of my execution will be recognised.

The specimens which I have selected are those which experience has shewn to excite the strongest emotions of pleasure and satisfaction in the great mass of observers of all ranks; whom I have always found to be most delighted by *comparatively large living objects*, seen with *medium powers*. In fact they seem to afford the same sort of gratification with a menagerie of living wild beasts on the large scale; and most certainly many of them wonderfully emulate the ferocity, voracity, cunning, and cruelty of the mammalia. They prey on each other, and fight with a degree of determined obstinacy not inferior to that of any beings whatever. They have likewise a thousand diverting pranks and humours, quite peculiar to themselves. In addition to these amiable and amusing qualities, they possess such a high degree of transparency, that their unique and beautiful internal machinery is as clearly perceptible as if they were made of glass; so that, without any dissection, we can unravel all the mysterious workings of their nature . . .

Editorial Endnotes

1 Chorea is a disease that causes involuntary muscle movements.
2 Jan Swammerdam was a famous seventeenth-century Dutch microscopist.

Editorial Headnote

11. Arthur C. Cole, *The Methods of Microscopical Research* (1895)

Guides to microscopy proliferated in the second half of the nineteenth century, catering to the needs of both professional scientists and hobbyists. While microphotography grew in importance, the drawing and painting of microscopic specimens were still sometimes considered a better means of recording their particular features. Arthur Cole pointed out that it had the added advantage of 'exquisite colouring', not yet attainable in photography (p. 8). Therefore, he devoted a long chapter of his *Practical Guide* to this kind of art, giving as much attention to aesthetics as he did to science. Although he made a living as a commercial supplier of prepared microscopic slides, he stresses here – in prolix and enthusiastic language – the subjectivity of those who fashion microscopic images in their own ways. *The Methods of Microscopical Research* originated as part of Cole's *Studies in Microscopical Science* (London: Bailliere, Tindall and Cox, 1883), but was subsequently issued separately.

11

'ON MICROSCOPICAL DRAWING AND PAINTING,' *THE METHODS OF MICROSCOPICAL RESEARCH*

Arthur C. Cole[1]

Source: Arthur C. Cole, *The Methods of Microscopical Research: A Practical Guide to Microscopical Manipulation*, 2nd ed. (London: Baillière, Tindall and Cox, 1895), ch. vii, 'On Microscopical Drawing and Painting', pp. 161–5, 173–6.

[pp. 161–5]

A great teacher has said 'Drawing should be considered not an accomplishment, but a necessity. Learning to draw is learning the grammar of a language. Anybody can learn the grammar, but whether you have *anything to say* is another matter.' To the naturalist this accomplishment is of great importance; accurate illustration adds to the value of written description. At every point the microscopist is sensible of its deeper significance. Such a control quickens the perception, excites exact observation, and creates an interest beyond research, admiration, or curiosity. The compactness of the vision presented by the microscope so rivets the attention, that changes, disclosures, development of activities, in organisms often lost and swept away, after cursory examination, rouse in a zealous observer an impatient desire to possess some power, beyond words, to place on paper a memorandum or record, however rough, of things rarely discovered under the same conditions. This ability is a result of practice. There is no royal road but that traversed by enthusiasm and earnestness. Sketches from the hands of a dexterous microscopist, marking first impressions, are often more valuable than, and superior to, the formal work of the mere draughtsman, who may not even *know* the significance of the subject, especially when the result is a replication of drawings made by the actual observer. He necessarily falls into one or other of two errors; he mends and improves, or obscures material points by drifting into formal monotony; a microscopical draughtsman must essentially be a microscopist, and work *direct from actual observation*, completely understanding the matter before him.

There are three well defined characteristics of microscopical representations, drawings of tissues, or minute organisms, requiring for elucidation high powers, delicate conditions of light, conducted under careful observation and technical skill, satisfying the highest biological research, in its progress demanding rigorous precision; then, rapid sketching, catching features, graphic memoranda;

DOI: 10.4324/9781003107835-12

without hesitation, or the assistance of the camera-lucida jotting down, and washing in, with tints, unexpected appearances, this readiness should be cultivated by those desirous of adding record to observation; many most important phases in the sequence of activities have been seen and passed over, when a few rough lines would have induced and helped further research, but beyond this tentative work, and the stern formality of scientific requirement, is a finished 'picture;' at this crucial point the capability of the microscopist and artist blend, involving knowledge of the subject, the arrangement of optical apparatus, judgment, and study in the methods of procedure. A drawing may be true in its scientific aspect, and possess artistic features of decided interest – the one may incorporate the other. The illustrations of Mr. Gosse's books are instances of this peculiar quality.[2] 'Still Life' has arrested the attention of artists of all time, from Missal Illuminators to Royal Academicians; such results have no scientific import, but like all art products, awaken gratification in appreciating the power applied in producing their essence, and without degrading the legitimate functions of the microscope, it is possible to extract from its revelations, models of exceptional charm and excellence, associated, moreover, with scientific value.[3] Although the bias of an expert microscopist and practised artist may not often touch the same mind, it is certain that when a keen perception is directed to complications of beauty, with rare conditions of light and effulgence of colour, the instrument becomes the very touchstone of artistic feeling, and beyond mere beauty (which, in visible nature, is inexhaustible) there are revelations of structural form, quaint elegancies, mysterious changes of tissues, and embryological developments, under radiances, hidden, not only from ordinary familiarity, but even from the cognisance of many who have not had the opportunity of exhausting the resources of a fine instrument, with all its accessories. It may be urged that few have the ability to approach art of this description, but the power of drawing quickly develops itself, especially when stimulated by special and eager interest, concentrated on special objects; no one led by inclination to contemplate what may be seen under such circumstances, can be destitute of an appreciation of art in its most exalted sense . . .

A microscopical drawing may be absolutely true, and an artistic grace secured, by preserving line for line what is actually presented, assuming the preparation to be fairly perfect; in other words, not drifting into a stilted diagrammatic style, or wandering from close observation, because the subject *appears* to have a certain regularity; no two cells, vessels, or fibres are absolutely alike; to give 'life' to a picture, every part of the structure should be a portrait, the pencil deviating from accuracy melts into falsity and confusion, *uniformity is fatal*, and obscures important differentiation of parts; again, in order to delineate what is expected, or wished to be seen, aiming at 'correction' is to be avoided; it is better to draw imperfections, if they be present, an overlapping or torn structure often reveals an important fact, so patent is this, that a 'fabricated' drawing may be detected in a moment, especially of diatomaceous or infusorial forms – a broken fragment, a solitary individual is the clue to a perfect whole, or group; such built up arrangements have no charm beyond technicality. A good representation possesses a mingled quality of accuracy and imperfection, a paradox, which stamps its value! . . .

[pp. 173–6]

In painting purely opaque objects under top light the treatment of background deserves attention; eggs of insects or parasites are generally attached to fragments of wood, leaves, cuticles, hair or feathers, it enhances the effect and beauty of a representation, if such details are carefully painted, and the rest of the field delicately stippled up with indian ink, to the edge of the circle.[4] This applied to many subjects – threads of algæ, or vegetable stems supporting such objects as fixed rotifera, polyzoa, &c., introduced into a drawing, add greatly to the interest and make most attractive pictures. Any prepared mount or specimen should be as perfect as possible, and *considerable experience* is necessary in order to decide what is fairly *good* as a preparation and *worth drawing*. Common objects of easy procurement from the woods, the garden, and the stream, are exquisite models for the draughtsman, their excellence, interest, and freshness are necessarily superior to even the admirable results now obtained by professional preparers, aided by mechanical appliances, and rare skill in the use of reagents and staining fluids . . .

Structure and its thoughtful exposition is the limit of draughtsmanship, and it is here that the photographic lens as a delineator fails; the superiority of work produced by a hand guided by cultivated observation as compared with a photograph is the operation of a mind capable of expressing combined and superimposed tissues, in having at command a control and adjustment of various planes of surfaces, and without militating against scientific truth, seeking for, and obtaining even picturesque effects . . . a draughtsman may arrange a minute and just perspective of parts, absent in a photograph, anticipating the presence of relative parts, and having at command the fine adjustment, he can feel his way, conscious that at the slightest touch a fresh point, perhaps an important revelation, flashes into sight, supplying a link to the better understanding of the whole.

Editorial Endnotes

1 Cole, in collaboration with another professional microscopist, John Ernest Ady, also produced a journal or serial publication with numerous coloured lithographic illustrations, *Studies in Microscopical Science*. It ran to only two volumes in 1883–4, but, as noted earlier, included the first version of the present work. It focused on histology, apparently as an aid to students: Arthur Cole's son Martin was Instructor to Practical Microscopy at the Birkbeck Institution in London, and scientists at Birkbeck contributed material to the journal.

2 Some of Philip Henry Gosse's popular books on marine organisms were illustrated with colour lithographs based on his own drawings from the microscope, notably *Actinologia Britannica: A History of the British Sea-anemones and Corals* (1860) and *Tenby: A Seaside Holiday* (1856). The drawings combined scientific accuracy with density and variety of forms, richness of colour, and feeling for pattern. Diana Donald, 'Introduction,' in Diana Donald and Jane Munro (eds.), *Endless Forms: Charles Darwin, Natural Science and the Visual Arts* (New Haven, CT, and London: Yale University Press, 2009), pp. 14–15. See also chapters 56 and 57 in the present volume.

3 Ariane Varela Braga, in 'Microorganisms, microscopes, and Victorian design theories', *British Art Studies* 21 (30 November 2021), has noted the likely influence of microscopic slides of such organisms on the decorative arts in the second half of the nineteenth century.
4 Cole recommended making drawings of microscopic creatures in a circular format, like the view through the microscope itself.

Editorial Headnote

12. Herbert Spencer, 'The Haythorne Papers No. vi. The Value of Evidence', *The Leader* (1853)

In this early article, Spencer discussed the nature of human psychology and cognitive processes as they are revealed in approaches to scientific research and illustration.[1] In the same year he sent a more abstruse and polemical essay on the same general theme to *The Westminster Review*; it was titled 'The Universal Postulate' and was later assimilated into his book *The Principles of Psychology*.[2] There he argued that valid human thought necessarily depends on irrefutable beliefs arising from sense data and experience, and the rejection of delusive 'metaphysical reasonings'. Spencer's choice of examples of delusion in his *Leader* article – legendary and fallacious ideas about barnacles in former centuries, which crystallised into fanciful images – may be related to the recent publication of Darwin's illustrated volumes on the *Cirripedia* (1851–4). Darwin's scientific discoveries about fossil and living species of cirripedes often seemed stranger than fiction, yet they were based on close visual study and analysis of material evidence, furthering the evolutionary theories that were to be presented in *On the Origin of Species* a few years later.[3]

Editorial Endnotes

1 David Duncan, *The Life and Letters of Herbert Spencer*, 2 vols. (London: Methuen, 1908), vol. 1, pp. 65–6.

2 Herbert Spencer, 'Article VII – The Universal Postulate', *The Westminster Review*, 60:118 (October 1853), pp. 513–50. Spencer, *The Principles of Psychology* (London: Longman, Brown, Green, and Longmans 1855).

3 Jonathan Smith, *Charles Darwin and Victorian Visual Culture* (Cambridge: Cambridge University Press, 2006), pp. 17, 52–60.

12

THE HAYTHORNE PAPERS NO. VI

The Value of Evidence[1]

Herbert Spencer

Source: Herbert Spencer, 'The Haythorne Papers No. VI. The Value of Evidence', *The Leader*, 4: 170 (25 June 1853) pp. 619–20.

To observe correctly, though popularly thought very easy, every man of science knows to be extremely difficult. Our faculties are liable to report falsely from two opposite causes – the presence of hypothesis, and the absence of hypothesis. To the dangers arising from one or other of these, every observation we make is necessarily exposed; and between the two it is scarcely possible to see any fact *quite* truly. A few illustrations of the extreme distortions arising from the one cause and the extreme inaccuracy consequent upon the other, will justify this seeming paradox.

Nearly everyone is familiar with the myth prevalent on our sea-coasts, respecting the Barnacle Goose. The popular belief was, and indeed is still in some places, that the fruit of trees whose branches hang into the sea becomes changed into certain shell-covered creatures, called barnacles, which are found incrusting these submerged branches; and further that these barnacles are in process of time transformed into the birds known as barnacle geese. This belief was not confined to the vulgar; it was a received doctrine amongst naturalists . . . In a paper contained in the *Philosophical Transactions*, Sir Robert Moray, describing these barnacles, says: 'In every shell that I opened I found a perfect sea-fowl; the little bill like that of a goose, the eyes marked, the head, neck, breast, wings, tail, and feet formed, the feathers everywhere perfectly shaped and blackish coloured, and the feet like those of other water-fowl, to the best of my remembrance.'[2] . . . Under the influence of a pre-conception, here is a man of education describing as 'a perfect sea-fowl' what is now seen to be a modified crustacean – a creature belonging to a remote part of the animal kingdom.

A still more remarkable instance of perverted observation is presented in an old book entitled *Metamorphosis Naturalis*, &c., published at Middleburgh in 1662.[3] This work, in which is attempted for the first time a detailed description of insect-transformation, contains numerous illustrative plates, in which are

DOI: 10.4324/9781003107835-13

represented the various stages of evolution – larva, pupa, and imago. Those who have even but a smattering of Entomology will recollect that the chrysalises of all our common butterflies exhibit at the anterior end a number of pointed projections, producing an irregular outline. Have they ever observed in this outline a resemblance to a man's face? For myself, I can say that though in early days I kept brood after brood of butterfly larvae through all their changes, I never perceived any such likeness, nor can I see it now. Nevertheless, in the plates of this *Metamorphosis Naturalis*, each of these chrysalises has its projections so modified as to produce a burlesque human head – the respective species having distinctive profiles given them. Whether the author was a believer in metempsychosis, and thought he saw in the chrysalis a disguised humanity, or whether, swayed by the false analogy which Butler makes so much of, between the change from chrysalis to butterfly, and that from mortality to immortality, he considered the chrysalis as typical of man – I cannot say.[4] Here, however, is the fact – that influenced by some preconception or other, he has shown the forms to be quite different from what they are. It is not that he simply thinks this resemblance exists – it is not that he merely says he can see it – but his pre-conception so possesses him as to swerve his pencil, and make him produce representations laughably unlike the realities.

These, which are extreme cases of distorted observation, differ only in degree from the distorted observations of daily life; and so strong is the distorting influence, that even the coolest man of science cannot escape its effects. Every microscopist knows that if they have conflicting theories respecting its nature, two observers shall look through the same instrument at the same object, and give quite different descriptions of its appearance.

From the dangers of hypothesis let us now turn to the dangers of no hypothesis. Little recognised as is the fact, it is nevertheless true that we cannot make the commonest observations correctly without beforehand having some notion of what we are to observe . . .[5]

Is it not clear, therefore, that to observe correctly is by no means easy? On the one hand, if we have a pre-conception, we are liable to see things not quite as they are, but as we think them. On the other hand, without a pre-conception, we are liable to pass over much that we ought to see. Yet we must have either a pre-conception or no pre-conception. Evidently, then, all our observations, save those guided by true theories already known, are in danger either of distortion or incompleteness.

It remains but to remark, that if this be so with *statical* phenomena, how much more must it be so with *dynamical* ones. If our observations are imperfect, in cases like the foregoing, where the things seen are persistent, and may be again and again looked at, or continuously contemplated, how much more imperfect must they be where the things seen are complex processes, changes, or actions, each of them presenting successive phases, which, if not correctly seen at the moments they severally occur, can never be correctly seen at all. Here the chances of error become immensely multiplied.

Editorial Endnotes

1 This essay was reprinted in an amended form as 'The valuation of evidence' in Spencer's *Essays: Scientific, Political & Speculative*, library ed., 3 vols. (London and Edinburgh: Williams and Norgate, 1891), vol. 2, pp. 161–7.

2 Spencer is referring to Sir Robert Moray, 'A Relation concerning Barnacles', *Philosophical Transactions of the Royal Society*, 137 (10 February 1678), pp. 925–7. Jessie Dobson, in 'Curiosities of natural history', *Annals of the Royal College of Surgeons of England* 22:5 (May 1958), pp. 330–42, discusses this work on p. 333.

3 Johannes Goedaert, *Metamorphosis et Historia Naturalis Insectorum*, 3 vols. (Middleburgh, 1662). The heads of the insect pupae in the engravings forming plates 1 and 24 are especially anthropomorphic. In plate 65, the heads of caterpillars look more like those of bears.

4 Bishop Joseph Butler in *The Analogy of Religion, Natural and Revealed, to the Constitution and Course of Nature* (1736), ch. 1, 'Of a future life', claimed that the metamorphoses of insects through their life stages might have a counterpart in the transformation of human beings in the hereafter.

5 Spencer's example of deficiency in observation, attributable to lack of prior knowledge, is his own failure to discern the true colours of shadows, until they were pointed out to him by an artist; these observations were then verified by reference to optical laws.

Editorial Headnote

13. Mrs. Hugh Blackburn [Jemima Blackburn], *Birds Drawn from Nature* (1868)

Jemima Blackburn came from an aristocratic Scottish family and married a professor of mathematics at Glasgow University. Her book of lithographic drawings was based on birdwatching within the couple's Roshven estate on the west coast of Scotland. She drew from life, free of the commercial constraints and representational conventions imposed on professional illustrators, and the work has a freshness and immediacy not seen in run-of-the-mill ornithologies. Her accompanying text often recorded birds' natural behaviour in wild flocks diving for fish, or in family groups, as she had observed and sketched it first hand. She always recorded punctiliously how a drawing had become possible: many birds were caught alive as models and afterwards released unharmed, and she emphasises the difference between such direct life studies and her occasional resort to freshly killed or stuffed specimens. The refined feeling for line, pattern, and flowing movement that characterises her lithographic drawings owes something to Bewick's *British Birds*, which she had delighted in since childhood, and she was perhaps also influenced by Audubon. A selection from the brief texts that accompanied the drawings exemplifies Blackburn's concern with authenticity in her records of bird life.

Figure 4 Jemima Blackburn, *Birds Drawn from Nature*, 1868, plate XXX, 'The Landrail' [corncrake], lithograph from her drawing. (Biodiversity Heritage Library)

13

BIRDS DRAWN FROM NATURE

Mrs. Hugh [Jemima] Blackburn

Source: Mrs Hugh Blackburn [Jemima Blackburn], *Birds Drawn from Nature* (Glasgow: James Maclehose, 1868), preface and selected commentaries, unpaginated.

The Drawings, of which a few are here engraved, have been made either from the living bird, or from specimens so fresh as to preserve most of the characteristic appearances of life, while the attitude and background have been studied from careful observation of the habits of the wild birds.

This has of course involved a good deal of trouble, and it is not likely that a single observer will have the opportunity, under these restrictions, of obtaining good drawings of the whole series of British Birds. Such considerations have no doubt induced most illustrators of the subject (even Bewick himself), to put up with a stuffed skin for a lay figure, and, apparently, to label drawings so made as 'from nature.'

But in the present instance the artist, without neglecting to refer to stuffed 'specimens,' has refused to be guided by them, in the belief that drawings *really* from nature (and such only) may be made to give a representation of nature more faithful in most essential points than the stuffed skin itself, even when newly set up by the most skilful workmen, and of course in a higher degree preferable to an idealised copy of the usual faded and withered denizen of a glass-case. Even in completeness it is surprising how soon a collection of drawings may be made to bear comparison with all but the greatest museums.

In order to carry out the same idea of interposing as few interpreters as possible between nature and the actual print, the drawings have been copied on to the stone (or zinc plate) by the same hand as made the original drawings, or in some instances the drawing has been made on the stone direct from nature.[1]

After what has been said it will be understood that the choice of subjects has been to some extent limited by circumstances. In many cases, however, it was thought better to give several plates illustrating points of interest in the habits and growth of one species, than to occupy the same space with others, for a complete history of which the materials have not yet been collected. But an untoward accident, which at the eleventh hour has befallen a number of the plates we had intended to include, has destroyed the links connecting some of our illustrations, and made them even less consecutive than they would otherwise have been. Yet

DOI: 10.4324/9781003107835-14

it is still hoped that this volume may be considered as so far complete in itself, or at all events as a contribution not without some value towards the illustration of the subject, whether or not opportunity be given to the same hand of continuing the series . . .

IX. The Sandpiper. We have found Sandpiper's nests in various positions on the ground, in the side of a bank, or at the foot of a tree, and once only actually in a low bush, but always near the shore. The young birds are able to leave the nest as soon as hatched, but remain near it for a few days, probably returning to it at night.

The nest sketched was in a bank, and the whole family were drawn from life. The old bird was caught by placing the young ones in an open cage, and shutting the door by means of a string as soon as she went in, which she did immediately on our retiring a dozen yards.

There is no perceptible difference of plumage between the male and female, but we assumed this to be the female. They were all restored to their home uninjured . . .

XXII. The Common Heron. The Heron, from which this head was drawn, was caught alive during a hard frost in Stirlingshire. He lived for a fortnight in a garret in the College of Glasgow, where he fished with great success for small herrings in a footpail. He always stood on one leg on a chair without perceptible motion for at least an hour after meals. He seemed quite contented with his lot, but when the mild weather returned he was liberated at the place where he had been captured . . .

XXX. The Landrail.[2] The Nest of the Landrail, is from nature, at Roshven. The nest was watched till one egg hatched, and the young bird then drawn from life. The next day the whole were hatched, and left the nest. The attitude of the old bird was studied from the life, but some of the details of the plumage were finished from a newly killed bird.

XXXI. The Common Snipe. The young Snipe was very carefully drawn from a live bird caught at Roshven in August, and returned safe to its mother. The bird was unquestionably the young of the Common Snipe, and the faithfulness of the portrait may be relied on; but, for some reason or other, it differed much both in form and colour from the plate in Mr. Gould's Birds of Great Britain.[3] The old bird is also from a live specimen, and the background represents the place where the young bird was caught.

Editorial Endnotes

1 One advantage of lithography as a graphic medium was that the artist could draw freehand directly on the lithographic stone surface, whereas copper engraving and etching, together with wood engraving, normally required the services of professional engravers.

2 The Landrail (see Figure 4) is the Corncrake.

3 John Gould's five-volume work, *The Birds of Great Britain*, was published in its entirety in 1873. Jemima Blackburn must have seen a separate plate of the snipe in advance of this collected edition, or her own work may have been reissued or added to sporadically: the snipe occurs in 'Part II' of *Birds Drawn from Nature*.

Editorial Headnote

13.1. J. B. [Jemima Blackburn], 'Cuckoo and Pipit', *Nature* (1872)

This article provided the context for Blackburn's famous drawing of a newborn cuckoo ejecting the young of the host species, meadow pipits, from the nest – behaviour which she had observed first hand. The use of initials disguised the author's sex, while an added address, 'The University, Glasgow' – her husband's institution – gave an impression of academic authority. Nevertheless, in the *Nature* article, there is a footnote reference to the author as 'Mrs. Hugh Blackburn' and to her illustrated storybook for children, *The Pipits*, in which this drawing was first reproduced, with moralising comments on 'the naughty, selfish bird' involved – an application that would have been unthinkable in a male naturalist. The image was adapted by John Gould for an illustration in his *The Birds of Great Britain*, vol. 3 (1873), without acknowledgement to Blackburn.[1]

Editorial Endnote

1 In *On the Origin of Species* (1859), Darwin discussed the ruthless behaviour of young cuckoos as an example of inherited instinct necessary for survival. In the sixth edition of *Origin* (1872), p. 214, he noted that a recent direct observation of a newborn cuckoo throwing out pipit fledglings (seemingly referencing Jemima Blackburn's drawing) had defeated John Gould's initial attempt, in the first issues of *The Birds of Great Britain*, to interpret such events in a benign way. However, when Gould subsequently published a collected edition of this work in 1873, he included in volume 3, as plate 68, a copy of Blackburn's drawing, falsely crediting himself as the artist. At the same time, he added to the drawing a figure of the mother pipit, supposedly watching the cuckoo's action and acquiescing in it.

13.1

CUCKOO AND PIPIT

'J.B.' [Jemima Blackburn]

Source: 'J.B.' [Jemima Blackburn], 'Cuckoo and Pipit', *Nature*, 5 (14 March 1872), p. 383.

Several well-known naturalists who have seen my sketch from life of the young cuckoo ejecting the young pipit (opposite p. 22 of the little versified tale of which I send a copy) have expressed a wish that the details of my observations of the scene should be published. I therefore send you the facts, though the sketch itself seems to me to be the only important addition I have made to the admirably accurate description given by Dr. Jenner in his letter to John Hunter, which is printed in the 'Philosophical Transactions' for 1788 (vol. lxxviii, pp. 225, 226), and which I have read with pleasure since putting down my own notes.[1]

The nest which we watched last June, after finding the cuckoo's egg in it, was that of the common meadow pipit (Titlark, Mosscheeper), and had two pipit's eggs besides that of the cuckoo. It was below a heather bush, on the declivity of a low abrupt bank on a Highland hill-side in Moidart.

At one visit the pipits were found to be hatched, but not the cuckoo. At the next visit, which was after an interval of forty-eight hours, we found the young cuckoo alone in the nest, and both the young pipits lying down the bank, about ten inches from the margin of the nest, but quite lively after being warmed in the hand. They were replaced in the nest beside the cuckoo, which struggled about till it got its back under one of them, when it climbed backwards directly up the open side of the nest, and hitched the pipit from its back on to the edge. It then stood quite upright on its legs, which were straddled wide apart, with the claws firmly fixed half-way down the inside of the nest among the interlacing fibres of which the nest was woven; and, stretching its wings apart and backwards, it elbowed the pipit fairly over the margin so far that its struggles took it down the bank instead of back into the nest.

After this the cuckoo stood a minute or two, feeling back with its wings, as if to make sure that the pipit was fairly overboard, and then subsided into the bottom of the nest.

As it was getting late, and the cuckoo did not immediately set to work on the other nestling, I replaced the ejected one, and went home. On returning next day, both nestlings were found, dead and cold, out of the nest. I replaced one of them, but the cuckoo made no effort to get under and eject it, but settled itself

DOI: 10.4324/9781003107835-15

contentedly on the top of it. All this I find accords accurately with Jenner's description of what he saw. But what struck me most was this: The cuckoo was perfectly naked, without a vestige of feather or even a hint of future feathers; its eyes were not yet opened, and its neck seemed too weak to support the weight of its head. The pipits had well-developed quills on the wings and back, and had bright eyes, partially open; yet they seemed quite helpless under the manipulations of the cuckoo, which looked a much less developed creature. The cuckoo's legs, however, seemed very muscular, and it appeared to feel about with its wings, which were absolutely featherless, as with hands, the 'spurious wing' (unusually large in proportion) looking like a spread-out thumb. The most singular thing of all was the direct purpose with which the blind little monster made for the open side of the nest, the only part where it could throw its burthen down the bank. I think all the spectators felt the sort of horror and awe at the apparent inadequacy of the creature's intelligence to its acts that one might have felt at seeing a toothless hag raise a ghost by an incantation. It was horribly 'uncanny' and 'grewsome.'

Editorial Endnote

1 'XIV. Observations on the Natural History of the Cuckoo. By Mr. Edward Jenner. In a Letter to John Hunter, Esq., F.R.S. Read March 13, 1788', *Philosophical Transactions of the Royal Society of London*, 78 (1788), pp. 219–37.

Editorial Headnote

14. Arthur Herbert Church, *Colour* (1891)

As the work of James Sowerby has already shown (see Chapter 3), the definition of colours in nature and explanation of the causes of their occurrence were significant problems for natural scientists in the nineteenth century. In 1871–2 Arthur Church, who was Professor of Chemistry at the Royal Academy, produced a study of the nature of colour that was intended to be helpful to naturalists, chemists, and physicists, as well as to artists and craftsmen, and this expanded edition appeared twenty years later. He discussed colour phenomena in the natural world, especially in relation to birds' feathers. Church proved experimentally that, in some birds, the colours of the feathers were inherent or pigmental, arising from chemicals in their bodies.[1] However, he also discussed the phenomenon of 'the *interference* of light waves' falling on birds' feathers: their differential refraction created iridescent or 'shot' colours, which change according to the angle of vision – known as structural colours. Such awareness of the diversity of causation and possible purposes in animals' colouring raised many new scientific questions, especially in the light of Darwin's theories of protective coloration (camouflage), and sexual selection. However, Church was as much interested in the aesthetic and affective qualities of colour as he was in its origination.

Editorial Endnote

1 Arthur Herbert Church, 'Researches on Turacin an Animal Pigment containing Copper', paper read 27 May 1869, *Philosophical Transactions of the Royal Society*, 159 (31 December 1869), pp. 627–36. Church gave the name Turacin to a red chemical pigment he found in the feathers of the Touracou or Turaco, a brightly coloured African bird.

14

COLOUR

An Elementary Manual for Students

Arthur Herbert Church

Source: Arthur Herbert Church, *Colour: An Elementary Manual for Students*, new ed., revised and enlarged (London, Paris, New York, Melbourne: Cassell, 1891), pp. 37, 56–8, 111–12, 188.

[p. 37]

The splendid metallic hues of the feathers of the humming-bird and the peacock and of the wing-cases of certain beetles; the rainbow hues of mother-of-pearl and many shells, of antique glass, of the precious opal, of imperfectly polished metals – all these beautiful phenomena are due to interference, and not – at least in the majority of instances – to any actual colouring matters. We have in these objects minute surface sculpturings, or striæ, or veins, or foldings, and it is by reflections or refractions among these microscopic mechanical textures that rays capable of interfering with each other are generated . . .

[pp. 56–8]

Many attempts have been made to classify colours, including under that designation not only all hues, with their shades, tints, and broken tints, but also white – a balanced or neutralised compound of two or more hues – and black – the negative correlative of light and colour . . . The real difficulty begins when we attempt the classification of hues: that is, of colours proper. Where can we find standards of comparison for all colours in respect of the three constants of colour – hue, purity, luminosity? . . . The difficulties in the way of classifying colours are augmented by the very great number of hues, with their shades and tints, possessed of varying degrees of luminosity, which the human eye is competent to distinguish . . . Add to these the hues produced by gradual increments or decrements in luminosity and the whole series of purples, and we reach a grand total of colours which must be measured by hundreds of thousands.

These high figures alone preclude the possibility of assigning names to any hues but those which are well known, and are separated by considerable intervals of wave-length. The dearth of well-defined colour-names in English, and the want of flexibility in the language as to the coinage of new designations, makes the question of colour nomenclature a most difficult one.

DOI: 10.4324/9781003107835-16

[pp. 111–112]

Endeavours have been made to show that in olden times the appreciation of colour, as distinct from that of light and shade, was very imperfect. The main argument is founded upon the limited vocabulary for various colours possessed by the oldest writers, and the vague usage of such terms as they employ.[1] But . . . when we discover that a keen sense of colour belongs to many groups of the lower animals, not only to mammals but to birds, fishes, and even insects, then we have very good reasons to doubt that the sense for colour in the human eye and brain is a development of the last few thousand years. The experimental proof, obtained by Rood, that the amount of time necessary for vision is the same, namely, one forty-billionth of a second, whether colour or merely light and shade be recognized, tends to show that the human sense for colour is as ancient as the human sense for tone[2] . . . This cultivation of the sense of colour is, however, rather psychological than physiological, rather mental than physical . . . We try to trace out the causes of the vast number of colour-sensations which we are continually receiving, but we constantly find that the cold methods of analysis fail to explain the mental appreciation with which we regard the astounding fertility of nature in its gifts of colour. We shall endeavour farther on to demonstrate how greatly our pleasure in colour depends upon an infinitude of most minute variations of tone and hue, which, by their suggestion of the wealth, variety and vastness of nature, and by their association with scenes and circumstances of enjoyment and delight, enrich our appreciation of the sensation of colour in a way which no mere optical demonstration of chromatic phenomena can ever completely trace'.

[p. 188]

The colours which adorn animals are distributed in a very strange and apparently capricious way, and, in many cases, show no correspondence with the structure of their bodies. These colours arise in great part from the minute sculpturing, reticulation and scoring of the surface, and not from definite colouring matters like those present in plants. The metallic colours of the humming-bird and the peacock must be attributed in the main to what may be called the optical structure of the web of the feathers: they are, in fact, *interference* colours relieved against a dark background, which owes its blackness to a black or dark brown pigment. Instances, however, do occur in which an actual pigment or colouring matter exists in, and may be extracted from, coloured feathers. Thus amongst the Touracos or plantain eaters of Africa there are no less than eleven species which owe their splendid crimson coloration to a definite pigment discovered by the present writer. This pigment is remarkable in many ways, notably in containing as an essential ingredient no less than 8 per cent. of metallic copper. And from other birds several other colouring matters, soluble in alcohol or in soda solution have been extracted. As a rule, these pigments are much more permanent than those of flowers.

Editorial Endnotes

1 The statesman William Ewart Gladstone had argued in his *Studies on Homer and the Homeric Age*, 3 vols. (Oxford: University Press, 1858), vol. 3, section iv, "Homer's

Perceptions and Use of Colour', pp. 457–99, that the *Iliad* and the *Odyssey* revealed a poor, undeveloped feeling for colour. Gladstone concluded that 'the perceptions so easy and familiar to us' in the nineteenth century arose from 'a slow traditionary growth in knowledge and in the training of the human organ' since Homer's time (p. 495). Gladstone's view was challenged by evolutionists like Grant Allen, who pointed out that many animals had a highly developed colour sense, which humans must always have shared and gradually refined.

2 Ogden Nicholas Rood, *Modern Chromatics, with Applications to Art and Industry* (New York: D. Appleton, 1879), p. 102.

Editorial Headnote

15. Marion Isabel Newbigin, *Colour in Nature: A Study in Biology* (1898)

Marion Newbigin was a biologist and a lecturer on zoology at the Medical College for Women in Edinburgh. Her book was partly a critique of the Darwinian interpretation of animals' colours as products of either natural or sexual selection – an interpretation particularly associated with the writings of Edward Bagnall Poulton (see Chapter 61 in the present work).[1] In Newbigin's view, the theory that colour was always either protective or a product of aesthetic selection by the females ignored the complexities of the biological and chemical phenomena involved in coloration. She was sarcastic about the mindset of 'field naturalists' and stressed the importance of laboratory research on actual specimens. As Church had also shown, such analysis of coloration, whether in birds' feathers or in insects' wings, revealed a great range of causative factors. Effects of colour might be 'constitutional' and 'pigmental' (arising from inherent chemical elements in the animal's body); or they might be 'structural' or 'optical' (arising from reflections of light from feathers or scales, seen from different angles of vision). Visual beauty might be just a fortuitous side effect of physiological processes unconnected with display: yet she did not deny that there *was* beauty in nature, of a kind that human beings responded to with joy.

Editorial Endnote

1 The polemical or corrective aspect of Newbigin's work (which becomes explicit in pp. 301–6) was highlighted in a review of it in *The Zoologist,* 4th ser., 3:691 (January 1899), pp. 33–4.

15

COLOUR IN NATURE

A Study in Biology

Marion Isabel Newbigin

Source: Marion Isabel Newbigin, *Colour in Nature: A Study in Biology* (London: John Murray, 1898), pp. 12–15, 148, 257.

[pp. 12–15]

Of *Objective Structural* colours, green and blue afford the best examples. Green seems to be usually produced by a combination of a yellow pigment and a structural modification, wherefore green feathers usually appear yellowish in transmitted light. The display of a blue colour again seems, at least in birds and probably in insects, to be always associated with the presence in the tissues of a dark-coloured pigment. A blue colour in the feathers of birds is always confined to certain parts of the feather, and its presence is associated with considerable modifications of feather structure. Blue is not however confined to the feathers, but may occur also on bare patches of skin, as in some of the Paradise birds, in the cassowary, etc. Curiously enough, a blue colour in the skin seems to be particularly unstable, fading as rapidly after death as does the blue colour in the abdomen of some dragon-flies.

The exact physical cause of green and blue colours is still doubtful, but the fact that the colours are structural is readily perceived both by the strong surface gloss and by the disappearance of the colour in transmitted light.

While unvarying blue and green tints in birds rather heighten the general effect than display in themselves great beauty, the *Subjective Structural* colours, on the other hand, display the most exquisitely varying tints, and it is to them that many birds and insects owe their wonderful flashing beauty. These colours glow with all the tints of the rainbow, and change with every changing ray of light . . . In birds their degree of development varies greatly, for we find them ranging from the dull greenish gloss of some of the female humming-birds to the gorgeous colouring of many of the males in humming-birds and birds of Paradise. Among birds metallic colour is apparently always associated with the presence in the feathers of dull brown or black pigments, which are necessary for the production of the colours. It is also associated with a modification of the feather structure which in many cases renders the feathers unfitted for the purpose of flight. Here, as in the

DOI: 10.4324/9781003107835-17

case of objective structural colours, the exact physical causation of the colours is unknown.

In insects the colours are equally bright, but have had little attention bestowed upon them; it is still doubtful whether the colours in them are or are not associated with the presence of dark pigment.

The presence of pigment is not, however, essential to the production of structural colours; the common earthworm, for example, exhibits a faint iridescence which is due to the presence of numerous fine lines on its colourless cuticle, these fine lines producing interference of light. Although the colouring is very slight in the earthworm, it is well known that some of the marine worms, *e.g.* the sea-mouse (*Aphrodite*), are covered with numerous bristles which exhibit brilliant iridescent colours. Again, the colours of mother-of-pearl are of course produced by structure only, without any assistance from pigment . . .

Structural colours are of extreme interest, not only on account of their wonderful beauty, but also on account of the difficult questions connected with their origin. It is to some extent possible to correlate pigment-production with the physiology of the organism, but this seems extremely difficult in the case of structural coloration. We may note, however, that structural colouring attains its greatest perfection among birds and butterflies, and both groups are noted for the extraordinary development of their cuticular structures. The delicate beauty of the sculpturing of butterflies' scales has been extolled by most possessors of a microscope, while savage and civilised races are alike in their admiration for the feathers of birds. The fact that organisms so widely separated as are birds and butterflies are alike in exhibiting both exquisite structural coloration and a wonderful development of structures arising from the cuticle, suggests that the structural colours are in origin merely a result of extreme differentiation of the cuticle, and therefore produced by the same cause which gave rise to this differentiation. The presence of brilliant iridescence in some of the mud-inhabiting worms is therefore not quite inexplicable, for here also we find that the cuticle shows a considerable amount of differentiation. We can also further understand how it is that the highest pitch of perfection is attained in birds and butterflies, when we consider that in both cases the colouring occurs in connection with structures which are of supreme importance to the species, that is, with the feathers of the bird and the scales, which are but outgrowths of the wings, in butterflies.

[p. 148]

Having regard to the small size of the scales [of butterflies], it will be readily understood that there is frequently great difficulty in determining whether a particular colour is due to pigment or structure; the fact that a scale showing structural colour frequently contains pigment in addition further complicates the matter. We thus find that there is much difference of opinion among observers as to the cause of particular colours . . . Making due allowance for difficulties of observation, it seems, however, certain that blue in butterflies is always a structural colour, while green, black, and white are at least usually due to structure. Other of the structural colours are readily recognised by their metallic brilliancy and changing glow, which give to the butterflies possessing them an appearance of surpassing beauty. Many will recall Mr. Wallace's description of how his heart beat fast and his brain reeled when his perseverance was rewarded, and he captured with his own hands one of the finest of these living gems in the Malay Archipelago.[1]

[p. 257]

The pigments of the egg-shells of birds have been investigated by several authors. The important points upon which all agree are first, that the colouring is due to definite pigments; and second, that these are derived directly or indirectly from hæmoglobin – results of much theoretic importance. The interesting point is not that derivatives of hæmoglobin should be used in coloration, but why, if vivid and beautiful colouring-matters do arise in this way, they should not be employed in the coloration of the feathers. It seems also generally admitted that even the ingenuity of that highly esteemed person, the field naturalist, is unequal to the task of explaining the colours of all birds' eggs upon the hypothesis of usefulness,[2] so that from the theoretical point of view these pigments are of quite special interest.

Editorial Endnotes

1 Alfred Russel Wallace, *The Malay Archipelago*, 2 vols. (London: Macmillan, 1869), vol. 2, p. 51: Wallace described his excitement in catching a bird-winged butterfly, which he named *Ornithoptera croesus*. The species is now known as 'Wallace's golden birdwing'. His account of the King Bird of Paradise on pp. 221–4 of this volume was, if anything, more ecstatic when describing its vivid colours and the unique 'ornaments' of its breast and tail feathers.

2 'Usefulness' in the sense of providing camouflage, etc. Birds' eggs are not always of a colour that blends in with their surroundings.

Editorial Headnote

16. William Chapman Hewitson, Letters to John Hancock, 1840s

Many Victorians, especially men, were passionate collectors of natural history specimens, whether of stuffed birds, birds' eggs, butterflies, beetles, shells, or flowers – a hobby that was taken up by people from a wide range of social classes, often through membership of local natural history societies and participation in their country outings. Many specialist dealers in animal specimens were also established. Some wealthy collectors would not rest until they had obtained specimens of *all* the species in a particular group, to make up a complete set, at any cost. These specimens would then be carefully identified, documented, preserved, labelled, ordered, and displayed in fine bespoke cabinets, for the admiration of visitors and of fellow collectors. Aesthetic taste in their presentation was as important as scientific rarity and completeness. This extravagant collecting mania certainly contributed to the extinction of many species in the wild across the world, and by the end of the nineteenth century it was coming under sustained attack by conservationists such as W.H. Hudson. However, private collections of natural specimens were often eventually gifted to museums, including the British Museum (Natural History), with benefits to scientific research. One such collector and donor was William Chapman Hewitson, a close friend of the naturalist and taxidermist John Hancock. Hewitson was himself a fine zoological draughtsman, who produced lithographic drawings of insects, birds' eggs, etc. for natural history publications. In a letter to Hancock of 24 December 1845, written from near Bristol, Hewitson reported on his collecting activities. In a further letter (undated, c. 1846–7), written from Kirkby Stephen in Cumbria, he requested Hancock's assistance in ordering a cabinet to house his specimens (Letters 0322 and 0327, Hancock archive, Newcastle, NEWHM:1996.H67).

16

LETTERS TO JOHN HANCOCK

William Chapman Hewitson

Source: William Chapman Hewitson, letters to John Hancock, 1840s. Hancock archive, Newcastle, NEWHM:1996.H67, nos. 0322, 0327.

6 Sion Place Clifton near Bristol December 24 1845[1]

My dear friend, . . . I have received a nest of eggs from Mr. Bond said to be those of Savi's Warbler and taken in Cambridgeshire. The eggs very like those of the Grasshopper Warbler but larger, the nest made entirely of flags. Mr. Bond knows nothing further about it except that the bird was shot from the nest. They have had the species in the British Museum from Cambridge some time. You know Mr. Bond & therefore I wish to ask you whether I may depend upon him & draw the egg[2] . . .

Will you tell me what you think the best material of which to make artificial bodies for butterflies – for the thorax it would be necessary to have something the pin would go through. I should like to show you some of the very elegant long tailed Swallowtails I have from Honduras – white with black bands like podalirius. Our man is going out again next month to Venezuela which is the best part of So. [South] America for butterflies[3] . . . I am busy resetting my butterflies and it is astonishing how it improves them – I have not forgot the shells I promised to send your brother[4] . . . Harrington had several of the pea great beetles you mention & several allied species all rare. He has sold all his Coleoptera to Argent. The first specimen of the species sold at Drury's sale brought £10 – a dealer here who got several from Africa sold them for £5 each . . . The dealer here got £30 for a rarer one of the same genus Goliathus.[5]

Kirkby Stephen[6]

My dear friend . . . I wrote to Sopwith oddly just before I got your letter & sent him £50 on account of the cabinet. I shall be very much obliged to you to make what enquiries you can about glass & as if you were doing it for yourself.[7] I shall also be greatly in your debt for modelling the beetles for Scott but why can he not carve as well from the real ones?[8]– If you outlive me the cabinet & all it contains (except a few that are desiderata to the British museum)[9] will be yours for I would grieve to let it fall into the hands of those that would not appreciate the things which have held so much the happiness of my life. I know that by saying this I should not increase your kind readiness to oblige me – in having it well done.

DOI: 10.4324/9781003107835-18

I mean now to rest upon my oars for some time with regard to my butterflies. I am going to spend so much more money at Oatlands that I am beginning to feel alarmed in earnest & wish I may not make myself unhappy[10] . . .

There is at present a large collection of Indian butterflies in London in the finest condition possible but such is their idea of the value that no one will buy them. – There was also a large collection of Brazilian ones in town when I left & amongst them some splendid new things but all so dear that their owner has taken them to Holland.[11] I have just completed my paper on my favourite genus of butterflies & have figured & described 12 new species for the Annals.[12] Harrington has been into Huntingdonshire with Bond collecting & has brought home some thousands of chrysalises of two or three species only . . .

Editorial Endnotes

1 Letter from William Hewitson to John Hancock, dated 24 December 1845.

2 Savi's Warbler nests in reedbeds, in this case among 'flags' or irises. 'Mr. Bond' is presumably James William Bond, who collected British insects in the area round London and kept a hand-written collecting journal between 1825 and 1858. Bond may have known Hewitson through shared entomological interests, but he was not an ornithological expert, and his plebian background may have made Hewitson inclined to be suspicious of his bona fides. Specimens of rare species had greater value if reliably sourced to a site in Britain. Hewitson would have been drawing the egg for his *Coloured Illustrations of the Eggs of British Birds*, 2 vols. (London: John van Voorst, 1846).

3 The dark kite-swallowtail from Honduras and elsewhere in Central America is slightly similar in its markings to the British species *Iphiclides podalirius* or scarce swallowtail. 'Our man' indicates a professional agent commissioned by Hewitson and others for a particular collecting project.

4 John Hancock's brother, Albany Hancock, was an expert on marine molluscs.

5 'Pea beetles' are weevils that eat peas and broad beans. 'Goliathus' is a genus of very large beetles from African jungles.

6 Letter from William Hewitson to John Hancock, undated.

7 This was an expensive glass-fronted display cabinet, destined to house Hewitson's butterfly specimens. Thomas Sopwith was a leading cabinet-maker and businessman in Newcastle upon Tyne (the home city of both Hancock and Hewitson himself), and he specialised in fine mahogany furniture. Sopwith was also recommended to clients like Hewitson by being an amateur geologist, and an active member of the Natural History Society of Northumberland, Durham, and Newcastle upon Tyne. The cabinet was designed by the artist William Bell Scott, with ornamentation carved by Robert Sadler Scott, and was assembled by Sopwith's firm c. 1846. It was apparently lent by Hewitson himself to the 1848 Newcastle Exhibition of Arts, Manufactures and Practical Science. See Rosamond Allwood, 'Thomas Sopwith of Newcastle 1803–1879', *Furniture History* 26 (1990), pp. 1–9.

8 William Bell Scott's design for the decoration of the cabinet evidently included appropriate natural motifs such as beetles, but the carver Robert Sadler Scott relied on Hancock for three-dimensional models to guide him in the rendering of entomological details.

9 Hewitson gave some of his collections of specimens to the British Museum (Natural History).

10 Oatlands was Hewitson's country mansion, which he later bequeathed to Hancock.

11 Collectors journeying in Asia and South America could often get very high prices for the rare specimens they brought back to Europe. Their number included many important naturalists, such as Alfred Russel Wallace and Henry Walter Bates, who stood in need of the income from such sales.

12 Hewitson's 'Descriptions of new species of Butterflies' was published in *The Annals and Magazine of Natural History* 20:133 (1847) as item XXIV, pp. 257–64, illustrated with his own lithographic drawings. The butterflies in question were of the family Nymphalidae, genus Heterochroa, from South America, many studied from specimens in Hewitson's own collection.

Editorial Headnote

17. Anon., 'Reports of Societies: Leicester Literary and Philosophical Society', *The Midland Naturalist* (1886)

Below the social level of rich specialist collectors like Hewitson, many amateur naturalists acquired objects that appealed to them as scientific curiosities or as things of visual beauty – scientific and aesthetic properties often being combined. The meetings of local natural history societies were occasions for the display and discussion of such collections among the members present, facilitating the exchange of information. This report from a meeting of the Literary and Philosophical Society of Leicester in 1886 is a good example.

17

REPORTS OF SOCIETIES

Leicester Literary and Philosophical Society – Section D, Zoology and Botany

Anon., The Midland Naturalist

Source: 'Reports of Societies: Leicester Literary and Philosophical Society – Section D, Zoology and Botany', *The Midland Naturalist*, 9 (1886), p. 284.

Attendance, eight (two ladies). The following objects were exhibited, viz.: by Dr. Cooper, dried plants from North Wales, including *Spiræa salicifolia*, apparently wild. By Rev. T.A. Preston, a set of beautiful glass models, by Blaschka, of Dresden, of an obelia, showing the natural size of the polypidom, the same greatly magnified, with the polyps in the cells, and the free medusæ in two stages; also models of several genera of sea anemones, and a few of Cole's microscopic slides. It was stated that the glass models could only now be got through Mr. Damon, of Plymouth, that the manufactory produces models of nearly a thousand species, but that the demand so much exceeds the supply that orders are rarely executed within twelve months, and small orders are scarcely attended to.[1] . . . By the Chairman, a metacarpal bone of *Bos longifrons*, the smallest of the old races of cattle, taken from the floor of the butcher's shop in the ancient Roman town of Uriconium, in Shropshire. The Chairman read a short paper on 'Rats, and the occurrence of the Black Rat in Leicestershire'; exhibiting a specimen of the black rat recently captured at a farm about a mile from Leicester. The Chairman suggested that it would be useful and interesting work for the members of the section to practise the art of setting up life-groups of invertebrate animals, showing the history and habits of the species. These being small and easily preserved, groups could be set up pictorially without the apparatus of a special workshop, and such groups would be novel and extremely useful.[2]

Editorial Endnotes

1 For 'Cole's microscopic slides', which were often highly decorative, see Chapter 11 in the present volume. Leopold and Rudolf Blaschka made glass models of marine

DOI: 10.4324/9781003107835-19

invertebrates, etc., which were sold to museums and collectors across Europe and America. In Britain Robert Damon acted as their agent, to filter and process orders. These models were expertly crafted objects that could not be mass produced. They were educational as museum exhibits, but private buyers often valued them for their sheer beauties of form and colour, Natural History Museum, 'Blaschka glass models: conserving art and science', *Institutional Archives*, 40 (Autumn 2005), and C. Giles Miller and Miranda Lowe, 'The Natural History Museum Blaschka collections', *Historical Biology* 20:1 (February 2008), pp. 51–62.

2 The chairman seems to be suggesting the creation of tabletop dioramas, which might have been useful for visual instruction in museums or schools.

Editorial Headnote

18. Revd John Christopher Atkinson, *British Birds' Eggs and Nests* (1867)

Schoolboys were encouraged to form their own collections of natural history specimens. Atkinson defended the taking of eggs from birds' nests, despite increasing public opposition to this practice, including the disapproval of some of Atkinson's friends (p. 3). He was, however, more indulgent towards the (supposedly) discriminating practices of his middle-class readers than he was towards the habits of 'some young loutish country savage' whose spoils could be seen in the 'long strings of blown birds' eggs festooned at cottage doors or hung over the cottage or farm-house mantel-piece' (pp. 4, 74). The first edition of *British Birds' Eggs and Nests* appeared in 1861 and was followed by a number of modified editions up to 1901.

18

BRITISH BIRDS' EGGS AND NESTS, POPULARLY DESCRIBED

Revd John Christopher Atkinson

Source: Revd John Cristopher Atkinson, *British Birds' Eggs and Nests, Popularly Described, with coloured illustrations by W.S. Coleman*, new ed. (London and New York: George Routledge & Sons, 1867), pp. 2–3, 14–16, 19.

[pp. 2–3]

The difficulty of making such a book useful to the systematic collector of eggs, however young, is not nearly as great as that of making it interesting to the many, who, though not inspired with the ambition of owning a real grand cabinet, and of arranging its manifold drawers with neatly ordered and ticketed egg-cards, are yet sensible of a real pleasure and enjoyment in noticing the nests and eggs of their numerous 'feathered friends,' and identifying such as may chance to be less familiarly known than the majority of those met with under ordinary circumstances . . .

[pp. 14–16]

The question, – Why are Birds' Eggs, in so many cases, so variously and beautifully ornamented? Why are their hues and markings made so attractive to look at? has often been asked, and two or three different answers or modes of answer have been suggested. I have seen the idea started that the design of such various colouring and marking is intended to facilitate concealment, by the adaptation of the general hue of the egg to that of the recipient or supporting substances. The theory is at least original and amusing; but unfortunately less happy than when applied to the plumage of the birds themselves that lay the eggs . . . Again, another answer to the question just noticed is, Eggs were made so beautiful, and so various in their beauty, to gratify and gladden man's eye. I don't dispute the fact that the beautiful shape, and the beautiful tints, and the beautiful markings do gratify and gladden the human eye and human heart too. I know they do, and in thousands of cases, and with a great, pure pleasure. But that is a very different thing from saying that God made them so for no other, or even for that purpose as a principal reason. How many thousands of eggs, for ten that are seen by man, escape all human notice whatever! How many millions upon millions in the old-world times before there were men to see them, must have had their fair colours, and delicate symmetry, and harmonious intermingling of hues, for no purpose whatever according to this view! No, no. Nature should not be read so. God made

DOI: 10.4324/9781003107835-20

the Beasts of the Field, and the Birds of the Air, and the Fishes of the Sea, and the Insects, and the Shells, and the Trees, and Herbs, and Flowers, all, as a rule, wonderfully, gloriously, harmoniously beautiful, because He is a God of order, and beauty, and harmony . . .

[p. 19]

As to mounting the eggs and labelling for insertion in the collection, much depends on taste. An ordinary 'printer's' card is as good for the purpose as anything, and a little very strong gum-water is the only other requisite. A little attention to placing the eggs symmetrically and neatly, and the use of a few gun-wads or halfpence or small wooden wedges, to retain the eggs, when accurately set in their true position, until the gum has had time to harden, are matters which will almost surely suggest themselves to any youthful egg-fancier who is only tolerably given to admiring the '*simplex munditiis*.'[1] As for labels, they may either be neatly written, or procured, at a very light cost, printed on purpose for such application.

Editorial Endnote

1 Elegant, without flashiness.

Editorial Headnote

19. A.H. Palmer, *The Life Of Joseph Wolf* (1895)

Joseph Wolf's views on his own role as an 'animal painter' were recorded by his friend and biographer Alfred Herbert Palmer, son of the artist Samuel Palmer. Wolf had begun to draw birds and other animals from life in his native Germany in the 1840s, seeking both exactitude and vitality. He settled in London in 1848 and soon established himself as a leading artist for animal subjects (see Figures 9 and 23). He was often employed by the Zoological Society of London and studied live animals in the Society's Gardens extensively.[1] However, he found that many scientific authors wanted only anatomical diagrams to elucidate their texts, and these brought him no credit as an artist. Conversely, his status as an imaginative fine artist was compromised by his employment as a scientific draughtsman. Wolf also complained to Palmer that the subtleties of his animal drawings were often lost in the process of technical translation, when they were engraved and printed as book illustrations. The spontaneity of his sketches of birds in flight and other transient effects of movement in nature was inimitable. The first extract given here refers to his early years, when he was drawing birds in the country near Koblenz.

Editorial Endnote

1 Karl Schulze-Hagen and Armin Geus (eds.), 'Joseph Wolf (1820–1899)', *Tiermaler/Animal Painter* (Marburg an der Lahn: Basilisken-Presse, 2000).

19

THE LIFE OF JOSEPH WOLF, ANIMAL PAINTER

A.H. Palmer

Source: A.H. Palmer, *The Life of Joseph Wolf, Animal Painter* (London and New York: Longmans, Green, 1895), pp. 43–4, 57–9, 107–9, 112–14, 124–5, 130–1, 182–3.

[pp. 43–4]

Some wood-cutters, as they felled a neighbouring oak-copse, saw a Woodcock fly off her eggs. The forester on duty told Wolf that the bird had returned, in spite of the destruction of the cover. Sketch-book in hand, and trembling all over with excitement, the artist crept up, sat down 'by inches,' and worked, as he says, 'like blazes,' till he had secured careful drawings from several points of view. If not altogether unique, such a chance was rare enough to shake a man's nerves who realized the beauty of the sight, and what the sketches were worth in days when 'snap-shot' photographs were unknown. The power to turn out careful studies under such circumstances arose partly from a habit of intense concentration when the time came for it, and partly from the perfect knowledge of the distribution of the feather tracts. 'It would otherwise,' says the artist, 'have been impossible. The light stripes on the backs of the birds of this genus are each composed of two lines of parti-coloured feathers; the light webs of which, joined together, form the stripes when the plumage is in perfect order. There are hundreds of sportsmen who have killed no end of Woodcocks who don't know anything about that. They don't know the beauty of them. Professed ornithological artists have made the mistake of representing the stripe as formed of one line of feathers.

[pp. 57–9]

I regret to say that a few of the men of science Wolf came across filled him with wonder . . . 'Some of the ornithologists don't recognise nature – don't know a bird when they see it flying. A specimen must be well dried before they recognise it.' He found also (which to him was much more serious), that his instincts and knowledge as an artist were at a discount among many of his new friends . . . 'If a thing is artistic they mistrust it. There must be nothing right in perspective. There must be nothing but a map of the animal, and in a side view. They are like those other naturalists who only know a bird when they handle the skin. It is impossible, for instance, for a mere museum man to know the true colour of the eyes' . . . The

DOI: 10.4324/9781003107835-21

result of this state of things may be seen in many a scientific work; but it has not always been the case. A few ornithologists, for instance, have proved themselves most appreciative and kindly employers of the artists upon whom, as they know, they depend so much for the interest and value of their labours. But Science and Art, though ostensibly united under the auspices of a government department, have, in certain branches, been well nigh divorced from each other.[1] The fault is not on one side . . . Artists have sneered at Science, and have treated her simplest laws with open ridicule . . . They have looked down from the sublime pinnacles of landscape art with openly avowed contempt upon the man who has devoted himself to any but the regulation animals and 'the regulation nest of a Chaffinch with Hedge Sparrow's eggs.' They have eagerly turned aside to welcome 'Impressionism' into their very midst; and have shaken their tresses not only at 'the objects of natural history,' but at Nature.[2]

[pp. 107–9]

The consciousness that, for the most part, artistic refinements were entirely thrown away on the naturalists and perhaps resented by them as impairing the accuracy of the drawings, disturbed him still. He says: – 'There have been very few among all my acquaintances among naturalists who could appreciate a drawing if it were ever so well done; and sometimes the better it was done, the less they liked it . . . There are naturalists who think a stuffed Falcon superior to the best picture which can be painted. How can you expect respect as an artist from a man like that? The scientific work consists merely of *portraits* of single figures. I was never satisfied with this, but tried to express action and life – to make the animals do something by which you could give the picture a name' . . . 'So among the artists,' he says, 'I shall be called a "naturalist," and among the naturalists, an "artist"' . . . That the mutual hostility or indifference I have already alluded to should continue to intervene between Science and Art is sad; and that the talent of such an artist as Wolf should be so curbed and fettered by the requirements of his scientific work that he keeps it rigidly distinct from that which, in the proper sense, is artistic, and finally does it, so to speak, in secret, is still more sad. When the man of science accords to the artist a small measure of that respect which he justly claims by reason of his own life-long study and devotion, a better day will dawn; though it will have dawned too late for the one man who has united, as they have never before been joined, the best attributes of Science and Art . . .

[pp. 112–14]

In the same category as the *Zoological Sketches*[3] must be placed the elaborate monographs of the Pheasants, the Birds of Paradise, and the *Felidæ* by Mr Daniel Giraud Elliott[4] . . . These volumes form an *édition de luxe*; that is to say, they in every way promote the discomfort of the would-be reader; who, in heaving them up upon the table, involuntarily wishes that the author's expenses had not been quite so liberally allowed . . . It is a large superficies of zoological art, to say the least of it. The birds, for the most part, are life-size, and the tails are so deftly manœuvred as the ladies' trains at a Drawing-room.[5] So many gorgeous plates of species that are often yet more gorgeous are somewhat overpowering.

We turn them over with fear and trembling . . . It is almost a relief to turn from the Pheasants and Birds of Paradise to the more sombre colouring of the Cats; a most interesting tribe . . . Although it is as much to the illustrations as to the letterpress of these monographs that Mr Elliott owed their subsequent reputation, a would-be student of Wolf's work should be warned against accepting them, any more than the *Zoological Sketches*, as thoroughly or even fairly representative; because it is work which, under no circumstances, will bear translation with impunity even by such skilled hands, to say nothing of the addition of colouring done at a low rate of remuneration.

All possible care was certainly taken that the translations should be good; and Mr Elliott used frequently to take his friend in a cab to the residence of the lithographic draughtsman, that Wolf might correct with his own hands, the drawings on the stone. A comparison with the original charcoal sketches, and that alone, will show why any attempt at translation must necessarily fail. I think it is doubtful whether the artist himself could have transferred to the stone *all* their refinement and vigour. They depend on subtleties which, in all probability, no other living man could fully understand, much less translate . . .

[pp. 124–5]

Passing over sixteen illustrations by Wolf in an edition of Æsop out of the hundred all ascribed to Tenniel on the title-page, we come to Captain Drayson's *Sporting Scenes among the Kaffirs*; published by Routledge in 1858 . . . 'Elephant-hunting in the Bush,' 'Sharp Practice,' and 'The Red Buck and the Sporting Leopard ' are the best.[6] In the last of these, the engraver (as we shall often find in parallel cases) has carefully cut a light halo round the foremost Buck, that there may be no mistake about the outline. It is curious how often this pernicious officiousness in clearing up everything that the artist has intentionally left doubtful, or in non-relief, or subdued occurs in wood-engraving. The determination to cut away the wood round dark or middle-tint forms – to sharpen everything up, seems to be a kind of irresistible mania which seizes the engraver, just as the opposite mania to obscure, and besmirch, by means of his fatal *retroussage*, rages within the mind of a printer of modern etchings[7] . . .

[pp. 130–1]

From feathers it is an easy transition to flight, and the representation of motion in birds. Here, also, every word Wolf has to tell us carries the greatest weight, if only by reason of the immense study he has given to the question. He says: – 'In the flight of birds you cannot give the relative rapidity of the movement of their wings. They always look soaring with the wings open. This is right with Eagles and Falcons and soaring species; but with Partridges and others in which the wings flutter, it looks wrong if they are drawn in a hard way. It can only be done in the way the spokes of a moving wheel are indicated.' Now it does not take the student of his work long to discover that whatever species of bird he represents in the act of flying, seems to *fly*, and further, that it flies in its absolutely natural manner. The Vultures in 'Morning' (the dead Lion subject), do not approach in the same manner as the Hooded Crows in 'Hunted Down' . . . How Wolf transfers all this to his canvas, how he secures the sense of various kinds of motion so successfully, the soaring, the fluttering, the laborious, the easy, it is hard to say; but that he does secure it, can, I think, be proved.[8]

[pp. 182–3]

It is obvious that in a great deal of his scientific work, such as his drawings for *The Proceedings* of The Zoological Society, *The Ibis*, and Elliot's *Monographs*, besides certain of his book illustrations, Wolf had found the Society's Menagerie indispensable. 'When I first began,' he says, 'I had no ideas except of European animals, but when I came to see the splendid species in the different Zoological Gardens, I changed my opinion.' The Gardens in Regent's Park soon became his studio and recreation-ground. But there were many dangers lurking in the study of animals kept in confinement, to say nothing of the constant distractions. It takes a man some practice to be able to concentrate his attention on such difficult points as the anatomy and actions of half a dozen active Ratels, trotting round and round and round again, or climbing up the wire; and to catch the unamiable expression of a misanthropic cat, when he is jostled by a crowd to whom an 'artist chap' is a perennial wonder, always worth an extra shove or two.

As a delicate hint to these people he tried the simple plan of stopping short, and drawing a Donkey's head or a Goose on the margin of his paper. He had found that a Monkey's head was too amusing, and defeated his object; but a Donkey never failed to make the people retire 'after they had digested the meaning of it'; not all at once, he says, but gradually.

Editorial Endnotes

1 The government Department of Science and Art, founded in the wake of the Great Exhibition of 1851, fostered technical and design education, partly through the augmentation of museum collections for study purposes. See the introduction to Part 4 in the present volume.

2 The complaint voiced by Wolf and Palmer – that fine artists now despised accurate representations of animals – probably reflects the growing taste for sketchier and more spontaneous impressions of nature, partly inspired by Japanese art. Wolf's kind of composed tableaux went out of fashion.

3 Wolf's *Zoological Sketches* were done for the Zoological Society of London, to picture the live animals in the Gardens.

4 In the 1870s to 1880s Daniel Giraud Elliot [Palmer misspells his name] wrote, and published by subscription, lavishly illustrated folios on the *Phasianidae*, the *Paradiseidae*, the *Felidae*, etc. The illustrated folios were drawn by Wolf, lithographed by J. Smit and J.G. Keulemans, and expensively hand-coloured. Palmer's lack of enthusiasm for the project signals the imminent demise of such luxury publications, which seldom went beyond a few issues or volumes. J.A. Allen, 'Daniel Giraud Elliot,' *Science*, n.s. 43:1101 (4 February 1916), pp. 159–62.

5 A 'drawing room' was a reception for ladies at Queen Victoria's court, where the guests would have worn gowns with elaborate trains.

6 Captain Alfred W. Drayson, Royal Artillery, *Sporting Scenes amongst the Kaffirs of South Africa*, illustrated by Harrison Weir, from designs by the author (London: G. Routledge, 1858).

7 Commercial engravers and printers developed their own graphic conventions, overriding the distinctive stylistic touches of individual artists. In 'retroussage', the fine lines of an etching were softened by letting ink in the grooves flow out onto the surface of the plate.
8 The reference is to Wolf's *The Life and Habits of Wild Animals* (see Chapter 43). This preoccupation with the problems of representing animals' movements in a static pictorial medium partly stemmed from the experiments of Muybridge and Marey in 'chronophotography' – the beginnings of film (see Chapters 20–3 of the present volume).

Editorial Headnote

20. Anon., 'Mr. Muybridge at The Royal Institution', *The Photographic News* (1882)

Eadweard Muybridge, whose original name was Edward James Muggeridge, was born in England but spent much of his life in America.[1] There, through the 1870s, he had developed a method of photographing animals and humans in movement, first shown to the world in 1878. The split-second phases of an action were recorded by a battery of cameras; their shutters were successively activated, using increasingly fast and sophisticated technical devices. When the resulting sequential images were copied by hand onto glass discs, then rotated and projected onto a screen in rapid succession, the animals' movements were recreated. There was an obvious link to the beginnings of cinematography, but Muybridge was equally interested in the implications of his work for artists. In his book *Animals in Motion* (1899 and later editions) he bluntly pointed out the fallacies, or the artistic license, in many recent pictures of horses trotting and galloping. His photographs were intended to provide a corrective – almost a pattern book – for the use of animal painters.[2] Nevertheless, many artists found his photographic images inexpressive and graceless: art, they believed, should be about more than scientific accuracy. Muybridge seems to have courted such controversy, especially in public lectures like this one at the Royal Institution, London, on 13 March 1882: there was showmanship and polemic as well as serious science and aesthetics.

Editorial Endnotes

1 Philip Brookman (ed.), *Helios: Eadweard Muybridge in a Time of Change* (Washington, D.C.: Steidl and Corcoran Gallery of Art, 2010).

2 Eadweard Muybridge, *Animals in Motion: an Electro-Photographic Investigation of Consecutive Phases of Animal Progressive Movements* (London: Chapman and Hall, 1902) (see Figure 5). This work centred on horses but included a variety of animals in the Philadelphia Zoo; there were also photographs of human beings in athletic action.

20

MR. MUYBRIDGE AT THE ROYAL INSTITUTION

Anon., The Photographic News

Source: Anon., 'Mr. Muybridge at the Royal Institution', *The Photographic News*, 26: 1228 (17 March 1882), p. 129.

Before a distinguished audience, which included H.R.H. the Prince of Wales, the Princess of Wales, and the three young Princesses, the Duke of Edinburgh – a distinguished photographer, it may be remembered – the Poet Laureate, the President of the Royal Society, and most of the managing body of the Royal Institution, Mr. Muybridge, of San Francisco, gave, on Monday, his first public demonstration in this country.[1] Mr. Muybridge might well be proud of the reception accorded him, for it would have been difficult to add to the *éclat* of such first appearance, and throughout his lecture he was welcomed by a warmth that was as hearty as it was spontaneous.

Mr. Muybridge wisely left his wonderful pictures to speak for him, instead of making the occasion the subject of a long oration. He showed his photographs one after another on the screen by the aid of an electric lantern, and modestly explained them in clear but plain language. In this way the demonstration was at once rendered entertaining as well as interesting.

Mr. Muybridge first explained his plan of securing such rapid pictures of animals in motion. He showed a representation of his 'studio' to begin with; it was like that portion of a race-course to be found opposite the grand stand. This latter building was, in effect, a camera stand, and a very grand one, into the bargain, for it contained twenty-four cameras in a row, the lenses a foot apart, all looking on to the course. As the animal passed, these cameras, with their instantaneous shutters, were fired off one after another by electricity. Thin linen threads, breast high, and a foot apart, were stretched across the course, and as the animal broke these threads, they, being connected, each of them, with a camera, brought about the exposure . . .

Mr. Muybridge, by way of comparison, first threw on the screen a series of artist's sketches of the horse in motion, some of them old-world designs of the Egyptians and Greeks, some very modern, including the principal animal from Rosa Bonheur's well-known 'Horse Fair.'[2] In no single instance had he been able to discover a correct drawing of the horse in motion, and, to prove his statement, he then threw on the screen several series of pictures representing the different

DOI: 10.4324/9781003107835-22

positions taken up by a horse as he walks, trots, ambles, canters, or gallops. One thing was very plain from Mr. Muybridge's pictures, namely, that when a horse has two of his feet suspended between two supporting feet, the suspended feet are *invariably* lateral; that is to say, both suspended feet are on the same side of the animal. This, no painter – ancient or modern – had ever discovered. Then the amble was found to be different from the canter, and the canter very different again from the gallop; although most people imagined that, to perform all these, the horse used his legs in the same fashion. Mr. Muybridge was at some difficulty to describe the amble, and it seemed at one time as if it would be necessary to call upon Mr. Tennyson to give a definition of it in his well-known lines: 'Property, property, property!' but he succeeded subsequently in defining the step very satisfactorily afterwards by means of his pictures.[3]

After Mr. Muybridge had shown his audience the quaint and (apparently) impossible positions that the horse assumes in his different gaits, he then most ingeniously combined the pictures on the screen, showing them one after another so rapidly, that the audience had before them the galloping horse, the trotting horse, &c. Nay, Mr. Muybridge, by means of his zoöpraxiscope,[4] showed the horse taking a hurdle – how it lifted itself for the spring, and how it lightly dropped upon its feet again. This pleasing display was the essence of life and reality. A new world of sights and wonders was, indeed, opened by photography, which was not less astounding because it was truth itself.

After these life-like pictures, it needed not Mr. Muybridge's dictum that to use a mild term it was 'absurd' to see a galloping horse depicted with all four feet off the ground, a simple impossibility. And if this held good of one horse, what must be said of ten horses, thus painted, as was the case in Frith's 'Derby Day,' which Mr. Muybridge projected on the screen by way of comparison, and which the clever photographer described as a miracle.[5]

Mr. Muybridge modestly calls his series of animals in motion – they include horse, dog, deer, bull, pig, &c. – simply preliminary results. They contain little or no half-tone, and are only proof of what may be done. What he desires now to secure, if he only receives sufficient encouragement, is a series of photographic 'pictures,' and these, with the experience he has now acquired, and with the gelatine process to help him, should be well within his reach.[6] We only trust this encouragement will be forthcoming, and that Mr. Muybridge will be tempted to carry on the difficult work he has commenced with such genuine success.

Editorial Endnotes

1 A similar address to the Society of Arts, 'Muybridge on the attitudes of animals in motion,' was published in *The Photographic News* 26:1243 (30 June 1882), pp. 373–5.

2 The French painter Rosa Bonheur's monumental painting *The Horse Fair* was shown at the Paris Salon in 1853. It is now in the Metropolitan Museum, New York. As early as 1878–9 Étienne-Jules Marey, who was also experimenting with chronophotography, gave a series of lectures which compared photographic images of horses in movement with depictions in famous art works of the past. Translations were published as 'A study in locomotion'. See especially *Nature,* 19 (27 March 1879), pp. 488–9.

3 As mentioned by the *Photographic News* reporter, Tennyson, the Poet Laureate, was in the audience for Muybridge's lecture. The reference is to his dialect poem 'Northern Farmer, New Style': an avaricious farmer riding on horseback tells his son to forget romance and think only of 'Proputty, proputty, proputty' – the words echoing the rhythm of his horse's legs.

4 Muybridge developed this instrument on the model of a child's toy called the 'zoetrope' or 'wheel of life'. Successive images of the stages of an animals' action when rotated seemed to merge and created the illusion of movement.

5 William Powell Frith's panoramic painting *Derby Day*, exhibited at the Royal Academy in 1858, shows a race in progress in the distance. Better examples of horses depicted with all four legs splayed out and off the ground simultaneously could have been found in the many eighteenth- and early nineteenth-century sporting pictures of hunts and steeplechases.

6 The 'gelatine process' indicates dry-plate photography, which provided greater detail of forms.

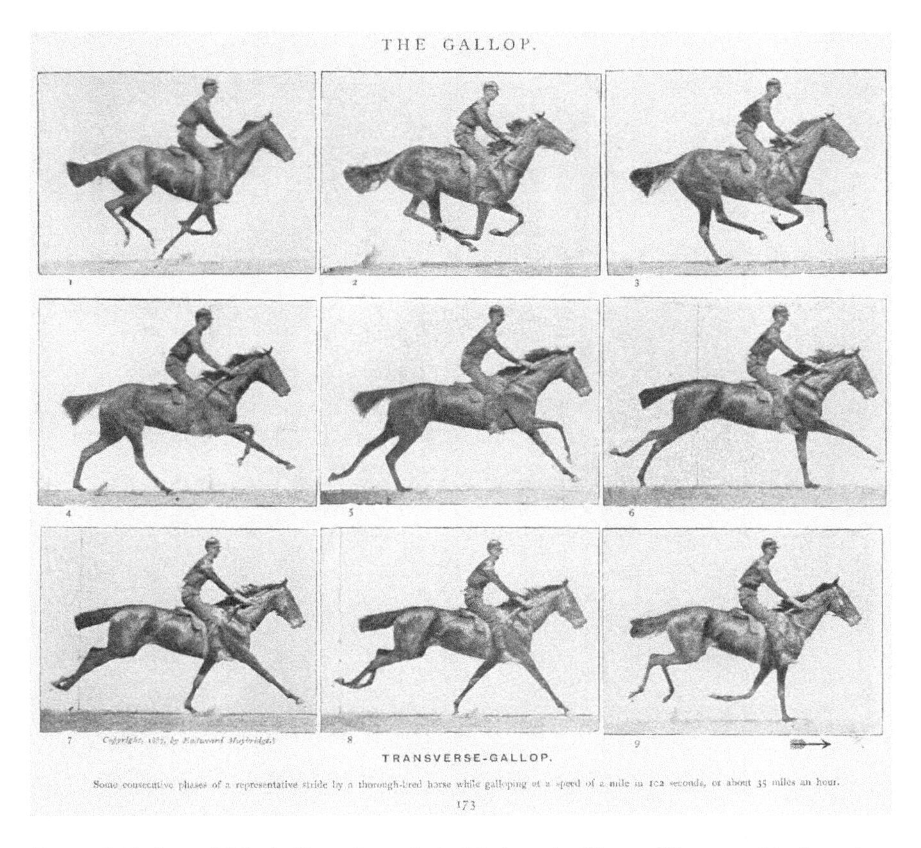

Figure 5 Eadweard Muybridge, *Animals in Motion: An Electro-Photographic Investigation of Consecutive Phases of Animal Progressive Movements* (London: Chapman and Hall, 1902), p. 173, 'Transverse-Gallop'. Muybridge's studies were carried out between 1872 and 1885. (Biodiversity Heritage Library)

Editorial Headnote

21. W.P. Adams, 'Muybridge at the London Institution', *British Journal of Photography* (1889)

Seven years after his first public performance in London, Muybridge was able to show a more sophisticated apparatus to a more knowledgeable audience. Apparently, the hall of the London Institution and other venues where Muybridge performed were always packed out, and 'when the animals were shown on the screen in actual (thaumatropical) motion it "brought down the house"'.[1]

Editorial Endnote

1 Report in *British Journal of Photography* 36:1529 (23 August 1889), p. 556. The word 'thaumatropical' is another allusion to an optical toy. In the case of the thaumatrope, two images of different stages of an action, reproduced on the two sides of a disc, appeared to merge and show movement when the disc was twirled round.

21

'MUYBRIDGE AT THE LONDON INSTITUTION,' *BRITISH JOURNAL OF PHOTOGRAPHY*

W.P. Adams

Source: W.P. Adams, 'Muybridge at the London Institution', *British Journal of Photography* 36:1546 (20 December 1889), pp. 826–7.

On entering the hall, the first thing that attracted attention was the apparatus which was to illustrate the lecture. There was an ordinary biunial lantern, and a lantern of rather novel construction. The body was elevated on brass pillars about eight inches high, and a lens was supported about three inches from the front by a single pillar fixed in the top left-hand corner. A box sliding in runners containing gear wheels, and provided with a boss to which the various discs were to be fixed, was in front of the camera, and the top of the discs, when in position, were [sic] between the lens and condenser.

Professor Muybridge was punctual . . . the first picture being projected on to the screen. This was a sketch of reindeer, made by primitive man. Professor Muybridge explained that this was remarkable for its correctness in showing the walk of the deer, and he referred to it again later after he had shown a number of his own results.[1]

Following on this, a description of the apparatus used in the investigations on animal motion was entered into. The battery of cameras consists of a long box divided into twelve or twenty-four parts, with a lens to each division. Plate holders are arranged at the back, and in front of the lenses in the exposing apparatus.

Each lens has its own shutter, an endless curtain on rollers. The shutters are liberated in turn by electricity . . . A track is specially arranged for the animals to traverse, and parallel to this a long battery of twenty-four cameras is arranged, so as to take the animal broadside on. Of these, twelve are found to be a sufficient number for most purposes. A second battery of twelve is placed at right angles to the first, to take a back view of the animal, and a third battery at 45° to the first takes the animal on the right shoulder. The shutters on these cameras work simultaneously . . . A chronograph is provided to register accurately the intervals of exposure, and the period of one phase in the animal's progression.

After describing the apparatus, Professor Muybridge showed a series of results obtained with it. The first slide showed twelve positions taken in each of the three

DOI: 10.4324/9781003107835-23

batteries simultaneously, illustrating a horse walking; then followed a number of pictures of different animals walking – horses, a camel, mastiff, cat, lion, tiger, coon (which, by-the-by, was walking along a pole as a fly does on the ceiling), buffalo, cow, goat, hog, sloth, and, lastly, a child crawling. These all follow the same law, as does every other animal but the ape – according to Professor Muybridge's observations – in the placing of the feet in walking. The universal law is this: the laterals on one side will be close together, while the others are extended in front and behind. Now the ape, walking on all fours, has the *diagonals* together, and the other diagonals extended in front and behind . . .

After the explanation of this law the reindeer of primitive man again appeared, and be it said to the honour of our ancient forefathers that they were perfectly correct in representing a quadruped's walk, while many artists of the present day, who certainly should have had greater facilities of observation, have left works of art (!) with flaring incorrectnesses.

There is one picture in the Louvre, a famous one, of a team of six oxen ploughing. In this picture six different ways of walking are portrayed, *one* of which, however, is correct.[2]

Miss Thompson's picture, the *Roll-call*, shows a horse walking in the correct attitude. Miss Thompson was laughed at by both artists and critics alike, as also was Meissonier for committing a similar crime.[3]

Horses trotting have all the feet off the ground at one period; this Professor Muybridge has proved to the edification of certain great lights of the turf, who maintained that a trotting horse had always one foot on the ground.

The most absurd error that has been perpetrated in the history of art is the common representation of a horse galloping. The impression usually given by observing a horse galloping is that it has all its feet drawn up under the body, but in paintings it is almost always depicted as having all four legs fully extended in such a manner as to offer no support to the body, and to preclude any possibility of its drawing up its feet in time to prevent its crashing to the ground. One picture of the Derby, which is well known, shows ten horses all with legs fully, nay, more than fully, extended. This picture is, perhaps, the most supremely absurd effort of the imagination ever committed to canvas. Fancy the remarkable coincidence of ten horses racing together, and being at the same moment all in the same position, and that position an impossible one! . . . A sketch, most crude, by North American Indians, on horn, representing horses galloping, shows the legs correctly drawn together under the body.[4] . . .

There is one conventional method of representing birds flying which is adopted by most artists, viz., with the wings extended upwards. Why this should be is strange; of course, it is the most artistic way to us now that we are accustomed to it, and any other position would look strange and unreal, but I, for one, greatly admire the variety and artistic taste of the Japanese, whose efforts in the representation of birds flying are now proved to be almost entirely correct.[5] In this point, as well as in others, we are decidedly behind the Japanese in art. The pictures of a white cockatoo shown by Professor Muybridge were most remarkable; the most striking position of the wings is when they are just finishing the downward stroke, a position the Japanese are very fond of, and in which the Egyptians always represented the sacred hawk. Just as the downward stroke is finished, it is an interesting fact that the feathers rotate simultaneously, and present only the edge to the resisting air until the upward stroke is finished, when they overlap again to give the fullest effect to the downward stroke . . .

We had horses walking, trotting, cantering, galloping, and jumping, with long flowing tails waving behind in the most lively manner, while the rider of the galloping horse flourished his whip with every sign of urging the animal to its utmost. A dog tore across the screen at full speed, and we could see how much the back helped in the work. Then an acrobat turned summersaults on the back of a galloping horse, his arms swinging backwards and forwards as he got up steam just before his leap. And finally a hawk flew over the screen, showing the whole of the most interesting motion of flight, even to the turning of the feathers when the discs moved slowly.

Editorial Endnotes

1 In his book *Animals in Motion: An Electro-Photographic Investigation of Consecutive Phases of Animal Progressive Movements* (London: Chapman and Hall, 1902), pp. 9–10, and elsewhere, Muybridge remarked on the extraordinary accuracy of depictions of running animals in prehistoric cave art.

2 This is another dig at Rosa Bonheur, whose painting *Ploughing in the Nivernais* (1849) is now in the Musée d'Orsay, Paris.

3 'Miss Thompson' is Elizabeth Thompson, now better known as Lady Butler. Her painting *The Roll Call*, 1874, a scene of the battlefield after the battle of Inkerman in 1854 during the Crimean War, is in the Royal Collection.

4 This is apparently another criticism of Frith. Again, Muybridge claims that ancient or tribal peoples were often more accurate in their perceptions of animals' movements than modern Europeans were.

5 Apparently, it was Adams rather than Muybridge who was here expressing admiration for Japanese art. Such enthusiasm was at its height in Britain in the 1880s–90s (see Chapters 72–4 in the present volume). The Japanese artists' impressions of spontaneous movement in nature seemed to offer a parallel with Muybridge's and Étienne-Jules Marey's chrono-photography.

Editorial Headnote

22. Anon., 'Muybridge's Photographs of Animal Motion', *Illustrated London News* (1889)

On the cover of this issue was a dramatic portrayal of Muybridge as a bearded sage, gesturing towards the lighted screen during his presentation at a Royal Society 'conversazione'. An accompanying article emphasised the important role of the University of Pennsylvania in sponsoring Muybridge's research from 1884 to 1887 and also supplied a great deal of technical detail about how his images were obtained.

22

MUYBRIDGE'S PHOTOGRAPHS OF ANIMAL MOTION

Anon., Illustrated London News

Source: Anon., 'Muybridge's Photographs of Animal Motion', *Illustrated London News* 94:2614 (25 May 1889), p. 647.

It is not too much to say that the discoveries already made, and those hereafter to be expected, by the incomparably more rapid instrumentality of photography, instead of the untrained human eye, will add greatly to the facts of zoological, anatomical, and biological science; to the resources of graphic art, and the instruction of draughtsmen, painters, and sculptors; and to the theory of athletic and gymnastic training, besides many other practical uses that may be made of this knowledge . . . The results of these ingenious labours are already shown in a collection of 781 beautiful plates, each illustrating the successive phases of a single action of human figures . . . horses, trotting, cantering, ambling, galloping, or leaping; mules, asses, oxen, dogs and cats, goats, lions, elephants, camels, buffaloes, and deer; pigeons, flying eagles, vultures, ostriches, cranes, and other birds. These plates, of a size 19 inches by 24 inches, are permanently printed by the Photo gravure Company, and are published in handsome portfolios, of one hundred, to be selected by any subscriber of twenty guineas. Several departments of the United States Government, nearly all the American Universities and Colleges, the chief institutions of Science and Art, and Public Libraries, as well as large numbers of private subscribers, have procured copies of this remarkable work. It has also been ordered for the Royal Academy, the Royal Society, and other institutions in England.[1]

Editorial Endnote

1 This was Muybridge's *Animal Locomotion: An Electro-Photographic Investigation of Consecutive Phases of Animal Movements*, 11 vols. (1872–85), issued by the University of Pennsylvania.

DOI: 10.4324/9781003107835-24

Editorial Headnote

23. Thomas Protheroe, 'Correspondence', *The Photographic News* (1882)

Not everyone who read about Muybridge's claims for his invention was as enthusiastic as the writers cited earlier. This correspondent to the *Photographic News* expressed the views held by many in artistic circles when he rejected Muybridge's criticism of painters for their inaccuracy in depicting animals in motion. Protheroe was himself a minor portrait and genre painter.

23

ATTITUDES OF ANIMALS IN MOTION

Thomas Protheroe

Source: Thomas Protheroe, 'Correspondence. Attitudes of Animals in Motion', *The Photographic News* 26:1247 (28 July 1882), pp. 445–6.

Dear Sir, – In reading the lecture delivered by Mr. Muybridge before the Society of Arts, one cannot but be struck with his refreshing assurance at the commencement, where he says that artists of all ages have been inaccurate in their 'notions' of depicting animals in motion. After reading the article, and seeing the pictures of the animals he has photographed in this month's *Century*,[1] I am of opinion that he is not warranted in his attempt to lecture artists.

An artist paints simply an *impression of motion* as he sees it, as it is impossible for him to see the sub-division of motion, or a single section of a stride; and until we are endowed with further visual powers, we must be content.

When a horse rises to a fence it is impossible to see him in the stiff awkward positions represented in the photographs. The pasterns look especially unreal, though they may be correct. Again, fancy a bird in flight painted with its wings folded under it, or a dog with his legs gathered together as if in a knot. These may be right photographically, but wrong artistically. To give a notion of a hunting field with horses and pack in full cry, they must be painted as we see them, with limbs stretched to their utmost, 'tearing away like mad.' . . . The lecture and illustrations are undoubtedly of great interest to the scientist or the curious as studies of analysis of motion; but beyond that, I fear, will be of little use. Probably they may be the means of starting a new school of fanatics in painting who will stand the chance of being laughed at for their pains in trying to depict, what may be right photographically, but is never seen with the naked eye . . . T. Protheroe

Editorial Endnote

1 George E. Waring, Jr., 'The Horse in Motion,' *Century Magazine* 24, n.s. 2 (July 1882), pp. 381–8.

Editorial Headnote

23.1. W.G. Simpson, 'The Paces of the Horse in Art, *Magazine of Art* (1883)

Simpson was even more vehement than Protheroe in insisting on a distinction between the aims of art and those of photography or science. Muybridge's images of galloping horses might be literally correct, but Simpson found them 'artistically valueless . . . so ungainly as to be only useful for caricature' (p. 203).

23.1

THE PACES OF THE HORSE IN ART

W.G. Simpson

Source: W.G. Simpson, 'The paces of the horse in art', *Magazine of Art* 6 (1883), pp. 198–203.

It is being hinted in many quarters . . . that a new era in animal painting is about to be inaugurated. It is not a renaissance we are to expect, but a revolution; for it appears that, except now and again by accident, artists from all time have wrongly represented the paces of quadrupeds. It will be asked, What artists, what sculptors are to figure as the leaders in this new departure? whose are the epoch-making names? There are none. It is the odograph and the camera which are to be crowned with laurels . . . The odograph enables Professor Marey to say of the frieze of the Parthenon that 'the greater part of the horses are represented in false attitudes.'[1] Modern works of art, he tells us, he will not permit himself to criticize; but it is evident that if he did so, the odograph would make sad havoc among them. Dr. Stillman,[2] as the prophet of instantaneous photography, foresees that before long all the famous paintings in which 'he [the horse] is a prominent figure in the gallop, will be relegated to the museums as examples of old masters, to illustrate the progressive stages in the development of art' . . . Scientific men, being in the habit of dealing with objective facts in their own province, are apt to attach too little importance to subjective impressions when they come out of it. Now in matters of art, the observer is of even more importance than the observed. In diagrams and sketches of things we have never seen, objective correctness is of the first importance. These are to convey new knowledge . . . A function of pictures is to revive and intensify former impressions; and I assert, without fear of contradiction, that neither Marey's nor Stillman's diagrams of galloping horses, treated never so skillfully, would revive recollections of that happy day we spent at Epsom. To us horses at full gallop *appear* extended. To the lover of art agreeing to this all is said. The scientific mind still asks the why.

Editorial Endnotes

1 The odograph was a wheeled device for analysing and measuring movement.

2 Jacob Davis Babcock Stillman's *The Horse in Motion as Shown by Instantaneous Photography* (Boston: Osgood, 1882) was published at the behest of the Californian millionaire Leland Stanford, who had earlier sponsored Muybridge's photographic experiments. In this work Stillman and Stanford connived to rob Muybridge of credit for his studies of movement, but their misrepresentation was later exposed.

DOI: 10.4324/9781003107835-26

Editorial Headnote

24. Richard Kearton, *British Birds' Nests* (1895)

The brothers Richard and Cherry Kearton were pioneers of wildlife photography, producing popular books on this subject for a lay public, especially for young readers.[1] Later, they both undertook lecture tours, using slide projection of photographs or actual moving film of animals and birds; the images were often hand-coloured for visual effect. The photographs in *British Birds' Nests* already reveal a gradual but significant change in attitudes to nature at the end of the nineteenth century: as Richard Kearton explained in 1896, 'This book is not intended to encourage the useless collecting of birds' eggs from a mere *bric-à-brac* motive, but to aid the youthful naturalist in the study of one of the most interesting phases of bird life'.[2] He explicitly supported recent legislation that empowered County Councils to introduce bird protection measures.[3] Traditional 'birds-nesting' (taking eggs from the nest) should, Kearton thought, be replaced by bird*watching* and wildlife photography. To entice boy readers, the Keartons constantly emphasised the daring, agility, and resourcefulness that wildlife photography required. The photographs of birds and their nests in the wild jolted the sensibilities of readers habituated to the idealising conventions of artistic imagery, which presented birds' nests as prettily framed motifs. In the Keartons' photographs, as in contemporary images by the American artist Abbott Thayer,[4] both nests and birds were often visually lost in their surroundings: the camera did not differentiate between them. Nevertheless, Kearton candidly explained the contrivances that were sometimes necessary to bring the living subject into sight and focus.

The 'Introduction' to *British Birds' Nests* by Richard Bowdler Sharpe (curator of bird collections at the Natural History Museum, London), stresses the book's innovative features.

Editorial Endnotes

1 W. R. Mitchell, *Watch the Birdie: The Life and Times of Richard and Cherry Kearton, Pioneers of Nature Photography* (Settle, UK: Castleberg, 2001).
2 Richard Kearton, *Birds' Nests, Eggs and Egg-Collecting* (London, Paris, New York, Melbourne: Cassell, 1905), preface, dated 1896, unpaginated.
3 Kearton, *Birds' Nests, Eggs and Egg-Collecting*, unpaginated.
4 On Thayer, see Diana Donald and Jane Munro (eds.), *Endless Forms: Charles Darwin, Natural Science and the Visual Arts* (New Haven, CT, and London: Yale University Press, 2009), pp. 111–5, with bibliographic references, p. 117, n. 54.

24

BRITISH BIRDS' NESTS . . . ILLUSTRATED FROM PHOTOGRAPHS BY C. KEARTON

Richard Kearton

Source: Richard Kearton, *British Birds' Nests: How, Where, and When to Find and Identify Them. Introduction by R. Bowdler Sharpe, LL.D. Illustrated from photographs by C. Kearton of Nests, Eggs, Young, etc., in their Natural Situations and Surroundings* (London, Paris, and Melbourne: Cassell, 1895). Bowdler Sharpe's *Introduction*, pp. vii–x, and Kearton's *Preface*, pp. xiii–xvi.

INTRODUCTION

[pp. vii–x]

This book certainly marks an era in natural history, just as Gould's 'Birds of Great Britain' and Booth's 'Rough Notes' did in the past.[1] The method of illustrating works on natural history has undergone as much development, as the illustration of the animals themselves has done in our public museums.[2] The works of the early part of the century were embellished with the faithful woodcuts of Bewick, or with coloured pictures of more or less merit. These were succeeded by the writings of Macgillivray, Yarrell, and Hewitson[3] . . . Yarrell was also a great naturalist, and his work was illustrated by the neatest of little woodcuts, which survive unto this day; but a candid critic must admit that the attitudes of many of the birds are strained and unnatural, and must have been taken from stuffed specimens . . .

The purchase of such works as those of Gould or Booth is beyond the compass of most of us . . . Mr. Kearton, therefore, steps in at the right moment with this book on BRITISH BIRDS' NESTS, and it will be some time before he finds a rival; for the photographs with which he and his brother have embellished the book are not only beautiful as photographs, but show us the nests and eggs of our birds *in situ*. I will not detract from the interest of the work by quoting from it; but the way in which these young naturalists have overcome the very serious difficulties presented by the task they undertook, proves that, in addition to the native British pluck, the true love of natural history is necessary to accomplish such a result as they have achieved. It is everything to show Nature as she really is, and here photography, the handmaid of science in the field, comes in. Artists will undoubtedly admire the illustrations, but the naturalist will love them still more, because they show him the nests of the birds as the authors discovered them; no

DOI: 10.4324/9781003107835-27

imaginary details, as is so often the case in illustrations of bird-life, but the actual nest itself, so that the perusal of the book is a birds'-nesting expedition.

PREFACE

[pp. xiii–xvi]
The great feature of the book lies in the unique character of its pictures. In this respect we can claim that it is the first practical attempt to illustrate a manual on the subject from photographs taken *in situ.* A glance through its pages will at once establish the valuable nature of this new departure. Of course, it must not be supposed that all the nests and eggs are to be seen exactly as represented in the illustrations; for many of them had to be partially exposed before a photograph could possibly be taken, and in some instances actually removed from holes, as in the case of the Wheatear, Starling, and Swallow . . .

No one who has yet to try this particular branch of photography, can possibly appreciate its troubles and disappointments. As an instance of the latter, my brother on one occasion travelled upwards of five hundred miles by rail, and dragged his camera at least twelve miles up and down a mountain side, in order to take a view of one bird's nest, and was defeated by the oncoming of a thick mist at the very moment he was fixing up his apparatus. The Golden Eagle's eyrie was photographed during the temporary lifting of a Highland mist, and considering the situation, and the unsatisfactory state of the light, has turned out very successfully.

The picture of the Solan Goose was obtained about four o'clock in the morning on Ailsa Craig, and so early in the season that the birds had not settled down seriously to the business of incubation; and is of especial value and interest to us on account of the adventures we encountered on that 'beetling crag.' In getting down to the edge of the cliff, my brother placed too much dependence upon the stability of a large slab of rock, which treacherously commenced to slither down the terribly steep hill side at a great pace directly it received his additional weight. He narrowly managed to save himself and the camera, with which he was encumbered at the time, from being shot over the lip of the precipice, and sustaining a fall of several hundred feet, into the sea below. We took five photographs of the Gannet sitting on her nest, each at closer range, and although she was ill at ease while all this was going on, by working deftly we established ourselves somewhat in her confidence, and got close enough to obtain the picture forming the frontispiece to this work. When everything was ready, as if by the malicious intervention of some unkind fate, the screw affixing the camera to the tripod suddenly dropped out, and the apparatus toppled over seawards. It was well on its way to what the Americans describe as 'everlasting smash,' when my brother, by a dexterous catch, stopped it from striking a piece of rock, off which it would have rebounded and finally disappeared over the cliff. By the aid of some strong feather shafts (the only materials available), we managed to fix up, after a fashion, our apparatus again, and whilst the artist held the camera on to the tripod, and the author, from a more secure footing, held the artist by the coat-tails on to the Craig, the picture was obtained, which I venture to think amply rewards us for our trouble.

Editorial Endnotes

1 On Gould and Booth, see Chapters 64–5 of the present work.
2 'Illustration' here means the display of stuffed specimens, especially in dioramas.
3 William MacGillivray's *History of British Birds* and William Yarrell's volumes with the same title were both classic works. For Bewick, see Chapters 5 and 6 of the present work, and for Hewitson, see Chapter 16.

Editorial Headnote

25. Richard Kearton, *With Nature and A Camera* (1897)

In this sequel to *British Birds' Nests*, Richard Kearton comments more explicitly on the fundamental differences between the idealising pictorial conventions of traditional natural history illustrations and the unvarnished reality of photographic images of bird life. At the same time, he enlarges on the practical difficulties that were then involved in photographing wild birds in their natural surroundings. The stated ideals of 'accuracy' and 'absolute truth' were difficult to attain with the photographic equipment and technology available in the 1890s, and colour photography was not yet possible. An element of contrivance was often necessary to get a good shot, when the intended subject was inconveniently active, distant from the camera or poorly lit. On a voyage to the island of St Kilda, the Kearton brothers succeeded in 'laying hands' on a St Kilda Wren (an endemic subspecies of wren found on the island) for Cherry Kearton to photograph, and Richard Kearton typically emphasises the adventures that this mission involved.

25

WITH NATURE AND A CAMERA
Being the Adventures and Observations of a Field Naturalist and an Animal Photographer

Richard Kearton

Source: Richard Kearton, F.Z.S., *With Nature and a Camera: Being the Adventures and Observations of a Field Naturalist and an Animal Photographer, illustrated by 180 Pictures from Photographs by Cherry Kearton* (London, Paris, Melbourne: Cassell, 1897), Preface pp. vii–x, and pp. 73–4.

PREFACE

[pp. vii–x]
Upon the appearance of my book – 'British Birds' Nests' – illustrated with photographs taken direct from Nature by my brother, many of those who reviewed it in the press suggested that I should write an account of our adventures and observations whilst wandering up and down the British Isles in search of subjects for our camera and note-book . . . We have slept for nights together in empty houses and old ruins, descended beetling cliffs, swum to isolated rocks, waded rivers and bogs, climbed lofty trees, lain in wet heather for hours at a stretch . . . waited for days and days together for a single picture, and been nearly drowned, both figuratively and literally; yet such is the fascination of our subject that we have endured all these and other inconveniences with the utmost cheerfulness.

We enjoy the gratification of having sent hosts of amateur photographers into the fields to study wild life for themselves, and hail with extreme pleasure their efforts towards the attainment of pictorial truth and accuracy. In this book we tell exactly and candidly how we work, and can only hope that the results we are able to show will still further stimulate a desire amongst those to whom we appeal to become better acquainted with the birds and beasts of our land.

Of course, we cannot hope to please everybody. Men who love the ideal and men who centre their affections upon absolute truth do not sit harmoniously at meat together. Whilst regretting our inability to meet the former entirely, we can say that we have always striven to make our illustrations as picturesque as possible; but a necessity of our mission has been to render effect subordinate to accuracy, and the value of this will, I think, be admitted upon comparing my brother's photograph of a Fulmar Petrel with any picture of the bird in existence made by a pencil.

DOI: 10.4324/9781003107835-28

Whilst the general public will, we hope, appreciate our efforts and the results we have obtained, the field naturalist and the practical photographer alone are in a position to understand the true character of our difficulties. The man who essays the task of photographing a wild bird in its native haunts, for instance, soon begins to think that, if he has not succeeded in solving the mystery of perpetual motion, he has discovered the creature possessing the secret. We have spent hours and hours and plates innumerable on some birds without obtaining a result about which we could get up any enthusiasm . . . I doubt not we shall be accused of adventurous foolhardiness. I must plead that we are English, and that our failing is a very common one amongst young fellows bred and born on British soil . . .

[pp. 73–4]

During the third week in June we did not see a single young Wren in St. Kilda, where such eggs as we had shown to us were quite fresh; but in Soa, which is only separated by a narrow channel, young birds were flying about the rocks almost as strongly as their parents. We succeeded in laying hands upon one, the adventurous particulars of whose capture will be related when I come to deal with our visit to Soa. My brother fixed up his camera and focussed the corner of an advantageously-situated crag, and when he had got his plate in and all ready, I quietly placed the bird upon it and kept my hands over the little creature until he was composed, then counting one, two, for my brother's signal, I swiftly withdrew. The pneumatic tube was instantly pressed, and the photograph, from which the accompanying picture has been made, was taken.

Editorial Headnote

26. Oliver Gregory Pike, *In Bird-Land With Field-Glass and Camera* (c.1902)

Several writers on wildlife in the late nineteenth century followed the Keartons in describing the pleasures of birdwatching and bird photography as alternatives to shooting or collecting, and they also stressed the plucky resourcefulness that such photography often required.[1] Oliver Pike's instantaneous action studies of birds in movement in their natural surroundings differed fundamentally from the picturesque compositions in traditional works on natural history, and Pike's production of still photographs led on to filmmaking (see Figure 24). In *Bird-land* his chatty and informative text – often making joking references to his stratagems and frustrations as a photographer – carried the message that birds should be cherished and studied, not killed. He aligned himself with W.H. Hudson and the [Royal] Society for the Protection of Birds, and openly criticised many of the destructive practices of specimen collectors, agriculturalists, field sportsmen, and gamekeepers.[2] *In Bird-land* was first published in 1900.

Editorial Endnotes

1 For example, Charles Dixon, in *Rural Bird Life, being Essays on Ornithology* (1880), recommended 'a first-class telescope or field-glass' and a notebook as essential items for the birdwatcher.

2 For W.H. Hudson and the Society for the Protection of Birds, see Chapters 66 and 69 in the present work. One edition of Pike's book was issued by the Religious Tract Society and praised by a reviewer as wholesome fare for 'Every boy and every man who loves birds': 'Christmas Books', review in *Manchester Guardian* (19 December 1907), p. 10.

26

IN BIRD-LAND WITH FIELD-GLASS AND CAMERA

Oliver Gregory Pike

Source: Oliver Gregory Pike, *In Bird-land with Field-glass and Camera*, 3rd popular edition (London and Leipsic: T. Fisher Unwin, c. 1902), pp. vii–xi, 4–5, 169–70.

[pp. vii–xi]

It has been my aim in the following pages to describe some phases of the country as they really appear, more especially those relating to the habits of birds as I have observed them. The book thus consists of facts and impressions, accompanied with photographs of birds and their nests in their natural surroundings, all being taken during recreative rambles in Bird-land. Readers may, therefore, regard themselves for the time being as companions in these excursions.

To such lovers of Nature as would like to add a camera to the other charms of country walks, some hints and advice may not be out of place.

There are several kinds of birds-nesting. With the heartless egg-collector, or the professional agent, who takes all the eggs to be found, I have no sympathy. These destroyers do more to exterminate our less common breeding birds than they themselves may have any idea of; otherwise, I think they would not do such injustice to the birds, as well as to those who derive pleasure from observing the habits of the feathered tribes. It is quite possible to enjoy the healthful pursuit of birds-nesting without in any way disturbing the birds' charming little homes, or causing the builders to desert their precious eggs. I prefer, when birds-nesting, to take a camera, and to photograph the nests, and so take away a lasting memorial which really gives more pleasure than mere possession of the eggs could ever yield.

For photographing nests, or birds while sitting, or feeding their young, I use a half-plate camera. A silent shutter is necessary, and mine is a Thornton-Pickard Time and Instantaneous pattern; I have fixed it inside the camera, attached to the front, with a thick padding of velvet between, which effectively deadens the slight noise which the shutter otherwise will make. If a shutter is used which makes noise enough to startle a bird, a very quick exposure is necessary; but if a silent one is used a slower exposure can be give, which in dull weather is a great advantage . . . Many little dodges have to be resorted to in order to overcome the disadvantages of shyness. Some birds tax our powers of resource and patience to the utmost; others are so confiding as to allow one to approach with a camera without apparently taking offence, or even much notice at all. When desiring to photograph a shy bird on its nest, it is a good plan to place a heap of dried grass or rubbish some distance away, and then to move this nearer at intervals of several hours, or even days in the case of some birds; and then, when near enough, to hide the camera underneath, the operator being either concealed with the camera or remaining some distance off with the pneumatic tube connection. By this means a photograph can often be obtained even of the most timid birds; although there are some which will still baffle all attempts to photograph them . . .

For taking occasional snap-shots of birds, I use what has been termed a gun-camera. This consists of a camera made on the 'reflector' principle, fixed on a gun-stock. The bird one wishes to photograph can be seen and focussed up to the moment of exposure; and for following restless birds, this offers great advantages over ordinary cameras. Mr. R.B. Lodge, of Enfield, was the first to use a camera of this description, fitted with a tele-photo lens.[1] To any one wishing to follow the new sport, as birds-nesting with a camera has been called, a gun-camera is a very useful acquisition, while it offers all the excitement of stalking a bird with a gun; the difference being that one's powers of woodcraft are taxed to the utmost, as a bird has to be approached much nearer than would be the case with an ordinary gun . . .

[pp. 4–5]

In the course of this work, it has been my aim to picture various kinds of birds in their own homes as I have been privileged to see them. Their every-day habits, or what might even be called their own manners and customs in their own wonderfully interesting little world, are depicted as I have been enabled to observe them. The practically endless variation makes it no less profitable than fascinating to gather one's facts, as far as possible, at first-hand from Nature herself.

[pp. 169–70]

What a difficult thing it is to obtain a picture of a Moor-hen on her nest! How I have tried, and tried again, to effect this, but have never been successful, although I have spent more time during the last three nesting seasons over these birds than over all others put together.

Last year there was a nest by a small waterfall on which the hen seemed to sit closely. I placed my camera on some rubbish that had accumulated in the water and covered it over with dead reeds, sticks, and other things, and then retired with the pneumatic tube to the top of a tree, where I thought I should be free from observation, while, at the same time, I should obtain a very good view of all going on below. Some time elapsed, but the Moor-hen would not enter her nest although keeping near. I waited until I was fairly cramped in my uncomfortable position; and patience had almost done her perfect work, when, suddenly, success seemed to be within measurable distance, for the bird was on the point of entering the nest. Just at the critical moment, however, a Wild Duck, with her interesting brood, came flapping over the waterfall and scared my Moor-hen away.

I descended from the tree making sundry vows never to try to photograph a Moor-hen again; but on second thought, and after the stiffness from sitting in the tree had worn off, I decided to try once more, and the next time to hide the camera in another place, while retiring to a distance of about one hundred yards, watching the movements of the bird with a field-glass. On this occasion the Moor-hen herself seemed to find some amusement in swimming round and round, as might have been imagined, for my edification, and, of course, always keeping just out of focus of the camera lens. These movements were continued until it became too dark to expose a plate, so that I removed the camera, leaving the heap of dead grass under which it was placed exactly as it had been.

Editorial Endnote

1 R. B. Lodge was another pioneering wildlife photographer of this era.

FIG. 36. "HOUR AFTER HOUR, DURING THE WHOLE DAY, THEY FOUGHT AGAIN AND AGAIN"

(*Page* 68)

Figure 6 George Murray Levick, *Antarctic Penguins: A Study of their Social Habits* (London: Heinemann, 1914), figure 36, showing male Adélie penguins fighting over a nest on their Antarctic breeding grounds; photographed by Levick in 1911. (Biodiversity Heritage Library)

Editorial Headnote

27. Dr. George Murray Levick, *Antarctic Penguins* (1914)

George Levick was a doctor and naturalist who took part in Captain Robert Falcon Scott's ill-fated 'Terra Nova' expedition to the Antarctic in 1910–13. He and other members of the 'Northern Party' were stationed at Ridley Beach, Cape Adare, over several months in 1911, and later endured fearful privations when stranded on 'Inexpressible Island', before eventually reaching a rescue ship.[1] Levick passed the time at Cape Adare by observing the gathering of Adélie penguins at the mating season, describing their behaviour as accurately as he could in a large notebook and photographing their actions, especially around nests in one chosen colony – giving both distance shots and close-ups (see our Figure 6).[2] He urged his companions to watch the birds too, but to 'disturb them as little as possible . . . it is most important to allow them to settle down naturally without interference from us', in the interests of a dispassionate scientific record.[3] However, in a subsequent article in *Nature*, Levick sometimes idealised the penguins' mating rituals in anthropomorphic terms, as did a reviewer of his book.[4] There was throughout a tension between Levick's emotional involvement with the birds and the increasing necessity to kill some of them for food. He was working in primitive conditions and could take only still photographs of the penguins. Nevertheless, his successive snapshots formed narrative sequences, often homing in on the experiences of individual birds through a day, and this highly original procedure anticipated the conventions of wildlife filming. The text of the book is a commentary on the photographic images, rather than the photographs being merely ornaments to the text. Elsewhere, another member of Scott's expeditionary party, the 'camera artist' Herbert Ponting, did take some brief cinematograph shots of Adélie penguins, which were later used in the film *The Great White Silence* (1924).[5] Levick's *Antarctic Penguins* was first published in 1914.

Editorial Endnotes

1 Lloyd Spencer Davis, *A Polar Affair: Antarctica's Forgotten Hero and the Secret Love Lives of Penguins* (New York and London: Pegasus Books, 2019), especially pp. 161–75, 322. George Murray Levick, *A Gun for a Fountain Pen: Antarctic Journal, November 1910–January 1912* (Perth: Freemantle Press, 2013).

2 Levick's manuscript notebooks with the photographs are now in the Natural History Museum, London.

3 Preface to a notebook which Levick supplied to his companions for their observations of penguin behaviour; quoted in Davis, *A Polar Affair*, p. 162. However, some of his observations of apparently aberrant sexual behaviour among the male birds were not published in *Antarctic Penguins*. Levick's more open manuscript account of 'The sexual habits of the Adélie penguin', dated 1915, is in the collection of the Natural History Museum's ornithology section at Tring.

4 In 'The nesting habits of Adélie penguins (Pygoscelis adellae)', *Nature* 93:2337 (13 August 1914), pp. 612–14, Levick writes of the birds as 'knights' and 'ladies'. A reviewer (anon.) of his book in *Nature* 94:2345 (8 October 1914), pp. 145–6, thought that the birds' conduct, 'altruistic and social . . . make a strong claim on our interest and sympathy'. Cf. also 'Levick's Antarctic Penguins', a review in an American journal, *The Auk* 32:3 (July 1915), pp. 372–3, noting the book's appeal to photographers as well as to ornithologists.

5 Herbert Ponting, *The Great White South, or, With Scott in the Antarctic* (London: Duckworth, 1923). Anne Strathie, *Herbert Ponting: Scott's Antarctic Photographer and Pioneer Filmmaker* (Cheltenham: The History Press, 2021).

27

ANTARCTIC PENGUINS

A Study of their Social Habits

George Murray Levick

Source: Dr. George Murray Levick, *Antarctic Penguins: A Study of Their Social Habits* (London: William Heinemann, 3rd impression 1915), pp. 25–6, 28–9, 38–40, 42–3, 67–9.

[pp. 25–6]

As I grew to know these birds from continued observation, it was surprising and interesting to note how much they differed in character, though the weaker-minded who would actually allow themselves to be robbed, were few and far between, as might be expected. Few, if any, of these ever could succeed in hatching their young and winning them through to the feathered stage.

When starting to make her nest, the usual procedure is for the hen to squat on the ground for some time, probably to thaw it, then working with her claws to scratch away the material beneath her, shooting out the rubble behind her . . . Sometimes the hollow is lined with a neat pavement of stones placed side by side, one layer deep, on which the hen squats, afterwards building up the sides around her. At other times the scoop would be filled up indiscriminately by a heap of pebbles on which the hen then sat, working herself down into a hollow in the middle.

Individuals differ, not only in their building methods, but also in the size of the stones they select. Side by side may be seen a nest composed wholly of very big stones, so large that it is a matter for wonder how the birds can carry them, and another nest of quite small stones. (Figure 14.)

Different couples seem to vary much in character or mood. Some can be seen quarrelling violently, whilst others appear most affectionate, and the tender politeness of some of these latter toward one another is very pretty to see. (Figure 13.)

[pp. 28–9]

When quietly on the march, both walking and tobogganing produce the same rate of progression, so that the string of arriving birds, tailing out in a long line as far as the horizon, appears as a well-ordered procession.[1] I walked out a mile or so along this line, standing for some time watching it tail past me and taking the photographs with which I have illustrated the scene. Most of the little creatures seemed much out of breath, their wheezy respiration being distinctly heard.

First would pass a string of them walking, then a dozen or so tobogganing. (Figure 15.) Suddenly those that walked would flop on to their breasts and start

DOI: 10.4324/9781003107835-30

tobogganing, and conversely strings of tobogganers would as suddenly pop up on to their feet and start walking. In this way they relieved the monotony of their march, and gave periodical rest to different groups of muscles and nerve-centres.

The surface of the snow on the sea-ice varied continually, and over any very smooth patches the pedestrians almost invariably started to toboggan, whilst over "bad going" they all had perforce to walk.

Figures 16, 17, 18 and 19 present some idea of the procession of these thousands on thousands of penguins as day after day they passed into the rookery.

[pp. 38–40]

A typical scene I find described in my notes for October 25 when I was out with my camera, and I mention it as a type of the hundreds that were proceeding simultaneously over the whole rookery, and also because I was able to photograph different stages of the proceedings as follows:

Figure 22 shows a group of three cocks engaged in bitter rivalry round a hen who is cowering in her scoop in which she has been waiting as is their custom. She appeared to be bewildered and agitated by the desperate behaviour of the cocks.

On Figure 23 a further development is depicted, and two of the cocks are seen to be squaring up for battle. Close behind and to the right of them are seen (from left to right) the hen and the third cock, who are watching to see the result of the contest, and another hen cowering for protection against a cock with whom she has become established.

Figure 24 shows the two combatants hard at it, using their weight as they lean their breasts against one another, and rain in the blows with their powerful flippers.

Fig. 25 shows the end of the fight, the victor having rushed the vanquished cock before him out of the crowd and on to a patch of snow on which, as he was too brave to turn and run, he knocked him down and gave him a terrible hammering.

When his conqueror left him at length, he lay for some two minutes or so on the ground, his heaving breast alone showing that he was alive, so completely exhausted was he, but recovering himself at length he arose and crawled away, a damaged flipper hanging limply by his side, and he took no further part in the proceedings. The victorious bird rushed back up the side of the knoll, and immediately fought the remaining cock, who had not moved from his original position, putting him to flight, and chasing him in and out of the crowd, the fugitive doubling and twisting amongst it in a frantic endeavour to get away, and I quickly lost sight of him . . .

[pp. 42–3]

Usually, as in the case I described above, one of the little crowd would suddenly 'see red' and sail into an opponent with desperate energy, invariably driving him in the first rush down the side of the knoll to the open space surrounding it, where the fight would be fought out, the victor returning to the others, until by his prowess and force of character, he would rid himself of them all. Then came his overtures to the hen. He would, as a rule, pick up a stone and lay it in front of her if she were sitting in her 'scoop,' or if she were standing by it he might himself squat in it. She might take to him kindly, or, as often happened, peck him furiously. To this he would submit tamely, hunching up his feathers and shutting his eyes while she pecked him cruelly. Generally after a little of this she would become appeased. He would rise to his feet, and in the prettiest manner edge up to her, gracefully arch his neck, and with soft guttural sounds pacify her and make love to her.

Both perhaps would then assume the 'ecstatic' attitude, rocking their necks from side to side as they faced one another (Fig. 26), and after this a perfect understanding would seem to grow up between them, and the solemn compact was made.

It is difficult to convey in words the daintiness of this pretty little scene. I saw it enacted many dozens of times, and it was wonderful to watch one of these hardy little cocks pacifying a fractious hen by the perfect grace of his manners . . .

[pp. 67–9]

One day, when the season was well advanced, I saw a violent altercation taking place between two penguins, one of which was in possession of a nest in a somewhat isolated position. The other evidently was doing his utmost to capture the nest, as whenever he got the other off, he stood on it. There were scarcely any stones in the nest, which contained one egg. I think from the way they fought that both were cocks.

For two reasons I make special mention of the occurrence, first, because of all the fights I ever saw this was the longest and most relentless, and, secondly, because the nest being in such an isolated position it seemed curious that there could be any mistake about its ownership. Such, however, seemed to be the case, and hour after hour, during the whole day, they fought and fought again . . .

I fetched my camera and photographed the birds as they fought (Fig. 36). As time went on, the weaker bird took longer and longer intervals to recover between his attacks, lying on his breast, with his head on the snow and eyes half closed, so that I thought he was going to die. Each time he got to his feet and staggered at his enemy, the latter rose from the nest and met him, only to drive him back again. When I saw them at about 10 P.M. (it was perpetual daylight now) both were lying down, the victor on the nest, the vanquished about five yards off. The next day one bird remained on the nest and the other had gone, and I do not know what happened to him.

Editorial Endnote

1 By 'tobogganing', Levick means sliding along the ice in a prone position: 'they fall forward on to their white breasts . . . and push themselves along by alternate powerful little strokes of their legs behind them' (p. 27).

Part II

THE HUNTERS AND THE HUNTED

Images of Conquest and Suffering in the Wild

INTRODUCTION

The nineteenth century saw a seismic upheaval in concepts of the order of nature and its relation to human existence. Once the long-extinct creatures which revealed an affinity with extant species and other evidence of evolutionary processes had come to light, natural theology – the belief that God created every animal in a perfect, final, and immutable form – was hard to maintain. The scientific exegesis of 'natural selection' or 'survival of the fittest' presented in Darwin's *On the Origin of Species* (1859), was an even greater threat to the old religious and philosophical constructs. Ruthless predation, internecine struggles for dominance, natural disasters that wiped out whole animal populations, or what Darwin himself once called (with grim humour) 'the clumsy, wasteful, blundering low & horridly cruel works of nature'[1]: these phenomena could now hardly be explained as the effects of man's disobedience to God in the Garden of Eden, or as God's benign interventions to prevent overpopulation of the earth.[2]

It was in this atmosphere of moral uncertainty that Edwin Landseer matured as an artist. Already in the 1840s and 1850s, he treated violence in nature – for example, fatal encounters between rutting stags – as the stuff of tragedy.[3] More often in his paintings, human hunters (of whom Landseer himself was one) were the destroyers – their actions presented sometimes as expressions of zestful energy, sometimes as causes of gratuitous animal suffering, with a troubled and unresolved vacillation between the two viewpoints. His painting of an otter hunt (see Chapter 36) is a case in point. It presents itself as a work steeped in European artistic traditions of animal representation, such as the seventeenth-century hunting scenes painted by Rubens and Frans Snyders. The composition is a classic pyramid, carrying the eye up through the melee of howling dogs – all slavering tongues and teeth – to the writhing otter on the huntsman's spear. The otter's form is echoed by the storm clouds and by a dead tree, which looks like a withered hand gesturing to the heavens, making nature itself a witness of the animal's fate.

DOI: 10.4324/9781003107835-31

The huntsman admittedly has a certain elegance of pose, as though Landseer was drawing a distinction between human psychology and the bestiality of the dogs with their bared fangs; yet we are made to understand that this huntsman is in fact the controlling mind amid the maelstrom of animal violence. As Landseer's correspondence with the Earl of Aberdeen reveals, this configuration was not imposed on the artist by a patron's relish for sporting kills. It was Landseer himself who decided to create an image of this scale, bold assertion and brutality: the same Landseer who, only a few years later, would break spectators' hearts with his painting of a dying hind and her orphaned fawn, *A Random Shot*.[4] Such contrasts in his imagery partly arose from his recognition of the differing sensibilities of the exhibition-going public – for example, women in particular were often repelled by scenes of cruelty and physical violence. Yet the paintings were also expressive of Landseer's own inner conflicts and unbounded cynicism, which Friedrich Keyl's records of their conversations (Chapter 42) clearly reveal. He was driven between tragedy and comedy, aggression and pathos, persecution of and identification with animal victims. Above all, he could conceive no state of being except the *physical* or material. If a god existed, he bore no resemblance to the Christian God (Landseer consistently refused to attend church) but was a malign force condemning both humans and animals to suffering and destruction. Landseer's paintings of dogs, notably, *The Old Shepherd's Chief Mourner*, sometimes express the agony of loss or they are charades and jokes about the indivisibility of human psychology from that of 'the beasts that perish'. On this reading of Landseer's oeuvre and of the comments of his contemporaries, it is difficult to understand why he is often referred to as a mere sentimentalist.

The ebullience of Landseer's paintings of animals, and his insistent emphasis on the physical substance of hair and fangs, certainly endeared him to some of the sporting lobby, as an evocation of lived experience (Chapter 37.1). Such pictures recalled the practices of the big game hunters – their drawings of the animals they had stricken and their hunting trophies: tusks, antlers, hides, and furs (see Chapters 28–31). However, these pictures were repellent to many art critics, such as William Michael Rossetti (Chapter 38), who thought that Landseer had, for money-making reasons, eschewed the high-minded symbolism that characterised the most impressive animal imagery of past ages in favour of gory physical detail, banal portraiture of pet dogs, and comic themes. Nevertheless, Landseer's sense of the tragedy inherent in both human and animal experience of the world proved to be a fertile source of ideas for the animal painters and taxidermists who followed in his wake. Rowland Ward's publicly exhibited taxidermy groups, inspired by contemporary paintings, dramatised wild animal life in Britain's vast tropical territories in all its violence and raw power, and on a grand scale (Chapter 35). Such compositions enjoyed a prestige which contrasts strongly with the lowly status of taxidermy in earlier times. Mr Venus, the backstreet taxidermist in Dickens's *Our Mutual Friend*, inhabits a dark little shop 'with a tallow candle dimly burning in it . . . a muddle of objects, vaguely resembling pieces of leather and dry stick', with odd bits of bone and 'two preserved frogs fighting a small-sword duel'.[5]

Rowland Ward, in contrast, ran a large firm in fashionable Piccadilly, attained national recognition, moved in aristocratic social circles, and died in 1912 worth over £147,000.[6]

In the works of some artists, the pessimism inherent in Landseer's view of nature becomes an almost perverse fatalism. Joseph Wolf, Bouverie Goddard, and John Trivett Nettleship often showed scenes of animal combat or predation where nature itself – in events such as forest fires, snowstorms, and floods – compounds the effects of 'survival of the fittest' (Chapters 43–4). The cinematic drama and vivid realism of these images owes something to the fact that live lions and tigers could now be studied in the Zoological Gardens, albeit in conditions very different from those encountered by their species in the wild.

The experience of visiting the zoo in fact gave rise to many thoughts and emotions, ranging from aesthetic delight to moral discomfort (see, for example, Chapters 64 and 89). Discomfort was greatest in observations of the apes – objects of special interest to anthropologists and natural scientists engaged in evolutionary speculations. For Landseer, apes and monkeys, like dogs (the latter being his daily companions in the studio), raised once again the problem of differentiating human mentality from that of other species, at least on any moral or spiritual plane. As early as the 1820s, he and his brother Thomas Landseer had already revived the old tradition of *singeries* as a disconcerting form of social satire (Chapters 46–7), but his *Sick Monkey* of 1870 presented more serious problems of interpretation and response, as though fingering a sore (Chapter 48). Similarly, the portrayal of his own dogs as *The Connoisseurs* watching him at work is a humorous conceit that nevertheless leaves the onlooker with an unsolved enigma (Chapter 49). If the notion of an immortal soul is discounted as delusive, what faculty (except greater cleverness and manipulative guile) remains to differentiate human beings from all the other mammals?

Notes

1 Darwin's letter to his friend Joseph Hooker, 13 July 1856, Darwin Correspondence Project, www.darwinproject.ac.uk/letter/?docId=letters/DCP-LETT-1924.xml accessed 20 November 2023. On images of the predatory pattern of nature in nineteenth-century British art, see Diana Donald, 'The "Struggle for Existence" in Nature and Human Society', in Diana Donald and Jane Munro (eds.), *Endless Forms: Charles Darwin, Natural Science and the Visual Arts* (New Haven, CT, and London: Yale University Press, 2009), pp. 81–99.

2 The idea that predation was devised by God as a means to keep species in balance was proposed by many religious writers, for example, Revd William Kirby (compare Chapter 55 of the present work) in his Bridgewater Treatise, *On the Power, Wisdom and Goodness of God as Manifested in the Creation of Animals and in Their History, Habits, and Instincts*, Treatise VII (London: William Pickering, 1835), vol. 1, pp. 11–12.

3 Landseer's painting *Coming Events Cast Their Shadow Before Them*, exhibited in 1844, shows one stag challenging another. *Night* and *Morning*, exhibited in 1853, show such a contest and its fatal outcome. Richard Ormond, *Sir Edwin Landseer* (Philadelphia Museum of Art and Tate Gallery, London, 1982), pp. 171–2, 178–9. Ormond, *The Monarch of the Glen: Landseer in the Highlands* (Edinburgh: National Galleries of Scotland,

2005), pp. 104–5. Diana Donald, *Picturing Animals in Britain 1750–1850* (New Haven, CT, and London: Yale University Press, 2007), pp. 96–9.

4 Landseer's *A Random Shot* depicts a wounded and dying female deer and her orphaned fawn. See Chapters 40 and 41 of the present work.

5 Dickens, *Our Mutual Friend* (1864–5), Chapter 7.

6 Christine E. Jackson, 'The Ward family of taxidermists', *Archives of Natural History* 48:1 (April 2018), pp. 1–13.

Editorial Headnote

28. Captain William Cornwallis Harris, *Portraits of the Game and Wild Animals of Southern Africa* (1840)

Cornwallis Harris was a British officer in the Indian army who was furloughed in southern Africa in 1836–7 and went on safari, shooting (it has been calculated) over four hundred big game animals on this one expedition.[1] The killing of elephants provided valuable ivory, the sale of which financed the enterprise, but Cornwallis Harris had a lust for pursuing and eventually killing animals, purely for the excitement and pleasure it gave him: an early example of the close connection between an imperialist mindset, bloodlust, possessiveness, and sensory arousal in Victorian sportsmen. His flowery account of the expedition in *The Wild Sports of Southern Africa* (1839) typified a new Victorian literary genre, which became very popular.[2] The *Portraits*, which was published a year later as a collection of his own drawings of African fauna, also established a tradition that lasted the century, producing sportsman-artists such as John Guile Millais (son of John Everett Millais). What Cornwallis Harris meant by 'first sketches . . . with the animal before me, in the scene of slaughter' becomes clear in his account of the fate of an eland.

Editorial Endnotes

1 John M. MacKenzie, *The Empire of Nature: Hunting, Conservation and British Imperialism* (Manchester and New York: Manchester University Press, 1988), pp. 94–6.

2 Captain William Cornwallis Harris, *The Wild Sports of Southern Africa; being the Narrative of a Hunting Expedition from the Cape of Good Hope, through the Territories of the Chief Moselekatse, to the Tropic of Capricorn* (London: John Murray, 1839). 'Moselekatse' was Mzilikazi of the Ndebele people. There were further editions of the book in 1841, 1844, etc. Diana Donald, *Picturing Animals in Britain 1750–1850* (New Haven, CT, and London: Yale University Press, 2007), pp. 178–80.

28

PORTRAITS OF THE GAME AND WILD ANIMALS OF SOUTHERN AFRICA, . . . FROM DRAWINGS BY THE AUTHOR

Captain William Cornwallis Harris

Source: Captain William Cornwallis Harris, *Portraits of the Game and Wild Animals of Southern Africa, Delineated from Life in their Native Haunts*, folio with coloured lithographic plates from drawings by the author, 1840, pp. v–vi, 24–5.

[pp. v–vi]

Africa, it is well known, is the great nursery of many of the most noble and interesting forms that exist in the animal kingdom . . . The grizzled Monarch of the forest – the stupendous Elephant – and the shapeless River Horse[1]; – the mailed Rhinoceros – the gaily painted Zebra – and the richly arrayed Ostrich; all claim alike some portion of her savage soil as the lot of their inheritance. An endless variety of grotesque and bulky ruminants also, offer to the keen disciple of 'the mighty Hunter,'[2] *quarrées* no less glorious than eccentric . . . The extensive field that yet remains unexplored of the great and mysterious Continent of Africa, doubtless contains a rich mine of hidden treasure, which in the progress of gradual development, will no doubt be one day fully exhausted. By the indefatigable exertions of modern travellers, the repositories of science have been already enriched with some of the choicest *exuviæ* of most of the interesting forms with which we are yet acquainted: and the enterprize of others, also, has stocked our menageries, like the ark of Noah, with living specimens of nearly every variety.[3] Widely different, however, is the graceful free-born of the desert, bounding exultingly in light and liberty over his native prairie, from the pampered cripple, pining in sad captivity, with sinews relaxed under the restraint of a prison-house. Yet it is from stunted subjects such as these, or worse still, from mummies and stuffed monstrosities, that the most popular illustrations of the African Fauna have heretofore been principally derived; – and so little likeness do some of the abortions and absurdities thus produced, bear to the brave originals, that it is frequently difficult, if not impossible, to trace in them the most remote resemblance to the actual works of the creation.

DOI: 10.4324/9781003107835-32

With the design, if possible, of supplying in some measure this palpable defect in our Zoological galleries, the portraits contained in the present series were originally undertaken. How manifold soever their imperfections, if viewed as productions of art, they can boast at least of being adorned with the beauties of truth, having all been delineated from living subjects, roaming in pristine independence over their native soil. 'To study animals with accuracy,' says the observant Buffon, 'we ought to view them in their savage state'[4] . . . Devoted to wood-craft from the cradle, my predilection for sylvan sports has afforded me all the opportunities, alluded to by the great Naturalist, of waxing intimate with the dappled denizens of the grove and waste to an extent, which abler artists and more finished Zoologists have necessarily been denied. I have beheld the venerable and half-reasoning Elephant browsing in native majesty among his own contemporary trees, 'in his huge strength impregnable;'[5] – have torn the much-prized ivory from his giant jaws, and plucked the horn from the saucy nose of the Rhinoceros. I have stripped the proud *spolia* from the shaggy shoulder of the 'King of Beasts, who clears the desert with his rolling eye;'[6] . . . my object has been to combine to the fullest practicable extent, information which might prove acceptable to the naturalist, the sportsman, and the lover of wild scenery. Adapted to one standard, and corrected by actual measurement, they comprise faithful portraits of every game quadruped yet known to inhabit Southern extra-tropical Africa . . . All the first sketches of my drawings were commenced either in the open air with the animal before me, in the scene of slaughter, or under the shelter of some neighbouring bush, and were completed upon my knees in the wagon, often amidst rain and wind . . .

[pp. 24–5]

Plate VI . . . Trusting to escape by mixing with the flying troops of Gnoos and Quaggas – which continually dashed across our path, or diverged on either side to admit of the passage of the chase – their [the Elands'] deep hairy dewlaps vibrated from side to side, and their pursy ribs quivered again with the unwonted exertion.[7] Notwithstanding their unwieldy shape, however, they had at first greatly the speed of our jaded and toilworn horses – covering the ground with a celerity truly surprising, and making the firm earth ring under their efforts to escape; but on being pushed, they presently exhibited symptoms of distress, and turning their beautiful heads, looked repeatedly over their plump shoulders to learn if they had not shaken off their persecutors. Finding us still at their heels, they shortly separated; their sleek coats turned first blue, and then white with froth, the foam fell in bell ropes from their open mouths, grease trickled from their nostrils, and the perspiration streamed from their lusty sides. The steeds came up hand over hand, and in another moment were abreast of the now labouring fugitives, whose pace gradually slackened till it had dwindled into a clumsy trot, when with their full brilliant eyes turned imploringly towards us – saying almost plainer than words could speak, 'Do pray now leave me alone,' – at the end of a mile, unresisting, each was laid low with a single ball.

How little resemblance did any of the portraits I had seen of this superb animal, bear to the ponderous original now lying at my feet! In place of the plethora for which the Eland is remarkable, the cunning artist must have surely striven to portray the features indicative of the last stage of a consumption! I was engaged in making a sketch of one of our noble victims, when the savages coming up, breathless with haste, proceeded with cold-blooded ferocity to stab the unfortunate and dying animal – stirring up the blood, and shouting with barbarous exultation as the tide of life gushed from each newly inflicted wound, – regardless alike of our remonstrances, and of the eloquent and piteous appeal expressed in the beautiful clear black eye of the mild and inoffensive Eland, whose tears might well have rung remorse from a far more ruthless disciple of Nimrod than myself, and have even caused him to sink the exultation of the sportsman in the feelings of the moralist.[8]

Editorial Endnotes

1 The 'river horse' is the hippopotamus.
2 The 'mighty hunter' was the mythic Orion – an allusion that is typical of Cornwallis's glorification of his sport.
3 The Zoological Society of London was founded in 1826 by Sir Thomas Stamford Raffles, with a menagerie which developed into the London Zoo.
4 Georges-Louis Leclerc, comte de Buffon's multi-volume *Histoire naturelle*, published in the mid-eighteenth century, was famous for its engraved illustrations, showing the various animals in imagined landscape settings.
5 A free quotation from James Montgomery's *The Pelican Island*, 'canto sixth' (1828).
6 Montgomery, *The Pelican Island*, 'canto sixth'.
7 The gnu or wildebeest and the quagga (a subspecies of zebra, hunted to extinction in the nineteenth century) evidently grazed with the eland.
8 The moral hypocrisy or double standards of this indictment of the Africans, who killed the stricken animal for food, strike the present-day reader.

Editorial Headnote

29. Anon., 'Portraits of the Game and Wild Animals', *Foreign Quarterly Review* (1845)

This is a eulogy on the beauties of the African landscape and its richly varied fauna, as the reviewer imagined it on the basis of sportsman-artist Cornwallis Harris's descriptions in *Portraits of the Game and Wild Animals of Southern Africa* (see Chapter 28 of the present work). Cornwallis Harris was, according to the reviewer, the first artist to represent the animals from life, in their natural surroundings, rather than against a contrived and conventional backdrop – at a time when the landscapes and animals of the Africa interior still seemed fascinatingly strange to Europeans. Yet the reviewer also noted that Cornwallis Harris lusted to kill the very creatures he found so seductive.

29

ARTICLE IX – PORTRAITS OF THE GAME AND WILD ANIMALS

Anon., Foreign Quarterly Review

Source: Anon., 'Article IX. – Portraits of the Game and Wild Animals of Southern Africa' [etc.] *Foreign Quarterly Review* 34:68 (1845), pp. 421–31.

Such is the scene over which the sportsman pursues his game in South Africa. Of the animals hunted we can say but little. Sir Cornwallis Harris has described them with the most graphic beauty, and added to his descriptions large lithographic portraits, which, for truth of delineation and delicacy of colouring, have never been surpassed. Nor is this all. Each animal is represented in a landscape resembling that in which he is found in nature; and as the features which extra-tropical Africa puts on in the southern hemisphere are peculiarly strange and magnificent, every illustration may be regarded as a rich pastoral piece . . . Beheld in wildernesses such as these, even the strangest animals appear at home. We are not surprised to view the quagga, or the gnoo, the giraffe, the oryx, or the black antelope, occupying the foreground of landscapes so singular. Africa has always enjoyed the reputation of being the mother of monsters; and if we group together in imagination the fantastic creatures portrayed in Sir Cornwallis Harris's 'Portraits of Game and Wild Animals,' couple together the tall and brilliantly painted camel-leopard[1] with the lumbering hippopotamus, resembling a huge cylinder of fat, supported awkwardly on stumps, and the ungainly rhinoceros, looking, in his corrugated skin, like a shrivelled hodman who has got into a coat a world too wide for him; if we place the slender leopard, agile, springy, light, and flexible as an eel, beside the cumbrous bulk of the elephant, striding along the plain, which seems to shake beneath him; if we set side by side the cerulean antelope and the lion, the springbok and the wild boar, the sassabe and the gnoo, the zebra and the eland, the minute humming bird and the gigantic ostrich – if we do this, we say, and compare the proportion and structure of the various animals, we shall probably conclude, that poetry has seldom fabled any thing more unlike our ordinary notions of reality than what nature has actually produced on the further extreme of the African continent.

That a sportsman like Sir Cornwallis Harris should enjoy a journey through such a region may easily be conceived; but the relentless hostility with which

DOI: 10.4324/9781003107835-33

he pursued his quarry, is scarcely to be accounted for on the same principles. He appears to have declared perpetual war against the whole four-footed race, and never to be happy but when engaged in thinning their numbers. His horse and his rifle are part of himself; he lives on powder and two-ounce balls. He stalks abroad in the morning, and death follows his footsteps. No sooner is the sun above the horizon, than the fatal rifle is at work, and throughout the day its report never ceases to be heard amongst the hills, or along the sunburnt face of the plain. Sometimes he dwells with a sort of rapturous admiration upon certain animals – upon the giraffe, for example, or that huge antelope, equalling a horse in size – and you begin to imagine that he longed only to gaze upon its beauty – to behold it move to and fro before him; to tame and make a pet of it, and lead it about over the wilderness as the ornament of his wandering kafila.[2] No such thing: he only wanted to kill it! He reminds us of the story of Zeus and Semele; he approaches with thunder and lightning the object of his affection, and destroys it through intense love. Could the ostrich or the zebra speak, however, it would exclaim, 'Heaven defend me from the preference of a sportsman!' But, after all, there is an unspeakable charm in excitement, and it is excitement that the hunter seeks, when, at break-neck pace, he pursues the flying game over hill and dale, dashes through breaks – or plunges into streams and quagmires . . . His magnificent volume is accordingly by no means what its exterior would seem to promise – a succession of poetical or pastoral pictures – but abounds everywhere with narratives of the most stirring interest, during the perusal of which, we expect to part company with our author, and behold him snapped up by a lion, – pen, pencil, and all . . .

Editorial Endnotes

1 The camel-leopard is the giraffe.
2 "Kaflia' is a variant of 'cafila', meaning a caravan.

Editorial Headnote

30. Roualeyn Gordon Cumming, *A Descriptive Catalogue of Hunting Trophies* (1851)

This was the catalogue of an exhibition held in London in 1851. It was housed in an improvised 'South African Museum' but later moved to the Great Exhibition in the Crystal Palace. Cumming's show featured his huge collection of animal trophies, furs, and native artefacts, derived from years of hunting in southern Africa, but it also included some spoils of his hunting expeditions in Scotland and North America.[1] The sensory impact of the animal exhibits seen at close quarters – their scale, voluptuous textures, and sheer strangeness – overwhelmed spectators. Cumming had recounted his adventures in *Five Years of a Hunter's Life in the Far Interior of South Africa* (London: John Murray, 1850), which ran to two volumes, with 'numerous spirited illustrations' of the most exciting, bloodthirsty, and dangerous hunts: the objects in the London exhibition provided incontrovertible material evidence of feats which many had doubted. The book was on sale in the exhibition and, like the catalogue, went through many further editions – an indication of its sustained popularity. Cumming also delivered public lectures on his experiences, with illustrations in the form of huge drawings by the artist Joseph Wolf. Although Wolf was often called upon for such work, he actually detested Cumming's wholesale and indiscriminate slaughter of animals.[2]

Editorial Endnotes

1 On Cumming, see John M. MacKenzie, *The Empire of Nature: Hunting, Conservation and British Imperialism* (Manchester and New York: Manchester University, 1988), especially pp. 28–30, 96–103. Diana Donald, *Picturing Animals in Britain 1750–1850* (New Haven, CT, and London: Yale University Press, 2007), pp. 178–80.

2 A. H. Palmer, *The Life of Joseph Wolf, Animal Painter* (London and New York: Longmans, Green, 1895), pp. 134–7. For Wolf, see also Chapters 19, 43, and 93 in the present work.

30

A DESCRIPTIVE CATALOGUE OF HUNTING TROPHIES, NATIVE ARMS, AND COSTUME, FROM THE FAR INTERIOR OF SOUTH AFRICA

Roualeyn Gordon Cumming

Source: Roualeyn Gordon Cumming, *A Descriptive Catalogue of Hunting Trophies, Native Arms, and Costume, from the Far Interior of South Africa, interspersed with Remarks on the Nature and Habits of some of the Principal Animals, and Anecdotes connected with the Manner of Hunting Them . . . the Property of and Collected by Roualeyn Gordon Cumming, Esq*. (published by the author in 1851, but issued in many versions, some undated).

'Prefatory Remarks', p. 2.

The visitor will observe that there is an immense number and variety of each of the objects enumerated in the Catalogue. All these specimens have been carefully selected, either on account of their unusual size, their uncommon beauty, or from some peculiar interest attached to them. The Bechuana arms and beautiful fur robes are the manufacture of tribes, inhabiting those parts of Southern Africa which are as yet comparatively unknown to the white man; but to which a peculiar interest now attaches, as in consequence of late geographical discoveries, they may soon open a fresh field to British industry.

The immense variety of trophies of the chase, tusks, antlers, horns, bones, skulls, teeth, &c. &c., are interesting to the sportsman, to the naturalist, and to the every day observer; from their extraordinary size, from the variety, or from their graceful forms. Each of these represents a select specimen of some fierce and formidable, or shy and wary animal, and most of them were obtained by undergoing perils, hardships, and fatigues, of which the gentlemen of England who live at home at ease can form but a faint idea.[1]

The elephant's tusks alone, which may appear to the passing observer but coarse uninteresting objects, are the finest of ivory, selected from the unbroken herds that from the earliest ages have roamed undisturbed, the desert solitudes of Africa. Coarse as they may appear, their value in the ivory market varies from £40 to £80 *each!*

'Catalogue of Mr. Gordon Cumming's Collection of Hunting Trophies, Native Arms & Costumes, 232, Piccadilly', extract from pp. 3–32.

DOI: 10.4324/9781003107835-34

Skin of Chetah, or hunting-leopard . . . Kaross, or native robe of skins of leopard[2] . . . Skull of Pallah[3]; a very graceful forest antelope of the far interior; it is of a delicate rufous colour, and remarkable for the elegance of its horns . . . Bechuana Shield, made of the hide of Buffalo . . . Skin of Leopard that cruelly mangled Mr. Orpen, a young man who accompanied Mr. Cumming on his last hunting expedition . . . Skin of an old Metsapallah, a species of rock serpent, killed in the territory of the chief Sichely, after a personal encounter, in which the hunter's weapon was a bough of a tree. The serpent measured 14 feet.[4] . . . Skin of Lion, shot in the act of charging; the bullet split his skull, when he pitched a somersault and fell lifeless at the hunter's feet . . . Tusks of male Elephant, which the hunter by judicious riding held in check without gun or dogs for several hours, until Mr. Cumming's after rider appeared with a rifle. He received 8 balls . . . Head of Black Wildebeest. This animal has the head of a buffalo, the mane and tail of a horse, and the legs of an antelope . . . Head of Giraffe. The only representative of about fifty fine specimens shot by Mr. Cumming in Africa. Cat Kaross, worn by Bechuana ladies of distinction . . . Pallah Kaross, worn by the Chief of the Baseleke . . . Silver Jackal Kaross, the winter robe of the Bechuanas . . . Around the room are placed coloured portraits of the various quadrupeds of Southern Africa, from the stupendous elephant down to the smallest antelope, with appropriate scenery, illustrative of the districts in which they are met with.[5]

Editorial Endnotes

1 Cumming deliberately echoes the well-known speech which Shakespeare gives to Henry V, rousing his men to battle: 'And gentlemen in England, now a-bed,/Shall think themselves accursed they were not here' (*Henry V*, Act IV, Scene III). He thus implies that big game hunting has the virtues of manliness and patriotic heroism.

2 A kaross is a cloak or sleeveless jacket made of animal skins.

3 The 'Pallah' is the impala.

4 This was probably the Southern African rock python.

5 These paintings may have been by Joseph Wolf and perhaps identifiable with those that Wolf provided to illustrate Cumming's lectures.

Editorial Headnote

31. Benjamin Silliman, *A Visit to Europe in 1851* (1854)

The entries in Roualeyn Gordon Cumming's 1851 catalogue *A Descriptive Catalogue of Hunting Trophies, Native Arms, and Costume, from the Far Interior of South Africa, interspersed with Remarks on the Nature and Habits of some of the Principal Animals, and Anecdotes connected with the Manner of Hunting Them… the Property of and Collected by Roualeyn Gordon Cumming* were chiefly intended to impress the reader with his courage, daring, and prowess as a hunter and with the richness of his spoils. However, visitors to the exhibition of these spoils evidently reacted in different ways. The American Benjamin Silliman – a natural scientist who taught at Yale University – was engrossed by the variety, vast scale, and tactile character of the specimens exhibited by Cumming (whose first name he misspells) – their sheer materiality and zoological interest – but came away from the exhibition with doubts as to the morality of such ruthless slaughter.

31

'AFRICAN TROPHIES,' *A VISIT TO EUROPE IN 1851*

Benjamin Silliman

Source: Benjamin Silliman, *A Visit to Europe in 1851*, 2 vols. (New York: G.P. Putnam, and London: Sampson Low, 1854), vol. 2, 'African Trophies', pp. 443–6.

– Mr. Roualyn Gordon Cumming, who passed five years of a hunter's life in the far interior of Southern Africa, and whose book was regarded by many as a romance, has accumulated a vast museum of trophies of his slaughtered animals, and this collection we have this day seen. The walls of a room, as I suppose, sixty or seventy feet long, and twenty-five feet high, are entirely covered with the spoils of the African forests and deserts wild. It is an exhibition which is almost terrific; as one can hardly fail to transport himself to those untamed regions where these animals roam at large. The skins of lions of both sexes and of various ages, are numerous in this museum. There are among them the hides of very old lions, with shaggy manes, long and dark, sometimes almost black, which fully answer to the pictures of the noble lion, as drawn by artists and naturalists. The orifices for the eyes, and the bullet-holes, by which the monarch of the forest fell, are also visible. The elephant makes a conspicuous figure, and especially his tusks, which are numerous, and some of them very large. I measured a pair, which were ten feet long . . . The value of the ivory in this collection is very great. The tusks on view here vary in value, from 40 to 80 pounds each, little short of 200 to 400 dollars a tusk. They are often very much worn by friction with the bushes. In old male elephants they are polished down at the end into a wedge or section. There are many spoils of the rhinoceros and hippopotamus; and their skulls and bones make a great figure here. The heads of the hippopotamus are of enormous size, and their teeth, too, are very much worn. The two-horned rhinoceros is of frequent occurrence; and the longer horn is always at the end of the nose. It is a very formidable weapon to every beast of the forest. I measured some of them, which were thirty-three inches long, and sharp at the vertex. There are heads and limb bones of giraffes. I measured a leg bone, which was fifty-two and a half inches long. The buffalo heads and horns are numerous, and also those of the African ox, with broad spreading horns. There are, for comparison, heads of the American bison, as well as of other members of the bos family, from various countries. Antelopes

DOI: 10.4324/9781003107835-35

are very numerous, and of many varieties. When living, they are not only fleet, but some of them are formidable, from their long, pointed, strong, and often twisted, horns . . . The room is hung all around with skins, and many of them are in the form of robes, or ornaments worn by the natives . . . Mr. Cumming has published two volumes containing the narrative of his perilous warfare against the wild animals. There is a high degree of romance in African scenes, among the forests and desert wilds, and we find our enthusiasm kindled by our sympathy with the amateur hunter . . . He appears, however, to have had no ulterior object in view, and we, after all, are disposed to take sides with the poor persecuted animals, and to feel that they were consigned to destruction for the sake of indulging a spirit of reckless adventure; although some additions have been made to their natural history by a long continued acquaintance with them in their native haunts.

Editorial Headnote

32. Anon., 'The Natural History of the Exhibition', *Illustrated London News* (1851)

The writer describes the 'natural history' objects which were shown as part of the Great Exhibition in the Crystal Palace, alongside the industrial and manufactured products. John Hancock's taxidermy groups were picked out for special mention as embodying a new quality of dramatic narrative. Composed in three dimensions like sculptural groups, his work represented a fusion of art and natural science.

32

THE NATURAL HISTORY OF THE EXHIBITION

Anon., Illustrated London News

Source: Anon., 'The Natural History of the Exhibition', exhibition supplement to the *Illustrated London News* 19:505 (26 July 1851), pp. 133–5 (p. 134).

In the Transept, just before the palms, are deposited by far the finest specimens of taxidermy in the Exhibition, those shown by Mr. Hancock.[1] They are all birds: the plumage is beautifully displayed; the natural tints preserved in all their freshness, and the characters and motions of each individual imitated with the knowledge of a naturalist, and the tact and skill of an artist. First, we have a hooded falcon, showing the paraphernalia in which the bird was equipped for hawking.[2] The animal itself is a noble specimen of a highly-bred and vigorous hawk. He wears his hood upon his head; the hood in question consisting of a close-fitting cap of leather, which completely blinds the bird and was only removed at the moment of flight. Its legs are manacled by jesses, stout thongs of leather, with which it was bound to the wrist, sitting upon the sportsman or sportswoman's hawking gauntlet. The next specimen is called the 'Struggle with the Quarry.' The falcon has towered above the prey, a fine vigorous heron, swooped down upon it, and with beak and claws struck deeply into the struggling bird; the twain have tumbled, a mere chaos of fluttering feathers and jerking limbs and claws, upon the earth. The struggle is painfully life-like; the heron, with its breast and throat torn by the hawk, and the red, raw, bleeding flesh seen amid the rumpled feathers, seems vainly jerking his long bill, and attempting with his strong wiry legs to hit off his antagonist, who is tearing him with beak and claws. The convulsive movements of the victim are represented with great truth: so contorted, indeed, are its members, its pinions, and limbs, that you must look attentively before you understand the position of the bird: the fierce impetuosity of the hawk is also very truthfully rendered. Still, like many of Landseer's finest pictures, the group is a painful one; indeed, we suspect that it is a blunder in any species of art to represent artificially a sight, which would wound our feelings if seen in reality.[3] Nay, even the keenest sportsman, although he knocks over his game without the slightest twinge of a humanitarian scruple, would possibly not wish to have continually before his eye a vivid representation of the sufferings of the wounded bird.

DOI: 10.4324/9781003107835-36

Close to the 'Struggle with the Quarry,' is the very clever 'Gorged Falcon,' which we have already pointed out as a triumph of expression in taxidermy. The stupid, blinking look of the bird – the half shut and dimmed eyes, and the oddly wrinkled cheek, with the indefinable expression of painful helpless repletion which pervades the whole individual, are all very cleverly caught up, and very effectively reproduced. The hawk sits, listlessly and half asleep, upon one leg – the other claw, still red from the slaughter, retracted by the involuntary tendency of the muscles up to the breast . . . Turning from a gorged hawk to a hungry vulture – the stuffed lammergeyer of the Alps is represented as perched upon the rocky jag of a bare mountain peak, searching with his fierce, wild, hungry eyes, the valleys and ravines below. The attitude of the creature is very graceful, and full of life and vigour.

Editorial Endnotes

1 The work of John Hancock was then little known outside his native Newcastle upon Tyne, and the Crystal Palace exhibits surprised the public.

2 There was some revival of interest in falconry in the Victorian era, including in Hancock's circle of patrons. His taxidermy groups in the 1851 exhibition represented an imagined narrative sequence of events, tracking the hawk's attack on the heron. They are now in the Great North Museum: Hancock in Newcastle, which Hancock himself helped to found and to which he gave many of his works (see Chapter 87).

3 As the writer points out, the painter Edwin Landseer often represented life and death struggles in nature which excited or potentially distressed the spectator: see Chapters 36–7 and 40–1 of the present work.

Editorial Headnote

33. Anon., 'Stuffed Animals in the Palace of Glass', *Athenæum* (1851)

The writer of this review thought that John Hancock's taxidermy groups at the Crystal Palace (1851) had raised the art of taxidermy 'into the region of picture' so that they acquired the cultural cachet of works of fine art.

33

STUFFED ANIMALS IN THE PALACE OF GLASS

Anon., Athenæum

Source: Anon., 'Stuffed Animals in the Palace of Glass', *The Athenæum*, no. 1234 (21 June, 1851), pp. 661–2.

The object of natural history is not only to describe the structure of animals, their external character, and their internal organization – but also to observe and describe the living habits and manners of the animated tribes that cover the surface of the earth. The skin and bones of an animal may serve for the one purpose, – but the living animal, or the attitudes and aspects of life, are necessary for the other. As it is impossible to bring living animals together in sufficient numbers to witness their habits, the naturalist has recourse to written descriptions, drawings, and stuffed specimens. Each of these has its advantages; but the latter gives a constant opportunity for examining what really belonged to the animal, – which the other two do not.

But the preserving of animals in such a way as to make them supply the greatest amount of information is, we have said, a work of Art, – and one that requires in the artist an intimate knowledge of the habits of the animals preserved as well as of the technical details of preparing and stuffing skins. Let any one who doubts that the art of preserving animals is one requiring the artist's eye, and admitting of great exercise of talent and genius, compare some of the specimens which we shall have to mention in the Great Exhibition with the ordinary wretched looking things that he will find in our Museums. He will see that the animal preserver has materials to deal with that are capable of producing effects almost as beautiful as the brush of the painter or the chisel of the sculptor. No one can look at the beautiful specimens of prepared animals by Mr. John Hancock, of Newcastle, exhibited in the Transept, without recognizing the mind of the artist as well as the hand of the taxidermist.

The three specimens illustrative of Falconry are most life-like, – and show how much can be done in this department of Art. The first specimen, representing the Falcon accoutred for his aerial strife, is interesting as affording opportunity of examining the mode of harnessing these birds for their battles in the air. In the second, the bird is seen struggling with his quarry: – and in the way in which Mr.

DOI: 10.4324/9781003107835-37

Hancock has set up the Falcon we have an excellent instance of how the dead animal may be made to assume the attitude of life. The helplessness of his prey, in the Heron which he has in his claws, is as well displayed as the fierceness of the Hawk. – In the third specimen, the Falcon is gorged. There he sits, with one of his eyes half shut, and his feathers in the loose condition indicative of muscular repose.

In addition to these specimens, Mr. Hancock exhibits several others. The Læmmer Geyer – the eagle of the Alps – is a noble example of that bird, expressive of its life and activity. A case of Cockatoos, in which they are surrounded by the plants and insects of a tropical forest, is an interesting combination of animal and vegetable forms. – A Sleeping Leopard is remarkable for its life-like repose. Amongst these examples will be found some in which the specimen is exhibited as dead, – and these show strikingly the artistic power which the taxidermist possesses of contrasting in his specimens death with life. The Dead Gull is an instance: – a specimen representing the living creature appearing as a mourner over its dead mate. – Such stories as these are somewhat new in the history of preserving dead animals; but they are well worthy the attention of those who have the arrangement of museums. The habits of many an animal may thus be indicated, and many an episode in animal life graphically told. The visitors to the approaching Meeting of the British Association, at Ipswich, will have an opportunity of seeing in the Museum there what may be done by a little artistic arrangement in such matters.[1] There, a group of Felidæ, instead of being set up in stiff and unnatural forms, are represented in various attitudes; and the case in which they are placed being fitted up with rocks and the background painted so as to represent a tropical scene, – the whole produces a very pleasing and instructive effect.[2] We would especially direct the attention of the Curators of the British Museum to this mode of arranging their animals. The present crowded mode of arrangement produces anything but an agreeable impression.

Editorial Endnotes

1 The annual meeting of the British Association for the Advancement of Science took place in Ipswich in 1851. The development of the public museum there had been fostered by the leading entomologist Revd William Kirby (see Chapter 55 in the present work) and by Revd John Henslow, Charles Darwin's mentor in his Cambridge years.

2 Apparently, there were already experiments in providing natural backgrounds to stuffed specimens, leading on to habitat groups or dioramas.

Editorial Headnote

33.1. Letter From Revd Robertson to John Hancock (1852)

Letters to Hancock testify to the impact of his new concept of taxidermy, as an enactment of a momentary drama – and it was not only sporting enthusiasts who admired his artistry. The Revd Frederick William Robertson was an intelligent and questioning preacher with a large following, but also a troubled and sick man (he died in 1853). He wrote to Hancock to express his ardent admiration for the latter's taxidermy groups shown in the Great Exhibition.

33.1

MANUSCRIPT LETTER TO JOHN HANCOCK

Revd Frederick William Robertson

Source: Revd Frederick William Robertson to John Hancock, 16 January 1852. Hancock Archive, Newcastle.

Dear Sir,

I wrote to Mr. Hewitson[1] in consequence of the advertisement in the Athenaeum to ask the price of the cases of stuffed birds in the Exhibition. It was far beyond my purse, but no more beyond the value of the birds themselves than the prices given for a Raphael or any other work of genius in painting.[2]

My object however, in writing to you now is this. The falcons & heron etc. struck me as so immeasurably superior to anything of the sort I had ever seen though I have seen much in Taxidermy, so living & inspired with the creative character of poetry that I am induced to take the liberty of asking whether you have published any work or observations in any periodical on the subject. I know that so far as the tact of observation & living sympathy with life go, no rules can teach – but there must be some thing that you could impart to the world which would elevate the study of ornithology & raise Taxidermy to the rank of one of the fine arts. I do not ask you to take the trouble of putting down on paper for a stranger & a mere amateur your principles of preserving, but confine my question to this whether any hints are published, or to be published.[3] And I am sure you would pardon the liberty if you knew how often I had gone to look at your birds, how long I staid [sic] before them & and how many I had sent there for the same purpose with enthusiasm.

I am your obd. Serv.[4]

Fred. W. Robertson

My address is the Rev. FW Robertson 60 Montpellier Road, Brighton.

DOI: 10.4324/9781003107835-38

Editorial Endnotes

1 William Hewitson was a close friend and patron of Hancock; see Chapter 16 in the present work.
2 Robertson here extravagantly compares Hancock with one of the most venerated Renaissance painters.
3 The nearest that Hancock came to the kind of 'observations' on taxidermy that Robertson envisaged was in the introduction to his *Fasciculus* (see Chapter 34).
4 'Obedient Servant'.

Figure 7 John Hancock, *A Fasciculus of Eight Drawings on Stone*, 1853, 'Struggle with the Quarry', drawn and lithographed by Hancock from a photograph of his own taxidermy group, and printed by Hulmandell & Walton. (British Library)

Editorial Headnote

34. John Hancock, *A Fasciculus of Eight Drawings on Stone* (1853)

While John Hancock always aimed at an impression of authenticity and natural action in his taxidermy groups, they really involved considerable artifice. In designing a series of large lithographs to record his Crystal Palace exhibits, he found that a further element of contrivance was necessary. His lithographic drawings (see Figure 7) were based not directly on the stuffed gyrfalcon and heron, but on large photographs of them, taken for the purpose, which Hancock refers to here as 'originals' or 'sun-drawings'. The tonal effects of such early photographs then had to be reworked after fresh study of the birds' actual plumage. Although Hancock wanted his images to be 'authentic', they were actually several removes from nature.

34

A FASCICULUS OF EIGHT DRAWINGS ON STONE, OF GROUPS OF BIRDS

John Hancock

Source: John Hancock, *A Fasciculus of Eight Drawings on Stone, of Groups of Birds, &c. . . . The whole being representations of Specimens Stuffed and Contributed by the Author to the Great Industrial Exhibition of 1851* (Newcastle upon Tyne: Published by the Author, 1853. Hullmandel & Walton, lithographic printers, London); published by subscription.

The drawings made from these originals are not intended to express their peculiar effect, the object being to copy them in such a manner as to attain authentic delineations of the stuffed birds in outline, general drawing and character. The photographs have therefore been faithfully copied in all that relates to these leading points; but the details of the plumage, &c., which in the generality of sun-drawings are more or less defective, have, to a considerable extent, been derived immediately from the specimens themselves. It was thought that in this way more correct representations could be produced than by any other means of the taxidermy exhibited by the Author.

For the purpose of ascertaining how plumage could be best represented on stone, several styles have been tried. That entitled 'Black Game and Ptarmigan' is the only drawing wholly executed in the ordinary chalk manner; the Dead Gull and the back view of the Læmmer-Geyer were both worked out on the 'wet principle,' the lights being produced by scraping as in Mezzotint[1]; the front view of the latter was done much in the same manner, only the stone was prepared dry as for a tint; the stump was also extensively used in several of the drawings, particularly that of the Hooded Falcon. This diversity of manner, it is feared, may injure, to some extent, that unity of character so desirable in a series of drawings like the present . . .

Respecting the subjects of the various drawings little need be said, as they, for the most part, speak for themselves. The 'Hooded Falcon,' the 'Struggle with the Quarry,' and the 'Gorged Falcon,' form a consecutive series illustrating falconry . . . None of the other drawings require explanation, except that of the Dead Gull (*Larus Minutus*), and of it a word or two will suffice, as it represents an incident that may be witnessed daily by those who frequent the sea-beach – A Gull has just been shot, and its companion is hovering over the dead bird, uttering its mournful cry, incapable of comprehending the fatal catastrophe, and heedless of its own imminent danger.

Editorial Endnote

1 Hancock presumably means that, within the areas of his lithographic drawing, which, when inked, would print dark, he had scraped away some of the oily crayoning to expose the stone surface. He wetted those exposed areas, along with the rest of the untouched surface. They would then repel the ink when printing, producing a flecked effect suggestive of plumage.

Editorial Headnote

35. Rowland Ward, *A Naturalist's Life Study in the Art of Taxidermy* (1913)

Ward's account of his 'life study' reveals the huge range of late Victorian big game hunting, and of the taxidermy businesses associated with it. His premises in the West End of London accommodated work on a near-industrial scale, and his international clientele encompassed princes and aristocrats, but also the proprietors of zoological museums. Products of the firm included 'Wardian furniture' – 'domestic ornaments' made from animal parts such as stuffed birds or elephants' tusks and feet.[1] However, Ward also created large, dramatised groups of tropical wildlife for viewing by the public. Working before photographs or films of live animals became available, he carefully studied the physique and movements of those in the London Zoo; and, as a friend of artists like Landseer and Heywood Hardy, he produced taxidermy spectacles that seemed to transmute their painted images of animal strife into three dimensions. His exhibited tableaux or dioramas apparently had the same kind of dense, piled-up compositions, filling the frame, that one sees in illustrations to popular books on zoology of the period. Those shown by Ward at the various international exhibitions held in London demonstrate above all the close connections between Britain's imperial dominance and a sense of entitlement, bravado, a taste for mass slaughter, and an obsession with violence and struggle in the natural world.

Editorial Endnote

1 A silver wedding present for the Prince and Princess of Wales in 1888 was 'a crocodile mounted by myself as a dumb waiter, with a wooden stool in its fore-paws' (*A Naturalist's Life Study*, p. 90).

35

A NATURALIST'S LIFE STUDY IN THE ART OF TAXIDERMY

Rowland Ward

Source: Rowland Ward, F.Z.S., *A Naturalist's Life Study in the Art of Taxidermy* (London: Rowland Ward, Ltd., 'The Jungle', 167 Piccadilly, W., 1913), pp. 70–2, 74–80, 85.

[pp. 70–2]

The grouping of animals amid surroundings in imitation of nature, as exemplified in the earlier Exhibitions held in London, was an original idea of my own, and one which afforded some of the earliest evidence that the public could be attracted by displays of this kind. In recent years the idea of grouping specimens amid imitation natural surroundings has gradually spread and developed, until it has attained its supreme development in the museums of America, which appear to have far greater funds and space for display at their disposal than is the case with similar institutions in our own country.[1]

The first large group which I modelled in the new style was the one known as 'The Combat' (see illustration), which was shown in the Scientific Inventions and New Discoveries section of the London International Exhibition of 1871. The group represented two red deer stags fighting with a fury common to this animal. I killed the stags in Richmond Park and skinned and cast them myself, and in modelling them I used R. Ansdell's famous engraving 'The Combat' for the subject.[2] 'To our thinking,' wrote one critic, 'the fierce animals seem to fight with deadly spirit. Tendon and muscle are strained to the utmost in the deadly struggle.' 'The fierceness of this fight *à l'outrance* is wonderfully rendered,' wrote another; 'the eyes and tongue of the victor being displayed with marvellous fidelity, and with an utter absence of that dull, listless unreality so generally characteristic of stuffed beasts. Nothing could represent intensity of agony better than the upturned gaze of the unfortunate animal stricken unto death'[3] . . .

'A Trying Moment' was the title I gave to a group which I mounted in 1875 in commemoration of the visit of the then Prince of Wales to India.[4] This group took the form of a tigress attacking a shikar elephant, and represented a scene which did actually occur during the royal visit. In my design the tigress had all four feet at work, supporting herself by one foot on one of the tusks, and viciously clawing with the other three into the quivering flesh. The elephant's trunk was raised,

DOI: 10.4324/9781003107835-40

indicating the trumpeting which told of the agony and terror it was enduring. I was able to heighten the general effect considerably by a new method of forming the artificial eyes, which I had invented and used for some time previously with great success . . .

[pp. 74–80]

From the point of view of displays designed to attract the interest of the general public, one of my greatest successes was achieved in the Colonial and Indian Exhibition held at South Kensington during the summer of 1886, when I had four distinct exhibits, two of which were in the Indian Court.[5]

The first of these took the form of a hunting scene, prepared for the late Maharajah of Cooch Behar. It represented a great group in the deep-grass jungle. A hunting elephant preceding the beaters had come upon the group of tigers, one of which had sprung upon him with a deadly grip; others were near or retreating in the tall grass and bamboo copse. I had been at a great disadvantage in arranging this for want of space; if I had had more room I could have given a greater depth to the jungle and more space for mountain scenes, and so have obtained a still better effect. Some of the animals were lent by the Maharajah, most of them having been shot by himself, in his own dominions, where there are the finest jungles for big game to be found in India. As providing some indication of the work entailed, I may mention that I gave thirty hours at a stretch to the preparation of one tiger. It is a curious fact, not generally known, that much of the expression on a tiger's face is gained by the disposition of the whiskers. I made a special study of that tiger from life – went to the Zoo and made a tiger snarl by rattling the bars, and afterwards fixed the whiskers on my mounted tiger in exact imitation. In addition to these there were several heads of the rhinoceros, whole reptiles, birds etc. . . .

The second and larger scheme, which was designated 'Jungle Life,' was installed at the instance of the Exhibition Commissioners in order to illustrate some of the more striking representatives of the fauna and flora of India as a whole. The idea I had to carry out was to group these representative animals and birds as picturesquely as possible in illustration of their habits . . . The late Maharajah of Cooch Behar (who died in 1911) said he would send what he could to help me to form the exhibit, and the then Prince of Wales (the late King Edward VII) also gave valuable assistance, and helped me to obtain some of the best trophies then existing, on loan from their owners. To achieve this object he made a signed request in *The Times*. We found we had a much larger task than we had any idea of at the start, for we were allotted a very large space just inside one of the entrances of the old Horticultural building, reaching right up to the roof. I enclosed the space in large sheets of plate-glass and canvas, and painted on the latter the foliage of the banyan tree . . . the whole scene was lit up with electricity inside . . . It was a set scene of all the Indian animals I could get hold of, and those I hadn't got I made! For instance, the sambur head had an artificial skin to it, and that is only one . . . I had a good opportunity of hiding the feet of some of the animals, for I went to Norfolk and got loads of Norfolk reeds and rushes, dead trees, and things of that description, to take the place of the Indian foliage which I was promised and did not receive until it was too late. I also made use of a number of trophies which I had in stock. Some very large snakes hung from the dead trees, and on the very top of the scene – at the roof, in fact – I put some ibex with their heads just appearing over the top of the rock-work. Portions of the 'Jungle' were draped with cloths painted to represent foliage and rocks, and there was also some imitation rock-work which gave me an excellent opportunity of concealing any portion of an animal I did not desire to expose. At the bottom were artificial pools with alligators, and overhanging creepers, all of which had to be made – some I had made in Paris, and the rest we did ourselves. Then the animals and birds had all to be prepared for the various positions they had to occupy. I was very anxious to get all the subjects together to see the effect, and help me to go on, for the idea was all in my head and I wanted to work it out. At length I was able to collect the majority of the exhibits and put them into a group. I could see at once that it was going to be a fine effect, and from that day I was sure of its being a success. The tigers came from Cooch Behar, but we had to get an elephant – or the 'Jungle' would not have been complete.

I hadn't a suitable Indian elephant, but I heard that Hagenbeck, at Hamburg, had a dangerous one that he was going to kill.[6] A friend of mine – a Dutch gentleman – said he would like to kill it when I told him I was going over to see whether it would suit me. So we went to Hamburg together, he taking a 477 rifle to shoot the elephant with. We saw the elephant, and although it wasn't as good as I wanted, I decided to have it. I went with my friend to Hagenbeck to witness the shooting of the elephant. I had expected that Hagenbeck would have taken it out of the town away from any crowds, but he had made the preparations for the 'elephant hunt' in a square of houses, and with people looking on all round us. It is true that it was in a poor neighbourhood, but I didn't want to be concerned in an affair of that kind . . . I told him if he killed the elephant I would take the skin, so he agreed to that. I was told afterwards that he strangled the elephant with a big chain, but neither my friend nor myself saw it. So that is how the elephant came into the 'Jungle.'

I put one of my Cooch Behar tigers on the elephant, and set up another tiger lying on its haunches just in front of the elephant, with its shoulder broken, and several other tigers were in the vicinity. I let this form one scene, and separated it from the other part of the 'Jungle' with Norfolk grass, and when the Indian grasses came – after my work was finished – I put some of them in the scene as well . . .

This 'Jungle,' the first one exhibited, was an enormous success, and it was inspected by many thousands of persons, over ten thousand visiting it on August Bank Holiday alone . . .

[p. 85]

Towards the end of June, 1892, I had the pleasure of exhibiting in Piccadilly the biggest bag of lions I have ever had – shot in one trip and by one individual, viz. Lord Delamere, of East African fame.[7] Two of the finest skins chosen from this bag of fourteen shot by his lordship on an expedition to Somaliland were mounted as though in the middle of a deadly combat. One of the lions, whose fore-paw was held in the other's powerful jaw, and whose sides were dripping blood where the sharp claws and fangs had struck him, was depicted as roaring in fierce agony. Locked together, the two great beasts seemed to be rolling down a sloping bank towards the spectators' feet.

The bigger of the lions, which had a magnificent mane, took two days in the killing. Wounded on the first day in an attack on Lord Delamare's man, he retired into a thick cover of reeds. On the second day, when all attempts to dislodge him – including fireworks and other devices – had failed, Lord Delamere determined to get at close quarters. He had an exciting quarter of an hour, the lion being at his lordship's very feet before the third shot laid him dead.

The group eventually found a home at Vale Royal, Lord Delamere's Cheshire residence, where even the ceilings are decorated with lion skins. Lord Cranworth, in his recently published book *A Colony in the Making*, mentions that Lord Delamere, single handed, has accounted for close on seventy lions, more than twice as many as stand to the credit of any other sportsman.[8]

Editorial Endnotes

1 Ward was probably thinking of the ambitious groups produced by Carl Akeley at the Field Museum in Chicago and by William Temple Hornaday at the American Museum of Natural History in New York. Karen Wonders, 'Habitat Dioramas: Illusions of Wilderness in Museums of Natural History', (PhD diss., Uppsala University, 1993 [Acta Universitatis Upsaliensis Figura Nova Series 25], pp. 148f.).

2 Richard Ansdell's painting *The Combat* of 1847 became well known through engravings. It showed two stags fighting to the death – a subject with many parallels in the work of Landseer.

3 Ward's taxidermy involved the creation of casts – essentially sculptures – of animals' bodies in the required active poses, which were then covered in their skins. This procedure created a greater sense of realism than the traditional stuffing of skins.

4 The Prince of Wales, the future King Edward VII, toured India between October 1875 and May 1876. If Ward dates his taxidermy group correctly, it was created before the prince's tour was complete and had the appeal of extreme topicality.

5 The Colonial and Indian Exhibition of 1886 was organised by a Royal Commission presided over by the Prince of Wales and featured arts, crafts, and manufactures from the Empire. See especially *Times*, 31 March 1885, pp. 3 and 9. Ward's representation of 'an Indian Jungle' was frequently mentioned in press reports.

6 Carl Hagenbeck was instrumental in the capture and import to Europe of large numbers of live tropical animals, which stocked his famous *Tierpark* near Hamburg. Nigel Rothfels, *Savages and Beasts: The Birth of the Modern Zoo* (Baltimore and London: Johns Hopkins University Press, 2002).

7 Hugh Cholmondeley, 3rd Baron Delamere, acquired vast estates in Kenya and hunted lions from the 1890s onwards.

8 Bertram Francis Gurdon, Baron Cranworth, *A Colony in the Making. Or, Sport and Profit in British East Africa* (London: MacMillan, 1912), p. 251.

Figure 8 Edwin Landseer, *The Otter Speared*, painted between c.1838 and 1844, oil on canvas, Laing Art Gallery, Newcastle upon Tyne. (Bridgeman Images)

Editorial Headnote

36. Letters From the Earl of Aberdeen to Edwin Landseer (1838, 1841)

The lengthy correspondence about Sir Edwin Landseer's painting of an otter hunt (see Figure 8), commissioned by the 4th Earl of Aberdeen, reveals an interesting tension between the ideas of the patron and those of the artist. The earl wanted a small, unassertive picture that would give pleasure to himself and his guests in the relaxed atmosphere of his Scottish home, Haddo House. Landseer, in contrast, planned a large, strenuous, and potentially disturbing work, one that combined brutal realism with historical echoes. It is striking that the earl, a man of wide culture and high political and social status (he was foreign secretary under Peel and later became prime minister), was as diplomatic as possible in his communications with Landseer, whose ideas ultimately prevailed – an outcome suggesting a privileged relationship with the aristocracy that was unusual for artists of the Victorian era. At the time of the second quoted letter, the earl was especially busy with affairs of state, but he seems to have invited Landseer to stay at Haddo House in his absence, in order to make progress with the painting. The letter conveys anxiety about the scale of the work that Landseer envisaged, but also anxiety not to upset him, following the artist's mental breakdown in 1840.

36

MANUSCRIPT LETTERS TO EDWIN LANDSEER

George Hamilton-Gordon, 4th Earl of Aberdeen

Source: George Hamilton-Gordon, 4th Earl of Aberdeen to Edwin Landseer, 27 November 1838 and 14 October 1841, manuscript letters in the National Art Library, Victoria & Albert Museum, London.

H: H: [Haddo House] Novr. 27th 1838

Dear Landseer,

By the Steam vessel today, I send a remarkably fine Roe buck's Head, which I have directed my Porter to take to you. I had remarked him, for some days, in the large wood on the other side of the river, and thought he was a very fine specimen of the animal. He was shot for me by Capt. John; and I send his head at once, because I do not think there is the least chance of my finding a better; although I hope you will come and try for yourself.[1] The Head has been pretty well preserved, by my Cook, with the exception of the eyes, which are too small, and squint abominably; but they are the best which could be found in Aberdeen.[2]

I am glad you approve of the introduction of a pony into the picture of otter hunting.[3] Decorated in the manner I mentioned, he will help to tell the story. You are very kind in undertaking the work at all, – and I should be most unreasonable if I expected it to be pressed forward, to the injury of other compositions. You will do what you think best, and what you can, with the greatest convenience to yourself.

We have said nothing about size. A certain degree of magnitude is necessary to do justice to the subject, and to the animals represented; but consistently with the attainment of this object, perhaps the less, the better. It will be a picture that I shall wish to <u>live with;</u> and I have no rooms, or walls, fit to receive a large work. You will know what is most desirable in this respect.

My notion of the composition would be, not to attempt a great landscape, but to have a bit of broken bank of the river, where the whole scene should take place.

I may also mention that it will be well to omit all the smooth fox hounds, and to stick to the genuine otter hound. This I am in fact doing myself. I have already discarded most of the fox hounds, and hope next year to take the field (or the water) with nothing but rough dogs.[4]

DOI: 10.4324/9781003107835-41

You will excuse me for throwing out these suggestions; but I feel very much interested about the work, which I fully anticipate will be one of the most beautiful you have ever produced.

Ever faithfully yours, Aberdeen.

Foreign Office Oct. 14th 1841

Dear Landseer,

I write a line to you at Haddo where I hope it will find you and the Captain. I fear an empty house will be but uncomfortable, at the same time, if you can find any amusement, of any kind, I trust you will stay there as long as there is any attraction. You ought to have good sport with the Roe deer, of which there must be many, for they have been much spared for the last two years. Of other game, I fear you will find but little.

I hope Lord John Scott may not have sent for the otter hounds, which I promised to lend him for the remainder of the season.[5] When I heard last from Haddo, he had not done so, and as the season is far advanced, it is possible that he may have given up his intention of sending his yacht for them to Aberdeen.

With respect to the picture, I am glad to find you are thinking about it, but I hope you will not be very much shocked, if I express a wish which I know you will not approve of.

I am quite certain that my pleasure in the picture will be greatly increased if it should be of small dimensions, instead of the half life size proposed. I think that size is always rather awkward to manage; and in the present case, even my room is an objection. What I mean to describe as my desire to see, are figures of the size of those in the beautiful picture you had in the Exhibition of 'Horses Watering' which I think you told me was painted for Mr. Marshall.[6] We might have two pictures of this size, for I think your first composition, with the hounds in the water, was admirable. Now, I know how much an Artist hates to have his subjects diminished, but you are wrong, and I am [sure] this will be more generally liked, as well as give me infinitely more pleasure. Indeed, I should not well know how to live with the other. Pray think of this, and make up your mind to it.

I hope you continue quite well, and think your Highland expedition has been the means [of] confirming your health. I wish most heartily that I could be with you, instead of being shut up in this abominable Tread Mill.

Ever most truly yours, Aberdeen.

Ly [Lady] Abercorn comes to London tonight.

Editorial Endnotes

1 The roebuck's head sent to Landseer may relate to his painting *Head of a Roebuck* and *Two Ptarmigan*, which is stylistically dateable to the 1830s and is now in the Art Institute of Chicago, or to *Young Roebuck and Rough Hounds* of 1840 (see Chapter 37.1).

2 The Earl meant that Aberdeen taxidermists could not supply artificial eyes of a quality equal to that obtainable in London.

3 Landseer's painting *The Otter Speared*, now in the Laing Art Gallery in Newcastle, was finished only in 1844, when it was exhibited at the Royal Academy. There was no pony in this final version of the composition. Richard Ormond, *Sir Edmund Landseer* (Philadelphia Museum of Art and Tate Gallery, London, 1981), pp. 184–7. Ormond, *The Monarch of the Glen: Landseer in the Highlands* (Edinburgh: National Galleries of Scotland, 2005), pp. 118–9. Diana Donald, *Picturing Animals in Britain, 1750–1850* (New Haven, CT, and London: Yale University Press, 2007), pp. 294–7. Daniel Allen, Charles Watkins, David Matless, '"An incredibly vile sport": campaigns against otter hunting in Britain, 1900–1939', *Cambridge Core* at www.cambridge.org/core/journals/rural-history/article, 3 March 2016.

4 The dogs in Landseer's painting are, in fact, all shaggy otterhounds, adding to the archaic and picturesque flavour of the painting.

5 Lord John Douglas Montagu Scott, who was briefly MP for Roxburghshire, was brother of the 5th Duke of Buccleuch. He was an enthusiastic hunter and interested in the breeding of sporting dogs.

6 This was *Horses at a Fountain*, shown at the Royal Academy in 1840.

Editorial Headnote

36.1. Anon., 'Fine Arts, Royal Academy', *The Literary Gazette* (1844)

Despite the Earl of Aberdeen's understandable conviction that Landseer's *Otter Hunt* was impossible to live with, it was acclaimed in the public sphere. The *Times*, for example, described the picture as being in Landseer's 'happiest style . . . one of the most attractive in the collection'.[1] *The Literary Gazette*'s reviewer was even more enthusiastic.

Editorial Endnote

1 Anon., 'Royal Academy of Painting', *Times*, 7 May 1844, p. 6. The reviewer's praise of *Otter Hunt* stands in contrast to art critic John Ruskin's indictment of the cruelty of the image and of the practice it depicts: *Modern Painters*, vol. 2, 1846, part 3, chapter 12, 'Of vital beauty'.

36.1

FINE ARTS, ROYAL ACADEMY

Anon., The Literary Gazette

Source: Anon, 'Fine arts, Royal Academy', *The Literary Gazette, and Journal of the Belles Lettres, Arts, Sciences, &c.*, no. 1425 (11 May 1844), p. 306.

No. 13. *The Otter Speared.* E. Landseer, R.A., – Snyders, eh? Snyders never beat this animated animal assemblage.[1] The huntsman, burning with fatigue and flushed with victory, holds up the fish-felon on the point of his spear, the shaft of which the fierce creature bites in dying revenge. Around, in every position and with every expression, are Lord Aberdeen's pack; all of them delightfully painted, and some of them – witness one little bright-eyed wire terrier on the left – perfect as life. The composition, too, is very fine; we sum up the beauty of this performance when we say it is one of Landseer's masterpieces . . . all life and spirit.

Editorial Endnote

1 Frans Snyders's paintings of the early to mid-seventeenth century, showing wild animals fighting with dogs in hunting scenes, were widely believed to have influenced Landseer and his contemporaries.

DOI: 10.4324/9781003107835-42

Editorial Headnote

36.2. Anon., 'The Royal Academy', *The Art-Union* (1844)

The *Art-Union*'s reviewer also focuses on the graphic realism of Landseer's painting, especially in the characterisation of the excited dogs.

36.2

THE ROYAL ACADEMY

Anon., The Art-Union

Source: Anon, 'The Royal Academy', *The Art-Union*, 6:67, supplementary no. (1 June 1844), p. 154.

East Room, no. 13. The Otter speared – portrait of the Earl of Aberdeen's Otter-hound, E. Landseer, R.A. A very large composition, and one which must rank among the most important productions of the entire career of this artist in his own peculiar walk of Art. It is, in short, a pyramid of dogs, formed thus: – We have a fragment of the river-bank, against which the huntsman of the pack is standing, bearing high above his head the otter, pierced by a long spear, which, of course, collects around him the whole pack of otter-hounds, some in the water at his feet, others on the bank above him, and others climbing and leaping around him. This picture far transcends all other efforts, ancient or modern, at portraiture of canine character. We are told it is (that is, in variety) a portrait of Lord Aberdeen's otterhound, which seems to be an animal of most grave and eremitical features, but very earnest in pursuit, and curiously formed for swimming. The picture is wonderful in colour.

DOI: 10.4324/9781003107835-43

Editorial Headnote

37. Anon., *Engravings . . . After the Designs of Sir Edwin Landseer* (1853)

The paintings, drawings, engravings, and book illustrations created by Edwin and Thomas Landseer in the 1820s had introduced a wholly fresh approach to the representation of animals. Energy, violent action, and physical realism were the keynotes, and the Landseer brothers often reworked animal pictures by the Old Masters in the light of their new ideals. A number of these early engravings were reprinted and issued together with an accompanying text commentary some thirty years later, in 1853. By then Edwin Landseer had become the most famous of animal painters, and he added some fresh graphic studies to the collection, engraved by his brother: dramatic scenes, such as savage fights between the big cats over their prey. The anonymous introductory text justified this hyper-realistic approach, pointing out the shortcomings of the Old Masters as regards zoological accuracy. However, it raised a question which runs through this collection of texts: does such literalism entail a loss of dignity and idealism in animal art?

37

ENGRAVINGS OF LIONS, TIGERS, PANTHERS . . . CHIEFLY AFTER THE DESIGNS OF SIR EDWIN LANDSEER

Anon.

Source: Anon., *Engravings of Lions, Tigers, Panthers, Leopards, Dogs &c, chiefly after the Designs of Sir Edwin Landseer, by his Brother, Thomas Landseer. Printed from the original plates published between 1823 and 1828* (London: Henry G. Bohn, 1853), pp. 1–3, 5.

[pp. 1–3]

That there has hitherto existed no good book of Engravings of the nobler wild animals, to assist the progress of the student in that department of Art, is to be regretted . . . of the ferocious TIGER tribe, and the lordly LION, we have nothing extant that would bear critical inspection, beyond a few detached prints: – nothing like a collection of figures, whose justness and accuracy of form, action, character, and expression, might be relied on . . . Even those after TITIAN and after RUBENS (the latter of whom has perhaps painted a greater number than any other of the old masters) are far more deficient in form, character, and expression, than is generally supposed, or than will be easily believed, by those who have not actually compared them with the Lions, Leopards, and Tigers of Nature.[1] They have been taken too much on the credit which attaches to the great names of their authors. – Nor is this intended to impugn the merits, as historical or poetical painters, of those distinguished Artists, but simply as an assertion of truth . . .

The Lions of RUBENS are *humanized.* We do not intend to discuss at length whether the ideality of allegorical painting required this: we only state the fact: yet the opinions which we felt at liberty to form on the subject, we felt at liberty to offer. So much in apology for using the licence of asserting that the heads of many of the Lions of RUBENS rather resemble those of frowning old gentlemen decorated with Ramillies wigs[2]; as if Nature's journeymen had made *manes*, and not made them well. There is a profusion of flowing and curling hair, which seems rather to solicit the unguents of the perfumer, than to have endured the torrid heats of the desert, or the rough storms of the forest. The shag of a Lion's mane is a very different sort of thing.

However such dressed Lions may be thought to accord with Allegory, they are demonstrably at variance with Nature. To be sure, what might become a Lion in

DOI: 10.4324/9781003107835-44

the procession of the Cardinal Virtues, might be rather unsuitable in his den, or within the precincts of those wild haunts, where he is accustomed to roam in his natural state . . .

Among the observers of this poetic improvement, or this natural and unpoetical deficiency, on the part of RUBENS, TITIAN, JULIO ROMANO, and other painters, both ancient and modern; and of the consequent *desideratum* on the part of the public, of a cabinet or library collection of the nobler wild animals in a state of Nature, so as to answer the purposes of reference, while they conduced to the pleasures of Taste, were Mr. EDGAR SPILSBURY[3] and Mr. THOMAS LANDSEER . . . They carried with them what, in those ancient masters, was meritorious in composition, attitude and chiaroscuro, and brought away, to the best of their ability – superadding it to, and blending it with, the above – accuracy of detail.

Every artist does best, that which he is best qualified and best disposed to do. In completing the number of plates that has been found necessary for the Work, Mr. EDWIN LANDSEER has chosen to proceed toward the same purpose, upon a different principle. He has gone, without any introductory medium, directly to the living animals, and has exhibited the savage manners and habits of these quadrupeds, according to his own ideas and observations . . .

[p. 5]

No. VI. In this group by Mr. EDWIN LANDSEER there is much of violent animal *Expression*, and Character fades before it, or rather, is absorbed in it. It tells a story of the past as well as the present, and is pregnant with a catastrophe not difficult to anticipate from the actions and expressions of the parties engaged. A FAWN has been seized by a LEOPARD, who has been despoiled of his prey by a more powerful TIGER. The Tiger in turn becomes the victim of an enraged LION.

The expression of the wounded Leopard is that of painful suffering mingled with dread. Together, they amount to agony. He shrieks while he submits. The Tiger is still enraged and resisting, though astounded with the power and suddenness of the Lion's attack. He is losing his energy of resistance, and is beginning to feel that all resistance is vain. He roars with anguish; while his expression is that of terror, and indignation not yet subdued.

The Lion, who has just made his thundering spring, appears conscious of having fatally seized his adversary, and luxuriates fearlessly in his victory; and with a powerful and just expression of carnivorous enjoyment. – Meanwhile the characters of the animals, severally, are faithfully and specifically represented.

Editorial Endnotes

1 This is perhaps a reference to works like Rubens's *Lion Hunt*, now in the Alte Pinakothek, Munich. In Titian's paintings, animals are rarely more than accessories to the main subject.

2 Ramillies wigs featured a pigtail tied with ribbons.

3 Rubens, Titian, and Guilio Romano were famed painters of the sixteenth and seventeenth centuries. Edgar Ashe Spilsbury was a surgeon who also made realistic animal drawings in the early years of the nineteenth century.

Editorial Headnote

37.1. Anon, 'The British Institution', *New Sporting Magazine* (1840)

The sheer physicality, energy, and tactile quality of Landseer's art clearly constituted a large part of its appeal to his fellow sportsmen, as is revealed by this review of a current exhibition at the British Institution. In the Landseer picture described by the reviewer, *Young Roebuck and Rough Hounds*, the dangling head of the dead deer is surrounded and licked by the dogs, which fill the frame. This work was acquired by John Sheepshanks and is now in the Victoria & Albert Museum.

37.1

THE BRITISH INSTITUTION

Anon., New Sporting Magazine

Source: Anon., 'The British Institution', *New Sporting Magazine*, 18:107 (March 1840), pp. 196–7.

No. 1. *Is* number one! – unapproachable by anything, except the animal painting by Maclise, in his Robin Hood.[1] It is the gem on the forehead of the exhibition. It is 'Young Roebuck and Rough Hounds,' by E. Landseer, R.A.; and oh! what skins! the picture would charm a furrier! The hound licking the wound in the neck – the wound itself – the quiet shaggy dogs in front – the deathful roebuck – and the solemn terrier, forming the black and back ground – are something more like an oil improvement upon the art of transferring nature to canvas as it has been done through light to paper,[2] than the common working of the imagination, the hand, and the brush!

Editorial Endnotes

1 Daniel Maclise, *Robin Hood and his Merry Men Entertaining Richard the Lionheart in Sherwood Forest*, 1839; now in Nottingham Castle Museum.

2 This seems to be a reference to the camera obscura, or perhaps to the beginnings of photography.

Editorial Headnote

38. William Michael Rossetti, 'Animal-Design and Landscape' (1863)

The author, a writer on art and brother of the artist Dante Gabriel Rossetti, explains that his subject is 'the arts of Animal-design and Landscape, with regard to some of the more salient characteristics of their treatment at the present day'. His article echoes art critic John Ruskin's views, as expressed in *Modern Painters*, in a critique of the 'minute' physical specificity of Edwin Landseer's art. While sportsmen enjoyed that quality of literalism, Rossetti compares it unfavourably to the grander and more monumental treatment of animal forms in earlier art.

38

ANIMAL-DESIGN AND LANDSCAPE

Aspects of their Contemporary Treatment

William Michael Rossetti

Source: William Michael Rossetti, 'Animal-design and landscape: aspects of their contemporary treatment', *Macmillan's Magazine*, 8 (May–Oct. 1863) pp. 116–23.

[pp. 118–20]

Most persons conversant with archaic or unsophisticated art have probably noticed its remarkable excellence in animal-design . . . As examples one may cite the Nubian lions in the Egyptian-room of the British Museum, than which nothing more mighty in conception and impression is to be done[1]; the Egyptian paintings in the same room, of a fowler hunting with a cat, and of the tribute of geese[2]; the stupendous lion-hunts and other animal-subjects of Assyrian sculpture[3]; Lombardic chases; early Gothic grotesques; or the perfect refinement, ease, spirit, and fancy, with which animals are treated in Japanese art of past and present time[4] . . . The facts that the animal form is easier to represent than the human, and that we are not so entirely familiar with the former as with the latter, count for something. Besides this, the amount of expression needed is much smaller and less subtle, and the forms are more amenable to a treatment so far conventional as to tend towards the decorative. And on this, in many instances, much of the excellence of the representation depends . . .

Without dwelling farther upon the particular qualities of archaic animal-design, to which my space would not suffice, it may be stated that the animal-design distinctive of the present time has wholly lost the conventional character referred to . . . As late as the times of Titian and Velasquez, and even Snyders and Jan Fyt,[5] the typical character of animal-design was kept up: a dog by Snyders is a dog of the pictorial breed, a representative of the canine in physical nature, so to speak: a dog to be used on the broad scale for the purposes of the picture, and dropped after his pictorial juices have been extracted. Heraldry, too, is by no means to be despised as a preservative of types of animalism. A lion rampant, a lion couchant, were often not lions at all, in an accurate sense; but they served to keep up an acute perception, in the artistic mind, of rampancy and couchancy as leonine conditions; and a deal of sturdy design, blending the typical and the arbitrary, is connected with leading notions of this sort. The tendency of our own day is wholly in the opposite direction.

DOI: 10.4324/9781003107835-46

It individualizes the animals; passes from types to genera, and so to species, varieties, and single specimens; and its outcome is the dog Toby, rather than the mammal Canis. This is the inevitable course for our animal-design to follow, in connexion with our design of all sorts. Its advantages of truth and nature are indisputable; but it sheds by the way some of the dignity and breadth of type of animal-life, preserved in the older styles.

One of its consequents is the minute attention to varieties of hide and surface – softness, downiness, wiriness, and so on – most true, as far as they go, and not to be lightly omitted, yet not truth of the highest kind. The pursuit of them betrays the art towards knicknackery, and often propels it over the brink.

On the whole, Landseer continues the most distinguished animal-painter of our time in Europe, and the one who has most thoroughly embodied and fixed the modern point of view for animal nature. He unites all the tendencies above indicated, though the precision of the style of painting which has arisen in England since his prime carries some of them to further or modified developments.[6] He is peculiarly modern, too, in the fullness of his sympathy with the real individual incidents and feelings of animal-life. His dog is not Snyders' dog – the sort of creature whose best known propensity is to snap in packs at a boar's ear, and get ripped up by its tusks. His dogs have each a personal character to maintain and exhibit, and will even become almost human, without ceasing to be canine. Landseer's specialty and eminence in this respect have been pointed out again and again, but cannot be omitted from mention when modern animal-art is in question.

Such principles of animal-designing, with all their manifest merits, have this disadvantage – that they tend to reduce animals from their grand typical proportion in art, and from their serviceableness for art in its larger or more abstract forms. What is the counteracting remedy? The movement of modern art forbids us to return to anything which can be fairly called conventional, unless in works of a monumental, architectural, or decorative character. The medium course, exactly corresponding to the demands of our time, seems to lie in a careful development of *zoological* character, as distinct from the conventional, on the one hand, and from the merely individual, with its ingenious personality and comparative tenuity of impression, on the other.[7]

Editorial Endnotes

1 Rossetti is referring to the ancient Egyptian red granite statues of lions, found in Nubia and brought to Britain by Lord Prudhoe. They are grandly simplified in treatment.
2 The British Museum's fragmentary wall painting of a fowler in the Nile marshes is from the tomb of Nebamun. His cat, a participant in the hunt, is drawn with a gracefully flowing, simplified contour.
3 This refers to the relief of a lion hunt from the palace of Ashurbanipal at Nineveh, which is also in the British Museum.
4 William Michael Rossetti was an early enthusiast for Japanese art. See Chapter 73 in the present volume.

5 These were artists of the sixteenth and seventeenth centuries.
6 Rossetti is probably thinking of the minute descriptions of nature that were characteristic of the Pre-Raphaelites and their school.
7 Artists such as Richard Friese and Wilhelm Kuhnert did adopt a more 'zoological' or quasi-photographic approach to animal painting. Their work could be described as wildlife art in a way that Landseer's was not (see Chapter 45 in the present work).

Editorial Headnote

39. Anon., 'Landseer's Lions', *Nature and Art* (1867)

An anonymous writer in this short-lived journal passed judgement on Landseer's great bronze sculptures of lions around Nelson's column in Trafalgar Square, London, which had just been unveiled.[1] Again, accurate physical detail and monumental dignity had proved difficult to combine.

Editorial Endnote

1 James A. Manson gives an account of the unveiling of the lions in *Sir Edwin Landseer, R. A.* (London: Walter Scott Publishing and New York: Charles Scribner's Sons, 1902), pp. 165–7.

39

LANDSEER'S LIONS

Anon., Nature and Art

Source: Anon., 'Landseer's lions', *Nature and Art*, 1 (1 March 1867), pp. 86–7.

In the centre of the great square of the capital of England, in the high place of national honour, round the base of the monument which commemorates the most characteristic achievement of our race, are four great masses of bronze wrought into lions, proud emblems for all future Englishmen, of courage and endurance and stately honour. If we say that we do not think Sir Edwin Landseer, to whom we owe these fine works, has risen to the height of such high argument, we in no way impugn his power to do other things. No man need be ashamed of failure in such an undertaking. It would seem almost as if the creation of great emblems was only possible in certain states of society and to certain races of men . . . When men constantly live in the presence of a spiritual world, where the phenomena of life are habitually regarded as the mutable types of some divine quality, we may hope to find an art capable of clothing an abstract idea in clear, tangible form. In the present day such a thing is almost hopeless, for in this matter taste and knowledge will not serve a man as guides. It is not given to us of the modern time to create such forms as the terrible creature that watches, calm, invincible, imperishable, within the walls of our Museum.[1] Who would see what the terror of a lion is, the terror of strength remorseless and just, may there find sufficient reason for saying that our English lions are not of the greatest art, nor indeed in any way fit to rank with the works in which national conviction has expressed itself in certain ages of the world. They are lions such as we have seen in our menageries, but not the British lion. Their manes, too, are rather soft and woolly – one does not see those large divisions where, when the great beast frowns, the hair divides and seams. Again, the uniform colour of the bronze does not render the terror of the fangs, and we think the expression of the mouth somewhat grimacing. The muzzle, also, is perhaps a little sharp for so large a work, which must necessarily be seen against a great background of confused objects. The eyes and forehead are certainly imposing, and wonderfully true to nature; the position of the ears forcible and yet unexaggerated, while the drawing of the head and neck generally is very exact. The finest part, however, of these statues is the back and loins; this portion is really grand, and, if the tail had been carried a little more out, would be as perfect as anything modern art has produced. The paws are not successful; they may be true to nature, but they are not right in art . . . Taking

DOI: 10.4324/9781003107835-47

the lions, however, for what they are, we must grant that Sir Edwin has worked here as well as he ever did. They have all his facility, his elegance of taste and sound knowledge of the form to be rendered. The forms are not of that typical perfection which makes us forget the individual. There is an attempt to render them vast by suppression of small details; but this has not been steadily kept in view, and the lines are rather blurred than sublime.

Editorial Endnote

1 The writer is perhaps referring to a Greek work, the Lion of Knidos (in modern Turkey), which entered the British Museum's collection in 1859.

Editorial Headnote

40. Anon., 'Landseer – Works of the Late Sir Edwin Landseer, R.A,' *British Quarterly Review* (1874)

This was one of many essays prompted by the retrospective exhibition of Edwin Landseer's art at the Royal Academy in 1874, following his death in 1873. Landseer's *physical* realism is again a talking point here, but the writer shows how it may be productive of differing emotions, depending on the thematic context. The aim is to situate Landseer's art within a traditional academic framework of ideas: a hierarchy which places human themes above mere animal portraiture, and high tragedy (whether human or animal) above humour. This extract begins with the writer's analysis of Landseer's painting style.

40

ARTICLE VIII – LANDSEER. – WORKS OF THE LATE SIR EDWIN LANDSEER, R.A.

Anon., British Quarterly Review

Source: Anon., 'Article VIII. – Landseer. – Works of the Late Sir Edwin Landseer, R.A.', *British Quarterly Review* 60:120 (1 October 1874), pp. 514–35.

We cannot understand how anyone can look at these studies and yet affirm that he was not a colourist in the sense of being able to transfer to canvas any hue of beast or bird. Every variety of animal texture; fur and feather, and shaggy hide; sleek marmot, brindled lion, downy softness of white rabbit and harsh splendour of tiger, iridescent glow of pheasant's breast, delicious mottling of wood-cock's wing and cool grey of teal and ptarmigan, green glistening flame of drake's neck and dark stippled russet of the grouse, roguish sparkle of fox's eye, crisp hair of skye terrier, and gloss and curl and tuft of hound and retriever; these, with every touch and tint that goes to body forth the deer from hoof to horn, were within the grasp of Landseer. On a purely technical matter we would not speak dogmatically, but to our thinking Landseer's sleight-of-hand in the management of colour reached its climax, first in the reclining tiger in the Van Amburgh picture (the one with the lamb in it),[1] and again in the Brazilian monkeys in Her Majesty's possession.[2] The light in both of [these] instances seems not so much to rest on the fur as to shimmer over it and through it, and, in the monkeys particularly, has a kind of electric quality – as if it would sparkle when you rubbed it – which, to us at least, is very wonderful. The monkey picture is exquisite also in its humour. The startled yet fascinated and scientific curiosity with which the little creatures, perched upon the pineapple, eye the wasp among the leaves, – they would like excessively to investigate the mystery, but cannot make up their minds that it would be safe, – is very amusing; and if Mr. Darwin, in his book on the relation between man and the lower animals is no fabulist, their expression is so true to monkey nature, that we almost wonder the picture escaped the great naturalist as an illustration and confirmation of his remarks on the dawning of curiosity upon the simian brain[3] . . .

It is to the earlier period of Landseer's art that the pictures which we must pronounce unworthy of him chiefly belong. In these he seems to have vied with Snyders, whose coarse hand did not deserve such homage from Edwin Landseer. He

DOI: 10.4324/9781003107835-48

was betrayed into painting one or two such subjects as the 'Otter Hunt.'[4] Workmanship more masterly can hardly be conceived. Not only are the dogs marvellously life-like, and, crowd of them as there is, sharply individualized, but the huntsman, who holds the writhing otter aloft on the spear, is most dramatically rendered. His thickset form and stalwart limbs, and rude strong face, suit his calling; and, as he bids the dogs keep down, you seem to hear his hoarse accents amid the yelling of the hounds and the rush of the stream. No right human interest or enjoyment, however, can be associated with the agonized writhings of a small animal that has no chance against its enemies; and Landseer appears to have lost liking for the picture, never finishing the companion-work. He passed on to nobler subjects, leaving it to others to paint the ferocity, terror, pain, and rage of the animal creation . . .

A drawing or a painting becomes a work of art in proportion as the spirit of man is breathed into it, – in proportion as it is charged with feeling, thought, or imagination . . . Classifying the pictures of Landseer by this test we find that, putting aside studies, we have to consider, in ascending order, first, his animal portraits and show pictures; secondly, his works of humour; and thirdly, his works of pure and great art.

If it is but seldom that the portrait even of a man or woman becomes a true picture, valuable to the world as well as to relatives and friends, still more rarely can we look for a work of art in the likeness of a dog or a horse. When a dog has been a friend, however, and when the painter has so felicitously suggested the simplicity and sincerity, the limited but faithful sympathy, of doggish friendship, that every observer can comprehend in some measure what it was to its master, a dog-portrait may be admitted to a place, though but a lowly place, within the temple of art. It is almost cruel to tell the hundreds of proud possessors of portraits of horses and hounds by Landseer, that their treasures can with difficulty be admitted to be pictures at all; but when we call to mind the time and energy squandered by this consummate painter in perpetuating the features of nags and lap dogs, our sensibilities become steeled upon the subject. The court and the drawing-room had too much, as we have already hinted, of Edwin Landseer. Princes and nobles petted him, and so they might; for with unapproached grace and brilliancy, he realized for them all that is piquant, sportive, and fascinating, in the companionship of the wealthy and high-born with the unreasoning creatures . . .

Let us not forget, however, that if Landseer painted too many fashionable pictures he did not paint these alone.

By his pictures of humour, we mean such works as 'The Travelled Monkey,' 'Laying Down the Law,' 'High and Low Life,' 'Dignity and Impudence,' 'Jack in Office,' 'The Catspaw,' and many others.[5] All the world has seen and enjoyed these, and they are too frequently regarded not only as eminently characteristic of Landseer, which they are, but as exhibiting his highest power as an artist, which they do not. We have heard it remarked by an epigrammatic critic that Landseer's power consists in putting human eyes into dogs' heads. Even Mr. Ruskin, who has on more than one occasion done frank justice to Landseer, seems to fall into the mistake of founding a general estimate of his art upon his works of humour.

'In our modern treatment of the dog,' says Mr. Ruskin, 'of which the prevailing tendency is marked by Landseer, the interest taken in him is disproportionate to that taken in man, and leads to a somewhat trivial mingling of sentiment, or warping by caricature; giving up the true nature of the animal for the sake of a pretty thought or pleasant jest. Neither Titian nor Velasquez ever jest; and though Veronese jests gracefully and tenderly, he never for an instant oversteps the absolute facts of nature. But the English painter looks for sentiment or jest primarily, and reaches both by a feebly romantic taint of fallacy, except in one or two simple and touching pictures, such as the "Shepherd's Chief Mourner"'.[6]

If Titian and Velasquez never jest, the fact is a proof of the limitation even of their imperial faculties . . . English humour, in its light caricaturing mood, was never more charmingly displayed than in the work of Cruikshank, Leech, and Doyle,[7] and it is a vein of the same national quality that shows itself in the gentle satire of Landseer. Of course he deliberately assumed, in this class of his works, the liberty of the caricaturist. He 'oversteps the absolute facts of nature'; and he does this, not in the earnestness of the highest imagination (which it is the prerogative of sovereign art to do) but in play . . . He has not, we say, confined himself absolutely to the facts of dog-life and monkey-life; but what caricaturist, what fabulist, has with skill so subtle adapted the facts of animal life to suit his purpose, or modified them less traceably? Who shall draw the line between animal character and human character, in such marvels of delicate irony and racy fun as 'The Travelled Monkey' or 'Jack in Office'?[8] Who shall say wherein the dogs of high vulgarity and of low vulgarity, the dogs of dignified reserve and of insolent familiarity, the sycophant dogs, the official red-tape dogs, the wise Lord Chancellor dogs,[9] the greedy dogs, the sentimental dogs, the puppy dogs, the good dogs, pass beyond the canine frontier, and ascend or descend into mere humanity? For our own part we never feel more deeply Landseer's exquisite and comprehensive knowledge of the lower creatures than when we carefully take note of his use of dog gesture, and dog expression, and dog propensity, to point his human moral. In no instance are his dogs more human than in the 'Jack in Office;' but every one of the troop has a look and demeanour not only markedly his own but characteristically doggish, and even the sycophant, who hopes with truly human whine and self-humiliation, to beg his way into Jack's favour and a share of the good things, has an irrefragably canine look about the paws[10] . . . In 'Our Poor Relations' the sick baby and its disconsolate mother are principal; the swarthy doctor in the back-ground, though there is the purest comicality and fine satire in the serene complacency with which he regales himself on the oranges provided for the invalid, is secondary. This also, however, is a picture of humour, and if, on the ground that pathetic humour is by nature higher than comic humour, it is maintained to be Landseer's best work of the kind, we shall not argue the question.[11] To the same class we assign the 'Highland Nurses,' painted about the time of the Crimean War, and dedicated to Miss Nightingale.[12] A wounded stag lies dying on the hill; two hinds hang over him, licking his wounds. This is a work of humour, because the action of the hinds is frankly impossible, but the humour is tragic, not comic. Landseer's pathetic vein was very delicate and sometimes deep.

These pictures, illustrative of animal emulation, of human courage or faithfulness, or of animal mimicry of human vices and foibles, may have a not merely accidental or fanciful connection – M. Taine would probably insist upon this connection as corroborative of his fundamental principle of literary philosophy[13] – with the historical characteristics of a period when science makes it her proudest boast to have unveiled those secret bonds of relationship by which, according to Darwin, Haeckel, and Huxley, the whole family of living things is linked together.[14] Those in which Landseer depicts animals as human pets or playthings have a general tendency to foster that kindliness of regard for the lowlier creatures in which people of the present day, not, perhaps, so theologically orthodox or metaphysically aspiring as former generations, may claim to have realized some small moral improvement[15] . . .

We have spoken of studies, portraits, show-pictures, and pictures of humour; we now approach the most important works of Landseer . . . First of all we take that picture which Mr. Ruskin selected, thirty years ago, as illustrating, with expressive eloquence of imagery and convincing clearness of discrimination, the difference between the language of painting and the ideas, or thoughts, or imaginative suggestions, which are the life of art. Mr Ruskin introduces it as 'one of the most perfect poems or pictures which modern times have seen.' Its name is 'The Old Shepherd's Chief Mourner.'[16]

> 'Here the exquisite execution of the glossy and crisp hair of the dog, the bright, sharp, touching of the green bough beside it, the clear painting of the wood of the coffin and the folds of the blanket, are language – language clear and expressive in the highest degree. But the close pressure of the dog's breast against the wood, the convulsive clinging of the paws, which has dragged the blanket off the trestle, the total powerlessness of the head laid, close and motionless, upon its folds, the fixed and tearful fall of the eye in its utter hopelessness, the rigidity of repose which marks that there has been no motion nor change in the trance of agony since the last blow was struck on the coffin-lid, the quietness and gloom of the chamber, the spectacles marking the place where the Bible was last closed, indicating how lonely has been the life – how unwatched the departure – of him who is now laid solitary in his sleep; these are all thoughts – thoughts by which the picture is separated at once from hundreds, as far as mere painting goes, by which it ranks as a work of high art, and stamps its author, not as the neat imitator of the texture of a skin, or the fold of a drapery, but as the Man of Mind'.[17]

. . . Another great picture is that entitled, with what we can well believe to have been no affected piety, 'Man Proposes, God Disposes'.[18] Again the landscape is wintry, but now we are in solitudes of thick-ribbed Polar ice. The only living things visible are two white bears, prowling for prey. One tears at some woollen fabric, blanket or shawl, which is frozen tight among the ice-blocks beside the fallen and shattered mast. A telescope lies on the snow. The other bear looks up to the icy sky, and snarls and howls, as if disappointed to find no morsel on the human skeleton whose ribs protrude from the snow. The visibility of this skeleton is the one blemish in the picture. It is a homage to the vulgar, of a kind into which Landseer was seldom betrayed. The pathos, the terrible meaning of the work, would have sunk more deeply into the heart without it, for imagination, roused by the frozen raiment and the telescope, would have seen with the mind's eye, keener in its vision than the eye of the body, what lay beneath the snow. But it is a noble picture. Man came here; nature crushed him, and ended him; hungry bears, ghastly, unhappy-looking, forlorn creatures, rend and snarl above his grave. It is the most original and impressive work ever suggested to artist by the tale, sad in its glory, melancholy in its heroism, of Arctic discovery and disaster.

In the 'Random Shot' man has been the minister of the pain that is suffered.[19] In 'Night' and 'Morning,' companion-pictures, there is a representation of that mysterious cruelty which recent science has shown to be interwoven with nature's general treatment of her forest-children, and of which they are themselves the ministers.[20] In the 'Night,' strong moonlight shivers through mist-wreaths that trail dimly along the hills in the wind, ruffling up the lake into stormy spray, and wrapping the landscape in gloom. Two stags occupy the foreground in mutual conflict; their knotted sinews, entangled horns, and bloodshot eyes express the last energy of impassioned rage. In the 'Morning,' all is changed. The clouds have trooped away, the wind has fallen, the lake, still as glass, looks up, like a glad, calm face, to take the sunrise. Beautiful upon the mountains are the feet of the dawn. The brave stags are dead, their limbs rigid as if cast in bronze, their antlers entangled in the final grapple, their eyes fixed in the last glare of defiance. And lo! there, creeping up the hill, fearless now of hoof or antler, the fox comes to breakfast on venison, and the mountain-eagle, winging its way across the lake, will have its share of the feast. So have the monarchs of the glen ended their duel. This is literal fact; a far deeper feeling than humour was in the heart of the painter when he executed the work; it is not fable, but epic.

Editorial Endnotes

1 Landseer's *Isaac Van Amburgh and His Animals* portrayed the American lion tamer in a cage with the snarling big cats. It was painted for Queen Victoria in 1839 and is still in the Royal Collection. Diana Donald, *Picturing Animals in Britain, 1750–1850* (New Haven, CT, and London: Yale University Press, 2007), pp. 192–3.

2 Landseer's *Brazilian Marmosets*, shown at the Royal Academy in 1842, was also painted for the Queen. Richard Ormond, *Sir Edwin Landseer* (Philadelphia Museum of Art and Tate Gallery, London, 1982), pp. 154–5.

3 Darwin discussed the force of curiosity in monkeys in his *Descent of Man*, 1871, part 1, chapter 3, 'Comparison of the mental powers of man and the lower animals'.

4 For Landseer's *Otter Hunt*, see Chapter 36 of the present work.

5 All these paintings are featured in Ormond, *Landseer* (see n. 2).
6 John Ruskin, *Modern Painters*, 1843, vol. 5, chapter 9, section 6.
7 George Cruikshank, John Leech, and Richard Doyle were all nineteenth-century comic draughtsmen.
8 For these works see Ormond, *Landseer*, pp. 58–9 and 104–5.
9 This is an allusion to Landseer's painting *Laying Down the Law*, shown at the Royal Academy in 1840, in which an imagined scene in the Court of Chancery is acted out by dogs. Ormond, *Landseer*, pp. 191–4. Donald, *Picturing Animals*, pp. 149–51.
10 On *A Jack in Office*: Ormond, *Landseer*, pp. 104–6. Donald, *Picturing Animals*, pp. 130–2.
11 For Landseer's *Our Poor Relations* or *The Sick Monkey*, see Chapter 48 of the present work.
12 Donald, *Picturing Animals*, p. 303.
13 Hippolyte Taine believed that literature embodied a response to contemporary historical events.
14 Charles Darwin, Thomas Huxley, and Ernst Haeckel (together with Alfred Russel Wallace) were the leading figures in the exposition of evolutionary theory.
15 The belief that human beings uniquely possessed an immortal soul was threatened by revelations of the evolutionary continuity of life forms – the kinship of animals and humans.
16 Ormond, *Landseer*, pp. 110–11. Ormond, *The Monarch of the Glen: Landseer in the Highlands* (Edinburgh: National Galleries of Scotland, 2005), pp. 68–9. Donald, *Picturing Animals*, pp. 154–8.
17 John Ruskin, 'Definition of greatness in art', *Modern Painters*, 1843, vol. 1, chapter 2, section 4.
18 Ormond, *Landseer*, pp. 207–8. Diana Donald, 'The arctic fantasies of Edwin Landseer and Briton Riviere: polar bears, wilderness and notions of the sublime': Tate Research Publications, *The Art of the Sublime*, 2013, at www.tate.org.uk/art/research-publications/the-sublime/diana-donald-the-arctic-fantasies-of-edwin-landseer-and-briton-riviere. The *British Quarterly Review* writer credits Landseer with genuine 'piety' in this work's title, but it is more likely to reflect his sardonic humour and pessimism.
19 On *A Random Shot*: Ormond, *Landseer*, pp. 172–3. Ormond, *Monarch of the Glen*, pp. 113–14. Donald, *Picturing Animals*, pp. 303–5. See also Chapter 41 of the present work.
20 Ormond, *Monarch of the Glen*, pp. 104–5. Donald, *Picturing Animals*, pp. 97–9. Diana Donald, '"The struggle for existence" in nature and human society', in D. Donald and Jane Munro (eds.), *Endless Forms: Charles Darwin, Natural Science and the Visual Arts* (New Haven, CT, and London: Yale University Press, 2009), pp. 81–99, on pp. 91–3.

Editorial Headnote

41. Anon., 'Landseer', *London Quarterly Review* (1874)

This article was also prompted by the Royal Academy's retrospective exhibition of Landseer's works, but additionally includes a response to F.G. Stephens's *Memoirs of Sir Edwin Landseer* (London: Bell, 1874), with biographical details of the artist. The reviewer exemplifies the wide variety of subject and mood in Landseer's art, its insights into animal psychology, and its connections with Darwinian science. However, it is evident that he feels the need to defend Landseer against charges of toadyism in relation to the aristocratic sporting set, and also of facile crowd-pleasing and vulgarity. The tastes of the cultural elite were already turning against Landseer's kind of pictorial realism.

41

LANDSEER[1]

Anon., London Quarterly Review

Source: Anon., 'Landseer', *London Quarterly Review* 42:83 (April 1874), pp. 49–70.

[pp. 58–62]

Now the first thing that strikes one in a review of Landseer's works is, that a large proportion of them aim at being something different – we will not for the moment say better – than transcripts of animal life, photographs of scenes in which animals play a more or less prominent part. Many of them are this, and this alone, no doubt. The line that divides his art from that of nearly all other animal painters, also separates his own pictures into two distinct classes. On one side of that line are his portraits of individual beasts . . . On the other side of the line are the pictures into which the artist has thrown a peculiar and very subtle charm, educing from his materials, not a direct moral lesson as sturdy William Hogarth would have done, but a power of awakening thought and feeling in others, of stirring them deeply – pictures now idyllic with all the simple happiness in mere living of the brute inhabitants of the field, now epic with their strifes and struggles, their wars and conquests, now dramatic with the play of their strange minds, so mysteriously like and yet unlike our own, now lyric with their joys and griefs – pictures, in short, which, as Mr. Ruskin said, in his healthy earlier admiration for the artist, are poems[2] . . . Practically, no one can fail to recognize that the motive, whatever it was, to which we owe the large portrait of *Voltigeur*, who won the Derby in 1850,[3] was not the same as the inspiration which gave us the *Random Shot*. There is no fault to find with the proportions, or sleek satin skin of the racer, or with the painting of the straw on which he stands, or of the two tortoiseshell cats who roll therein. The technical skill is admirable. But these things neither waken, nor were meant to waken, any responsive chord of feeling in the spectator's mind, unless, possibly, he happened to be a jockey or a betting man. They are quite prosaic. Now turn to the *Random Shot*.[4] A doe, stricken by some untoward ball, has painfully toiled to the summit of a snow-clad slope, and then, after a few, a very few ineffectual struggles, fallen down to die. She lies upon her side, her eyes glassy in death, her limbs stiffening with the cold. Her fawn, a poor dappled little slender brown beastie, has followed her, and now tries to draw from the old motherly fount the drops of sustenance she shall enjoy no more. Such are the simple elements of the picture. But what are words to describe the pitiless beauty

DOI: 10.4324/9781003107835-49

of the evening rose-flush upon the snow, the cruel coldness of the blue shadows and rarefied still air, the fair desolateness of the whole scene? All nature seems to mock the sufferings of these two hapless innocent creatures – the one just dead, the other doomed to die – and smiles on heedless of their fate. The frosty shadows creeping upwards from the lower hills will be almost a relief from the unfeeling splendour of the sunlight.

It is in the works of which this is a noble specimen – works in which the poetry of animal life, running so curiously parallel to the poetry of human life, is strikingly embodied, that Landseer's originality is, to our thinking, most shown. The older masters painted animals but sparingly, and seldom introduced them as a principal element in their pictures . . . So again, among modern animal painters he holds a most distinct place. He has imitators, no doubt, like Mr. Riviere – certainly not rivals . . . Messrs. Ansdell and Cooper represent fairly the average standard of animal painting.[5] But in none of these is there Landseer's vein of poetry; not one has seen so far into brute nature, and passed by so entire a transmigration into the beast's soul, into its limited blind feeling, so simple and often so strong, and its groping rudimentary reasonings.

Of course we are perfectly aware of the counter-accusation that has been brought against the painter in this matter. It has been said, over and over again – for the remark once made seemed too acute to be allowed to drop – all this pretended insight is a mere *ad captandum* trick. Landseer seemed to be revealing the animal's inner mind, and unvailing what may be called its personality, when in fact he was only putting a man's mind into the form of an animal. His beasts are no more beasts than those of Æsop or La Fontaine. They might just as well, for any truth to their real natures, allow their 'rank tongues to blossom into speech,' and conclude with an improving moral.[6] Now, in answering this objection, we are, in some sense, impeded by the many-sidedness of Landseer's art. Animals may be treated in several ways. They may be considered, according to the mode just indicated, as mere pegs, on which to hang caricatures of humanity; some, on the other hand – as Swift for instance – have regarded them as the nobler type of beings, of which humanity itself was the caricature, the contrast between the Yahoo and the equine creatures with the unpronounceable name being very forcibly insisted upon.[7] The Darwinites look upon them as men in a more or less partial state of development; and most of us, whether or not we have any theory to account for the resemblance, must recognise in them the rudiments of a mind and conscience akin to our own. By all these aspects of his subject Landseer was at various times impressed. It *is* true that in some, not many, of his pictures, the animal is not really, essentially, an animal at all . . . The *Laying Down the Law*, and *Diogenes and Alexander*, and *Jack in Office* are confessedly – their very names imply it – scenes that have had their counterpart in human life. But here a very important distinction has to be drawn. The scene is human – in the case of the *Laying Down the Law* we confess altogether too artificial for our taste – but the dogs are not human.[8] Everyone who has lived in the familiar intercourse of affection with these beasts, and watched them habitually and narrowly, will bear us out when we say that the expression of face and attitude in all these various hounds and bull-dogs, terriers, spaniels, and nondescripts, are perfectly possible and very characteristic. No one, of course, has ever seen quite so effective a *tableau vivant* as is formed by some of these groups. But astute and foxy-looking dogs, dogs of a courtier-like solemnity, dogs proletarian and mendicant, dogs pompous and overbearing, dogs refined and gentlemanly, dogs vulgar and demoralized – in short, all the wonderful assortment of canine creatures to be found on the master's canvasses – these one may recognise as thoroughly and amazingly real . . . If the *Monarch of the Glen* reminds one faintly of a human gallant, vain of his successes with the fair sex, or the *Sick Monkey* recalls a suffering child, it is because similar causes produce similar results, and because the deer, the ape, and man have somewhat in common.[9]

[p. 64]

Then there are deer, too, in every variety of circumstance – stags locked in deadly combat for the lordship of their frightened herds, or bellowing defiance at one another across a moon-lit lake, or breasting the angry waters in a vain attempt to escape from the pursuing hounds, or turning round on those hounds, and keeping them at bay in majestic fury; or wearily reaching, faint, dripping, and yet saved, some desired haven of refuge; or, lying down, wounded and dying, amid kindly and helpful does. And besides these animals, what shall we say of horses, goats, sheep, oxen, pigs . . . monkeys, lions, polar bears, and numerous others, down to hedgehogs, to say nothing of feathered fowl innumerable? This is indeed a menagerie, a happy family,[10] a zoological garden, a compendium of animated nature; but the variety is not more singular – nay, is less so – than the completeness and individuality of each representation . . .

[pp. 68–70]

We have already spoken of the *Random Shot*. There is no faltering here, but a difficult and unusual effect of light rendered with peculiar delicacy, the whole in perfect keeping. So also in the *Hunted Stag*, that poor 'strong swimmer in his agony,' who has just overturned one of the pursuing dogs, and strains every nerve to escape from the second, there is no shortcoming to deplore.[11] The vigour of the action, the arrowy directness with which the fierce beast makes for the deer's throat, the despair in the upturned face with its glaring eyeballs, the boiling of the water around the combatants, the storm that is lashing the lake into angry foam – all these are not more admirable than the powerful painting and colour. Nor in the *Stag at Bay*, as he stands in his pride, knee-deep in water, fronting his foes and compelling their respect,[12] – nor again in the *Event in the Forest*, where the fox and the eagle are gathering together at the fall of an antlered monarch of the glen, who lies prone amid the wintry rocks[13] – nor in these, nor in the painter's other similar great works of poetical art, do we think the characteristic fault is to be found. Nor yet finally in that which, according to our judgment, is his greatest picture, pregnant with bitter meaning as a chapter in Ecclesiastes, sad with the unfulfilled projects of life, cheered but by the rays of an eternal and uncertain twilight, the picture which shows how *man has proposed and God disposed,* – how the men who steered northward, in manly enterprise and hope, seeking the great undiscovered passage, have found no resting place even for their bones amid the weird translucent iceheaps, and make but a meal for the hungry bears.[14]

There are certain critics who regard popularity as the unpardonable sin . . . All we wish to show is that there is a certain class of art, and that the very greatest, which is universal in its appeal, and rises superior to intellectual class distinctions, and that in railing against popularity we are in danger of overlooking this truth . . . But in power of drawing and painting animal life, of expressing insight into animal character and sympathy with animal feeling, in the divine faculty of casting a halo of poetry over his subject – in these he has never been surpassed.

Editorial Endnotes

1 The *London Quarterly Review* is a different journal from the *British Quarterly Review* featured in Chapter 40.
2 The writer refers here to Ruskin's eulogy on Landseer's painting *The Old Shepherd's Chief Mourner*, which is now in the Victoria & Albert Museum.
3 Landseer's portrait of the successful racehorse Voltigeur was commissioned by the animal's owner, Lord Zetland, and shows the horse in his stable with two playful cats as companions.
4 Richard Ormond, *Sir Edwin Landseer* (Philadelphia Museum of Art and Tate Gallery, London, 1982), pp. 172–3. Ormond, *The Monarch of the Glen: Landseer in the Highlands* (Edinburgh: National Galleries of Scotland, 2005), pp. 113–14. Diana Donald, *Picturing Animals in Britain, 1750–1850* (New Haven, CT, and London: Yale University Press, 2007), pp. 303–5. Sportsmen were supposed to avoid killing the female animals, but in deer drives, when the whole herd ran in front of the guns, it could hardly be avoided. From one of Friedrich Keyl's notes on his conversations with Landseer (27 November 1869), it is clear that the latter himself took part in shoots on deer drives (see Chapter 42).
5 For Briton Riviere see Chapters 52–4 in the present collection. Richard Ansdell and Thomas Sidney Cooper were also animal painters, Ansdell being particularly well represented in the collection of the Walker Art Gallery, Liverpool.
6 Aesop and La Fontaine wrote fables in which animals take on human characteristics. The quotation is from Robert Browning's poem 'Caliban upon Selebos', which in turn alludes to Shakespeare's *The Tempest*. The bestial Caliban, subject to the will of Prospero, here aspires to eloquent articulacy.
7 In Part IV of Jonathan Swift's *Gulliver's Travels* (1726), Gulliver encounters the 'Houyhnhnms' – intelligent speaking horses who exert wise rule and control over the 'Yahoos' (human beings).
8 For Landseer's *Laying Down the Law*, see Chapter 40 of the present work, n. 9.
9 For *The Monarch of the Glen*, see Ormond, *Landseer*, pp. 174–5. Ormond, *Monarch of the Glen: Landseer* (Edinburgh: National Galleries of Scotland, 2017). For *The Sick Monkey*, see Chapter 48 of the present work.
10 'Happy families' were cages containing assorted animals, including carnivores, that appeared to co-exist peaceably without conflict or predation. The cages were pitched by showmen in the London streets, in the hope of receiving coins from intrigued passersby.
11 The quotation is from Byron's *Don Juan*, canto II, stanza 53. *The Hunted Stag* is now generally known as *Deer and Deerhounds in a Mountain Torrent*. Ormond, *Landseer*,

p. 81. Ormond, *Monarch of the Glen*, pp. 54–5. Donald, *Picturing Animals in Britain*, pp. 96–8, 299.

12 For *The Stag at Bay*, see Ormond, *Monarch of the Glen*, pp. 114–15.

13 For *An Event in the Forest*, see Ormond, *Monarch of the Glen*, pp. 124–6.

14 For *Man Proposes, God Disposes*, see Chapter 40, n. 18. The picture referred to the loss of Sir John Franklin's expedition, which had set out to discover the 'northwest passage' – a potential sea route north of Canada and Alaska to the Pacific Ocean.

Editorial Headnote

42. Edwin Landseer's Conversations With Friedrich Keyl

Some of artist Edwin Landseer's conversations with Friedrich Keyl were recorded by the latter, in manuscripts that are now in the Royal Archives, Windsor Castle. Keyl, an animal painter and zoological illustrator, had been a pupil or studio assistant of Landseer and was often invited back to his house in the later 1860s. Keyl seems to have jotted down notes or 'memos' of their conversations after he got home, perhaps with the idea of writing a memoir of Landseer at a later stage. However, Keyl himself died in 1871, and none of the manuscripts were ever published. They are often very difficult to decipher and contextualise but do nevertheless throw light on Landseer's psychology and moods in his later years. The vitality, sociable charm, and humour of his youth and middle years had gradually given way to a bitterly cynical state of mind, an ingrained pessimism, and his passionate but conflicted feelings about wild animals took on a dark tone. Many of these conversations, often in the presence of other visitors, were gossip about the art world and high society, but Landseer's hostility to religion, his general cynicism, and his strong views on art and science also emerge.

In the first quoted passage, Landseer relived his experience of deerstalking in the Scottish Highlands, giving Keyl a dramatic blow-by-blow account of the pursuit of a stag with the dog Lassie, and apparently acting out the stag's movements and expressions as he spoke: he both hunted it and identified with it. He also detached, preserved, and stuffed the stag's head, later using it as a model when painting his huge *Deer of Chillingham Park*, for the Earl of Tankerville's dining room – a work of which Keyl was privately critical. As mentioned, Landseer scoffed at conventional religious faith and made unfeeling jibes about the religious works which Keyl illustrated. Yet he was apparently just as critical of Darwinism and of theorising about nature in general: a dismissiveness which Keyl attributed to Landseer's lack of formal education and consequent unwillingness to engage in scientific or philosophical debates. His affectionate intimacy with his dogs, who were his daily companions, comes over clearly, though their relationships with him are sometimes expressed with mordant humour. Charles Dickens's famous public readings from his novel *Oliver Twist*, especially the account of Bill Sikes's murder of Nancy and his flight from justice, tailed by his dog, prompted a discussion of how faithful such a dog would actually be to a brutal owner.

42

LANDSEER'S CONVERSATIONS WITH FRIEDRICH KEYL IN 1866–70

Source: Keyl's manuscript notes of his conversations with Landseer. Friedrich Keyl

31 August 1866 (MS.RA VIC/ADDX14/2O/1)

. . . So they go back to place of shot measuring the 20 or 50 yards I forget . . . and then Lassie examines every trifle every blade [of grass] at last Carr says I think we may say the Deer is safe now, put a string round her neck & away . . . They follow it & find him in the water – the bitch before him (But I cannot write the Imitation of voice & gesture & expression of the very Animals the Deer head up & neck, eye faintly rolling in Corner, the very ears seemed to go back). He broke his neck by a Bullet & so ended him. – You will see the head when it comes in about a fortnight & if you had been with me you would have agreed it was so beautiful . . . Many graphic remarks came in between illustrated by his small expressively beautiful hands (yet they are manly) how for instance when the hinds suspect who[?] are on the watch all with their Ears up they stand motionless – hundreds of Gnats Flies Midges settle about their eyes, Ears, Nostrils, but they never blink nor wince, stand motionless till satisfied, they at last will shake their heads stoop down to find the grass again. Then you must not move either till they move or the hind gives a bark, and all is over . . . (all this is imitated to perfection) . . . In stalking Sir E. says you must always look where you tread the Deer hears & distinguishes the snapping of a twig by man's foot. Patience and this overcoming difficulties make the pleasure . . . there are only two Places the size of a half Crown in a Deer's head where you kill & I have seen the greatest Cruelty committed by firing at head – A Deer with his Jaw dangling, the Dogs tearing out & eating his tongue of the poor Deer yet getting away . . . He thought whether it was insensibility lower organisation or extreme vitality which enabled Deer to overcome wounds as he does . . .

9 April 1867 (MS. RA VIC/ADDX14/20/3)

The Deer picture had all his great Qualities, but I had not the heart seeing how dejected and tired he was to tell him I thought the head of the Stag too small for body and in his desire for breadth the body of Fawn losing itself in frame is too thick its neck too short.[1] The Stag's head itself is lovely in Character & Drawing the Antlers moderate – I presently asked him whether it was the old Stag he stalked (whose skin he had prepared) he said he used him as a foundation . . .

DOI: 10.4324/9781003107835-50

Timidity is not want of courage. A Deer will run away as long as he can so will the Bull. But at bay fights with great skill and Courage and dies without a sigh. They also ran upon Jaques and the weeping Deer[2] which led to scent question & pear-shaped Cavity.[3] He told me Millais, Ansdell and Elmore had been[4] . . . He feared the things would look too sketchy and he would be hauled over the Coals. They said only let them get in their places and they will look the most finished things there . . . Sir E. sent for Lassie – who had been confined to Stable on account of being in a state. – She jumped into his Arms like Myrtle used to do, then he said into her ears if you will be so foolish you must be shut up & was so nice with her. Praised her as a sitter, put her down, Stuck a Brush in her mouth one in each hind leg &c.[5] . . . He then said how he had kept all sorts of Dogs – How he had two Pointers, (I was very keen then he said) the best in all England – I suppose you saw a picture I painted of them life-size, every hair was painted[6] – Somebody gave me 60£ for it, and it has been sold since for I believe 1200 . . .

7 November 1867 (MS. RA VIC/ADDX14/20/6).

Sir E.: Nobody sees Deer on the hill, though they stand before you – I do, because I know the colour, texture and where to look for them. You will find that all animals who are prolific and greatly destructive to agriculture are soon seen and at any distance. Rooks for instance are Black, Rabbits have the white Fur which tells the moment they move. But animals that are game and scarcer assimilate to their haunts. Nobody can see a Woodcock among Ferns – I believe it was from struggle for life, but I forget how, he drifted on to say, that God in Creating Made a mistake and his world too small, and in order to get rid of his (men) creatures invented religion – and religious wars, in which they exterminate each other and have from all time[7] . . . Small talk on the Schwabe's whom he had seen in Marochetti's Studio at time of modelling the Lions.[8] He said: Our world is but a young one – I told Lutyens so the other day[9] – Time is quite a relative Idea – The Butterfly thinks its life a long one. The World is now full of Barbarism . . .

. . . the Otter occasionally will go for a mile or two as straight as a Fox. – I was surprised – he said not at all – it is the built [sic] of a Stoat or Weasel. Miss Jessi[10] thought it lived in the water. – He: It only goes in to fish, when hungry. The Cairn of an Otter is beautifully lined with soft things and as dry and as warm as can be. – like the Ptarmigan are under their rocks . . .

Also of Revd J.G. Wood's Natural History of Bible Drawings[11] – He said why of Bible? A Catch penny I suppose. – I said it comprised a familiar Group of Animals which everybody knew and was interested about, that Wood had something new to say on things – He: how do you treat them: I explained – he said: – Well if a School boy is to learn from it I should do as Bewick did and draw the Animal.[12] I could only reply the Book was meant for mature Readers too – that it would become a Sunday book – as Hark the Vespers hymn is stealing became a Sunday piece . . . I then told him how the Book of Job was the first Expression of a feeling for Natural history in those days and had a similitude with the beginnings of Art – as a long time always elapses ere the Art or the Science were the chief motive for a book or a Picture . . .

Naturalists are no use – Owen and all these people only write Latin descriptions of the animal & when you get them translated there is nothing in them.[13] When I kill an Animal I always try to get to know it as well as I can. But they never tell one or try to find out how a fish sees for instance he swims upright at the Bottom of a pool how does he see & distinguish the fly that tempts him most on the surface of the water 12 or 15 feet overhead. – The eye of a Snake is a little motionless Slit – covered with horny scale and yet a Python 20 feet long dashing from his lair a distance of 15 feet at the most vulnerable part of the passing Prey and killing it with the greatest Accuracy must be a good Marksman – I said this knowledge was chiefly a Catalogue one, but that for instance Revd. J.G. Wood had some such things to say. – I then told him how harpooning Crocodile & Ostrich hunt for same work had taken me to Mr Baines the African traveller and how much I liked his things[14] – how new they were and how every where Nature finds cover & safety for its creatures . . .

6 January 1869 (MS. RA VIC/ADDX14/20/8)

I told him how I was worried by the intermittent bark and yelp of a very pretty blue Skye Terrier opposite my window – how would he like that – this led to his saying he disliked so-called blue in Dogs, even in Greyhounds, and that it was a meagre colour. He liked brown yellow black a generous colour all mixed together. He thinks he will have a smallish black and tan Spaniel and give away Browny who spends her life only in eating and sleeping and getting fat – he is sure to take her up some day by the tail and dash her against the wall – Spaniels are so good in Colour and are attached . . . Nothing can exceed his picturing beauty and the loyalty of Lassie. Absence makes no difference to her, nor does it to Tracker – He will lay for hours on his chair in the Painting room – vide previous Memos – . . . and nothing moves but what he gives a low little growl . . . We then harked back to Dogs and Myrtle whose blue was broken with brown brindle. – He: She was the best of all Dogs . . . Reminiscences came of Punch (which he said he gave to Lady Rachel Russell) the Campden Hill Spaniel – Pickle Lord E. Russell's yellow Terrier a little stupid. I told him I thought most so called Skye & Scotch Terriers Pecksniffs of Dogs.[15] Then I told him . . . how Wilkinson's Persian Russian Greyhound . . . seeing the hare ~~go~~ wriggle through a Gate he thought he must do so too and lost his advantage – beating himself after a mighty jump & effort to get up to her to a Standstill. He smiled and said Well done Hare . . .

25 February 1869 (MS. RA VIC/ADDX14/20/9).

He took opposite sides in all we started . . . He then asked me if I knew any of the modern Philosophers – what are their Names. Huxley how old is he about 50, told him how nice [?] he was over the first dead porpoise he dissected. Then I said there is Darwin, Wallis [sic], Mr. Blyth[16] . . . He: all these men who know Latin Names can bother the Public very much, but they know really nothing and have no observation of living things. He thought that our Lord had got in a bother with Man – whom he perhaps created and was responsible for to somebody more powerful – and so he allowed every thousand years some fellow to start up with a new religion . . . and he prevents their speaking one Language and so gets rid of them by war & disease & hunger. We discussed Darwinist Ideas of Creation, he thought I had it all at my fingers Ends but he could not agree . . .

22 March 1869 (MS. RA VIC/ADDX14/20/10).

Sir E.'s want of reading and Education makes him constantly take up opposite sides in talk – as a certain smartness of repartee is soon obtained. He can not argue properly nor follow argument. Looking at Laying down the Law & Stag at Bay at same time. Good as the first is – it is cocquettish [sic] & artificial and below the 2d [17] . . . Wolf told me how somebody had said to him Sir E's Art is admirable his Natural History abominable[18] . . . Talk began about Dickens's readings, to which he and some friends had been[19] . . . He left out the bit with Dog. He thought (I praised it as a true bit of observation) Dogs with their loving devoted nature did not sit in judgement on the acts of their master. I replied I never thought so, but that the Dog of a Ruffian who had to take his own line of action so much & by kicks & blows had become an observer of temper, would not come because he thought from Sykes's manner and tone it would not be safe. – He thought first oh yes he would unless he showed him a stick but after a time agreed to my notion and said it had not occurred to him in that light and he thought it was good.

5 February 1870 (MS. RA VIC/ADDX14/20/13).

At Windsor – Miss Davis's quiet little room thought of Random Shot & the curious Coincidence with my fawn & dead Doe[20] the latter was suggested through crust on deep snow freezing . . . lots dying from hunger & exhaustion & lesion of their feet by hard Crust which broke in at every Step. I had not the Pluck to make it Snow – which he had (also falsely constructed Shadows) The original Drawing has no snow one of his Chalks – Highland Sport written underneath – The Scheme of Light & Shade and Colour carried the day over literality – and as he told me the Speculation – Springs parental love – never failing the lacteal Springs dried up &c. &c. It is one of his most refined bits of Pathos . . .

Editorial Endnotes

1 Landseer's *Deer of Chillingham Park, Northumberland* and *Wild Cattle of Chillingham* were companion pictures destined for the 6th Earl of Tankerville's dining hall at Chillingham Castle; both were exhibited at the Royal Academy in 1867. Richard Ormond, *Sir Edwin Landseer* (Philadelphia Museum of Art and Tate Gallery, London, 1982), pp. 210–12.

2 In Shakespeare's *As You Like It*, act 2, scene 1, 'The melancholy Jaques' reportedly sympathised with the sufferings of a hunted and wounded stag, whose 'big round tears/ Coursed one another down his innocent nose'.

3 It was claimed that this cavity in a stag's skull allowed it to be shot and killed outright, rather than being mangled and made to suffer a slow death.
4 John Everett Millais, Richard Ansdell, and Alfred Elmore were fellow artists, preparing works for the opening of the annual Royal Academy exhibition.
5 In the margin of the manuscript, Keyl has here sketched a 'vignette' of the dog lying on her back with the brushes tied to her legs – captioned 'looked too much like skewers'.
6 *Pointers* was shown at the Royal Academy in 1820, when Landseer was only seventeen. Ormond, *Landseer*, p. 52.
7 Despite Landseer's posture of hostility to Darwin and Darwinism, and his sense of a world out of joint, he had evidently absorbed the theory of concealing coloration as an aspect of 'the struggle for life'.
8 Landseer's bronze lions for the Nelson monument in Trafalgar Square, London, were cast in the studio of the sculptor Baron Carlo Marochetti.
9 The soldier, sportsman, and artist Charles Augustus Henry Lutyens was a close friend of Landseer and named his son, who became a leading architect, Edwin Landseer Lutyens.
10 'Miss Jessi' was Jessica, Landseer's sister and housekeeper.
11 Keyl was one of a team of artists working on the illustrations to the Revd John George Wood's *Bible Animals: Being a Description of Every Living Creature Mentioned in the Scriptures, From the Ape to the Coral, with One Hundred New Designs* by W.F. Keyl, T.W. Wood and E.A. Smith (London: Longmans, 1868).
12 Landseer is suggesting that the illustrations should show the animals alone, in a clear profile view, as in Bewick's *A General History of Quadrupeds*, 1790. However, *Bible Animals*, like Wood's other illustrated books, has exciting action scenes – cf. Chapter 93 in the present work.
13 Richard Owen and, later, Darwin, Huxley, and other leading natural scientists became the objects of Landseer's dismissive scorn. It is true that the study of animal behaviour in the wild was then in its infancy, but, as Keyl remarks, Revd Wood sought to evoke it, drawing on explorers' narratives.
14 Thomas Baines accompanied David Livingstone on his African journeys and was an original painter of animals in the wild. Diana Donald, *Picturing Animals in Britain 1750–1850* (New Haven, CT, and London: Yale University Press, 2007), pp. 177–8, with bibliographical references on p. 341, n. 97.
15 Dickens's Mr. Pecksniff in *Martin Chuzzlewit* is a self-serving hypocrite.
16 'Wallis' is Alfred Russel Wallace. Edward Blyth was a zoologist who worked on Indian ornithology.
17 Keyl prefers Landseer's scenes of life in the natural world to the comic anthropomorphism of works like *Laying Down the Law*, an imagined scene in the Court of Chancery acted out by dogs.
18 The artist Joseph Wolf rejected Landseer's kind of humorous play-acting in animal representations. See Chapters 19 and 43 in the present collection.
19 Dickens staged dramatic public readings from his own novels: the account of Bill Sykes's murder of Nancy and its aftermath in *Oliver Twist* was especially famous. Evidently some passages about Sykes's relationship with his dog were cut from the live narration.
20 Keyl compares his own realistic image of a doe and her fawn, frozen to death, with Landseer's much more artful and famous *A Random Shot*, revealing that the latter was largely a work of the imagination. Ormond, *Landseer*, pp. 172–3. Donald, *Picturing Animals*, pp. 303–5.

Figure 9 Joseph Wolf, *The Life and Habits of Wild Animals*, 1874, 'The Struggle', lithograph from Wolf's drawing. (Biodiversity Heritage Library)

Editorial Headnote

43. Joseph Wolf, *The Life and Habits of Wild Animals* (1874)

The artist Joseph Wolf (see also Chapters 19 and 93) worked on this project with the Whympers, who were high-quality wood engravers, and with the American zoologist Daniel Giraud Elliot, who wrote commentaries on the images.[1] However, Wolf himself evidently invented these scenes of animals in conflict or distress, so typical of the period. There is here an intrinsic pessimism and fatalism about the workings of nature, which makes harsh weather itself an enemy; and some episodes are presented as high tragedy, investing the animal victims with a quasi-human consciousness. 'The Struggle' (see Figure 9) describes a trial of strength between a tiger and a crocodile in their native Indian habitat, while 'Hunted Down' is about the suffering and death of a hunted hare.

Editorial Endnote

1 Daniel Giraud Elliot also authored and published expensive zoological folios, illustrated by Wolf and others. See Chapter 19 of the present work, n. 5.

43

THE LIFE AND HABITS OF WILD ANIMALS[1]

Joseph Wolf

Source: Joseph Wolf, *The Life and Habits of Wild Animals Illustrated by Designs by Joseph Wolf, engraved by J.W. and Edward Whymper. With Descriptive Letter-press by Daniel Giraud Elliot, F.L.S., F.Z.S.* (London: Alexander Macmillan, 1874), pp. 9–13, 39–41.

[pp. 9–13]

. . . Having now given a cursory review of the two creatures depicted in our illustration, we will witness the mode by which they became engaged in the tremendous struggle which will end only in the death of one of them. The sun is just rising, flooding the eastern sky with golden light, and rousing the feathered inhabitants of the forests from their slumbers. Shaking the dew, that lies in diamond drops, from off their brilliant plumage, they awake the echo of the woods with their morning songs of praise; whilst sated with the results of his nightly foray, and in the company of his mate, the jungle's fierce monarch turns towards the stream to quench his thirst, before seeking a lair in which to dream away the unwelcome day. Noiselessly they thread the well-known thickets, unmindful now of the many active forms of joyous life around them. The playful monkey swings his supple body to the branch above, and, unregarded, chatters forth his mingled rage and fear at the passing figure of his most dreaded foe. The stream is reached, and, more cautious than her lord, the tigress stops to take a look beyond the leafy screen; but he steps at once into the water and commences to lap it into his mouth. Lying close to the shore, its eyes with their stony glare alone exposed, a crocodile has lain, perhaps for hours, patiently waiting for such an opportunity as now presents itself. With an imperceptible movement, that gives not the slightest ripple to the surface, the scaly legs are drawn towards the body, and as the tiger stoops again to the water, with a rush so rapid as to defy the eye to follow it, the powerful reptile seizes the unfortunate animal's head in its armed jaws. With a half-stifled roar of rage and surprise, the tiger endeavours to withdraw himself from the cruel grasp, while his foe, lashing the waters into foam, strives to drag him into the stream, unheeding the heavy blows the tiger deals it with its paw, the sharp claws of which however glance harmlessly from off the mailed-covering of the reptile's head. Step by step the animal is dragged away from the bank, struggling against

DOI: 10.4324/9781003107835-51

his horrible fate with the energy of despair; but as the water deepens, his power of resistance grows feebler, while the crocodile at home in his native element, redoubles its exertions, and forcing the tiger's head beneath the stream, by a few quickly repeated, powerful efforts disappears with its prey to the bottom of the river. – A few fast-widening circles spreading towards the opposing banks – a few bubbles brilliant in rainbow hues, floating with the tide, and perhaps an occasional, ominous red spot rising to the surface, are the sole remaining witnesses of the terrible, deadly struggle that had just terminated . . .
[pp. 39–41]

HUNTED DOWN

The members of the Crow Family are generally associated with gloomy thoughts and funereal events, chiefly perhaps from their dress of black that seems to array them in a garb of mourning . . . we associate with these birds the saddest period of the year, when all the flowers have drooped and died, and nature, bereft of her summer beauty, awaits the joyful resurrection of the spring-time. No poor wearied creature, sinking under the fierce blast, wounded perhaps, need hope to escape these pilferers; for quickly spying it out they stoop around it, only delaying their attacks until the evidence of all active life is gone . . . Night is drawing slowly on, the sun is setting in clouds and thick mist, and the wind moans sadly over the cheerless landscape . . . At such a time, one would suppose, every animal would keep under shelter, and that nothing but the pangs of hunger could induce any of the wild dwellers of the woods to brave the chill blast that is sweeping over the face of the land. But, yonder, moving slowly, evidently in pain, one small limb hanging useless, struck perhaps by the pellets from some sportsman's gun, a wounded hare is seeking some friendly shelter to hide herself from the cutting wind, and her no less relentless pursuer. How she must long for the warm form,[2] from which she was so suddenly startled but a short time since, by the dog which had discovered her retreat, and where she had sat thinking perhaps of the moon-light night in the pleasant summer-time, when she had played upon the soft green sward – and then, as the snow went whirling by, nestled all the closer in her warm nest.

But the spot she is accustomed to regard as home (for even the lower animals have such to which they constantly resort) is far away now, and weary with her efforts to escape, and faint from the deadly wound, she struggles on, if only perchance she may reach a place of safety. And now she can go no farther, and by the side of a slender stalk, that of itself can give no protection, she has drawn herself up, and with her long ears laid upon her back remains exposed to all the severity of the approaching winter's night. Alas! poor pussy,[3] not even there can you be left at peace; for the scavengers of the air have already found you out, and with wonderful instinct have discovered your failing strength, and come swiftly, with many a boding croak, to sweep over your crouching form. Well they know that soon your bright eye will grow dim, and undeterred by even any semblance of life, they may work their will upon that which was only lately so replete with vigour, and graceful activity. Yes, you start! for their funereal wings almost touch you as they brush closely by, as if the ill-omened birds could not restrain their impatience, nor wait until that gentle head should sink upon the snow. The wind as it rushes by soughs through the branches singing a requiem, and with a rough kindliness tosses the feathery flakes around, as if it would shield the drooping animal in an unsullied shroud; then, as the darkening night drives the winged enemies to seek their own shelter, the blast, more friendly than any of the poor thing's fellow creatures, will hide the lifeless form in a pure white covering, that the rising sun shall cause to glow in his flashing rays.

Editorial Endnotes

1 A.H. Palmer, *The Life of Joseph Wolf, Animal Painter* (London and New York: Longmans, Green, 1895), pp. 198–209. Diana Donald, *Picturing Animals in Britain, 1750–1850* (New Haven, CT, and London: Yale University Press, 2007), pp. 92–4.
2 A form is a hollow in the ground that a hare makes for itself as a shelter.
3 A hunted hare was often referred to as 'pussy', and often assumed to be female.

Editorial Headnote

43.1. Anon, 'Christmas Books', *Times* (1873)

The *Times* reviewer of Joseph Wolf's *The Life and Habits of Wild Animals* entered fully into the drama and tragedy inherent in Wolf's images of the natural world and recognised their echoes of contemporary scientific theory on 'the survival of the fittest'.

43.1

CHRISTMAS BOOKS IV

Anon., Times

Source: Anon, 'Christmas Books IV', *Times*, 25 December 1873, p. 4.

A number of Fine Art publications – indeed, some of the best of the season – still claim our notice. Foremost among these we must place Wolf's *Wild Animals* (Macmillan) – a magnificent volume, the illustrations of which are alike admirable as drawings and as specimens of the art of the wood-engraver. They are drawn by Mr. Joseph Wolf, who is not only a famous artist of picture-books, but one of the best animal painters of his day. These drawings well exhibit the marvellous skill with which he depicts not only the outward forms, the fur and hair and feathers of the animal kingdom, but the very soul and character of the wild creatures which inhabit them. The subjects of his pictures are chosen with artistic skill, and each one of them testifies to a close study and accurate knowledge of the habits of birds and beasts. Mr. Wolf is also an acute observer of nature, and his pencil may be depended on, whether it sketches forest or mountain, field or flood. Each of his pictures tells a story, and seizes hold of some episode in the lives of its creatures which brings vividly before us the conditions of their daily existence. The combats and captures, the escapes and ambuscades, so admirably given in the different drawings, are a forcible picture of the never-ending struggle for existence among the animal creation. The principle of the sacredness of life is recognized by man alone, and perhaps it would be impossible to separate him from the lower animals by a sharper definition than this. Each of Mr. Wolf's pictures is a delightful lesson in natural history. The gorilla, swinging from a branch by his long arms, and searching the forest with his fierce eyes, while his mate makes off with her little one in her arms, rabbits bolting into their hole, an owl with its claw already in the fur of one of them; a struggle between a tiger and a crocodile; a bear at bay over the body of a dead hunter; a fish-hawk seizing its prey, that has swum too near the surface of the calm water of a highland loch; a boar bated by wolves, – such, and suchlike, are the subject of the twenty illustrations. If we may venture on criticism of such admirable work, we would ask Mr. Wolf whether the tiger which the crocodile has seized by the head at the water's edge is not too fat and comfortable-looking, and whether he ought not to have been drawn leaner in the flank, especially as in such a terrible tussle, at the moment when the crocodile's jaws are closing on his head, his muscles would be contracted by an indrawn breath and by his violent efforts to release himself? Is it also quite right that the lynx, who is waiting to spring on some goats, should be so many feet above them as the comparative size of objects in the drawing would seem to show that he is? But these are little matters, and we could fill a column with praise of the inimitable truth with which the artist has put on paper the inward nature as well as the outward appearance of the creatures he has drawn. The choice of subjects is very clever, and nothing can be finer than the picture of a lion raising his head from a dead antelope to roar at the lightning. The wood engraving is by Messrs. J.W. and Edward Whymper; they have never done better work, and it would be hard to match it anywhere. The letter-press is no mere inventory of the engravings, but consists of some most pleasant chapters of natural history, written by Mr. D.G. Elliot, the well-known American naturalist. As we close this exquisite volume, we cannot help thinking what pleasure it would have given Sir Edwin Landseer to turn over its pages.

Editorial Headnote

43.2. Anon., Review of Wolf's *Life and Habits of Wild Animals* in *The Art Journal* (1874)

This reviewer also aimed to bring out the excitement and pathos of Joseph Wolf's imagined scenes.

43.2

REVIEW OF WOLF'S *LIFE AND HABITS OF WILD ANIMALS*

Anon., The Art Journal

Source: Anon., 'Wolf's *Life and Habits of Wild Animals*', *The Art Journal* 36, new series 13 (1874), pp. 31–2.

Rarely, if ever, have we seen animal-life more forcibly and beautifully depicted than in this really splendid volume. As a painter of the untamed beasts of the forest and the wild feathered tribes of the air, Mr. Wolf has long made himself conspicuously known in this country, and in this series of illustrations he seems to have put forth all the power of his art to produce a variety of pictures of the most attractive kind. They are far more than the mere representations of certain phases of natural history; they are highly picturesque scenes in which the animal or the bird is a principal actor. To point out a few examples to elucidate our meaning: 'A Hairbreadth Escape' shows a magnificent owl which has swooped down upon some rabbits that have just reached the entrance of their hole under the snow-covered ground, on one of which he has fixed his talons, when a fox makes its appearance and scares the bird from its prey. 'The Struggle' represents two tigers that have come down from the jungle to drink at a stream, where one of them is instantly seized by a huge alligator,[1] which has a firm grip of the tiger's head. 'At Close Quarters' shows a wild boar attacked by dogs. 'Gleaners of the Sea' is a most beautiful picture, in which appears the hull of a wrecked vessel tossed on the waters, with a flock of sea-gulls skimming about, and picking up any waifs or strays of food floating from the unfortunate ship. Another subject of a somewhat similar kind, only a wintry landscape and not a sea view, is called 'Hunted Down;' a poor wounded hare, struck by the sportsman's gun, has seated itself near a patch of faded thistles, waiting death, an event foretold by the advent of numerous crows preparing themselves for a feast on her body. 'Maternal Courage' shows the flight of a huge bird of the vulture tribe from an attack on a young chamois, which its mother has successfully repelled.[2] A grand composition is 'The King of Beasts,' a mighty lion startled, as he stands ready to dispose of an antelope, by the thunder-clap and vivid flash of lightning from a sky of deep gloom: the head of the lion is grandly depicted.

DOI: 10.4324/9781003107835-53

Editorial Endnotes

1 The term 'alligator' is more properly applied to species found in the Americas.
2 Diana Donald, 'The "Struggle for Existence" in Nature and Human Society' in Diana Donald and Jane Munro (eds.), *Endless Forms: Charles Darwin, Natural Science and the Visual Arts* (New Haven, CT, and London: Yale University Press, 2009), pp. 94–5.

Editorial Headnote

44. 'The Extra Supplement. "Lions Fighting"', *Illustrated London News* (1873)

The engraver of Heywood Hardy's scene of fighting lions was John Greenaway, who specialised in animal subjects. Landseer's zest for extreme, often brutal realism and physicality in painting wild animals inspired many artists following in his wake, such as Heywood Hardy, Bouverie Goddard, John Trivett Nettleship, and Richard Friese. Their paintings were novel in the zoological knowledge they embodied – being often based on direct studies of living animals in the London Zoo. However, their academy exhibits took on an increasingly histrionic character, seeking to escape from the lowly category of 'mere' animal painting by emulating the high drama of the biblical and historical pictures which surrounded them in Royal Academy shows. As in Wolf's *Life and Habits of Wild Animals* (Chapter 43 of the present work), tragedy arises from 'survival of the fittest', the predatory pattern of nature, and the destructiveness of the elements. Themes taken from biblical or classical epics and romantic poetry were thus infused with Darwinian ideas. Such pictures did not make for restful viewing: they were probably intended to gain publicity for the artists by attracting the attention of exhibition reviewers, print publishers, and magazine editors, rather than appealing to private buyers of art works.

44

THE EXTRA SUPPLEMENT. "LIONS FIGHTING"

Anon., Illustrated London News

Source: 'The Extra Supplement. "Lions Fighting"', *Illustrated London News*, 63:1770 (2 August 1873), pp. 94–5.

In the catalogue of the Royal Academy Exhibition, whence we engrave this notable picture by Mr. Heywood Hardy, and where it forms a leading attraction, there is no title to the work properly speaking, and we must apologise to the artist for the prosaic heading which for convenience sake we give to these observations. Mr. Hardy uses only, by way of title or motto, the lines from Homer's 'Iliad' –

> Fierce as conflicting fires the combat burns,
> And now it rises, now it sinks by turns.[1]

These lines will suggest some duration and some vicissitudes in this terrific contest between two full-grown males of one of the strongest and fiercest species of the feline tribe; whereas a painter's representation is limited to a single moment, unless, indeed, he adopt the mediæval licence of rendering a number of successive incidents in one and the same composition. Surely, however, a combat of such fell determination between two such blood-thirsty antagonists cannot long endure; surely this must be the final bout between the savage creatures; even feline tenacity of life cannot hold out much longer; and this leonine embrace must prove the last death struggle. One king of beasts – he with the blackish mane and fringe to his tawny coat, like his lately-deceased majesty the 'old lion of the Zoo' – seems to have decidedly the best of it. His face is being frightfully mauled, but he has his fangs deep in his enemy's throat, and we feel that the vultures that hover and swoop in the mid-distance will not be disappointed of their prey. How is it that the representation of a fight between wild beasts always seems to excite keen sympathy and speculative interest from childhood upwards? Is it that the latent combative instincts of our own once savage nature are thereby excited – as by the old sports of the Coliseum arena, the bull-fighting in the Spanish ring, the tiger-hunting in India, and milder sports nearer home? The scene of this tremendous encounter at nightfall is, we presume, the African desert, on the border of the

DOI: 10.4324/9781003107835-54

jungle, where grow only rank grass and a few starry asphodels. The cause of the quarrel is not far to seek – a female was at the bottom of it, as of many combats between bipeds, and this is a duel à outrance[2] between jealous rival pretenders to female favour. Mark how the lioness slinks about the devoted combatants, how she seems to sniff the bloody tussle with keen relish, ready to submit at once to the victor! A word of warm praise is due, in conclusion, to the painter for the knowledge of animal character, the vigour and mastery of execution displayed in this picture, and that on a scale seldom attempted by contemporary artists. It is unquestionably one of the most admirable works by a young painter exhibited in recent years, and holds its own even beside our recollection of similar subjects by Rubens, Snyders, and other great animal painters.[3]

Editorial Endnotes

1 The quotation is from Alexander Pope's translation of Homer's *Iliad*, Book XVII, lines 420–1. Heywood Harvey thus endows his lions with the heroic courage of human warriors in Homer's epics. An equally grandiose but less successful work by Heywood Harvey was his painting of the animals entering Noah's ark (1876).

2 'To the death'.

3 The seventeenth-century Flemish artists Peter Paul Rubens and Frans Snyders both painted large scenes of animals being hunted or in fierce conflict.

Editorial Headnote

44.1. Anon., 'The Royal Academy Exhibition', *The Art Journal* (1877)

The subjects of animal paintings exhibited by Bouverie Goddard at the Royal Academy in the 1870s also epitomised the Victorians' sense of intrinsic violence in nature, often treated as the stuff of tragedy. They included an illustration to Milton's epic poem *Paradise Lost*: the original sin of Adam and Eve destroyed the harmony of Eden and engendered ferocious predation in the natural world. Goddard's *Struggle for Existence*, in contrast, referred directly to contemporary Darwinian theory on survival of the fittest through natural selection, though the incident it depicts is purely imaginary.

44.1

THE ROYAL ACADEMY EXHIBITION

Anon., Art Journal

Source: Anon., 'The Royal Academy exhibition', *The Art Journal* 39, new series 16 (1877), p. 186.

When we enter Gallery No. II., looking straight before us, our eye falls on the group of sweet young girls who, as G.D. Leslie, R.A., shows us in his soothing and cajoling way, have been gathering cowslips. One has need of some gentle reassurance of this kind when one looks to the canvas above, and sees what sad confusion 'The Fall of Man' (100) made throughout all animated nature: Bouverie Goddard displays in it, no doubt, much knowledge of animal life, and of feline nature especially. But we do not see here so much 'signs of woe that all was lost' as ramping and raging among the wild beasts of the field at 'completing of the mortal sin original.'[1] This picture, as a *tour de force* in the way of animal painting, is grand enough; but it would form a very disturbing element if hung in a room where a nervously imaginative man lived.

Editorial Endnote

1 Goddard's histrionic work illustrates Milton's *Paradise Lost*, Book IX, lines 782–4. It was believed that the original sin of Adam and Eve in disobeying God caused animals to forsake their former peaceable ways. They turned to predation and warfare, alienated from God and from humanity.

DOI: 10.4324/9781003107835-55

Editorial Headnote

44.2. Anon., 'Pictures of the Year', *Magazine of Art* (1878–9)

Like Goddard's *Fall of Man*, this work of his (shown at the Royal Academy in 1879) is imbued with a sense of inescapable violence and brutality in the natural world.

44.2

PICTURES OF THE YEAR – IV

Anon., Magazine of Art

Source: Anon, 'Pictures of the year – IV', *Magazine of Art* 2 (1878–9), p. 217.

A grim and a great animal-picture is Mr. Bouverie Goddard's 'Struggle for Existence.' It illustrates a law of the community of wolves, who, it seems, engage every year in a deadly civil war whereby all the weaker members are slaughtered, while the 'fittest survive'. Malthus would recognise in the social economy of these hungry tribes the ideal of his system. Mr. Goddard's work is full of the spirit and vigour of the scene.[1]

Editorial Endnote

1 This work is now in the Walker Gallery, Liverpool. Diana Donald and Jane Munro (eds.), *Endless Forms: Charles Darwin, Natural Science and the Visual Arts* (New Haven, CT, and London: Yale University Press, 2009), p. 83. The economist Thomas Robert Malthus's *Essay on the Principle of Population* (1798) had influenced Darwin and many other nineteenth-century thinkers on the 'survival of the fittest'.

DOI: 10.4324/9781003107835-56

Editorial Headnote

44.3. Anon., 'The Royal Academy', *Times* (1879)

Although Bouverie Goddard's work was apparently hung high on the wall of the Royal Academy's exhibition room, its bold style still commanded attention.

44.3

THE ROYAL ACADEMY (CONCLUDING NOTICE)

Anon., Times

Source: 'The Royal Academy (concluding notice)', *Times* (6 June 1879), p. 4.

Bouverie Goddard's 'Struggle for Existence' (689) – a savage combat among a group of wolves in the snow – has immense vigour, and, fortunately for the painter, is less injured in effect by high hanging than the other victims of skying already referred to. There is no animal painting in the exhibition to compare with this for power and spirit. Whether a hungry herd of wolves would thus resolve itself into a series of free worrying matches we know not. Some experts have said 'No.' Mr. Nettleship's 'Tiger and Boa,' lying side by side, harmless, under the paralyzing terrors of a flood (187), from its subject, cannot show the testing quality of movement.[1] The tiger's skin is very good in texture and colour.

Editorial Endnote

1 The artist John Trivett Nettleship specialised in imaginary scenes of the big cats and polar bears on the prowl. In this painting, the animals' common danger from a natural catastrophe is also a typical theme of the period.

DOI: 10.4324/9781003107835-57

Editorial Headnote

44.4. 'The Royal Academy Exhibition. Third Notice', *The Art Journal* (1879)

Nettleship's work again exemplifies Victorian artists' emphasis on violence and danger in the natural world, fatefully augmented by the hostile elements – in this case wild weather and floods. Such works invited comparison with epic biblical subjects like Leighton's *Elijah*, which apparently hung nearby.

44.4

THE ROYAL ACADEMY EXHIBITION. THIRD NOTICE

Anon., Art Journal

Source: 'The Royal Academy exhibition. Third notice', *The Art Journal* 41, n.s. 18 (1879), p. 149.

Immediately over Sir Frederick Leighton's noble composition of 'Elijah in the Wilderness' . . . hangs a remarkable fine picture of a life-sized tiger, which, in the company of a great serpent, has got adrift on a log, and is now at the mercy of the boundless flood. This picture is called 'Fear,' and the author is J.T. Nettleship, an artist whose steady progress in his profession we have from time to time recorded with pleasure. The blue waste of water, backed by the blue-green sky, with the black barred tawniness of the helpless tiger, whose magnificent bulk is in such close proximity to the no less terrible coils of the boa constrictor, make up a composition in form and colour at once impressive and original.

DOI: 10.4324/9781003107835-58

Editorial Headnote

45. Anon., 'A New Animal Painter: Richard Friese', *The Art Journal* (1886)

This article served as a commentary on the plate of Friese's 'The Brigands of the Desert', which appeared in this number of *The Art Journal*. The work of Friese represented a move towards a more modern idiom of 'wildlife' art, influenced by photography as well as by studies of animals from life in the zoos.

45

A NEW ANIMAL PAINTER
Richard Friese

Anon., Art Journal

Source: Anon., 'A new animal painter: Richard Friese', *The Art Journal*, n.s. (June 1886), pp. 161–4.

An animal painter who does not wish to confine himself to cattle and horses, dogs and cats, must either go and study in the desert, or frequent that highly civilized substitute for the desert, a zoological garden. The Regent's Park has been the sketching-ground of many of our painters, from Landseer down to Mr. Nettleship . . . Berlin has its group of German students. Of these latter Herr Friese has been for some years among the most assiduous, and the sketches which illustrate this article are some evidence of his diligence and ability in observing the ways of wild creatures at rest and in motion . . . Sometimes it will be a lion springing upon an antelope; sometimes a fight between two powerful children of the desert; sometimes a dead victim, with its conqueror or the birds of prey at work upon its body . . . Again, we have the monarch of the desert indulging in a kingly nap, and our readers will not want to have explained to them how utter is the sense of repose and delightful unconsciousness which is presented by this admirable figure. Or, again, we have the tiger creeping stealthily towards its prey, in an excellent drawing of the animal at the moment when his tigerishness is conspicuous; or we have the capital sketch of a leopard resting in a tree, in an attitude which one may fairly suppose would hardly be restful to any creature less supple and muscular than this beautiful compound of tranquillity and fierceness. In point of fact, the attitude is extremely characteristic, and the leopard and his spotted brethren may often be seen in just such a position by any one who chooses to watch them though the hours of a summer afternoon in our own Zoological Gardens . . .

We may now turn from Herr Friese's sketches to his picture. It is of large dimensions; the lion and lioness are of life size. It is at once bold and highly finished in execution, and, as a picture should, it embodies the studies of months in the elaboration of its details. There is no need to describe it, for it tells its own story – a caravan (just suggested in the picture) is halting below, and a lion and lioness are creeping over the rocks to reconnoitre, and perhaps to find a good opportunity for a spring on some horse or camel of the wandering Arabs. With some disregard of probability, the artist has represented the 'Brigands of the Desert' as plying their

DOI: 10.4324/9781003107835-59

unholy calling by daylight, whereas their habits generally lead them, as every one knows, to look out for prey at night-time . . . As to the artistic qualities of the picture, nothing need be said of its dramatic success, nor of the force and accuracy of the drawing. The catlike silence and caution of the lion as he advances for the spring has never been better rendered; as one gazes one fancies almost that these great creatures are but the cats we know, seen through some magnifying medium, so still and silent is their advance. In colour the picture is dominated by the idea that its action takes place in full sunlight, and consequently the prevailing tone is light. A darker picture gives more scope for bringing out the grandeur of the lion; but on the other hand Herr Friese, by giving us his creatures in the full blaze of day, has taken the opportunity for displaying his great skill as a draughtsman to the best advantage.

Figure 10 Thomas Landseer, *Monkey-ana; Or, Men in Miniature. Designed and Etched by Thomas Landseer* (London: Moon, Boys, and Graves, 1828), engraving and etching. (Bridgeman Images)

Editorial Headnote

46. Anon., Testimonials, *Monkey-Ana; or, Men in Miniature* (1828)

At just the time in the 1820s when Edwin and Thomas Landseer were injecting a new vitality into the depiction of wild animals (see Chapter 37 of the present work), Thomas, probably assisted by Edwin, reworked the old tradition of *singeries* – images of monkeys 'aping' human behaviour – and took it into new territory. His etchings combined energetic zoological realism with mordant satire on contemporary morals. The monkeys exhibit all of humanity's worst traits as brutal hunters, charlatans, fops, social climbers, cruel petty officials, brawlers, political agitators, etc. – their facial expressions exploiting the likenesses between human and simian features (see Figure 10). Only one image shows an admirable trait in human and simian behaviour – a 'widowed' monkey mourning over her dead companion.[1] The prospectus for the whole set, printed within the publication, quoted several 'Testimonials' or press reviews of the first issues which throw light on contemporary responses to Landseer's imagery. A selection is given here.

Editorial Endnote

1 Diana Donald, *Picturing Animals in Britain, 1750–1850* (New Haven, CT, and London: Yale University Press, 2007), pp. 123–5.

46

TESTIMONIALS, LANDSEER'S *MONKEY-ANA*

Anon.

Source: Anon. testimonials, *Monkey-ana; Or, Men in Miniature Designed & Etched by Thomas Landseer* (London: Moon, Boys and Graves, 1828): a set of twenty-five prints, issued in six parts, n.p.

'This is the Age of Monkeys! Men in real life seem to ape the tribe, which appears to be but a degraded species of themselves; and how close the resemblance is to be found, may be seen by an examination of these spirited Etchings of Landseer. Each part has four designs, exhibiting different situations and characters in life, and shewing the union which exists, or would exist were Monkeys similarly placed, between this semi-biped and quadruped and ourselves. – These things of Mr. Landseer, pictures of every day occurrences but slightly caricatured, are well drawn and as well engraved.'

Gentleman's Magazine.

'These Monkeys are every one of them truly valuable creatures. Some of them contain in their hairy faces – as the mean oyster encloses the rich pearl – a valuable moral; one which we may take away with us, and make food for thought. What has been said of Hogarth's works, we may frequently apply to Mr. Landseer's – at first we smile at them, but seriousness succeeds. The suddenness with which the eye necessarily meets them begets laughter; we see at first but grotesque shapes, mere touches of caricature; the impression is but momentary, and we have thought more deep from the humour which heralded them. MONKEYANA cannot but add to the well-earned reputation of Thomas Landseer.'

Sunday Monitor.

'If these satires on "poor human nature" are not always agreeable to our taste and feelings, we are nevertheless compelled to acknowledge their truth and spirit. – Of the mechanical execution of these etchings it is almost useless to speak: the force, freedom, and precision of Mr. Landseer's graver are everywhere acknowledged.'

London Weekly Review.

DOI: 10.4324/9781003107835-60

Editorial Headnote

47. *Monkeyana* (1828)

This anonymous work is not simply a commentary on the social satire in Thomas Landseer's prints. Rather, it exposes and plays on the anxieties that similarities between men and primates actually aroused – anxieties that would be continuously augmented over the next thirty years, even before the publication of Darwin's *On the Origin of Species*. As Edwin Landseer would later do in a teasing spirit, it raises the possibility that the 'higher' animals can recognise the subjects of scientific illustrations and art works – and may even appraise them aesthetically.[1] Varying but intelligent responses to two-dimensional images become the basis of an argument that animals are *not*, as theologians had argued, mere automata activated by God-given instincts: they actually share many human traits.

Editorial Endnote

1 See also Chapter 49 of the present work, Landseer's *The Connoisseurs*.

47

MONKEYANA

Anon.

Source: Anon., *Monkeyana. This Work may be considered as an accompaniment to the highly Talented Plates, Just Published, by that celebrated Artist Landseer* (London: W. Reeves, 1828), pp. 33–6, 53–6.

[pp. 33–6]

The oran outan was discovered in a flannel gown reclining in a low chair, with his feet on a stool, busily employed turning over the leaves of Buffon[1]: on reaching the delineations of the different kinds of monkeys, he became deeply interested and chattered to himself; his interest was converted into intense pleasure on coming to an engraving of his species, he pointed to the print, then patted himself, grinned, and looked at those around him, while he chattered in a tone and manner different to what he had ever been heard to utter. Though this instance is sufficient to shew the capability of the tribe to *admire*, if not to appreciate, works of art, it is by no means as conducive as the following circumstance.

The favourite monkey of a celebrated amateur and connoisseur, who usually inhabited the gallery where some of the most splendid works of the greatest painters were suspended, and where many precious gems were enclosed in cases, had certainly opportunities of observing the various gestures of the delighted amateurs who visited this splendid collection. According to the writer, the monkey Pug having escaped from his chain and basket, tried to pick the fruits in a Van Huysum still life, then hurled a mirror at it.[2] He went through the usual amateur manual exercise before a Rubens, gabbered at a Caravaggio, and did so very naughty an act on a questionable [drawing] by Raphael, that W.W – flew with his umbrella at poor Pug . . .

[pp. 53–6]

Cursory Reflections and Collateral Examples on the Preceding Memoir. The author of 'Annaline or Motive-Hunting,' at page 107, volume 1 says, that 'Instinct is an impulse implanted by Providence which compels every animal of the same species, when unrestrained and under the same circumstances, to perform the same operations.'[3] If this definition is correct, the arguments which might be raised on it are too numerous and profound for these memoirs; therefore a few of the general results, &c., will be given.

It is clear, that all monkeys do not, under similar circumstances, act as Pug and Meike: it follows that these illustrious examples of their species did not act from

DOI: 10.4324/9781003107835-61

instinct. Then from what could they act; from memory, reasoning, and reflection? Undoubtedly. But these are mental operations, since they are not material; in other words, they are derived from what we call mind or soul, for the words are synonymous in common parlance; the soul or mind is without parts, that is immaterial, and according to the great philosophers, necessarily immortal, (as to second causes) in other words, the natural causes, which produce decomposition in all combinations of matter, cannot destroy that which has no parts to be acted on. It follows that Pug and Meike, and all other creatures which evince any of the *effects* of mind, must possess an immaterial *cause*, indestructible by any known natural powers. Monkeys and other animals are *taught*. Now, no masses, or combinations of matter can be instructed: mind alone can receive instruction, or remember the information communicated, it follows logically, that all teachable creatures have, for all we can tell, an immortal principle'[4] . . .

Editorial Endnotes

1 Georges-Louis Leclerc, comte de Buffon, wrote a classic multi-volume *Histoire naturelle* with pictorial illustrations, published from 1749 onwards.

2 Jan van Huysum was a famous early eighteenth-century flower and fruit painter. The mirror hurled by the ape satirises the idea that such art is 'the mirror of nature'. The affectations of 'amateurs' or art connoisseurs are also being mocked in this passage.

3 Anon. [Laetitia Matilda Hawkins], *Annaline; Or, Motive-hunting: A Novel*, 2 vols. (London: James Carpenter & Son, 1824), vol. 1, pp. 107–8. Two of the characters in the novel discuss whether animals have not only individuality but also 'consciousness and memory', and possibly immortal souls.

4 This argument could be read another way: as a mischievous attempt to insinuate that neither humans nor other animal species are immortal. That view would certainly be accordant with what is known of Edwin Landseer's opinion – cf. Chapter 42 of the present work.

Editorial Headnote

48. Anon., 'The Royal Academy Exhibition', *Times* (1870)

Edwin Landseer's painting *The Doctor's Visit to Poor Relations at the Zoological Gardens*, later known simply as *The Sick Monkey*, was shown at the Royal Academy in 1870, and its Darwinian implications, implicit in the phrase 'poor relations', were immediately recognised.[1] In *The Descent of Man* (1871), Darwin was to discuss the extent to which non-human animals, especially primates, give evidence of a capacity for cooperative or altruistic actions comparable with that of humans. He claimed that in zoos 'Orphan monkeys were always adopted and carefully guarded by the other monkeys, both males and females', even if they were of a different species. Primates also sometimes (but not always) appeared to manifest sympathy with the sufferings of other creatures.[2] Landseer's painting shows one monkey tenderly nursing another, while a third one tucks into fruit, apparently unconcerned. It is quite possible, however, that the artist and the scientist were drawing on common sources, as suggested by the passage from Frank Buckland's article in Chapter 48.2. Landseer's pictorial drama was deliberately difficult to interpret; it perhaps reflected his own inner conflicts – his vacillations between sentiment and cynical pessimism with regard to the workings of nature; and, like Darwin, he was partly reliant on earlier witnesses and narrators for observations of authentic animal behaviour.

Editorial Endnotes

1 The original painting is in a private collection. There is an engraving of it published in 1875 by William Henry Simmons.

2 Charles Darwin, *The Descent of Man, and Selection in Relation to Sex*, 2nd ed. (London: John Murray, 1879), Part I, ch. 3, 'Comparison of the Mental Powers of Man and the Lower Animals' (Penguin Books edition, 2004, pp. 91, 125–6.) Darwin even mentions (*Descent*, p. 93) the ball – apparently a familiar plaything in the monkeys' cage in Regent's Park – which Landseer shows in the foreground of his painting.

48

THE ROYAL ACADEMY EXHIBITION (FIRST ARTICLE)

Anon., Times

Source: Anon., 'The Royal Academy Exhibition (First Article)', *Times* (30 April 1870), p. 12.

If Sir Edwin had meant to vindicate the Darwinian theory of human descent, he could not have more pathetically pleaded the claims of our simious ancestors than in the picture (265) of the 'Doctor's Visit to poor relations at the Zoological Gardens.' A selfish little black monkey, in rude health, is deep in the rind of one orange, while he grasps another between his hind-hands. But in the straw below, the Doctor – an old brown monkey so christened in the Gardens – is tenderly nursing a poor little patient in the last stage of consumption, whose wasted cheek is laid on the Doctor's bosom, while the sunk eye seems to look up into his for comfort, and to find it. This is quite the most pathetic picture in the Exhibition, and will go to more hearts than all the tragedies, high or humble, painted this year.

DOI: 10.4324/9781003107835-62

Editorial Headnote

48.1. Anon., 'An Inhuman Doctor', *Times* (1870)

The writer of this letter to the *Times* claims to offer clarification of Landseer's subject, but its ambiguity may actually have been deliberate on the part of the artist.

48.1

AN INHUMAN DOCTOR[1]

Anon., Times

Source: Anon., 'An Inhuman Doctor. To the Editor of the Times', letter signed by 'A disciple of Darwin', *Times*, 4 May 1870, p. 6.

Sir, – The history of the past is but too often open to suspicion and doubt; happily, the pen of the contemporary writer, if led into error, may at once be corrected. I am sure that the author of the able article on the Royal Academy in your columns of Saturday will not take it amiss if I state that he has, doubtless under the bewildering influence of kindly emotions, misapprehended the true pathos of Sir Edwin Landseer's 'Doctor's visit to poor relations in the Zoological Gardens.' May I ask you, for the sake of truth, to find space for the correct version of the sad passage in monkey life which it represents?

The little invalid is in its mother's (not 'the doctor's') arms, and still clings to the breast, yet has not strength to suck; but 'the doctor' – which and where is 'the doctor' at this trying moment? – the doctor is the gentleman in black, well known to frequenters of the gardens, who has been called in, but who, heedless of his poor feverish patient, diverts the golden fruit from its intended purpose, and heartlessly sucks the oranges himself.

When this sad story is understood, will any mother's eye in gallery No. 4 resist the appeal for a tear?

Editorial Endnote

1 An unsigned manuscript of this letter to the *Times* is among Landseer's papers in the National Art Library, Victoria & Albert Museum, London, MSL/1962/1316/289. It is not in Landseer's handwriting but was presumably sent with his blessing.

DOI: 10.4324/9781003107835-63

Editorial Headnote

48.2. Frank Buckland, 'My Monkeys', *Animal World* (1869)

Buckland's amusing account of his pet monkeys, which appeared in the first issue of the Royal Society for the Prevention of Cruelty to Animals' magazine *Animal World*, provides a context for Landseer's painting of *The Doctor's Visit*.

48.2

MY MONKEYS – "THE HAG" AND "TINY"[1]

Frank Buckland

Source: Frank Buckland, 'My Monkeys – "The Hag" and "Tiny"', *Animal World* 1 (1 October 1869), p. 3.

If monkeys are kindly treated they will be found to be most affectionate animals. They have so many ideas in common with our own species that, in my opinion, they are the most interesting of all pets. I have two monkeys, of whom I am exceedingly fond. Their names are 'The Hag' and 'Tiny.' The Hag's original name was 'Fanny,' but she has so much of the character of a disagreeable old woman about her that I call her 'The Hag.' Tiny is a very little monkey indeed, not much bigger than a large rat. My friend Bartlett brought her to me from the Zoological Gardens as a dead monkey; she was 'as good as dead' – a perfect skeleton, and with but little hair on her.[2] She arrived tied up in an old canvas bag. I put her into The Hag's cage. The old lady at once 'took to her,' and instantly began the office of nurse; she cuddled up poor Tiny in her arms, – made faces and showed her teeth at anybody who attempted to touch her. Tiny had port-wine negus, quinine wine, beef-tea, egg and milk – in fact, anything she could eat; and The Hag always allowed her to have 'first pull' at whatever was put into the cage. In time Tiny stood up, then began to run, her hair all came again, and she is now one of the most wicked, intelligent, pretty little beasts that ever committed an act of theft. Steal? Why, her whole life is devoted to stealing, for the pure love of the thing.

Editorial Endnotes

1 *Animal World* was read by the Darwin family. In 1863–4 Emma Darwin had corresponded with the RSPCA over the cruelty of the steel traps set by gamekeepers and other matters.

2 Frank Buckland was an eccentric zoologist who worked extensively on behalf of the animals in the Zoological Gardens. Abraham Dee Bartlett was the zoo's superintendent. Wilfrid Blunt, *The Ark in the Park: The Zoo in the Nineteenth Century* (London: Book Club Associates, 1976), pp. 96–105.

DOI: 10.4324/9781003107835-64

Editorial Headnote

48.3. Anon., 'Minor Topics', *The Art Journal* (1875)

It is clear that the subject of Landseer's painting remained an enigma, but this ambiguity did not lessen its appeal to the public.

48.3

MINOR TOPICS

Anon., Art Journal

Source: Anon., 'Minor Topics', *The Art Journal* 37, n.s. 14 (1875), p. 319.

Two notable pictures by the late Sir Edwin Landseer were on view for a short time at the gallery of the Messrs. Graves, in Pall Mall. The one was a life-sized portrait of 'Lady Emily Peel and her favourite dogs.' . . . The other work is a finished example of Sir Edwin's latest manner, and when exhibited in the Royal Academy in 1870 was called 'The Doctor's Visit to Poor Relations at the Zoological Gardens;' but is now more fittingly named 'The Sick Monkey.' It was painted for the late Thomas Baring, Esq., for three thousand guineas, and was bequeathed by him to Lord Northbrook.[1] We stand before a monkey's cage, and on the perch facing us sits a black-coated fellow eating an orange which he holds with his forepaws, while he grasps another with his toes. He affects no concern for the poor sick animal in the tawny yellow coat, which a sympathetic monkey of quite another kind, seemingly, has taken upon herself the office of nursing, as they lie lovingly together among the straw; but probably he is on the watch for intruders or disturbers of his sick friend, and we do our brother an injustice. We need scarcely add that the sympathetic droop of the muscles of the mouth in the nurse is almost human in its tenderness without any suggestion of caricature, and that the creatures are painted with the most consummate mastery of brush.

Editorial Endnote

1 This astonishing sum paid for the painting by the banker Thomas Baring indicates the value that was placed on even Landseer's more eccentric productions.

DOI: 10.4324/9781003107835-65

Editorial Headnote

48.4. Caleb Scholefield Mann, Notes Interleaved in A Copy of *The Works of the Late Sir Edwin Landseer* (1874)

Mann's handwritten additions to the *Works* date from c. 1874–7. It is not clear whether he was noting down his own impressions of the *Sick Monkey* or transcribing a passage from another printed source.

48.4

MANUSCRIPT NOTES IN A COPY OF *THE WORKS OF THE LATE SIR EDWIN LANDSEER*

Caleb Scholefield Mann

Source: Caleb Scholefield Mann, four volumes of MS notes and extra-illustrations, interleaved in a copy of the Royal Academy exhibition catalogue, *The Works of the late Sir Edwin Landseer*, 1874, in the National Art Library, Victoria & Albert Museum.

This picture is the merest toy imaginable. But how many years of patient, earnest, loving work and study must have been given to the acquirement of that marvellously keen insight and that astounding facility of hand which mark every touch in this exquisite little work. The story is rather painful than otherwise, for the baby monkey which the melancholy chimpanzee is nursing, is evidently dying; and the 'Doctor' – one of the most glossy and most impudent of ring tailed monkeys ever beheld – is in every lineament, as well as in the base action he is committing – an unmitigated scoundrel. Certain 'hospital comforts' – oranges to wit, have been brought for the sick monkey's use; and this medical adviser – shame upon him – has 'collared' the delicious fruit, and sucks one orange while he holds another between his hind paws ready to be consumed when the first is exhausted. Is this commonly decent kindness to one's '*Poor relations*?' Technically speaking the picture is distinguished by an extreme slightness of execution – but whilst a hundred contemporary animal painters could have done more by way of '*finish*' not one would have done half as much in the way of dramatic effect – and it is not too much to say that it has delighted both the learned and unlearned.

DOI: 10.4324/9781003107835-66

Figure 11 Edwin Landseer, *The Connoisseurs: Portrait of the Artist with Two Dogs*, oil on canvas, 1865. (Royal Collection Trust/Bridgeman Images)

Editorial Headnote

49. Anon., 'Exhibition of the Royal Academy', *Times* (1865)

Landseer's *The Connoisseurs*, shown in the Royal Academy exhibition of 1865, was a self-portrait of a novel kind, which he presented in a jocular spirit to his friend the Prince of Wales in July 1867: it is still in the Royal Collection (see Figure 11). Landseer here shows himself at work on a drawing from life of an unseen motif, which is presumably situated where we, the spectators, are standing, outside the picture space. As he portrayed animals more often than he portrayed humans, this implication is disconcerting, and Landseer has heightened the unease, or the comedy, by showing two dogs (possibly Lassie and Myrtle) watching and appraising his progress intently – perhaps as discerning experts in animal anatomy and character. We know from Keyl's notes (see Chapter 42 of the present work), that Landseer's favourite dogs did, in fact, spend their days lounging in his studio. Here their heads are brought into very close proximity with his, inviting the spectator to compare them in physiognomy and expression. The picture may be a joke about the pretensions of art critics, but it also chimes with nineteenth-century debates about the mental powers of animals, and especially of dogs – including their ability to recognise the subjects of two-dimensional images.

49

EXHIBITION OF THE ROYAL ACADEMY

Anon., Times

Source: Anon., 'Exhibition of the Royal Academy', *Times* (29 April 1865), p. 12, on Landseer's exhibits.

. . . But his raciest picture is his own portrait, with an intent look, hard at work, with drawing-board and portecrayon, while a sagacious colley and a noble retriever look with a concentration as complete and an insight as penetrating as their master's. It is wonderful how Sir Edwin, without in the least forcing the human character on the dog, or *vice versâ*, has contrived to give a family likeness to himself and his canine companions. One sees at once that in Sir Edwin's mysterious relationship to the dog lies the secret of his command of the family '*canis*' on canvas, and his power of penetrating their thoughts, works, and ways; and, on the other hand, in the same tie is the secret of the dog's wonderful understanding of Sir Edwin.

DOI: 10.4324/9781003107835-67

Editorial Headnote

49.1. Anon., 'Fine Arts, Royal Academy', *Athenaeum* (1865)

While anthropomorphic representations of animals are familiar to today's public from a host of films, animated cartoons, and children's books, Landseer's contemporaries were often bemused by the characterisation of the dogs in his paintings, especially when, as here, they are implicitly credited with aesthetic discrimination as well as with intelligence.

49.1

FINE ARTS, ROYAL ACADEMY

Anon., Athenæum

Source: Anon., 'Fine Arts, Royal Academy', *Athenæum*, no. 1958 (6 May 1865), p. 627.

We are a little disappointed with Sir E. Landseer's portrait of himself in the admirably humorous picture styled *The Connoisseurs* (152); its flesh-painting is too white, as well as 'pinky', to be true to nature; looking flabby, it is opaque and rather coarse; but the dogs who look over his shoulder at the sketch he is making, and supply the title to the picture, are perfect. Canine meditation and the results on a dog's face of critical habits were never even thought of before, much less ever painted, as they are here. The dog to our right will not, it seems, give a hasty verdict in favour of his master's work; that on our left will, like other critics, follow his neighbour. If anything could justify a man's wish to be a dog, it would be that he might be painted by Sir Edwin Landseer.

DOI: 10.4324/9781003107835-68

Editorial Headnote

49.2. Anon., 'The Royal Academy', *Art Journal* (1865)

The reviewer notes the fact that illustrations of talking animals in fables and children's stories could be seen as antecedents to Landseer's art.

49.2

THE ROYAL ACADEMY

Anon., Art Journal

Source: Anon., 'The Royal Academy', *Art Journal* (1 June 1865), p. 171.

'The Connoisseurs' may serve as a signal example of what has been termed, though not with verbal accuracy, the painter's 'anthropomorphism,' or, in other words, the transfer of human character to the brute creation – a practice which is pushed to its furthest extreme in Kaulbach's illustrations to 'Reineke Fuchs.'[1] 'The Connoisseurs' are, in fact, two dogs, who with eye of thoughtful yet self-complaisant critics, are looking over the sketch upon which the painter, Sir Edwin Landseer himself, is at work. This idea is a palpable hit. It must be confessed that the execution is a little heavy, and the picture is conspicuous for the absence of colour.

Editorial Endnote

1 Wilhelm von Kaulbach provided the engraved illustrations for *Reineke Fuchs (Reynard the Fox)* in an edition of 1845, where Reynard dominates the dramatic action.

DOI: 10.4324/9781003107835-69

Editorial Headnote

50. George J. Romanes, *Animal Intelligence* (1882)

The questions which Landseer's pictures had playfully raised, as to the extent of kinship between human and animal minds, were often seriously discussed by natural scientists in the later nineteenth century. Acceptance of Darwin's evolutionary theories led to a more searching analysis of animal cognition. Darwin's friend and disciple Romanes wrote a groundbreaking work on animals' mental processes, but his interpretations of them were sometimes criticised as anthropomorphic. Due to the dearth of controlled experiments on animal intelligence, Romanes's sources were often other people's anecdotal accounts of their pets' behaviour, which tended to be fondly wishful. One key area of research was the capacity of the so-called higher species of animals – especially primates and dogs – to recognise representations of other beings, as Landseer's painting of *The Connoisseurs* implied.

50

ANIMAL INTELLIGENCE

George J. Romanes

Source: George J. Romanes, *Animal Intelligence* (London: Kegan Paul, Trench, 1882), pp. 453–6.

Mr. R.O. Backhouse writes to me:-

My dog is a broken-haired rabbit-coursing dog, and is very intelligent. I took him one day to an exhibition of pictures and objects of interest, among which were statues and a bust of Sir Walter Scott. It was a local exhibition, and . . . some one had to sit up all night as a guard. I volunteered, and as we were looking about . . . my dog suddenly began to bark, and made as if he had found some one hiding. On looking round I found that it was the bust of Sir Walter Scott standing among the flowers, and in which he evidently recognized sufficient likeness to a human being to think the supposed man had no business there at so late an hour.

I adduce this instance because it serves as a sort of introduction to the more remarkable faculty which I cannot have the least doubt is manifested by some dogs – the faculty, namely, of recognising portraits as representing persons, or possibly of mistaking portraits for persons.

Mr. Crehore, writing to 'Nature' (vol. xxi, p. 132), says:-

A Dandie-Dinmont terrier, after the death of his mistress, was playing with some children in a room into which was brought a photograph (large) of her that he had previously never seen. It was placed upon the floor leaning against the wall. In the words of my informant, who witnessed it, the dog, when he suddenly caught sight of the picture, crouched and trembled all over, his whole body quivering. Then he crept along the floor till he reached it, and, seating himself before it, began to bark loudly, as if he would say, 'Why don't you speak to me?' . . .[1]

Lastly, my sister, who is a very conscientious and accurate observer, witnessed a most unmistakable recognition of portraits as representative of persons on the part of a small but intelligent terrier of her own. At my request she committed the facts to writing shortly after they occurred. The following is her statement of them:-

I have a small terrier who attained the age of eight months without ever having seen a large picture. One day three nearly life-sized portraits were placed in my room during his absence . . . When the dog entered the room he appeared much alarmed by the sight of the pictures, barking in a terrified manner first at one and then at another. That is to say, instead of attacking them in an aggressive way with

DOI: 10.4324/9781003107835-70

tail erect, as he would have done on thus encountering a strange person, he barked violently and incessantly at some distance from the paintings, with tail down and body elongated, sometimes bolting under the chairs and sofas in the extremity of his fear, and continuing barking from there . . . He continued in this state for nearly an hour, at the end of which time, although evidently very nervous and apt to start, he ceased to bark . . .

It will have been observed that in all these cases the portraits, when first recognised as bearing resemblance to human beings, were placed on the floor, or in the ordinary line of the dog's sight. This is probably an important condition to the success of the recognition. That it certainly was so in the case of my sister's terrier was strikingly proved on a subsequent occasion, when she took the animal into a picture-shop where there were a number of portraits hanging round the walls, and also one of Carlyle standing on the floor. The terrier did not heed those upon the walls, but barked excitedly at the one upon the floor. This case was further interesting from the fact that there were a number of purchasers in the shop who were, of course, strangers to the terrier; yet he took no notice of them, although so much excited by the picture. This shows that the pictorial illusion was not so complete as to make the animal suppose the portrait to be a real person; it was only sufficiently so to make it feel a sense of bewildered uncertainty at the kind of life-in-death appearance of the motionless representation.

Editorial Endnote

1 C.F. Crehore, 'Intellect in Brutes', *Nature*, 21 (11 December 1879), p. 132.

Editorial Headnote

51. Conwy Lloyd Morgan, *Animal Life and Intelligence* (1891)

In this book, written for a lay readership engaged with the new scientific ideas, the author discusses the more complex question of whether animals could recognise the subjects of pictures and could nevertheless understand the distinction between images and realities. He was equally interested in a related problem – that of interpreting animals' expressions and responses, and hence penetrating their minds: a problem that was central to animal painting by artists like Landseer, John Trivett Nettleship, and Briton Riviere. Lloyd Morgan's ideas were later developed in his *Introduction to Comparative Psychology* (London: Scott, 1894).

51

ANIMAL LIFE AND INTELLIGENCE

Conwy Lloyd Morgan

Source: Conwy Lloyd Morgan, *Animal Life and Intelligence* (London: Edward Arnold, 1891), pp. 340–1, 400, 403.

[pp. 340–1]

The fact that dogs may be deceived by pictures shows that they may be led through the sense of sight to form false constructs, that is to say, constructs which examination shows to be false. Through my friend and colleague, Mr. A.P. Chattock, I am able to give a case in point. I quote from a letter received by Mr. Chattock: 'Your father asks me to tell you about our old spaniel Dash and the picture. I remember it well, though it must be somewhere about half a century ago. We had just unpacked and placed on the old square pianoforte, which then stood at the end of the dining-room, the well-known print of Landseer's 'A Distinguished Member of the Humane Society.'[1] When Dash came into the room and caught sight of it, he rushed forward, and jumped on the chair which stood near, and then on the pianoforte in a moment, and then turned away with an expression, as it seemed to us, of supreme disgust' . . .

[p. 400]

Some time ago I ventured to stroke the nose of a little lion-cub which had tottered, kitten-like, to the bars of its cage. 'I wish,' I said shortly afterwards to a distinguished animal painter, 'you could have caught the look of conscious dignity (I speak anthropomorphically) with which the lioness turned and seemed to say, "How dare you meddle with my child!"' 'I have seen such a look and attitude,' said Mr. Nettleship; 'but I attributed it, not to pride, but to fear.'[2] Mr. Romanes quotes, as typically illustrative of an 'idea of caste,' the case of Mr. St. John's retriever, which struck up an acquaintance with a rat-catcher and his cur, but at once cut his humble friends, and denied all acquaintanceship with them, on sight of his master . . .

[p. 403]

My object is to show that it is possible for two observers to regard the same activities of animals, and read into them different psychological accompaniments. Throughout the sections of Mr. Romanes's work which deal with the emotions, I feel myself forced at almost every turn to question the validity of his inferences.

DOI: 10.4324/9781003107835-71

From all that I have said in the last chapter, it will be gathered that I am not prepared to credit our dumb companions with a single *sentiment*. A sense of beauty, a sense of the ludicrous, a sense of justice, and a sense of right and wrong, – these abstract emotions or sentiments, *as such*, are certainly impossible to the brute, if, as I have contended, he is incapable of isolation and analysis.

Editorial Endnotes

1 Landseer's painting of a Newfoundland dog, *A Distinguished Member of the Humane Society* (1838), became very popular through Thomas Landseer's engraving of it, but it seems unlikely that a dog would react to a black-and-white reproduction of the work.

2 John Trivett Nettleship was interested in the depiction of animals' mental states – see Chapter 44.3 of the present work.

Editorial Headnote

51.1. Anon., 'The Critics' – Painted By T. Earl' (1853)

This witty picture by Thomas Earl showed two dogs looking closely at an engraving of Landseer's *Laying Down the Law*. It is supposedly a high-quality 'proof' engraving of the work, propped up in a portfolio, with a magnifying glass to hand for scrutiny of the finer details. Again, therefore, dogs act the part of judicious connoisseurs of representational art, with the added twist that here 'real' dogs are looking at the anthropomorphised dogs in Landseer's courtroom scene.

51.1

"THE CRITICS" – PAINTED BY T. EARL

Anon., Illustrated London News

Source: Anon., '"The Critics" – Painted by T. Earl', *Illustrated London News* (19 February 1853): wood engraving and commentary, pp. 144–5.

The other animal piece now under notice, which we engrave, is by T. Earl, and is entitled 'The Critics.' Here we have a couple of rough terriers intently scanning the merits of an engraving from one of Landseer's well-known and favourite dog pieces; amongst the various animals represented, in which they fancy they recognise an old acquaintance or rival. The joke perhaps is not founded on fact – not perhaps true to nature; but *si non e vei* [sic] *e ben trovato* – the features and expression of the two dogs speak for the correctness of their portraiture; and it is impossible to contemplate their interesting occupation without participating in their feelings.

DOI: 10.4324/9781003107835-72

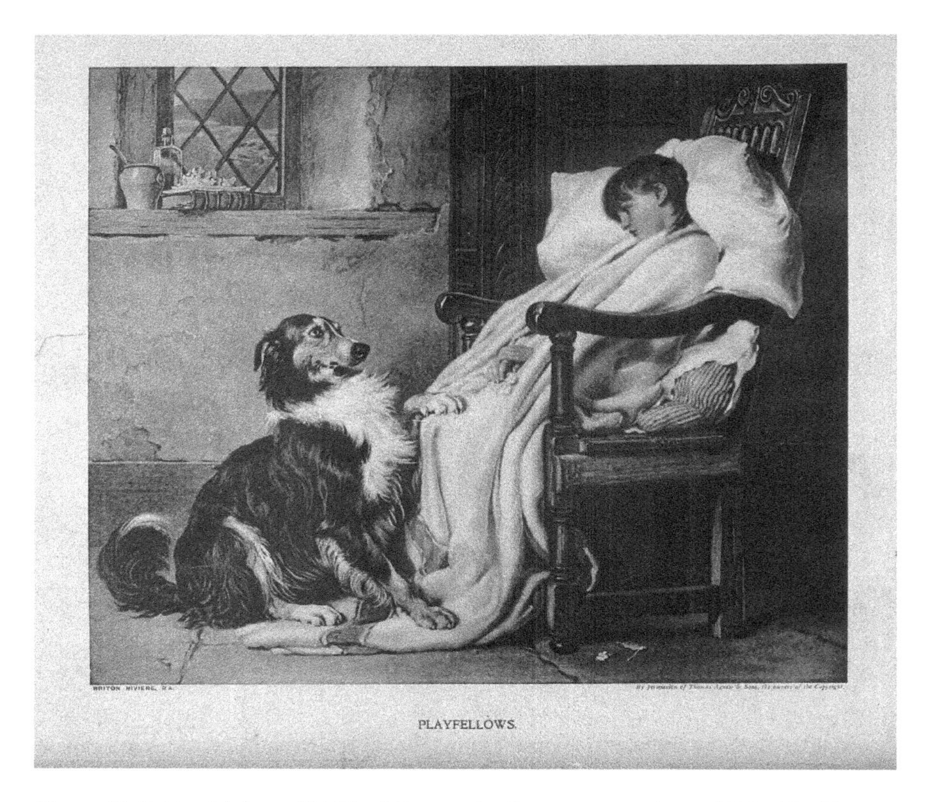

Figure 12 Briton Riviere, *Old Playfellows*, print from an engraving published by Thomas Agnew, of the painting exhibited by Riviere at the Royal Academy in 1883. The title poignantly suggests that the child is now too ill to play with the family's devoted dog. (Wellcome Library, Wikimedia Commons)

Editorial Headnote

52. Letter From Briton Riviere To Elinor Mary Bonham-Carter (1871)

The Bonham-Carters were friends of both the artist Briton Riviere and the Darwin family, and they helped to put Darwin in touch with Riviere. Thus, the latter's thoughts about animals' expressions in this letter to Miss Bonham-Carter were the prelude to his involvement with the illustration of Darwin's *The Expression of the Emotions in Man and Animals* (1872). To this work he contributed some studies of dogs' movements, expressive of various emotions.[1]

Editorial Endnote

1 Charles Darwin, *The Expression of the Emotions in Man and Animals*, 3rd ed., ed. Paul Ekman (London: Harper Collins, 1998), ch. V, 'Special Expressions of Animals', pp. 121, 400, 418. Phillip Prodger, 'Illustration as strategy in Charles Darwin's "The Expression of the Emotions in Mam and Animals"', in Timothy Lenoir (ed.), *Inscribing Science: Scientific Texts and the Materiality of Communication* (Stanford: Stanford University Press, 1998), pp. 140–81: Prodger here emphasises the value to Darwin of having Riviere's name associated with the book. Cf. also Prodger's *Annotated Catalogue of the Illustrations of Human and Animal Expression from the Collection of Charles Darwin* (Lewiston and Lampeter: Edwin Mellen Press, 1998). Jonathan Smith, *Charles Darwin and Victorian Visual Culture* (Cambridge: Cambridge University Press, 2006), 'Darwin's faces 1', pp. 179–213. Diana Donald, '"A mind and conscience akin to our own": Darwin's theory of expression and the depiction of animals in nineteenth-century Britain' in Diana Donald and Jane Munro (eds.), *Endless Forms: Charles Darwin, Natural Science and the Visual Arts* (New Haven, CT, and London: Yale University Press, 2009), pp. 195–213.

52

LETTER TO ELINOR MARY BONHAM-CARTER, 26 JUNE 1871

Briton Riviere

Source: Letter from the artist Briton Riviere to Elinor Mary Bonham-Carter, 26 June 1871.

Dear Miss Bonham Carter,

. . . I shall be very glad indeed if anything out of my small stock of information can be of any use to Mr. Darwin.

My experience is that a dog always puts its ears back when it 'grins' or 'smiles'. I believe that the grin denotes pleasure and a dog never shows pleasure without putting its ears back. Of course there is a grin that shows rage but in this too the ears are always laid back.

When I say that the grin or smile shows pleasure I mean pleasure of a kind that excites the affections, the sight sound or smell of any one that the dog loves.

Pleasure that excites mere interest, however intense such as that caused by – rats, game, the approach of food, &c., has an opposite effect upon the ear, viz, causes the dog to erect it. You can easily prove this by speaking to a dog that is listening or has its interest otherwise excited in such a manner as to cause the ears to be erected. Directly he hears your voice (if he cares for you) he will drop and lay back his ears into the form that they take in the ordinary expression of affection, but when you cease to speak he will re erect them into that of interest . . .

The grin in its full extent is not common so far as I know, but the beginning of it, viz, a slight drawing up of the upper lip just behind the canine teeth is very common and is always I believe part of the expression that denotes pleasure (of the kind mentioned above). Indeed of that expression I should call putting the ears back and down the first important characteristic, common to *all dogs*, and catching up the lip the second important characteristic, common in a less or greater degree to most dogs of a sensitive & affectionate disposition more especially to those that love the approbation and company of their masters. But I believe that there are many dogs of the most affectionate disposition that have not any sign of this upward contraction of the lip.

With the expression of the eye in some of these canine smiles & its exquisite tenderness you are yourself no doubt well acquainted. One thing more I have

DOI: 10.4324/9781003107835-73

noticed which is, that the grin will remain sometimes after the expression of affection has been changed to one of interest and the lip will still be kept up perhaps caught by some of the protuberances above the teeth. If you are going to take your dog for a walk he will grin & put back his ears from affection, then he will prick his ears from interest & excitement at the prospect of the walk and the ears will change more quickly than the mouth.

This is a difficult matter to write about for with me it is so much a matter of mere feeling & I fear too much so for my remarks to be of any service to Mr. Darwin.

Editorial Headnote

53. Anon., 'How I Paint My Animals: an Hour With Briton Riviere', *Chums* (1897)

Chums was a weekly magazine for boys, and in this interview with its unnamed 'representative' Riviere explained his aims and his difficulties as an artist when drawing live animals. He made close studies of their actual movements and expressions, but in his paintings such observations of animal behaviour often took on an element of anthropomorphism, pathos, or humour (see Figure 12). The *Chums* article was illustrated with a photograph of Riviere, taken by the firm of Barrauds.

53

HOW I PAINT MY ANIMALS

An Hour with Mr. Briton Rivière, RA

Anon., Chums

Source: Anon., 'How I Paint My Animals: An Hour with Mr. Briton Rivière, R.A.', *Chums*, 5:256 (4 August 1897), p. 790.

Mr. BRITON RIVIERE, the famous Royal Academician, began to paint wild beasts almost before his crawling days were over, and it may be safely assumed that what he does not know about animals and their ways is of no account whatever.

But not only does Mr. Riviere paint savage beasts, he is also a busy painter of tame ones, and it will be news to the readers of 'CHUMS' that many rich people take their pet poodles to eminent artists to have their portraits painted just as if they were human beings. The counterfeit presentment of a dog, like some portraits of some human beings by great artists, is often of greater value than the original in the flesh.

I had the privilege the other afternoon (writes a representative) of enjoying an hour's conversation with Mr. Briton Riviere on the subject of his work.

The dog and the lion are Mr. Riviere's favourite animals. When you come to think of it, it is rather strange that he should have any favourites among the four-footed creation, considering that, as a rule, animals show no marked (teeth-marks always excepted) leanings towards artists of any kind, and demonstrate their dislike to sitting for their portraits by chewing the easel.

'I have always been a great lover of dogs,' said Mr Riviere on my asking him to tell me how in the world he manages to keep them sufficiently quiet when they come to him as models, 'but I have worked at them so much that I've grown tired of having them about me. As you can understand I go through such worry and anxiety with them in the studio, that when the sitting is at an end I have had enough of them. However, you can never paint a dog unless you are fond of it. Of this I am perfectly convinced. Dogs are so restless that unless you are patient and good-tempered your efforts in presenting them on canvas will be wholly in vain.

'You have to wait a long time, even with a skilled assistant, before you can get the exact attitude you want. Then there is the difficulty of getting a sufficiently skilful assistant. Some people never learn how to hold a dog. It is essential to have someone who is sympathetic, one who is fond of dogs . . . you may think you will never get them in the attitude you want, but you will if you wait.

DOI: 10.4324/9781003107835-74

'In drawing an animal you must be able when it is in any attitude to evolve something like the attitude which you have in your mind. When a dog is not sitting as I want it I still go on painting and then when it assumes the attitude I have been waiting for I can, if necessary, correct or modify what I have done. To paint animals you must be able to do this; and, further, when you have the right attitude you must work at railroad speed. Animal painting necessitates the most rapid work' . . .

'As regards wild animals you must take them as you can. There is not much difference between them with respect to the trouble one experiences in getting them to sit. Of course, all the cat tribe are troublesome – more so than large placid animals, like the elephant. The fact is, the only way to paint wild animals is to gradually accumulate a large number of studies and a great knowledge of the animal itself, before you can paint your picture. I may tell you that I paint from dead animals as well as from live ones. I have had the dead body of a fine lioness in my studio. If I wanted a dead animal I should always go to the Zoo for it; I have done a great deal of work in the dissecting rooms at the Zoological Gardens from time to time.'

'What about painting special portraits of dogs, Mr. Riviere?'

'I have done a great number. The animals are brought here and stay for their sitting and go away at the end of it. Very few dogs will sit still for longer than two hours . . . An intelligent dog will do much better at the second or third sitting than at the first, and I've known dogs who have been very keen on coming to the studio. They've enjoyed sitting' . . . 'Some animals look uneasy and sulky, and I have had a few who have been very troublesome because they didn't like being looked at. I have to be exceedingly cautious at times not to arouse an animal's suspicions by letting him see that I am looking at him. Possibly you are not aware that the best way to make an animal uncomfortable is to look at him. Wild animals very often resent being gazed at. A wild animal not finding himself watched might naturally think he had escaped observation. On the other hand, if he sees you looking at him, he probably suspects that it is a question of a fight – that if he doesn't kill you, you will kill him. The old theory of looking an animal in the eye is totally wrong. So far from quelling an animal it brings it upon you. I've never been attacked by an animal but I had a mad dog in my studio on one occasion. The man took it away and it died during the night.' . . .

'It is well known that no one can write Latin verse unless he begins in his teens. It is the same with painting. The purely voluntary work which goes with the love of painting can't be done too early. When very young there is a certain quality in the powers of observation which is never found in one who has passed his teens. With respect to birds and animals I have known instances of young children seeing what adults experience great difficulty in seeing. There is a remarkable power of observation in the young . . . I believe a man very often works with his training and knowledge upon the intuition and inspiration that he acquired when very young indeed. I believe that in the first years of observation one lays up an immense store. I know I have worked on the knowledge of animals which I intuitively stored when a boy'.

Editorial Headnote

54. Walter Armstrong, 'Briton Riviere', *The Art Annual* (1891)

Armstrong commends Riviere's depiction of animals for its relative freedom from anthropomorphism. Yet his scenes of animal life in the wild were still invested with high drama and passion.

54

BRITON RIVIERE (ROYAL ACADEMICIAN). HIS LIFE AND WORK, THE ART ANNUAL

Walter Armstrong

Source: Walter Armstrong, 'Briton Riviere (Royal Academician). His Life and Work', from *The Art Annual*, 1891 (London: Art Journal Office, 1891), pp. 24–5.

Speaking of him broadly as an artist, Riviere's strong points are his sympathy with animals, his pleasant sense of colour, his directness of conception, and his fine vein of poetry. The first of these saves him from that besetting sin of the English *animalier*, the dressing up in human sentiments, and the setting among human conditions, of the lower animals.[1] His sympathy with dogs is too thorough to permit of their degradation into half-taught actors. He paints them for what they are, a symbol of what man was once, the rough material of civilisation with virtues and vices yet unblunted by convention; embodiments of the crude elemental passions, controlled only by the habit of respect for such a substitute for providence as man can offer and canine nature understand; and he paints other animals in the same spirit as dogs, seeking not solely the great tragic possibilities within their skins, as Barye did,[2] but understanding that even the more dangerous brutes, like that most fearful beast of all, man, are, for the most part, domestic – happy in a shallow sort of way, and by no means so full of hostility to other *feræ naturæ* as their looks suggest. Nearly alone among animal painters does Mr. Riviere withstand the temptation to dress a lion in conscious dignity, a tiger in conscious ferocity, a dog in conscious intelligence; with but a single exception, so far as I can remember – I mean the 'King and his Satellites' – his animals give their minds to the business in hand.[3] They never pose or think of themselves. This is all the more to Riviere's credit as, like Landseer and unlike Swan,[4] he nearly always paints them at moments when man has a finger in the pie. His interest, in fact, is in the animal's real self. His studies of anatomy have been very thorough. For a long time past he has been occupied on a leonine *écorché*,[5] which will, when complete, be of great value to future students.

DOI: 10.4324/9781003107835-75

Editorial Endnotes

1 Armstrong was probably thinking of works by Landseer and his followers when criticising anthropomorphism in animal painting. By the 1890s Landseer's style was going out of favour with art critics.

2 Antoine-Louis Barye created dramatic bronze sculptures and paintings of the big cats and other fierce carnivores attacking their prey.

3 In *The King and His Satellites*, shown at the Royal Academy in 1884, a male lion on the prowl is tailed by a pack of wolves, who presumably hope to assist or to profit from the kill.

4 John Macallan Swan was an animal painter.

5 An écorché was the body of a dead human or animal with the skin removed, for study of the underlying anatomy.

Part III

THE AESTHETICISATION OF NATURE

INTRODUCTION

In the Victorian era, the tonalism of seventeenth- and eighteenth-century art gave way to an explosion of colour and natural detail. Pre-Raphaelite paintings like Millais's *The Blind Girl* poignantly pictured the joys of *seeing* first hand the fleeting beauties in nature, an experience of which the blind beggar girl, her eyes closed, is deprived. She cannot take pleasure in the sight of a tortoiseshell butterfly which has alighted on her shawl, nor in the momentary appearance of a double rainbow, which is watched by her companion.[1] There is a direct contemporary parallel to such images in scientific works like Philip Gosse's books on sea life, with their vivid, detailed and finely composed illustrations (see Chapters 56–7). Yet in the later nineteenth century the beauty of the natural world – seemingly the most timeless and uncontroversial of topics – became a cause of contention among scientists and writers on aesthetics. It was not so much that beauty proved difficult to define. On the contrary, it was widely assumed (including by Darwin)[2] that animals and human beings had many shared tastes when it came to colours, shapes, and patterns. Rather, it was that the *causes* or *functions* of beauty in animals divided opinion.

For fundamentalist Christian believers, the beauty of plants and animals was a gratuitous expression of the moral beauty of the Creator, to which human beings could joyfully respond. William Kirby, the great defender of natural theology, celebrated the intricate structures and colours of insects as a gift from God, deserving the most poetic figures of speech that he could invent (Chapter 55); and Gosse, though fully conscious of the predatory habits of various marine creatures, described them with an ecstatic pleasure born of his faith in the harmony of the whole system of nature. A belief in nature as the source of all virtue and beauty in art is the leitmotiv of art critic John Ruskin's writings – whether he was writing about the subject matter of paintings or the forms of architectural ornament. Hence, it seemed to him that 'refinement of perception' was the foundation of artistic practice:

> You cannot so much as once look at the rufflings of the plumes of a pelican pluming itself after it has been in the water, or carefully draw the contours of the wing either of a vulture or a common swift, or paint the

DOI: 10.4324/9781003107835-76

> rose and vermilion on that of a flamingo, without receiving almost a new conception of the meaning of form and colour in creation.[3]

Such close study engendered love and reverence for the natural world and precluded any dismissal of animal representations as a merely subordinate aspect of art. In *Proserpina* (1879), Ruskin was even more vehement in his dismissal of 'the speculations of modern science' on animal forms and colours.

> All these materialisms, in their unclean stupidity, are essentially the work of human bats . . . among whom, for one-sided intensity, even Mr. Darwin must be often ranked. . . . If I had him here in Oxford for a week, and could force him to try to copy a feather by Bewick, his eyes might be opened to the subtleties of natural beauty, and their true meaning.[4]

However, Darwin and his 'unclean' followers remained adamant: the colours and markings of animals were important functional features, not ornaments contrived by God for the delectation of humankind. They had evolved to offer protection either as camouflage (blending in with the natural environment) or through mimicry (developing a protective likeness to some inedible species). Alternatively, they might have evolved in male animals, especially in birds and insects, through the tastes, and therefore the mating preferences, of the females of the species in question – a phenomenon that Darwin named 'sexual selection'. In the decades that followed the publication of his *Descent of Man* (1871), the arguments on these points among scientists were increasingly complicated by discoveries about the nature of coloration in the animal kingdom. Colour might be optical (an effect of the play of light on the surfaces of feathers or scales) or pigmental (inherent to the animal in question as part of its chemistry). In the latter case, it was sometimes argued, there might not be any necessary connection with either disguise *or* sexual selection. As scientific knowledge was extended to the study of fauna in more remote geographical areas, and regional variations in the characteristics of particular species were discovered, understanding of the significance of coloration became ever more difficult to attain with any certainty.

Debates over the causation and purpose of colour often pitted laboratory scientists against field naturalists or ecologists, with inconclusive outcomes (see Chapters 14–15). However, it seemed increasingly clear to writers of this time that the sense of colour and pattern evolved by animals over the millennia had been transmitted to humans through evolution and had then been raised by successive generations of civilised peoples to higher levels of sophistication. A disciple of Darwin, science writer Grant Allen, in his books *Physiological Aesthetics* (1877) and *The Colour-sense: Its Origin and Development. An Essay in Comparative Psychology* (1879), tracked this supposed ascent in standards of taste:

> [O]ur object must be to trace back the pleasure which man experiences from the deft combination of red and green and violet, in painting or in decorative art, to a long line of ante-human ancestry, stretching back indefinitely through geological ages.

This grand evolutionary progression encompassed

> the yellow, blue, and melting green of tropical butterflies; the magnificent plumage of the toucan, the macaw, the cardinal-bird, the lory, and the honeysucker; the red breast of our homely robin; the silver or ruddy fur of the ermine . . . the rosy cheeks and pink lips of English maidens; the whole catalogue of dyes, paints, and pigments; and, last of all, the colours of art in every age and nation,

culminating in the refined sensibilities of modern European aesthetes. Such highly developed tastes might even 'rank with the moral feelings'.[5] It was just such tasteful appropriations of nature's living forms which preoccupied artists like Henry Stacy Marks (Chapter 70) and fin de siècle designers such as Charles Annesley Voysey (Chapter 76). Moreover, the rise of *japonaiserie* from the 1860s onwards represented a feeling for wild nature and its fleeting beauties which was utterly disassociated from the jaded stylistic conventions of European art (Chapters 72–4).

Alas, the evolutionary process of derivation from animals' feeling for beauty could also, as Grant Allen noted, have malign consequences:

> And now, in our barbarous civilisation, millions of humming-birds from Trinidad and South America come yearly to Europe for the bonnets of our English ladies. . . . The bird-of-paradise forms a regular article of commerce; grebe and swans' down line our mantles and jackets.[6]

On this analysis, tastelessness and moral insensitivity were closely associated; and, conversely, an appreciation of nature's *living* beauties, when coupled with a sense of their increasing fragility, was thought to be the most effective preventative to such mindless, cruel destruction. This was the approach taken by ornithologists like Edmund Selous (Chapter 68) and by the leaders of the newly founded Society for the Protection of Birds, notably W.H. Hudson, for whom both caged and stuffed creatures were an abomination (Chapter 66). The Society offered a lecture kit for the use of voluntary speakers all over the country, consisting of a script and an eclectic collection of illustrations in the form of lantern slides (Chapter 69). Their miscellany of 'high' art, Japanese prints and drawings, book illustrations, and photographs of birds in their natural environment represented just the kind of interplay between science, aesthetics, and environmentalism which Hudson, Grant Allen, and other writers of the time sought to construct.

Notes

1 John Everett Millais, *The Blind Girl*, 1854–6, now in Birmingham Art Gallery. Jason Rosenfeld and Alison Smith, *Millais* (London: Tate Publishing, 2007), pp. 102–3. While the distribution of light and shade in seventeenth- and eighteenth-century paintings often suggested hierarchies of importance among the figures depicted, the colourism of mid-nineteenth-century British painting is expressive of a greater equality of value or interest, as regards both social groups and species.

2 For example, in *The Descent of Man, and Selection in Relation to Sex*, 2nd ed. (London: John Murray, 1877), Part II, ch. 13, 'Secondary Sexual Characters of Birds', Darwin enthuses about the 'artistically shaded ornaments' of the male Argus pheasant's plumage. 'These feathers have been shewn to several artists, and all have expressed their admiration at the perfect shading' (p. 398). Indeed, Darwin suggests that birds 'have nearly the same taste for the beautiful as we have' (p. 359). See Jonathan Smith, 'Evolutionary Aesthetics and Victorian Visual Culture' and Jane Munro, '"More Like a Work of Art than of Nature": Darwin, Beauty and Sexual Selection', both essays in Diana Donald and Jane Munro (eds.), *Endless Forms: Charles Darwin, Natural Science and the Visual Arts* (New Haven, CT, and London: Yale University Press, 2009), pp. 237–91.

3 Ruskin, Inaugural Lecture, 'The relation of art to use', in 'Lectures on Art,' iv (1870), para. 113, in *The Works of John Ruskin*, eds. E.T. Cook and Alexander Wedderburn, 39 vols. (London: George Allen, 1903–12), vol. 20. Ruskin's ideas are discussed more fully in the general Introduction to the present work.

4 Ruskin, *Proserpina. Studies of Wayside Flowers* (1879), vol. 1, ch. 4, in *Works of Ruskin*, vol. 25, p. 263. Ruskin was a great admirer of Bewick's art. See Diana Donald, *The Art of Thomas Bewick* (London: Reaktion Books, 2013), pp. 201–7.

5 Grant Allen, *The Colour-sense: Its Origin and Development. An Essay in Comparative Psychology* (London: Trübner and Co., 1879), pp. 2, 5, 223.

6 Ibid., p. 241.

Editorial Headnote

55. William Kirby and William Spence, *An Introduction to Entomology* (1818)

The *Introduction* was an authoritative and ground-breaking scientific work which began publication in 1815. The main author, Revd Kirby, was assisted by his fellow-entomologist William Spence, who was also an economist and political commentator. The work eventually ran to four volumes and went through many editions; it was used extensively by Darwin. The Revd Kirby was an enthusiast for his subject, seeking to rescue the study of insects from prevailing charges of 'littleness' or triviality. As a profound believer in natural theology, he wished to demonstrate the divinely inspired intelligence, creativity, and beauty of insects.[1] These qualities were to be complemented by the poetic beauty of Kirby's writing, exemplifying the inseparability of natural science and aesthetics in the eighteenth and early nineteenth centuries. While the relaxed epistolary form of *An Introduction to Entomology* follows the example of Revd Gilbert White's *Natural History of Selborne* of 1789, Kirby's literary style is more elaborate and figurative than White's.

Editorial Endnote

1 William Kirby contributed a title to the series of Bridgewater Treatises, intended to vindicate natural theology in the face of threats to Christian belief: *On the Power, Wisdom and Goodness of God as Manifested in the Creation of Animals and in their History Habits and Instincts* (London: William Pickering, 1835). Kirby laid less emphasis on the *hierarchy* of nature than many writers of his generation, such as J.C. Loudon. The latter, introducing his newly established *Magazine of Natural History* (May 1828, p. 3), enthused about 'the powers of the Author of nature, exerted in various degrees and for various purposes, through all the different orders of animated nature' until one reaches man, the 'most perfectly formed of all animals'.

55

AN INTRODUCTION TO ENTOMOLOGY

William Kirby and William Spence

Source: William Kirby and William Spence, *An Introduction to Entomology: Or Elements of the Natural History of Insects, with Plates*, 3rd ed., 4 vols. (London: Longman, Hurst, Rees, Orme and Brown, 1818), vol. 1, 'Introductory Letter', pp. 6–28, and 'Habitations of Insects', pp. 481–4.

[pp. 6–28]

Should you, as I trust you will, feel a desire to attend to the manners and economy of insects, and become ambitious of making discoveries in this part of entomological science, I can assure you, from long experience, that you will here find an inexhaustible fund of novelty . . . But numerous other sources of pleasure and information will open themselves to you, not inferior to what any other science can furnish, when you enter more deeply into the study. Insects, indeed, appear to have been nature's favourite productions, in which, to manifest her power and skill, she has combined and concentrated almost all that is either beautiful and graceful, interesting and alluring, or curious and singular, in every other class and order of her children. To these, her valued miniatures, she has given the most delicate touch and highest finish of her pencil. Numbers she has armed with glittering mail, which reflects a lustre like that of burnished metals; in others she lights up the dazzling radiance of polished gems. Some she has decked with what looks like liquid drops, or plates of gold and silver; or with scales or pile, which mimic the colour and emit the ray of the same precious metals. Some exhibit a rude exterior, like stones in their native state, while others represent their smooth and shining face after they have been submitted to the tool of the polisher: others, again, like so many pygmy Atlases bearing on their backs a microcosm,[1] by the rugged and various elevations and depressions of their tuberculated crust, present to the eye of the beholder no unapt imitation of the unequal surface of the earth, now horrid with mis-shapen rocks, ridges, and precipices – now swelling into hills and mountains, and now sinking into valleys, glens, and caves; while not a few are covered with branching spines, which fancy may form into a forest of trees.

What numbers vie with the charming offspring of Flora in various beauties! some in the delicacy and variety of their colours, colours not like those of flowers evanescent and fugitive, but fixed and durable, surviving their subject, and

DOI: 10.4324/9781003107835-77

adorning it as much after death as they did when it was alive; others, again, in the veining and texture of their wings; and others in the rich cottony down that clothes them. To such perfection, indeed, has nature in them carried her mimetic art, that you would declare, upon beholding some insects, that they had robbed the trees of their leaves to form for themselves artificial wings, so exactly do they resemble them in their form, substance, and vascular structure; some representing green leaves, and others those that are dry and withered. Nay, sometimes this mimicry is so exquisite, that you would mistake the whole insect for a portion of the branching spray of a tree . . .

In fishes the lucid scales of varied hue that cover and defend them are universally admired, and esteemed their peculiar ornament; but place a butterfly's wing under a microscope, that avenue to unseen glories in new worlds, and you will discover that nature has endowed the most numerous of the insect tribes with the same privilege, multiplying in them the forms, and diversifying the colouring of this kind of clothing beyond all parallel. The rich and velvet tints of the plumage of birds are not superior to what the curious observer may discover in a variety of *Lepidoptera;* and those many-coloured eyes which deck so gloriously the peacock's tail are imitated with success by one of our most common butterflies. Feathers are thought to be peculiar to birds; but insects often imitate them in their antennæ, wings, and even sometimes in the covering of their bodies. – We admire with reason the coats of quadrupeds, whether their skins be covered with pile, or wool, or fur, yet are not perhaps aware that a vast variety of insects are clothed with all these kinds of hair, but infinitely finer and more silky in texture, more brilliant and delicate in colour, and more variously shaded than what any other animals can pretend to.

In variegation insects certainly exceed every other class of animated beings. Nature, in her sportive mood, when painting them, sometimes imitates the clouds of heaven; at others, the meandering course of the rivers of the earth, or the undulations of their waters; many are veined like beautiful marbles; others have the semblance of a robe of the finest net-work thrown over them; some she blazons with heraldic insignia . . . Nor has nature been lavish only in the apparel and ornament of these privileged tribes; in other respects she has been equally unsparing of her favours. To some she has given fins like those of fish, or a beak resembling that of birds; to others horns, nearly the counterpart of those of various quadrupeds. The bull, the stag, the rhinoceros, and even the hitherto vainly sought for unicorn, have in this respect many representatives among insects. One is armed with tusks not unlike those of the elephant; another is bristled with spines, as the porcupine and hedge-hog with quills; a third is an armadillo in miniature; the disproportioned hind legs of the kangaroo give a most grotesque appearance to a fourth; and the threatening head of the snake is found in a fifth. It would, however, be endless to produce all the instances which occur of such imitations; and I shall only remark that, generally speaking, these arms and instruments in structure and finishing far exceed those which they resemble . . .

The sight indeed of a well-stored cabinet of insects will bring before every beholder not conversant with them, forms in endless variety, which before he would not have thought it possible could exist in nature, resembling nothing that the other departments of the animal kingdom exhibit, and exceeding even the wildest fictions of the most fertile imaginations. Besides prototypes of beauty and symmetry, there in miniature he will be amused to survey (for the most horrible creatures when deprived of the power of injury become sources of interest and objects of curiosity), to use the words of our great poet,

> . . . . all prodigious things
> Abominable, unutterable, and worse
> Than fables yet have feign'd, or fear conceiv'd,
> Gorgons, and Hydras, and Chimæras dire . . .[2]

The lord of the creation plumes himself upon his powers of invention, and is proud to enumerate the various useful arts and machines to which they have given birth, not aware that 'He who teacheth man knowledge' has instructed these despised insects to anticipate him in many of them. The builders of Babel doubtless thought their invention of turning earth into artificial stone, a very happy discovery; yet a little bee had practised this art, using indeed a different process, on a small scale, and the white ants on a large one, ever since the world began. Man thinks that he stands unrivalled as an architect, and that his buildings are without a parallel among the works of the inferior orders of animals. He would be of a different opinion did he attend to the history of insects: he would find that many of them have been architects from time immemorial; that they have had their houses divided into various apartments, and containing staircases, gigantic arches, domes, colonnades, and the like; nay, that even tunnels are excavated by them so immense, compared with their own size, as to be twelve times bigger than that projected by Mr. Dodd to be carried under the Thames at Gravesend.[3] The modern fine lady, who prides herself on the lustre and beauty of the scarlet hangings which adorn the stately walls of her drawing-room, or the carpets that cover its floor, fancying that nothing so rich and splendid was ever seen before, and pitying her vulgar ancestors, who were doomed to unsightly white-wash and rushes, is ignorant all the while, that before she or her ancestors were in existence, and even before the boasted Tyrian dye was discovered, a little insect had known how to hang the walls of its cell with tapestry of a scarlet more brilliant than any her rooms can exhibit,[4] and that others daily weave silken carpets, both in tissue and texture infinitely superior to those she so much admires . . . If we think with wonder of the populous cities which have employed the united labours of man for many ages to bring them to their full extent, what shall we say to the white ants, which require only a few months to build a metropolis capable of containing an infinitely greater number of inhabitants than even imperial Nineveh, Babylon, Rome, or Pekin, in all their glory?

That insects should thus have forestalled us in our inventions, ought to urge us to pay closer attention to them and their ways than we have hitherto done, since it is not at all improbable that the result would be many useful hints for the improvement of our arts and manufactures, and perhaps for some beneficial discoveries. The painter might thus probably be furnished with more brilliant pigments, the dyer with more delicate tints, and the artisan with a new and improved set of tools . . . Nor is the fact so extraordinary as it may seem at first, since 'He who is wise in heart and wonderful in working' is the inventor and fabricator of the apparatus of insects; which may be considered as a set of miniature patterns drawn for our use by a Divine hand . . .

And shall we think it beneath us to study what he hath not thought it beneath him to adorn and place on this great theatre of creation? Nay, shall we extol those to the skies who bring together at a vast expense the most valuable specimens of the arts, the paintings and statues of Italy and Greece, all of which, however beautiful, as works of man, fall short of perfection; and deride and upbraid those who collect, for the purpose of admiring their beauty, the finished and perfect chef-d'œuvres of a Divine artist! May we gaze with rapture unblamed upon an Apollo of Belvedere, or Venus de Medicis, or upon the exquisite paintings of a Raphael or a Titian, and yet when we behold with ecstasy sculptures that are produced by the chisel of the Almighty, and the inimitable tints laid on by his pencil, because an insect is the subject, be exposed to jeers and ridicule?

But there is another reason, which in the present age renders the study off Natural History an object of importance to every well-wisher to the cause of Religion, who is desirous of exerting his faculties in its defence . . . no department can furnish him with more powerful arguments of every kind than the world of insects – every one of which cries out in an audible voice, There is a God – he is Almighty, – all-wise, all-good – his watchful providence is ever, and every where, at work, for the preservation of all things.

[pp. 481–4]

. . . I pass on to the habitations formed by insects in their perfect state,[5] which have in view the education of their young as well as self-preservation, describing in succession those of *ants*, *bees*, *wasps*, and *Termites* . . . The nest of *Formica brunnea*, Latr. [Latreille] is composed wholly of earth, and consists of a great number of stories, sometimes not fewer than forty, twenty below the level of the soil, and as many above, which last, following the slope of the ant-hill, are concentric. Each story, separately examined, exhibits cavities in the shape of saloons, narrower apartments, and long galleries which preserve the communication between both. The arched roofs of the most spacious rooms are supported by very thin walls, or occasionally by small pillars and true buttresses . . . Having traced the plan of their structure, by placing here and there the foundations of the pillars and partition-walls, they add successively new portions: and when the walls of a gallery or apartment which are half a line thick are elevated about half an inch in height, they join them by springing a flattish arch or roof from one side to the other. Nothing can be a more interesting spectacle than one of these cities while building. In one place vertical walls form the outline, which communicate with different corridors by openings made in the masonry; in another we see a true saloon whose vaults are supported by numerous pillars; and further on are the cross ways or squares where several streets meet, and whose roofs, though often more than two inches across, the ants are under no difficulty in constructing, beginning the sides of the arch in the angle formed by two walls, and extending them by successive layers of clay till they meet: while crowds of masons arrive from all parts with their particle of mortar, and work with a regularity, harmony, and activity, which can never enough be admired. So assiduous are they in their operations, that they will complete a story with all its saloons, vaulted roofs, partitions and galleries, in seven or eight hours.

Editorial Endnotes

1 In ancient Greek mythology, Atlas was a giant holding up the sky and was often identified with lofty mountains.
2 A quotation from Milton's *Paradise Lost*, Book 2: these are the creatures which Nature breeds in hell.
3 In 1798 the engineer Ralph Dodd had published *Reports . . . Of The Proposed Dry Tunnel, Or Passage, From Gravesend, in Kent, to Tilbury, in Essex; Demonstrating Its Practicability.* The idea that some species of animals had, under divine direction, preceded human beings in various inventions was popular among religious writers. See, for example, Revd John George Wood's *Nature's Teachings: Human Invention Anticipated by Nature*, 1877.
4 This is perhaps a reference to the Kermes or the Cochineal insect.
5 The 'perfect' state of the insect is the imago or last stage of development.

Figure 13 Philip Henry Gosse, *Actinologia Britannica: A History of the British Sea Anemones and Corals* (London: Van Voorst, 1860), plate III, chromolithograph from a coloured drawing by Gosse. (Biodiversity Heritage Library)

Editorial Headnote

56. Anon., 'Gosse's Sea-Side Holiday', *British Quarterly Review* (1856)

The anonymous reviewer lists four recent publications by the naturalist Philip Henry Gosse, but focuses on the most popular of them – *Tenby: A Sea-side Holiday* (London: John Van Voorst, 1856). Gosse played a large part in creating the mid-Victorian fashion for aquaria. As a fervent fundamentalist Christian, he treated the visual beauties of marine animals – illustrated in *Tenby* with lithographs from his own watercolour drawings – as reflections of the perfect goodness of their Creator. Yet there was an evident difficulty, both for author and reviewer, in reconciling this facet of natural theology with the pattern of ruthless predation among marine animals that *Tenby* revealed. As an example, the reviewer cited Gosse's description of some species of sea anemones: he had noted their 'flower-like forms and beautiful hues', but also the penetrative 'missile filaments' by which they killed their prey, apparently inflicting 'great agony' in the process.[1]

Editorial Endnote

1 'Gosse's Sea-side Holiday', p. 50.

56

'GOSSE'S SEA-SIDE HOLIDAY', REVIEW

Anon., British Quarterly Review

Source: Anon., 'Gosse's Sea-side Holiday', *British Quarterly Review* 24:47 (July 1856), 'Article II', pp. 32–53.

But if the observer is startled by discovering the existence of such a grim machinery of death, he must remember that to each of the proprietors it is the machinery of life. It is not for us to touch upon that terrible problem, why the law of destruction occupies so prominent a place amongst the great statutes of nature. This kind of legislation is too deep for man, and it becomes him, therefore, whilst he remembers how his own sins have provoked the curse under which the world writhes, to mark well the marvellous skill displayed in the adjustments of that curse, so that it shall ever be tempered with mercy, and alleviated by tokens of creative beneficence and love.[1] Taking that law, therefore, as it stands, and admitting it as one of the great facts of our planet that some animals must perish that others may be supported, who can think of the lavish provision which has been made to enable the meanest zoophyte to obtain its daily food without feelings of the profoundest surprise? Who can think of the Divine Wisdom, descending, as it were, into the depths of the ocean, and working its wonders amongst creatures which are destined to live and die in a region where night reigns, and where human intelligence rarely dives? If mortals had been making a world, they would never have dreamt of finishing-off the inferior orders with the same care and polish as the superior. Their elephants would have been clever, and their lions magnificent. Their butterflies might have been beautiful toys for the children, and their horses splendid porters for the men. But their beetles would have been poor; their spiders would have spun the clumsiest webs . . . their polypes would either have been wholly neglected, or their fabrication would have been intrusted to apprentice hands, with instructions to get them up in the cheapest fashion possible. But how different is the reality! Nowhere can we discover any symptoms of haste, or any instances of crude and imperfect workmanship. Those living atoms, which the unaided eye can rarely detect, are found, when examined, to be as exquisitely moulded as if the animalcule stood at the head, instead of the foot, of creation. Well might Professor Forbes remark, 'that the skill of the Great Architect of nature is not less displayed in the construction of one of these creatures than in the building-up of a world.'[2]

If mere beauty of appearance is in question, the waters need not yield the palm of loveliness to the land. The deep has its butterflies as well as the air. Fire-flies flit through its billows, as their terrestrial representatives dance and gleam amidst the foliage of a tropical forest. Little living lamps are hung in the waves, and pour out their silvery radiance from vital urns which are replenished as fast as exhausted. The transparency of some of the inhabitants of the waters gives them an appearance of fairy workmanship which is perfectly enchanting . . . But, not to dwell upon the beauty of the mechanism, is there not something fascinating in the idea of crystalline creatures? Suppose we had transparent horses, or diaphanous dogs, or cats with a glass exterior, which would permit the circulation of the blood, and the working of the organs, to be distinctly seen?

Stranger still, the explorer will learn that the very *worms* which dwell on the shores, or live in the bed of the ocean, are sometimes models of elegance and of gorgeous painting. Hear what Mr. Gosse says on this subject: –

> 'The worms present many points of popular interest. One is the great splendour of colour displayed by many of them. The *Serpulæ* and *Sabellæ* exhibit in their radiating coronets of breathing-organs, not only the most exquisite forms and the most beautiful arrangement, but often glowing hues, usually disposed in bands or lines of spots. The *Pectinaria* carries on his head a pair of combs that seem made of burnished gold. The *Phyllodoces* are of various tints of green, sometimes very bright, relieved by refulgent blue, as of tempered steel. But it is in the rainbow hues that are reflected from many members of this class that their chief glory lies; for the bodies of many of the *Eunicidæ* and the *Nereidæ* glow with changing colours of great brilliancy, and their inferior surface displays the softer tints of the opal or the pearl. The sea-mouse (*Aphrodita*), one of the most common as well as the largest of our worms, is clothed with a dense coat of long bristles, which are fully as resplendent as the plumage of the humming-bird.'
>
> – *Marine Zoology*, p. 84.[3]

Perhaps there is more truth than the ancients suspected in the myth which represented the Goddess of Beauty as rising from the foam of the sea.

Editorial Endnotes

1 It was traditionally believed that the original sin of Adam and Eve had cursed the natural world, giving rise to its cruel predatory system.

2 Edward Forbes was a geologist and naturalist, with a special interest in marine biology and in links between natural science and the arts of design. In 1852 he lectured to students at the government's Department of Practical Art on 'The variety and symmetry of animal forms' and 'The symmetry of radiated animals'.

3 Philip Henry Gosse, *A Manual of Marine Zoology for the British Isles* (London: John van Voorst, 1855), part 1, p. 84.

Editorial Headnote

57. Edmund Gosse, *The Life of Philip Henry Gosse* (1890)

Here the writer and literary critic Edmund Gosse describes the beautiful depictions of sea creatures which served as a basis for the lithographic illustrations in his father's books.[1] Their perfectionism was an expression of Philip Gosse's belief in the divine origin of the creation (see Figure 13).

Editorial Endnote

1 Ann Thwaite, in *Glimpses of the Wonderful. The Life of Philip Henry Gosse 1810–1888* (London: Faber and Faber, 2002), discusses his difficult relations with Edmund, later recounted by the latter (apparently with some misrepresentations) in his book *Father and Son* (1907).

57

THE LIFE OF PHILIP HENRY GOSSE

Edmund Gosse

Source: Edmund Gosse, *The Life of Philip Henry Gosse* (London: Kegan Paul, Trench, Trübner, 1890), pp. 338–41.

As a zoological artist, Philip Gosse claims high consideration. His books were almost always illustrated, and often very copiously and brilliantly illustrated, by his own pencil. It was his custom from his earliest childhood to make drawings and paintings of objects which came under his notice . . . The remarkable feature about these careful works of art was that, in the majority of cases, they were drawn from the living animal.

His zeal as a draughtsman was extraordinary. I have often known him return, exhausted, from collecting on the shore, with some delicate and unique creature secured in a phial. The nature of the little rarity would be such as to threaten it with death within an hour or two, even under the gentlest form of captivity. Anxiously eyeing it, my father would march off with it to his study, and, not waiting to change his uncomfortable clothes, soaked perhaps in sea-water, but adroitly mounting the captive on a glass plate under the microscope, would immediately prepare an elaborate coloured drawing, careless of the claims of dinner or the need of rest. His touch with the pencil was rapid, fine, and exquisitely accurate. His eyesight was exceedingly powerful . . .

In *A Naturalist's Rambles on the Devonshire Coast* (1853) he first began to adorn his books with those beautiful and exceedingly accurate coloured plates of marine objects which became so popular a part of his successive works. These were drawn on the stone by himself, and printed in colours by the well-known firm of Hullmandel and Walton with very considerable success. The plates of sea-anemones in this volume, though surpassed several years later by those in the *Actinologia*,[1] were at that time a revelation. So little did people know of the variety and loveliness of the denizens of the seashore, that, although these plates fell far short of the splendid hues of the originals, and moreover depicted forms that should not have been unfamiliar, several of the reviewers refused altogether to believe in them, classing them with travellers' tales about hills of sugar and rivers of rum. Philip Gosse himself was disgusted with the tameness of the colours, to

DOI: 10.4324/9781003107835-79

which the imperfect lithography gave a general dusty grayness, and he determined to try and dazzle the indolent reviewers. Consequently, in 1854, in publishing *The Aquarium*,[2] he gave immense pains to the plates, and succeeded in producing specimens of unprecedented beauty. Certain full-page illustrations in this volume, the scarlet Ancient Wrasse floating in front of his dark seaweed cavern; the Parasitic Anemone, with the transparent pink curtain of *delesseria* fronds behind it, the black and orange brittlestar at its base; and, above all perhaps, the plate of starfishes, made a positive sensation, and marked an epoch in the annals of English book illustration. In spite of the ingenuity and abundance of the 'processes' which have since been invented, the art of printing in colours can scarcely be said to have advanced beyond some of these plates to *The Aquarium* . . .

Philip Gosse as a draughtsman was trained in the school of the miniature painters[3] . . . He had no distance, no breadth of tone, no perspective; but a miraculous exactitude in rendering shades of colour and minute peculiarities of form and marking. In late years he was accustomed to make a kind of patchwork quilt of each full-page illustration, collecting as many individual forms as he wished to present, each separately coloured and cut out, and then gummed into its place on the general plate, upon which a background of rocks, sand, and seaweeds was then washed in. This secured extreme accuracy, no doubt, but did not improve the artistic effect, and therefore, to non-scientific observers, his earlier groups of coloured illustrations give more pleasure than the later. The copious plates in *A Year on the Shore*, though they were much admired at the time, were a source of acute disappointment to the artist.[4] There exists a copy of this book into which the original water-colour drawings have been inserted, and the difference in freshness, brilliancy, and justice of the tone between these and the published reproductions is striking enough. The submarine landscapes in many of these last examples were put in by Mrs. Gosse, who had been in early life a pupil of Cotman.[5]

Editorial Endnotes

1 Philip Henry Gosse, *Actinologia Britannica: A History of the British Sea Anemones and Corals* (London: John Van Voorst, 1860).
2 Philip Henry Gosse, *The Aquarium: An Unveiling of the Wonders of the Deep Sea* (London: John Van Voorst, 1854).
3 Philip Gosse's father, Thomas, was a painter of portrait miniatures.
4 The book's correct title is *A Year at the Shore* (London: A. Strahan, 1865).
5 Philip Gosse's second wife, Eliza, had been taught by John Sell Cotman, the landscape watercolourist.

Editorial Headnote

58. James Shaw, 'Feeling of Beauty Among Animals', *Athenæum* (1866)

This short article related to a paper which the Scottish schoolmaster and amateur naturalist Shaw had delivered to the Dumfriesshire and Galloway Natural History and Antiquarian Society during its 1864–5 session. It was subsequently published in full in this Society's *Transactions* in 1867 (see Chapter 59 of the present work). Shaw felt that his ideas were vindicated by some passages in the fourth edition of Darwin's *On the Origin of Species* (1866), and he idolised Darwin himself. They corresponded occasionally during the years 1865–8, and Darwin cited Shaw's *Athenæum* article in the first edition of *The Descent of Man*, in a section on the 'decoration' of male birds, relating to the theory of sexual selection.[1]

Editorial Endnote

1 Charles Darwin, *The Descent of Man and Selection in Relation to Sex*, 2 vols. (London: John Murray 1871), vol. 2, chapter 13, p. 71.

58

FEELING OF BEAUTY AMONG ANIMALS

James Shaw., The Athenæum

Source: James Shaw, 'Feeling of beauty among animals', *The Athenæum*, 2039 (24 November 1866), p. 681.

I have been led to conclude from experiments which I have made, and from other observations, that certain animals, especially birds, have not only an ear for fine sounds, but also a preference for the things they see out of respect to fine colours or other pleasing external features. To begin with ourselves, the pleasure which we derive from a certain class of objects is universal and well marked; even when man becomes animalized this instinct is never lost, but only undergoes modification. Christian babes and cannibals are equally vain of fine clothes, and have a similar passion for beads and glittering toys. Carlyle suggests that the love of ornament rather than the desire of comfort was at the origin of clothes.[1] It is chiefly among birds, when we consider the case of animals, that a taste for ornament and for glittering objects, often very startling and human-like, is to be found. The habits of the pheasant, peacock, turkey, bird of paradise, several birds of the pigeon and crow kind, and certain singing birds, are evidence. The Australian satin bower-bird is the most remarkable of that class which exhibit taste for beauty or for glittering objects out of themselves, that is, beauty not directly personal; collecting, in fact, little museums of shells, gaudy feathers, shining glass, or bits of coloured cloth or pottery. It will be found with many birds that fine plumes, a mirror and an admirer, are not altogether objects devoid of interest.

Another consideration leading me to the same conclusion, is the fact that beauty in animals is placed on prominent parts, or on parts which by erection or expansion are easily, and at the pairing season, frequently rendered prominent, such as a crest or tail. A spangle of ruby or emerald does not exist, for instance, on the side under the wing, which is seldom raised, of our domestic poultry. Such jewels are hung where man himself wears his, on the face and forehead, or court attention, like our own crowns, trains, shoulder-knots, breast-knots, painted cheeks, or jewelled ears. I cannot account for the existence of these gaudy ornaments to please man, for nowhere are they more gorgeous than in birds which live in the depth of the tropical forest, where man is rarely a visitor; I cannot account for them on the principle that they do

DOI: 10.4324/9781003107835-80

good to their possessors in the battle for life because they rather render them conspicuous to their enemies, or coveted by man. But when I consider that the beauty of these beings glows most brightly at the season of their love-making, and that most observers agree that the female is won partly by strength, partly by gestures, and partly by voice, and that the male, whose interest it is to be most attractive, is often in his wedding-suit, the most gaily decorated, it seems to me that beauty, through a wider range than has yet been generally acknowledged, is accessory to love.

Butterflies, it is true, have gay patterns on the under wing, but this rather strengthens than diminishes the force of my argument, for with them, in a state of rest, the wings are folded erect, whereas others of that class, as moths and hawk moths, whose wings, when at rest, are either inclined, horizontal, or wrapped round the body, have only the upper side of the wings beautiful. It is to be noticed also that these creatures, out of the three states in which they exist, are only remarkable for beauty in that state in which they seek their mates, and whoever compares many of their males (as that of the orange-tip) to the females will find that gaudy colouring also favours the former. These delicate and ephemeral creatures are often to be observed flying lazily, as if aware of their splendour, and as if giving time that it might be seen.

Among fishes it is amusing to watch the combats of male sticklebacks for the females, which can be witnessed in an aquarium, and to note how the victor waxes brilliant in hue, and the vanquished, if he survive, wanes greatly in splendour. Fishes, and more especially insects, are often destroyed through the strange attraction which light has for them.

Birds are sometimes caught, especially larks in France, through the same allurement; and those very fire-flies, whose luminosity is so pretty to us, I have no doubt find it attractive to themselves. They are caught by means of their eagerness for light by those West Indian ladies who use them as jewels for their head-dress at a dance.

I am much strengthened in the conclusions at which I have arrived on this subject by the reference made to it by Mr. Darwin in the fourth edition of his work on Species, a copy of which has just now reached me.[2] The selection of beauty in their mates by some animals is there made to follow from their appreciation of it, so that effect and cause mutually throw light on each other. Some profound and interesting remarks are further added by the author, explanatory, on scientific grounds, of the origin of flowers, which strike me, although the remarks are very brief, as being the first likely solution of what has been for ages an inscrutable problem.

Editorial Endnotes

1 Thomas Carlyle, *Sartor Resartus*, first published in book form in 1836, Book 1, ch. 5, 'The World in Clothes'.

2 Charles Darwin, *On the Origin of Species*, 4th ed. (London: John Murray, 1866), ch. 6, pp. 240–1.

Editorial Headnote

59. James Shaw, 'The Appreciation of Beauty By Animals', *Transactions of the Dumfriesshire & Galloway Natural History and Antiquarian Society* (1867)

The lecture which the schoolmaster and amateur naturalist James Shaw delivered to his local natural history society, in a session chaired by its president, Sir William Jardine, was more overtly polemical than the *Athenæum* article (Chapter 58 of the present work) and apparently sparked much debate. Shaw intended to debunk the argument put forward by the Duke of Argyll,[1] that colour, pattern, and beauty in nature were gifts from God for the pleasure of mankind; and at the same time Shaw's equation of human and animal tastes implicitly negated the Ruskinian belief that beauty was a moral quality. Shaw's rebuttal of providentialism came *before* Darwin's full presentation of his theory of sexual selection as a cause of beauty in animals in *Descent of Man* (1871).

Editorial Endnote

1 George John Douglas Campbell, 8th Duke of Argyll, *The Reign of Law* (London: Alexander Strahan, 1867).

59

THE APPRECIATION OF BEAUTY BY ANIMALS

James Shaw

Source: James Shaw, 'The appreciation of beauty by animals', *Transactions and Journal of the Proceedings of the Dumfriesshire & Galloway Natural History and Antiquarian Society, Session 1864–65* (Dumfries: 1867), pp. 65–70.

The question of the origin and preservation of vegetable and animal beauty is one which deserves more attention than it has yet received . . . But if beauty merely existed for man – if he were the only creature for whom it had charms, then well might we wonder at the prodigality of nature, which, through all times and places, spreads this rich legacy, altogether heedless whether the most gifted of her sons be present to admire or not. It has been said in well-known lines:-

> 'Full many a flower is born to blush unseen,
> And waste its sweetness on the desert air.'[1]

Yet not only in the solitudes of the tropical forest but in the awful solitudes dimly pictured out by the geologist or revealed betimes by the microscope, flowers, and colours, and patterns of symmetry exist in all their glory, far out of our reach in space or time, and accusing nature of waste or prodigality if man alone is supposed conscious of her charms.

And so we have a distinguished writer (see *Reign of Law* by Duke of Argyll), removing the question from the naturalist to the theologian as formerly people did with the earthquake and the eclipse. Doubtless, we may believe that God makes his works beautiful to please himself, and yet try to find out whether the creatures are pleased with it as well.

For if in a thousand cases beauty is hid from human eyes, are we safe to assume or deny that it is hid from *all* eyes? Very many observations go to strengthen the notion that the inferior animals share with the lords of creation in rejoicing at the sight of their eyes and at the hearing of their ears. The infant who, in its nurse's arms, smiles and attempts to clutch the light, suggests comparisons with the moth or bird that often become victims to the same allurement. The lady who spends hours at her mirror, on her toilet, invites analogies with many birds and

DOI: 10.4324/9781003107835-81

quadrupeds which show similar pride in personal decoration; and with the inferior animals as with man, the most loving and the most lovely are not the least distinguished for the development of these tastes.

Take, for instance, that gorgeous animal the Bird-of-Paradise. Naturalists, who have observed it caged, have given us many glowing accounts of its behaviour. It is said to spend hours surveying its splendid self, jealous lest the least stain should darken the glory of its plumage, while, stretching out its pinions, it cleans in succession every tuft within reach of its bill. Its admiration of its own image in picture or mirror elicited the wonder of the spectators. It has been observed to caw with satisfaction at the completion of its toilet, and look archly at the onlookers as if ready to receive all the admiration that it considers its elegant form and display of plumage demand, of which, says a naturalist, 'it appears as proud as a lady of her full ball costume.' . . .

It would scarcely be safe in presence of such testimony to deny this lovely bird all æsthetical faculty. Evidently here too we have a connoisseur. The eye which is delighted with cleanliness, gracefulness, and colour, has its preferences. He who asks of what avail is beauty, of what avail are plumes of green and blue, of spangles of the ruby, or spangles of the emerald in the struggle for life, may be answered thus: if the love of beauty be so powerful in this bird as to neutralize the demands of appetite, we may well infer that at the pairing season the loveliest birds will be attracted towards each other, and thus the charms of beauty greater than that of strength secure for itself a perpetuity in the battle of life . . . Every one must have noticed that wonderful renewal of ornament in plumage, that wedding suit, as the French call it, which spring bequeaths to all the feathered tribes, suggesting to the most superficial observers that fine feathers play a part similar to fine garments with a human bride. What we have already said of the Bird-of-Paradise will have been understood by every one who has paid attention to the Peacock. We have admired the gracefulness of this bird's curving neck, its hues of gold and azure, green and brown, the eyelike or moonlike spots on its train dissolving or growing brighter – its metallic lustre intermixing with its gloomier tapestries, and the delicate crest of it faintly set with stars, but what is more to the point, we could not deny that the Peacock was sharing our feelings, that it was strutting about, and by means of powerful muscles was displaying itself to advantage, and that by its participation in human sentiments it has succeeded to make itself proverbial for ostentation and for pride. Both these animals are fond of a mirror, and the first became courteous to a picture of itself . . .

The Bower-bird of Australia is perhaps the most striking instance of the appreciation of beauty, the desire to conserve it, as any which we could select. Its extraordinary tunnels, which are its bridal chambers, are made with wonderful neatness of architecture, and the entrances profusely garnished with gay feathers of parrots, easily picked up in Australia, with sea shells, with pebbles, coloured bits of rags, or pottery, or whatever odd scrap that glitters which the animal can most readily pick up. In this tunnel it struts ridiculously until it attracts its mate, which, at the pairing season, it easily does, and then the two gallop in and out most merrily . . .

We have all observed the child's passion for flowers. Can it be anything more than coincidence, or is it that beauty is attractive to the beautiful that humming-birds and butterflies are so often found hovering around flowers, which are their rivals in gorgeousness? It seems as if the conspicuousness and sometimes the form (as in the bee-orchis) of those gaudily-coloured petals, as Mr. Darwin remarked, may be a decoy for the purpose of making insects the agents for intercrossing the seed[2] . . . Here, then, are facts worth comparing. The savage's adoration of light – the civilized man's confession of its beauty, distinct from its use, in his expensive illuminations when princes marry or victory is won – the insect's passion for it, which seems to intoxicate it and to overleap its more cautious instincts – until by long eager seeking, and selecting of the feeblest spark, those fairy tapers have been developed in its very organization in those regions where the sun conspired with the insect's own appetancy.

Space forbids us to take up the subject of the effects of light and loveliness of colour or form on quadrupeds, or we might tell some stories of pretty cats and vain apes in clothes.

Our deductions are but tentative, and by no means account for the grand phenomenon of vegetable and animal beauty, but merely afford hints as to its agency and development. Beauty is wide spread, but so, be it recollected, are eyes – eyes fashioned after a manner wonderfully like our own, and, no doubt, having preferences in the things which they see. Low down in the kingdom of nature, in star fishes, in molluscs, we still meet with the optic nerve and the faculty of sight; and if beauty be a solace, beauty meets those eyes even when the waves and billows hide it from the sight of man.

Editorial Endnotes

1 A quotation from Thomas Gray's 'Elegy Written in a Country Churchyard', 1751.

2 Charles Darwin, in his work *On the Various Contrivances by which British and Foreign Orchids are Fertilised by Insects* (London: John Murray, 1862), concluded that bee orchids were generally self-fertilising. However, as Shaw notes, it was also suggested that the similarity of the lower petal to the form of a bee was significant.

Editorial Headnote

60. Philip Henry Pye Smith, 'The Descent Of Man', *Nature* (1871)

In his first article reviewing Darwin's *Descent of Man* in *Nature* (6 April 1871, pp. 442–4) Pye Smith, a prominent physician, academic, and lecturer on comparative anatomy and zoology, had appraised Darwin's views on human evolution. In this second article he gives a sympathetic but sometimes quizzical account of Darwin's theory of sexual selection, accepting the contrasts in notions of beauty and good taste among animal species and human groups.

60

'THE DESCENT OF MAN', REVIEW

Philip Henry Pye Smith

Source: Philip Henry Pye Smith, 'The Descent of Man', second review article in *Nature* 3 (13 April 1871), pp. 463–5.

Among birds the rivalry of beauty has led to far more striking results than has the rivalry of strength. Foremost of these is the power of song, which, in accordance with the law of the least waste, is usually confined to birds of inconspicuous colours, while the combination of the harsh note with the magnificent plumage of the peacock is a familiar converse example. The object of the adornment of birds is conclusively proved by its being, as a rule, confined to males, and often to them only during the breeding season, as well as by the pains they take to exhibit their beauties to the hens. The difficulty is to show the precise way in which the results have been attained by gradual selection. In two remarkable instances, the wings of the Argus pheasant and the train of the peacock, Mr. Darwin succeeds in tracing the gradations in the same bird or the same family by which these wonderful and elaborate ornaments have been brought to their present perfection. The woodcuts which illustrate these gradations are unfortunately too numerous to be reproduced here; they are admirably drawn, and convey the impression of the feathers as nearly as is possible by the means employed. Indeed, we may here remark that throughout these volumes the original cuts, generally of details of structure, contrast very favourably with the figures of species taken from Brehm's 'Thierleben,' which are feebly drawn and ill-engraved[1] . . .

Among mammals sexual selection has chiefly operated by increasing the size and strength of the males, and furnishing them with weapons of offence; but besides allurements to the senses of smell and hearing, this class offers not a few instances, especially among the Quadrumana, of brilliant colouring being developed as a secondary sexual character. Here also we have the most striking instances of the production of defensive organs by the same process, as in the manes of lions, the cheekpads of some of the *Suidæ*,[2] and possibly the upper tusks of that ancient enigma, the barbirusa. Lastly, it is in the class of mammals that we meet with cases of what may be called primary sexual ornament, as in *Cercopithecus cynosurus*, which makes one wonder, with a thankful wonder, why such

DOI: 10.4324/9781003107835-82

apparently obvious results are not more common.[3] We must, however, admit that such adornment is not more disgusting, nor that of which we copy a figure more ludicrous, than the personal decoration of savages.[4] Sir Joshua Reynolds says that if a European in full dress and pigtail were to meet a Red Indian in his warpaint, the one who showed surprise or a disposition to laugh would be the barbarian.[5] But who could stand this test when meeting *Semnopithecus rubicundus* or *Pithecia satanas?*

We must admit, notwithstanding such anomalies, that, on the whole, birds and other animals admire the same forms and colours which we admire, and this, perhaps, may be admitted as an additional argument in favour of their kinship with us. Some of the ugliest creatures (like the hippopotamus) appear to have been quite uninfluenced by sexual selection, while the magnificent plumes of pheasants and birds of paradise are undoubtedly due to its operation. That it has occasionally led to unpleasing results in birds and monkeys of aberrant taste, is no more strange than that all savages do not carve and colour as well as the New Zealanders, or that most Englishmen admire ugly buildings and vulgar pictures. The prevailing aspect of nature is beauty, and the prevailing taste of man is for beauty also. The *means* by which natural beauty has been attained are various. Natural selection is one, by which the healthiest, and therefore the most symmetrical forms survive the rest. Protective mimicry is another, by which fishes have assumed the bright colours of a coral garden and butterflies the delicate venation of leaves. Flowers again have in many cases obtained their gay petals and fantastic shapes from the advantage thus gained for fertilisation by insects. The successive steps which have led to the graceful forms and brilliant tints of shells, to the intricate symmetry of an echinus-spine or a nummulite,[6] these are as yet untraced even in imagination.

But that many of the most striking ornaments of the higher animals, and almost all those which are peculiar to one sex, have been developed by means of sexual selection, is a conclusion which can no longer be distrusted. There remain doubtless many exceptions to be accounted for, many modifying influences to be discovered; but the existence of a new principle has been established which has helped to guide the organic world to its present condition. Side by side with the struggle for existence has gone on a rivalry for reproduction, and the survival of the fittest has been tempered by the success of the most attractive.

Editorial Endnotes

1 For the first edition of *Descent of Man*, Darwin borrowed his illustrations from a popular German work on zoology, Alfred Edmund Brehm's multi-volume *Illustriertes Thierleben* of 1864–9. However, he also commissioned some engravings of the markings on Argus pheasant feathers, which related to his theory of sexual selection. Pye Smith was not the only reviewer of Darwin's *Descent* to criticise the Brehm images. Therefore, for the second edition of the book, Darwin commissioned new illustrations by T.W. Wood, many showing male birds in courtship displays. Jonathan Smith, *Charles Darwin and Victorian Visual Culture* (Cambridge: Cambridge University Press, 2006), ch. 3, 'Darwin's birds', pp. 92–136. Smith, 'Evolutionary aesthetics and Victorian visual culture',

and Jane Munro, '"More like a work of art than of nature": Darwin, beauty and sexual selection', both essays in Diana Donald and Jane Munro (eds.), *Endless Forms: Charles Darwin, Natural Science and the Visual Arts* (New Haven, CT, and London: Yale University Press, 2009), pp. 237–91.

2 Wild boars and warthogs, etc.

3 Pye Smith is referring to the prominent red rumps of many mandrils and baboons.

4 The illustration shows the head of the *Semnopithecus rubicundus* monkey, with a dark red face and hair rising stiffly to a point.

5 Sir Joshua Reynolds, *Discourses on Art*, ed. Robert R. Wark (New Haven, CT, and London: Yale University Press, 1959), Discourse VII (1776), p. 137.

6 Nummulites are a kind of fossilised extinct marine organism.

Editorial Headnote

61. Edward Bagnall Poulton, *The Colours of Animals* (1890)

Poulton, who was Hope Professor of Zoology at Oxford, was also a keen Darwinian: this book developed theories about animal coloration which had been presented in *Descent of Man* and were much debated by subsequent writers. The existence of protective or warning coloration in animals was relatively uncontroversial, although the complexities of causation were increasingly apparent (see Chapters 14–15 of the present work). However, Darwin's view that the conspicuous colouring and patterning of the males of some species had evolved as an effect of sexual selection by the females was still contested, even by Alfred Russel Wallace.[1] There was always a danger of anthropomorphism – the presumption that aesthetic tastes characteristic of humans (particularly the refined tastes which Poulton associated with the educated classes) were shared with other species; and this could lead to circular arguments. Poulton was principally an entomologist, and he notes that any bright colours on insects that had been developed through sexual selection would normally be hidden when the creature was in self-protective mode – for example, a butterfly with folded wings. They can thereby be differentiated from warning colours, which are meant to advertise as clearly as possible that the insect is poisonous or inedible.

Editorial Endnote

1 Alfred Russel Wallace, *Darwinism: An Exposition of the Theory of Natural Selection with Some of its Applications* (London: Macmillan, 1889), ch. 10, 'Colours and ornaments characteristic of sex'.

61

THE COLOURS OF ANIMALS
Their Meaning and Use

Edward Bagnall Poulton

Source: Edward Bagnall Poulton, *The Colours of Animals: Their Meaning and Use, especially Considered in the Case of Insects* (London: Kegan Paul, Trench, Trübner, 1890), pp. 190, 316–18, 320.

[p. 190]

Warning colours

. . . But quite apart from these considerations, the Warning Colours can be distinguished by the subordination of every other feature to that of conspicuousness. Crude patterns and startling strongly contrasted colours are eminently characteristic of a warning appearance, while the colours and patterns produced by courtship include everything that is most beautiful in insects. The two kinds of appearance differ as an advertisement differs from a beautiful picture: the one attracts attention, the other excites admiration . . .

[pp. 316–18]

The necessity for Recognition can never explain the aesthetic value of the results produced.

It may also be urged that the beauty of the colours and patterns displayed in courtship can never be explained by this principle. For the purposes of recognition, beauty is entirely superfluous and indeed undesirable; strongly marked and conspicuous differences are alone necessary. But these, which are so well marked in Warning Colours, are not by any means characteristic of those displayed in courtship.

If an artist, entirely ignorant of natural history, were asked to arrange all the brightly coloured butterflies and moths in England in two divisions, the one containing all the beautiful patterns and combinations of colour, the other including the staring, strongly contrasted colours, and crude patterns, we should find that the latter would contain, with hardly an exception, the species in which independent evidence has shown, or is likely to show, the existence of some unpleasant quality.

DOI: 10.4324/9781003107835-83

The former division would contain the colours displayed in courtship and when the insect is on the alert, concealed at other times.

The immense difference between the two divisions, the one most pleasing, the other highly repugnant to our æsthetic susceptibilities, seems to me to be entirely unexplained if we assume that the colours of both are intended for the purposes of recognition. But these great differences are to be expected if we accept Mr. Darwin's views; for the colours and patterns of the latter division appeal to a vertebrate enemy's sense of what is *conspicuous*, while those of the former appeal to an insect's sense of what is *beautiful*. It is, of course, highly remarkable that our own æsthetic sense should so closely correspond with that of an insect. I believe, however, that it is possible to account for this wonderful unanimity in taste.

Our standards of beauty have been largely created for us by insects

Our standards of beauty are largely derived from the contemplation of the numerous examples around us, which, strange as it may seem, have been created by the æsthetic preferences of the insect world. One of the most fruitful inquiries originated by Darwin has been the renewed investigation of the marvellous relation between insects and flowers, a subject which had been previously attacked by Sprengel in 1793.[1] Darwin's work has been extended by others, and especially by Hermann Müller.[2] As the result of these investigations it is now well known that the fertilisation of flowers has been largely carried on by insect agency, and that insect preferences have decided as to the colours and patterns which prevail among the wild flowers of any country. This is now generally admitted, and as Mr. Wallace himself points out, 'we have abundant evidence that whenever insect agency becomes comparatively ineffective, the colours of the flowers become less bright, their size and beauty diminish, till they are reduced to such small, greenish, inconspicuous flowers as those of rupture-wort (*Herniaria glabra*).'[3]

But if this conclusion be accepted, if the beauty of flowers has followed so completely from insect selection, are we not compelled to admit that insects possess an aesthetic sense – a sense which could discriminate between the slightly different attractions displayed by suitors, just as we all admit that it has discriminated between the slightly different attractions displayed by flowers?

[p. 320]

The habits of Bower-birds as evidence for the existence of an aesthetic sense

The habits of the Australian Bower-birds are further evidence for the existence of a strongly-marked aesthetic sense in birds. Just as certain females are gratified by the display of personal adornment on the part of their suitors, others are pleased by the display and arrangement of beautiful or curious objects collected in the bowers. The latter are built on the ground and are intended for courtship alone, the nests being formed in trees. They are often very elaborate structures, and each species decorates its bower in a different manner. The Satin Bower-bird collects brightly coloured feathers, bleached bones, and shells: 'these objects are continually rearranged, and carried about by the birds whilst at play.' The Spotted Bower-bird lines its bower with tall grasses, kept in place by round stones which are brought from great distances, together with shells. The Regent bird makes use of bleached shells, blue, red, and black berries, fresh leaves, and pink shoots; 'the whole showing a decided taste for the beautiful'.

Editorial Endnotes

1 Christian Konrad Sprengel, *Das entdeckte Geheimniss der Natur im Bau und in der Befruchtung der Blumen* [The secret of nature discovered in the structure and pollination of flowers] (Berlin: F. Vieweg, 1793).
2 Hermann Müller, *The Fertilisation of Flowers,* trans. D'Arcy W. Thompson (London: Macmillan, 1883).
3 Wallace, *Darwinism,* ch. 11, 'Flowers the product of insect agency', p. 332.

Editorial Headnote

62. Sarah Stickney, *The Beautiful in Nature and Art* (1866)

Sarah Stickney (afterwards Sarah Stickney Ellis), a fervent evangelical Christian, wrote advice books for women, instructing them in their duties as wives, mothers, and daughters. She was also a novelist and essayist, with a particular interest in animal protection. Furthermore, she was an amateur artist and art lover who believed that young women should be taught to draw from nature – as a source of joy, self-education, and religious reverence, not as a mere genteel accomplishment (compare Chapter 77.1 of the present work).[1] *The Beautiful in Nature and Art* is partly a history of art, partly a presentation of the glories of nature as God's handiwork, which it was the duty of all artists to observe intensely and draw faithfully. Ignoring the interpretation of nature's destructive cruelties presented in Darwin's *On the Origin of Species* seven years earlier, she emphasises, in a Ruskinian spirit, the 'beauty . . . always before us in the open book of nature, and which is always accessible to us in the lesson-book of art' (pp. 5–6).

Editorial Endnote

1 Examples of Stickney's own drawings of horses, showing the emphasis on pure outline which is recommended in *The Beautiful in Nature and Art*, are reproduced in Diana Donald, *Women Against Cruelty: Protection of Animals in Nineteenth-century Britain*, 2nd ed. (Manchester: Manchester University Press, 2020), pp. 153–4.

62

THE BEAUTIFUL IN NATURE AND ART

Sarah Stickney

Source: Sarah Stickney, *The Beautiful in Nature and Art* (London: Hurst and Blackett, 1866), pp. 20–1, 26–8, 190–201.

[pp. 20–1]

Every object drawn, or otherwise represented by art, must have a definite outline, either expressed or understood; it must be true to its own distinctive shape and character, or it loses its identity. The student soon sees this, and in order to make a true outline or shape, looks again and again at the object which is to be truly copied.

Who that has ever attempted to draw a dove and found it a duck, or a rose and found it a cabbage, has not been stimulated by painful experience to look more earnestly at doves, and roses in general, so as to discover what really is the truth respecting them? Or who, in drawing a greyhound and finding it a sheep, has not endeavoured to fix in remembrance those light proportions and beautifully curving lines which render the greyhound one of the most graceful of animals?

[pp. 26–8]

Nothing can be more simple and trite than to speak of a love of beauty being inherent in our nature. But when we speak of beauty as being governed by laws, and as forming an important constituent in the order of creation, as holding a real place, and a very prominent one, in the designs of our Creator of our universe, we enter upon more questionable ground, because we have to do with those delicate and often dimly perceptible boundary lines by which the visible and material is separated from the ideal . . . The usefulness of the material world, and the manner in which nature yields up her stores to the service of man, is not more in accordance with the laws that govern our universe than the manner in which natural beauty delights the eye and cheers and animates the heart of man.

[pp. 190–201]

As an illustration . . . let any one sit down, without the objects before her, to draw a horse, a dog, or any other animal, with which she is perfectly familiar, but which she has never looked at with any particular reference to its form or outline. The most skilful hand is apt, under such circumstances, to deviate widely from the truth, nor can the eye, in most cases, see how the fault might be corrected.

DOI: 10.4324/9781003107835-84

But if the learner in art should be anxious about this matter of correctness, as all learners must be in order to their own success, having tried many times upon the horse, for example, and failed, she will begin to look earnestly, and observantly, at horses in general, and so will learn in time not only to see the beauty of this animal, but will become sensible of its graceful symmetry, and of the wonderful adaptation of its general structure to the circumstances in which it has to act. We perceive by such observation how one form of this animal indicates the quality of swiftness, another that of strength. And so on through all the animal creation, we become cognizant even of race and rank, as well as of those nice distinctions, according to which some are valued, and others despised.

I have chosen a horse for my example, simply because of a certain exactness of form required in the delineation of animals in general, and especially in that of the human face and figure. A landscape may deviate from nature in a thousand ways, and be a landscape still, but all animals must be true to their natural form, or they lose their identity, and represent really nothing. With such subjects a correct outline is of the highest importance, and we need to look well and thoughtfully at such objects in nature, or it is impossible that we should ever draw them correctly.

As regards correctness of observation, and the extent to which this can be cultivated, we find examples amongst those whose business leads them to consider minutely the distinctive forms of animals, and in the habits of some savage tribes, whose perceptions are quickened to the finest and most exact discrimination . . . Indeed, there are many ways in which our faculties become stimulated and sharpened, almost unconsciously to ourselves sometimes. Affection is one of these . . . In recommending so earnestly to the young student to look carefully and observantly out upon nature, I cannot forget the variety of forms which present themselves, and how perplexing these may at first appear as a whole. But variety is not vagueness, though on a slight view it may sometimes look like it; nor is abundance confusion. It is true that in our daily walks we are surrounded by this variety and abundance, so that we cannot gather a flower, nor mark the outline of a cloud, nor watch the unfolding of the butterfly's wings, without perceiving something graceful and exquisite in form; but of all these, and ten thousand attractive subjects besides, the outline of each is true to its own nature, and never runs into confusion with any other.

In our delineations of all these there must consequently be exactness, simply because nature is always true to her own forms in their different orders and varieties . . . It is scarcely more necessary to consider the truth of symmetry and proportion, when copying works of art than when drawing from nature; and yet how much more care is generally disposed by the learner upon a church than upon a cow, a tree, or a mountain . . . It has always appeared to me unlikely that the habit of drawing from masses of broken timber and masonry should ever bring the eye of the student into close acquaintance with the truth of pure outline, and yet this truth is the first principle out of which the perfection of art must grow[1] . . . Amongst flowers, a primrose or a lily may afford appropriate practice; a bird, also, is an excellent subject; and when considered with regard to form, there are few outlines more perfect than those which mark the back and breast of a bird, including always the exquisite curve of the neck. The wing of a bird, also, whether expanded for flight, or folded in repose, is an admirable study for any one who wishes to acquire facility of hand in the drawing of free and graceful lines.

It is impossible to pay much attention to painting or sculpture without seeing that this form of the wing of a bird has been always a favourite, especially in ancient art. In poetry, also, how many touching and graceful figures are supplied by the idea of a wing – its swiftness – its shadow – its tender brooding care. According to all the most popular representations of art, angels have wings, and from our earliest infancy we learn to associate this form with all those messages of love and mercy of which we delight to imagine these celestial beings are the bearers . . .

Many interesting studies of a scientific nature might very pleasantly be attached to the drawing of natural objects, according to their peculiar characteristics of vegetable or animal life, as in the case of birds, beasts, and plants . . . Earth, air, and ocean are full of forms of beauty. We have only to watch a cloud in the heavens, or to pick up a shell on the sea-shore, to feel how rich and abundant is the world we inhabit in subjects for delightful contemplation. Can anything, for example, be more perfectly graceful than the forms of many kinds of shells? Here we have, again, the folded scroll-like shape, with often the most curious embellishments of incrustation mingling with tints so rich and mellow, and yet so delicate, as to mock the garden's luscious fruits, and rival the tender bloom of the softly tinted rose. No wonder that the Greeks in their graceful mythology so often associated these forms in some way or other with their representations of gods and goddesses, or assigned to Venus herself an appropriate birthplace and cradle in the ocean wave . . .

So soon, however, as the eye and the hand have become sufficiently practiced, attention may be drawn to the characteristics of form in motion. And here we find another range or aspect of beauty, which can only be traced out by careful observation. What, for example, can equal the action of the horse for power and gracefulness combined? Almost all animals have some beauty in their movements when enjoying a condition of liberty and health. The undulating line, if we could only mark it, which is made by the flight of a bird through the air, is one of extreme gracefulness. The flapping of the great wings of a bird of prey before it raises its dark form from the rock; the bound of the antelope; the antics of the kitten; and the ecstatic welcome of the dog when the well-known step returns – all these are manifestations of form under varieties of motion, which the eye must learn to detect, and the mind to lay hold of, before the hand can become properly skilled in delineating their characteristic outlines.

Editorial Endnote

1 Stickney is thinking of the conventional kinds of 'picturesque' churches, ancient ruins, or rustic cottages which were often chosen as motifs by amateur artists.

Figure 14 E.A. Maling, *Song Birds and How to Keep Them* (London: Smith Elder, 1862), frontispiece, ‘Song Birds’, anonymous colour lithograph, perhaps by the author, depicting an idealised bird cage or aviary. (Biodiversity Heritage Library)

Editorial Headnote

63. E.A. Maling, *Song Birds and How to Keep them* (1862)

Many Victorian town dwellers kept caged birds – imported tropical species or trapped British songbirds – but not all could have afforded the expensive accessories that Miss Maling recommends (see Figure 14). She assures her readers that it is possible to combine the happiness and well-being of the captive birds with the aesthetic pleasure of their owners, creating the figment of a rural idyll. Thus, she credits the birds themselves with an appreciation of pretty surroundings and describes in detail how to accommodate them tastefully – the colours of the birds' plumage harmonising with their contrived quasi-pictorial settings.

63

SONG BIRDS AND HOW TO KEEP THEM

E.A. Maling

Source: E.A. Maling, *Song Birds and How to Keep Them* (London: Smith, Elder, 1862), pp. 109–12, 128.

[pp. 109–12]

Any wood susceptible of polish could be employed. Maple looks well, but in boudoirs or drawing-rooms it would generally be better to let it match the furniture or the window-frame itself; whatever is the material, it must be solid, with no veneers or inlaying in any part that the birds can get at . . .

Nothing adds so much to the birds' delight as well as to their beauty, as having a sort of shelf, about five inches wide, on which a box full of roses, myrtles, and other plants may stand, forming a hedge of foliage between them and the window.

Hanging baskets of plants near to the cage adds also much to its attractiveness, and the bath may be made the prettiest of room ornaments.

I have a cage of this kind that stands along a very large deep plant case, generally full of the gayest flowers, and it is very delightful in the morning to see the sun shining among the flowers, and the birds in a perfect tremble of song and happiness.

For very small and beautiful birds, such as the charming Waxbills, or Averdavatts,[1] nothing does better than a cage of maple or of satin-wood, with little silvered wires. These birds are really worthy of a pretty home, and their grains of millet are harmless; they do not make any litter, and are pretty to stand upon a table. A bell-shaped cage, with a fairy rose-tree, or some very small plant in it, looks well; a pot should be fitted into a wooden or gutta percha floor with a rim all round, and the bell-shaped cage would then drop down over it, fitting to the rim; while the perches should rather *go through* the tree than over it.

A similar arrangement does charmingly for Wrens. They delight particularly in a little fir-tree, on which they can perch and hop up and down. They do best of all, however, in a finely-latticed enclosure of *wood* instead of wire (fine wicker almost like basket-work); and in winter the safest plan is to let them fly about the room and nestle into boxes filled with the softest moss . . .

If Larks are kept, they are seldom happy, but perhaps in a long high cage they may be least unhappy. A piece of strong net, or of some green material should

DOI: 10.4324/9781003107835-85

be strained over the top, to prevent the poor bird from striking against the cage should he attempt to rise up and sing. The white linen advised by some writers, should never be used; and to be away from the fresh green fields, and from the blue clear air, is quite bad enough, without the further torture of a wall of white-wash to blind him with the glare. Larks soar without perching, so that perches are not wanted.

[p. 128]

Birds are so very fond of seeing anything moving, that there should be a vine trained about their windows, the branches waving outside, and the flickering shadow will delight them much. Swings are also valuable playthings. I like to have them all round, here and there, especially so placed as to show the birds against a background of green leaves. They also look well on a level with hanging flower baskets, which are great ornaments in, or rather outside, an aviary, the framing carried across a little way out, from one corner post to the other along the front, being just the thing on which to hang them.

The higher the side rows of trees, and the lower the front one of plants, the better pleased will be the inhabitants of the place; who are as fond as can be of gay colours and pretty, cheerful-looking homes.

Editorial Endnote

1 The waxbill is a small sub-Saharan African species that was popular as a cage bird.

Editorial Headnote

63.1. Anon. [Major Egerton Leigh], *Pets, A Paper* (1859)

Egerton Leigh's survey of contemporary pet-keeping embodies a darker view than that of Maling. Londoners' demand for caged birds to brighten and beautify their homes was ruthlessly exploited.

63.1

PETS, A PAPER

Anon. [Major Egerton Leigh]

Source: Anon. [Major Egerton Leigh], *Pets, a Paper. Dedicated to all who do not spell Pets – Pests. Read at the Mechanics' Institution at the Music Hall, Chester* (London: Longman, Brown, Green, Longmans and Roberts, and Manchester: George Simms, 1859).

There are few that would ever imagine the number of cage-birds disposed of in the metropolis, and they may be divided into those bought entirely for their song, like the nightingale, thrush, blackbird, linnet; those kept for their song and plumage, namely the canary, bullfinch, goldfinch, &c.; the imitators of the human voice, as the parrot, magpie, starling and raven; and those kept solely for their plumage, like the love-birds, and other rainbow-tinted denizens of sunny climes. . . . Seven thousand linnets, three thousand bullfinches, seven thousand goldfinches . . . fifteen hundred chaffinches, seven hundred greenfinches, two hundred nightingales (alas! for they are very difficult birds to keep alive in a cage), six hundred redbreasts, three thousand five hundred thrushes, fourteen hundred blackbirds, one thousand canaries, fifteen hundred starlings, five hundred magpies and jackdaws, three hundred red-poles, one hundred and fifty black-caps, and two thousand *duffed* birds are supposed to be annually sold in the streets of the metropolis, the value of which, including parrots, would produce a yearly sum of more than five thousand pounds sterling.[1]

Some of my hearers may not know the meaning of the term '*duffing.*' There are some twenty 'duffers' in London, men who earn their livelihood by 'duffing,' *i.e.* painting common birds (like sparrows and greenfinches) to represent some foreign sort, or to invent some non-existing breed. An old canary, faded and worn out with age, is re-dyed with queen's yellow; blackbirds are imbued with a deeper tint by using the soot off the frying-pan; a common parrot is painted marvellous hues, and its legs and beak varnished; in fact, as one of the 'duffers' confessed, 'the more outlandish a bird is made to look the more chance there is of selling it.'

DOI: 10.4324/9781003107835-86

Editorial Endnote

1 The activities of commercial bird-trappers were an early target of the [Royal] Society for the Protection of Birds, and protective legislation was gradually introduced. Tony Samstag, *For Love of Birds: The Story of the Royal Society for the Protection of Birds, 1889–1988* (Sandy: RSPB, 1988). Diana Donald, *Women Against Cruelty: Protection of Animals in Nineteenth-century Britain*, 2nd ed. (Manchester: Manchester University Press, 2020), pp. 268–73.

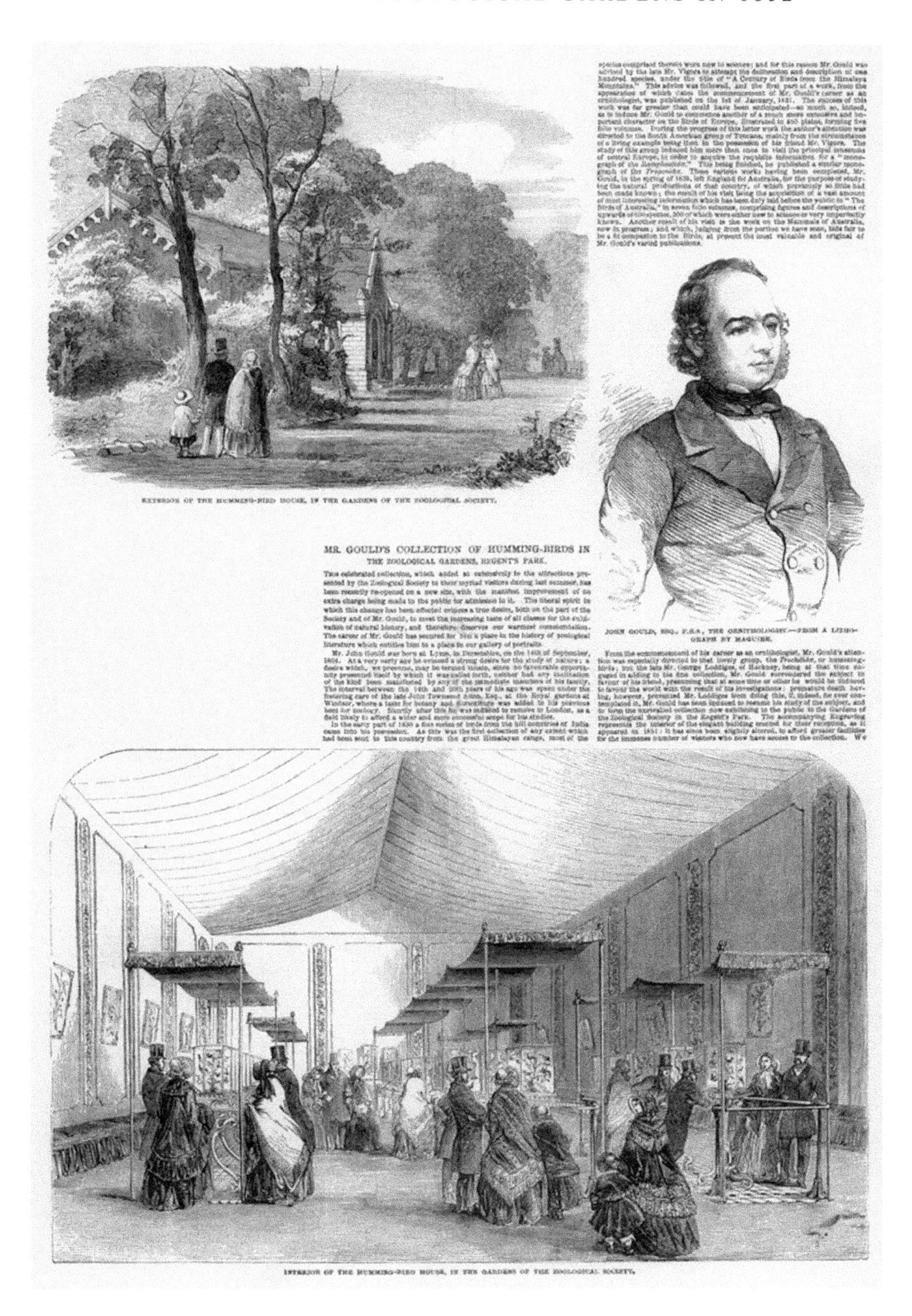

MR. GOULD'S COLLECTION OF HUMMING-BIRDS IN
THE ZOOLOGICAL GARDENS, REGENT'S PARK.

Figure 15 'Mr. Gould's collection of humming-birds in the Zoological Gardens', *Illustrated London News* 20 (12 June 1852), p. 457. (Bridgeman Images)

Editorial Headnote

64. 'A Glance at the Zoological Gardens in 1852', *Bentley's Miscellany* (1852)

This report on the activities of the Zoological Society of London in Regent's Park suggests the blend of scientific research, public education, crowd-pulling novelties, entertainment, and commercial promotions that was involved. Aesthetic appeal was all-important, and so a display of stuffed hummingbirds designed by the ornithologist John Gould, who had bought up these precious specimens, was a key attraction. In a set of elegant hexagonal glass cases with light metal frames in black and gold, the birds were shown perching, flitting, and hovering as though alive.[1] First opened to the public in 1851, Gould's display was originally conceived as an accompaniment to the Great Exhibition.[2] However, it was installed in a more permanent building in the Zoological Gardens in 1852[3] (see Figure 15) and used to promote Gould's monograph on hummingbirds, then in process of publication. This was a lavishly illustrated five-volume folio, with hand-coloured lithographs.[4]

Editorial Endnotes

1 Jane Munro, '"More like a work of art than of nature": Darwin, beauty and sexual selection' in Diana Donald and Jane Munro (eds.), *Endless Forms: Charles Darwin, Natural Science and the Visual Arts* (New Haven, CT, and London: Yale University Press, 2009), pp. 253–91. Munro illustrates (p. 258) one of the surviving cases of Gould's birds, which are now all in the collection of the Natural History Museum, London.

2 'Mr Gould's collection of humming birds', *Times*, 11 June 1851, p. 7: visitors who came to the Zoological Gardens to see the collection included international royalty, but also 'the most distinguished names in science and in art'. Cf. also 'Mr. Gould's collection of humming-birds at the Zoological Society's Gardens, Regent's Park', *Illustrated London News*, 18 (31 May 1851), p. 480, recording 'the most gorgeous effect of colour which can possibly be imagined'. Isabella Tree, *The Bird Man: The Extraordinary Story of John Gould* (London: Barrie & Jenkins, 1991), pp. 157–77. Takashi Ito, *London Zoo and the Victorians 1828–1859* (London: The Royal Historical Society and the Boydell Press, 2014), pp. 132–3.

3 The display in its new setting was illustrated in 'Mr. Gould's Collection of Humming-birds in the Zoological Gardens, Regent's Park', *Illustrated London News* 20 (12 June 1852), p. 457.

4 John Gould, *A Monograph of the Trochilidæ, or Family of Humming-birds*, 5 vols., published by the author, 1849–61. An *Introduction* to the series with scientific data on the various species was issued in 1861.

64

A GLANCE AT THE ZOOLOGICAL GARDENS IN 1852

Anon., Bentley's Miscellany

Source: Anon., 'A glance at the Zoological Gardens in 1852', *Bentley's Miscellany* 31 (1852), pp. 622–4, 626–8.

[pp. 622–4]

During the year 1851, the Zoological Gardens, Regent's Park, were visited by six hundred and sixty-seven thousand, two hundred and forty-three persons, and though a large portion of this vast multitude may have gone to them merely as a show, yet the spectacle witnessed within their boundaries, cannot fail to have exercised a beneficial and humanizing influence. Many thousands will pass through them again this year, and as important alterations and additions have been made, some account of them may not be unacceptable . . .

We now proceed to speak of the novelties; and that which will no doubt form the chief focus of attraction during the coming season is Mr. Gould's collection of humming birds, which has been replaced in a handsome wooden building to the left of the long walk, and not far from the elephant-house. It is now thrown open to the public. The general effect of the interior of the building is very elegant; the walls are principally covered with delicate green paper divided into compartments, by emblematic flowers; in the centre of each compartment is a beautiful painting, and to these we shall presently more particularly refer. The lower third of the walls is at present stained a dark oak; but this will probably be altered, as it deadens the brilliancy of the birds. These, numbering about two thousand, are arranged in hexagonal glass cases, down the centre and around the sides of the room.

It was curious to see how language was last year ransacked for words expressive of their beauty. The heavens and the earth were alike brought under contribution: they were compared to little suns, to stars, to gems, to metals, to the most brilliant flowers, and goodness knows what besides.[1] As we are not aware that our vocabulary of words of admiration was increased (though it well might have been) by the Great Exhibition, we will not attempt to draw on an exhausted mine, merely saying that the humming-birds must be seen for their beauties to be appreciated. Not the least remarkable point is the marvellous ingenuity displayed,

DOI: 10.4324/9781003107835-87

not merely in the general arrangements of the contents of each case, but in the attitudes of the birds themselves, every individual being placed in just that position best adapted to exhibit his especial beauty.

Branching off from the large apartment is a small chamber of much interest. In it is a stand containing the complete set of Mr. Gould's works, comprising no less than sixteen imperial folio volumes, superbly bound in green morocco and gold. A faint idea may be formed of the value of these books, when we state that the 'Birds of Europe' extend to five volumes, price 76*l.* 8*s.*, and that the 'Birds of Australia' fill seven volumes, amounting in value to 115*l.* the set: and this reminds us that had these works been published by 'the trade,' the price would have been much higher to admit of the enormous discounts allowed to the booksellers.[2] The necessity for keeping the price down to the lowest figure consistent with the choicest art, was the main inducement which led the author to take on himself the formidable risk of publication.

Magnificent though the works mentioned be, they are surpassed by a work now in course of publication by Mr. Gould, the 'Monograph of the Trochilidæ, or Humming-Birds,' for the execution of which the collection was formed. In the words of its founder, 'Having acquired the most extensive and valuable collection extant of these lovely ornithological gems, together with much valuable information as to their habits and economy, the author has determined on publishing a monograph of a family of birds, unequalled for their variety of form and colouring, and for the gorgeous and unrivalled brilliancy of their hues, which after a long series of experiments he is at length enabled, by an entirely new process of colouring, to represent almost equal to nature, and the beauty of which is exciting the admiration of every one to such an extent that the "Monograph of the Humming-Birds" bids fair to be the most popular of his productions.'[3] We are not acquainted in the whole range of literature with a more charming or instructive object for the wealthy than this gorgeous work, and as the number of copies is limited, we apprehend there will be no small competition for them.

We have mentioned the beautiful drawings with which the walls of the large room are ornamented. They are the illustrations of a work about to be published by Mr. Gould, on the Toucans, a singular and brilliant class of birds frequenting the same districts and woods as the humming-birds.[4] In the time of Linnæus not more than five or six species were known, whereas, in this work upwards of fifty are displayed, almost all being from the great range of the Andes . . .

Near to the eagle-aviary may be seen in process of erection a miniature Crystal Palace, intended for a Piscinarium (if we may coin a word). Its interior will be surrounded with glass tanks filled with water, and supplied with sand, pebbles, &c., and in these fish of various sorts will be kept.[5] Who can tell but that this may be the germ of a great and novel feature in Natural History, whereby the habits of fish will become as well known as those of birds and beasts; and perhaps the day may come when the main attraction to which the public will flock will be 'the Whale and her Calf,' 'the Great Shark from Port Royal,' or possibly 'the Mammoth Turbot presented by the Lord Mayor of London.' . . .

[pp. 626–8]

The grand aviary at the extremity of the gardens, on the left of the main entrance, was one of the happiest conceptions of Mr. Mitchell.[6] There, almost as free as in nature, may be seen the rarest birds . . . At this season the aviary rings with harmony, for there are collected birds from all parts, many of whom are now either building their nests or sitting on their eggs. We may mention the rock thrush of Germany, the Indigo birds of North America, the wild canary, the Baltimore oriole, grass parrakeets from Australia, bronze-winged pigeons and crested pigeons from Australia, crowned pigeons from Java, red-billed pigeons from Senegal, curassows from South America, quails from California, the whydah bird from South Africa, frankolins from the same, tinamoos from South America, and a host of others too numerous to mention. These constitute a most happy family, and their habits may be studied, and movements watched with interest and advantage, by the artist and the naturalist. This is no small boon, for there are few who, like Humboldt or Gould, would go to the uttermost parts of the earth to study the natural history of the country, but there are many who, prompted by strong instincts, yearn after nature, though their lot is cast in this huge smoky city.

Editorial Endnotes

1 The writer probably had in mind Dickens's hyperbolical review, 'The tresses of the day star', *Household Words* 3:65 (21 June 1851), pp. 289–91.

2 Gould, *The Birds of Europe*, 5 vols., 1837; *The Birds of Australia*, 7 vols., begun in 1840, but all dated 1848. These works and others by Gould were glowingly reviewed by 'W.M.' (probably Gould's coadjutor William Martin) in a long article in *The Westminster Review* 35:2 (January–April 1841), pp. 271–303.

3 Gould boasted that he had managed to reproduce the brilliant metallic effect of hummingbird feathers by applying semi-transparent oil colours and varnish over gold leaf.

4 Gould, *A Monograph of the Ramphastidœ or Family of Toucans* (London: the author, 1852–4). An earlier edition had been published in the mid-1830s.

5 The writer here refers to the zoo's new installation, designed and stocked by Philip Henry Gosse: the word 'aquarium' was not yet familiar. Ann Thwaite, *Glimpses of the Wonderful: The Life of Philip Henry Gosse* (London: Faber and Faber, 2002), pp. 178–9, 185.

6 David William Mitchell was the Zoological Society's first salaried secretary, appointed in 1847. He had a flair for visual spectacle, fostering a sense of intimate encounter with the animals.

Editorial Headnote

65. E.t. Booth, *Catalogue of the Cases of Birds in the Dyke Road Museum, Brighton* (1896)

Edward Thomas Booth, a man with inherited wealth, had assembled this comprehensive collection of British bird specimens, housing it in a purpose-built private museum adjacent to his house in Brighton. A catalogue details the contents of the various cases – early examples of what would now be called habitat groups or dioramas. Reconstituted family groups of birds of each species were arranged in recreated 'natural surroundings', an approach then described as 'artistic taxidermy', giving the effect of framed three-dimensional pictures. The aim was to feature both sexes, mature and immature birds, with all their variations in plumage. Booth brought out the first edition of a catalogue in 1876 but died in 1890, bequeathing the museum and its cases of birds to the town. This 1896 edition of the catalogue provides a 'History of the Collection' written by the Brighton naturalist and collector Arthur Foster Griffith, explaining Booth's intentions.

65

CATALOGUE OF THE CASES OF BIRDS IN THE DYKE ROAD MUSEUM, BRIGHTON

E.T. Booth

Source: E.T. Booth, *Catalogue of the Cases of Birds in the Dyke Road Museum, Brighton. Giving a Few Descriptive Notes, and the Localities in which the Specimens were found*, 2nd ed. (Brighton: King, Thorne, and Stace, 1896), ed. and intro. by A.F. Griffith. 'History of the Collection', pp. viii–ix.

The collection of birds bequeathed to the town of Brighton by the late Mr. Edward Thomas Booth is unique in two respects. No bird which was not obtained by Mr. Booth himself was allowed to form part of the collection . . . Kent, the bird stuffer and barber at St. Leonards, first taught him how to stuff and case his birds, and from the very commencement his ideal was to form a collection of birds set up in accordance with their natural surroundings; an ideal which he was afterwards able to reduce into actual practice, thus being the first to exhibit not merely a collection of stuffed birds, but rather a true representation of bird life and haunts; an example which the liberality of other lovers of birds has enabled the authorities of the Natural History Museum at South Kensington to worthily imitate.[1]

His early hunting grounds were the marshes near Rye, which in those days were comparatively little disturbed. But he soon extended his range to the Broads of Norfolk, the Highlands and sea lochs of Scotland and other favourite resorts of birds. Some idea of the closeness of his powers of observation can be obtained by reading this volume; but in his so-called 'Rough Notes,' a work which he revelled in, one is equally delighted with the freshness of the letterpress and the wealth and beauty of the illustrations. In fact, he never grudged either trouble or expense in connection with birds, whether to obtain specimens, to set them up when obtained, or to illustrate them and describe their habits . . . Looking through his memorandum books (very few of which unfortunately still exist) one recognises afresh what an immense amount of labour and disappointment he had to put up with in order to win the successes which usually came to him in the end.

DOI: 10.4324/9781003107835-88

Editorial Endnote

1 Dioramas were introduced at the Natural History Museum in the 1880s, under the supervision of the director, William Flower (see Chapter 87), and of Richard Bowdler Sharpe. As seen here, the latter fully acknowledged their debt to Booth.

Editorial Headnote

65.1. E.T. Booth, *Rough Notes on the Birds* (1881–7)

The artist Edward Neale specialised in wildlife subjects, and this book contains coloured lithographs from his drawings of some of the birds which ended up in Booth's museum. They had been 'collected' by Booth himself through wide-ranging travels in England and Scotland, accompanied by a large party of servants and gamekeepers. The adult birds were shot or trapped, but often the immature fledglings were caught alive and nurtured until they attained the state of plumage which Booth wanted for his featured specimens, then killed and stuffed. Since all the birds in the collection had been tracked in the wild and killed by Booth himself, often with great difficulty or physical danger, they were, in a sense, sporting trophies, even though taxidermy brought them back to an imagined life in fictive family groups. Thus, Booth's *Rough Notes* recall the narratives written by big game hunters, and, like them, he often made sketches of the terrain where the birds had been found – his visual data serving to guide the composition of Neale's plates and the design of the museum cases.

65.1

'INTRODUCTION', ROUGH NOTES ON THE BIRDS OBSERVED DURING TWENTY-FIVE YEARS' SHOOTING AND COLLECTING IN THE BRITISH ISLANDS

E.T. Booth

Source: E.T. Booth, *Rough Notes on the Birds Observed during Twenty-five Years' Shooting and Collecting in the British Islands, with Plates from Drawings by E. Neale, taken from Specimens in the Author's Possession*, 3 vols. (London: R.H. Porter and Dulau, 1881–7), vol. 1, 'Introduction', dated May 1887, pp. iii–iv.

More years than I anticipated have been spent in describing the habits of the birds procured and the production of the coloured Plates for 'Rough Notes.' During the time which has elapsed several other birds have been obtained, and it is now necessary that twenty-five years, instead of twenty as at first stated, should be given as the period over which my observations extend.

The assistance of the men well trained in the use of ropes, from the Bass Rock in the Firth of Forth and other quarters, whom I took with me, rendered the work of reaching the nests of the Golden Eagles on the mainland, and the White-tailed Eagles on the Western Islands, remarkably easy, all our attempts to descend the rocks or cliffs being made without mishap. While in pursuit of Skuas, Fulmars, and other Gulls in the North Sea, I was luckily able to hire some of the most powerful double-engine tug-steamers employed at Yarmouth, and we met with very good sport, shooting and obtaining specimens . . . To search thoroughly over the high tops of the Highland mountains where the Ptarmigan pass the winter months is by no means easy. Being, however, well acquainted with the parts of the hills they frequented, no accidents occurred, though, no doubt, we had some rather narrow escapes.

Little beyond what has come under my own observation is given in 'Rough Notes'; much information, however, is recorded that was picked up from those whose occupations have given them opportunities for making observations on the birds frequenting the hills in the most remote parts of the Highlands, on the marshes and low grass-lands in the fens, and also at sea in the fishing-luggers . . . I am aware that naturalists have so frequently drawn attention to what they are pleased to style the ignorance displayed by gamekeepers, that they would utterly condemn all information acquired from such sources. During the time passed searching over the moors and also knocking about in stormy weather at sea I have, however, learned much concerning the habits of many scarce species, that I have subsequently proved to be correct, from keepers and foresters, as well as from fishermen and coast-gunners.

Few remarks concerning the changes of plumage through which the various species pass are given, unless the birds are several years in assuming their last attire. As most carefully coloured drawings of the soft parts and plumage of Eagles, Ospreys, Kites, Harriers, Goosanders, Gannets, Skuas, as well as a few other species, were made for this work, having been taken either from life or at the time the birds were obtained, Mr. Neale has been enabled to give the most accurate representations of the various stages through which several species pass.

Editorial Headnote

65.2. R. Bowdler Sharpe, 'Ornithology at South Kensington', *The English Illustrated Magazine* (1887)

Richard Bowdler Sharpe, curator of the ornithological collections at the Natural History Museum in London, explains how the pictorial dioramas there, with all their 'artistic', crowd-pulling, and educational advantages, owed much to the examples of John Hancock and of E.T. Booth, who provided prototypes for the new approach. This was despite Booth's stated disdain for 'scientific' naturalists.

65.2

ORNITHOLOGY AT SOUTH KENSINGTON

R. Bowdler Sharpe

Source: R. Bowdler Sharpe, 'Ornithology at South Kensington', *The English Illustrated Magazine* 5:51 (December 1887), pp. 165–75.

The credit of having broken away from time-honoured tradition in the mode of mounting animals in this country is certainly due to Mr. John Hancock, who taught how to combine scientific accuracy and artistic feeling.[1] Mr. Hancock's name is a password throughout England, wherever taxidermy is mentioned, and in London his ablest representative has probably been Mr. A.D. Bartlett, the well-known superintendent of the Zoological Gardens, to whom we owe many of our most beautifully mounted specimens in the bird gallery.[2] But the first to suggest this combination of art and taxidermy *for an entire museum* was undoubtedly Mr. E.T. Booth, of Brighton, whose collection of British birds in the Dyke Road Museum, still remains one of the sights of England, and is not surpassed in interest by any Natural History Exhibition in the whole world. Here may actually be seen our native birds in their haunts, arranged in cases throughout a long gallery, every species being represented as in a wild state with corresponding natural accessories, reproducing as nearly as possible the surroundings as they were when the birds were alive, and representing the scenes sketched by the collector at the time of capture. Many years before we actually saw Mr. Booth's collection, its fame had reached our ears, and the idea seemed to us to indicate what the museum of the future ought to be; thus we lost no opportunity of advocating this system of artistic taxidermy in all our public lectures. At Leicester the notion was well received, and some groups of British birds were mounted under the auspices of the Natural History Committee of the Town Museum, until by the appointment of Mr. Montagu Brown as the curator of the museum, Leicester obtained the services of a taxidermist as skilled as he is energetic, and the result has been that the system of natural mounting has been extended to the entire collection of birds, so that not only British, but foreign, species are represented with their familiar surroundings in a state of nature.[3]

DOI: 10.4324/9781003107835-90

Editorial Endnotes

1 For John Hancock and his connections, see also Chapters 16, 32–4, 71, and 87 in the present work.
2 The effect of the displays in the Natural History Museum may be judged from drawings made by Maud Clarke, which were reproduced in Bowdler Sharpe's article. There is more spaciousness and movement than in Booth's ensembles.
3 Montagu Browne [not Brown, as spelt by Bowdler Sharpe] explained his methods in *Artistic and Scientific Taxidermy and Modelling: A Manual of Instruction in the Methods of Preserving and Reproducing the Correct Form of all Natural Objects* (London: Adam and Charles Black, and New York: Macmillan, 1896).

Editorial Headnote

66. W.H. Hudson, *Birds and Man* (1901)

Hudson was a novelist, a travel writer, an essayist, and a naturalist who campaigned on behalf of the Royal Society for the Protection of Birds in its formative early years, strengthening the protection movement through his wide ornithological knowledge, literary gifts, moral passion, and intellectual authority. He viewed nature as a beautiful and autonomous realm, full of movement and evanescent effects of light and colour, not as a material resource to be plundered by sportsmen and collectors. Thus, his reaction to the 'artistic' taxidermy in Booth's museum was very different from that of Bowdler Sharpe.

66

BIRDS AT THEIR BEST

William Henry Hudson

Source: William Henry Hudson, *Birds and Man* (London, New York, Bombay: Longmans, Green, 1901), ch. I, 'Birds at their best (By way of Introduction)', pp. 1–8, 13–20.

[pp. 1–8]

Years ago, in a chapter concerning eyes in a book of Patagonian memories,[1] I spoke of the unpleasant sensations produced in me by the sight of stuffed birds. Not bird skins in the drawers of a cabinet, it will be understood, these being indispensable to the ornithologist, and very useful to the larger class of persons who without being ornithologists yet take an intelligent interest in birds. The unpleasantness was at the sight of skins stuffed with wool and set up on their legs in imitation of the living bird, sometimes (oh mockery!) in their 'natural surroundings.' These 'surroundings' are as a rule constructed or composed of a few handfuls of earth to form the floor of the glass case – sand, rock, clay, chalk, or gravel; whatever the material may be it invariably has, like all 'matter out of place,' a grimy and depressing appearance. On the floor are planted grasses, sedges, and miniature bushes, made of tin or zinc and then dipped in a bucket of green paint. In the chapter referred to it was said, 'When the eye closes in death, the bird, except to the naturalist, becomes a mere bundle of dead feathers; crystal globes may be put into the empty sockets, and a bold life-imitating attitude given to the stuffed specimen, but the vitreous orbs shoot forth no lifelike glances: 'the "passion and the fire whose fountains are within" have vanished', and the best work of the taxidermist, who has given a life to his bastard art, produces in the mind only sensations of irritation and disgust.'[2] . . .

This, then, being my feeling about stuffed birds, set up in their 'natural surroundings,' I very naturally avoid the places where they are exhibited. At Brighton, for instance, on many occasions when I have visited and stayed in that town, there was no inclination to see the Booth Collection, which is supposed to be an ideal collection of British birds; and we know it was the life-work of a zealous ornithologist who was also a wealthy man, and who spared no pains to make it perfect of its kind.[3] About eighteen months ago I passed a night in the house of a friend close to Dyke Road, and next morning having a couple of hours to get

DOI: 10.4324/9781003107835-91

rid of I strolled into the museum. It was painfully disappointing, for though no actual pleasure had been expected, the distress experienced was more than I had bargained for. It happened that a short time before, I had been watching the living Dartford warbler, at a time when the sight of this small elusive creature is loveliest, for not only was the bird in his brightest feathers, but his surroundings were then most perfect –

> The whin was frankincense and flame.[4]

His appearance, as I saw him then and on many other occasions in the furze-flowering season, is fully described in a chapter in this book; but on this particular occasion while watching my bird I saw it in a new and unexpected aspect, and in my surprise and delight I exclaimed mentally, 'Now I have seen the furze wren at his very best!'

It was perhaps a very rare thing – one of those effects of light on plumage which we are accustomed to see in birds that have glossed metallic feathers, and, more rarely, in other kinds . . . But his colour was no longer that of the furze wren: seen at a distance the upper plumage always appears slaty-black; near at hand it is of a deep slaty-brown; now it was dark, sprinkled or frosted over with a delicate greyish-white, the white of oxidised silver; and this rare and beautiful appearance continued for a space of about twenty seconds; but no sooner did he flit to another spray than it vanished, and he was once more the slaty-brown little bird with a chestnut-red breast.

It is unlikely that I shall ever again see the furze wren in this aspect, with a curious splendour wrought by the sunlight in the dark but semi-translucent delicate feathers of his mantle; but its image is in the mind, and, with a thousand others equally beautiful, remains to me a perfect possession.

As I went in to see the famous Booth Collection, a thought of the bird I have just described came into my mind; and glancing round the big long room with shelves crowded with stuffed birds, like the crowded shelves of a shop, to see where the Dartford warblers were, I went straight to the case and saw a group of them fastened to a furze-bush, the specimens twisted by the stuffer into a variety of attitudes – ancient, dusty, dead little birds, painful to look at – a libel on nature and an insult to a man's intelligence.

It was a relief to go from this case to the others, which were not of the same degree of badness, but all, like the furze wrens, were in their natural surroundings – the pebbles, bit of turf, painted leaves, and what not, and, finally, a view of the wide world beyond, the green earth and the blue sky, all painted on the little square of deal or canvas which formed the back of the glass case.

Listening to the talk of other visitors who were making the round of the room, I heard many sincere expressions of admiration: they were really pleased and thought it all very wonderful. That is, in fact, the common feeling which most persons express in such places, and, assuming that it is sincere, the obvious explanation is that they know no better. They have never properly seen anything in nature, but have looked always with mind and the inner vision preoccupied with other and familiar things – indoor scenes and objects, and scenes described in books. If they had ever looked at wild birds properly – that is to say, emotionally, the images of such sights would have remained in their minds; and with such a standard for comparison, these dreary remnants of dead things set before them as restorations and as semblances of life would have only produced a profoundly depressing effect.

We hear of the educational value of such exhibitions, and it may be conceded that they might be made useful to young students of zoology, by distributing the specimens over a large area, arranged in scattered groups so as to give a rough idea of the relationship existing among its members . . . As things are, these collections help no one, and their effect is confusing and in many ways injurious to the mind, especially to the young. A multitude of specimens are brought before the sight, each and every one a falsification and degradation of nature, and the impression left is of an assemblage, or mob, of incongruous forms, and of a confusion of colours . . . These objects in a museum are not and cannot be viewed emotionally, as we view living forms and all nature; hence they do not, and we being what we are, cannot, register lasting impressions . . .

[pp. 13–20]

A man walking by the water-side sees by chance a kingfisher fly past, its colour a wonderful blue, far surpassing in beauty and brilliancy any blue he has ever seen in sky or water, or in flower or stone, or any other thing. No sooner has he seen than he wishes to become the possessor of that rare loveliness, that shining object which, he fondly imagines, will be a continual delight to him and to all in his house, – an ornament comparable to that splendid stone which the poor fisherman found in a fish's belly, which was his children's plaything by day and his candle by night. Forthwith he gets his gun and shoots it, and has it stuffed and put in a glass case. But it is no longer the same thing: the image of the living sunlit bird flashing past him is in his mind and creates a kind of illusion when he looks at his feathered mummy, but the lustre is not visible to others.

It is because of the commonness of this delusion that stuffed kingfishers, and other brilliant species, are to be seen in the parlours of tens of thousands of cottages all over the land. Nor is it only those who live in cottages that make this mistake; those who care to look for it will find that it exists in some degree in most minds – the curious delusion that the lustre which we see and admire is in the case, the coil, the substance which may be grasped, and not in the spirit of life which is within and the atmosphere and miracle-working sunlight which are without.

To return to my own taste and feelings, since in the present chapter I must be allowed to write on Man (myself to wit) and Birds, the other chapters being occupied with the subject of Birds and Man. It has always, or since I can remember, been my ambition and principal delight to see and hear every bird at its best. This is here a comparative term, and simply means an unusually attractive aspect of the bird, or a very much better than the ordinary one. This may result from a fortunate conjunction of circumstances, or may be due to a peculiar harmony between the creature and its surroundings; or in some instances, as in that given above of the Dartford warbler, to a rare effect of the sun. In still other cases, motions and antics, rarely seen, singularly graceful, or even grotesque, may give the best impression. After one such impression has been received, another equally excellent may follow at a later date: in that case the second impression does not obliterate, or is not superimposed upon the former one; both remain as permanent possessions of the mind, and we may thus have several mental pictures of the same species . . .

Of hundreds of such enduring images of our commonest species I will here describe one before concluding with this part of the subject.

The long-tailed or bottle-tit is one of the most delicately pretty of our small woodland birds, and among my treasures, in my invisible and intangible album, there were several pictures of him which I had thought unsurpassable, until on a day two years ago when a new and better one was garnered. I was walking a few miles from Bath by the Avon where it is not more than thirty or forty yards wide, on a cold, windy, very bright day in February. The opposite bank was lined with bushes growing close to the water, the roots and lower trunks of many of them being submerged, as the river was very full; and behind this low growth the ground rose abruptly, forming a long green hill crowned with tall beeches. I stopped to admire one of the bushes across the stream, and I wish I could now say what its species was: it was low with widespread branches close to the surface of the water, and its leafless twigs were adorned with catkins resembling those of the black poplar, as long as a man's little finger, of a rich dark-red or maroon colour. A party of about a dozen long-tailed tits were travelling, or drifting, in their usual desultory way, through the line of bushes towards this point, and in due time they arrived, one by one, at the bush I was watching, and finding it sheltered from the wind they elected to remain at that spot. For a space of fifteen minutes I looked on with delight, rejoicing at the rare chance which had brought that exquisite bird- and plant-scene before me. The long deep-red pendent catkins and the little pale birdlings among them in their grey and rose-coloured plumage, with long graceful tails and minute round, parroty heads; some quietly perched just above the water, others moving about here and there, occasionally suspending themselves back downwards from the slender terminal twigs – the whole mirrored below. That magical effect of water and sunlight gave to the scene a somewhat fairy-like, an almost illusory, character.

Such scenes live in their loveliness only for him who has seen and harvested them; they cannot be pictured forth to another by words, nor with the painter's brush, though it be charged with *tintas orientales*; least of all by photography, which brings all things down to one flat, monotonous, colourless shadow of things, weary to look at.

Editorial Endnotes

1 Hudson, *Idle Days in Patagonia* (London: Chapman and Hall, 1893), ch. 12, 'Concerning eyes'. Hudson had been born and grew up in Argentina. In this chapter he evoked

the blazing passion in the eyes of predatory animals and birds, contrasting it with the deadness of glass eyes in taxidermy specimens. On Hudson as a campaigning conservationist: Conor Mark Jameson, *Finding W.H. Hudson: The Writer Who Came to Britain to Save the Birds* (London: Pelagic Publishing, 2023).

2 By Hudson's account, in this chapter of *Idle Days in Patagonia*, Gould's stuffed hummingbirds (see Chapter 64 of the present work) also gave him this sense of revulsion. Here he slightly misquotes Coleridge's 'The passion and the life, whose fountains are within', from *Dejection: An Ode*.

3 For Booth's museum, see Chapter 65.

4 A quotation from the opening stanza of Algernon Swinburne's *The Tale of Balen* (1896).

Editorial Headnote

67. Eleanor Vere Boyle, 'A Plumage League', *Times* (1885)

In the last two decades of the nineteenth century, appreciation of the beauties of birds was linked to a growing detestation of shooting, especially when it served the feather trade. In the mind of this upper-class writer, who was a whimsical author and illustrator, vulgar nouveau-riche taste and sins against nature were closely associated. Here Vere Boyle welcomes current moves to establish a group that would campaign against the use of birds' feathers in hats and in dress trimmings. Such initiatives led up to the founding of the Society for the Protection of Birds in 1889.

67

A PLUMAGE LEAGUE

Eleanor Vere Boyle

Source: Eleanor Vere Boyle, 'A Plumage League', letter to the editor, *Times* (25 December 1885), p. 5.

Sir, – I hail with intense thankfulness the letter from Mr. F.O. Morris in *The Times* of Dec. 18.[1] 'The Plumage League' which he so admirably suggests is in effect precisely what I have for years been blindly groping after and vainly trying to get established – namely, an association for the disestablishment of beautiful birds as ornaments for ladies' hats or costume. Many are the ladies whose sympathies I have tried vainly to enlist. All of them have given their opinion most emphatically that any association for discarding the use of beautiful plumage as head gear and for other trimmings would fail, unless the Paris fashions and London milliners chose to be on our side, and the following observation has more than once been added, 'If we are to give up feathers why not furs also?' Mr. Morris reasons in the kindest and most gentle way. Alas! he little knows the hardness and the utter impracticability of some of us when fashion is in question. But these are the days of leagues, and the Plumage League must and will be a success. It will have, also, the immense advantage of appealing to all classes and to no special party. The barbarous fashion of wearing the stuffed skins of beautiful innocent birds has become nothing less than a vice. Where in former years one bird was enough to trim a hat, now half-a-dozen at least are required. Not content with Nature's gold and enamelled jewel work in such masterpieces as the ruby-crested, emerald-breasted humming bird, she is insulted by the vulgar art of the trade; and the wings and tails of these gems of loveliness are now encrusted with worthless gilt. I have counted as many as 30 rare and exquisite humming birds displayed in one shop window, their native brilliancy desecrated with Judson's gold.[2] The amusement of looking at shop windows at Christmas time is ruined for the many lovers of birds by the ostentation of bird murder we are forced to witness. A few days ago in Bond-street, amid the holocaust of birds of every kind, one ghastly arrangement lay on the velvet-covered window shelf alone in all its horror. It was a spray of five goldfinches, wired so as to be worn across the bodice of a dress. In the windows of almost every shop throughout the London streets there are English and foreign birds of every variety of brilliant colour or sober mezzotint. They are made up

DOI: 10.4324/9781003107835-92

in bunches for hats, towering up 12 or 14 inches high, or they are laid across the brim, as if dead, with wide-open glass eyes. Robins and bullfinches and tom-tits (mixed up with kittens) are fixed in distorted imitation of life upon plush photograph frames. There is no end to the tasteless use now made of birds. Nothing can be more contrary to the canons of true taste than this fashion of wearing the dead bodies of birds upon one's head or dress. No instance of such a fashion can be pointed to in any of the older and nobler examples of costume which remain to us in pictures and engravings. The only parallel exists in the savage who ornaments himself with the scalps of his slain enemies.

The Plumage League will do much to check the world-wide slaughter of birds. Meanwhile, however, it is to be feared that Nature will herself enter her unanswerable protest. By-and-by there will be no more beautiful wild birds remaining to be destroyed, either in Great Britain or anywhere else.

I remain, Sir, yours obediently, Eleanor Vere C. Boyle. Huntercombe Manor, Maidenhead.

Editorial Endnotes

1 Revd Francis Orpen Morris was a popular writer on birds and one of the group campaigning against the use of feathers in millinery in the 1880s. Tessa Boase, *Mrs Pankhurst's Purple Feather: Fashion, Fury and Feminism – Women's Fight for Change* (London: Aurum Press, 2018), pp. 72–3, 84–5. Diana Donald, *Women Against Cruelty: Protection of Animals in Nineteenth-century Britain*, 2nd ed. (Manchester: Manchester University Press, 2020), p. 256. Helen Louise Cowie, *Victims of Fashion: Animal Commodities in Victorian Britain* (Cambridge and New York: Cambridge University Press, 2022), pp. 17–54.

2 'Judson's Gold Paint, The Best Substitute for Gold Leaf' was marketed in the 1880s.

Editorial Headnote

68. Edmund Selous, *Beautiful Birds* (1901)

The author was the brother of Frederick Courteney Selous, who was a big game hunter, but their attitudes to the natural world could not have been more different. Edmund Selous was the author of *Bird Watching* (also published in 1901), which inaugurated a new genre of nature writing, recording his impressions and insights as he watched bird behaviour in the field.[1] *Beautiful Birds*, in contrast, was one of the books he wrote for children, and Selous adopts a much more emotional tone, which nevertheless seems to be tinged with irony or sarcasm. He pleads with his young readers to fight against the trade in birds' feathers for millinery – even suggesting they should make direct emotional appeals to their own guilty mothers. He begins by describing the colouristic beauties of birds, especially the tropical ones.

Editorial Endnote

1 Edmund Selous, *Bird Watching* (London: J.M. Dent, 1901). David Elliston Allen, *The Naturalist in Britain: A Social History* (Harmondsworth: Penguin Books, 1978), pp. 231–3, 238. Diana Donald, *Women Against Cruelty: Protection of Animals in Nineteenth-century Britain*, 2nd ed. (Manchester: Manchester University Press, 2020), p. 269.

68

BEAUTIFUL BIRDS

Edmund Selous

Source: Edmund Selous, *Beautiful Birds*, 'with many illustrations by Hubert C. Astley' (London: J.M. Dent, 1901), pp. 5–18.

Now it is about some of those birds – the very beautiful birds of all – the most beautiful ones in the whole world – that I am going to tell you . . . Indeed, I sometimes wish that those very beautiful birds were not quite so beautiful as they are. You will think that a funny wish to have, but there is a sensible reason for it, which I will explain to you. Perhaps if they were not quite so beautiful, not quite so many of them would be killed. For, strange as it may seem to you – and I know it *will* seem strange – it is just because the birds *are* beautiful that hundreds and hundreds, yes, and thousands and thousands, of them are being killed every day. Yes, it is quite true. I wish it were not, but I am sorry to say it is. People kill the birds *because* they are beautiful. But is not that cruel? Yes, indeed it is, very, very cruel. It is cruel for two reasons: first, because to kill them gives them pain; and secondly, because their life is so happy. Can anything be happier than the life of a bird? Surely not. Only to fly, just think how delightful that must be, and then to be always living in green, leafy palaces under the bright, warm sun and the blue sky. For I must tell you that these birds we are going to talk about live where the trees are always leafy, where the sun is always bright and the sky always blue . . .

So, as it is cruel to kill the birds, and as they are not nearly so beautiful when they are dead as they are when they are alive, and as the world is full of tender-hearted women to love them and plead for them and to say, 'Do not kill them,' perhaps you will wonder why it is that they are killed. I will tell you how it has come about. When Dame Nature had imagined all her beautiful birds, and then cut them out of that wonderful stuff of hers – the stuff of life – with her marvellous pair of scissors, she said to her eldest daughter – whose name is Truth – 'Now I will leave them and go away for a little, for there are other places where I must imagine things and cut them out with my scissors.' Truth said, 'Do not leave the birds, for there are men in the world with hard hearts and a film over their eyes. They will see the birds, but not their beauty, because of the film, and they will kill them because of their hearts, which are like marble or rock or stone.' 'They are,

DOI: 10.4324/9781003107835-93

it is true,' said Dame Nature, 'and indeed it was of some such material that I cut them out. I had my reasons, but you would never understand them, so I shall not tell you what they were. But there are not only my men in the world; there are my women too. I cut *them* out of something very different. It was soft and yielding, and that part that went to make the heart was like water – like soft water. I made them, too, to have influence over the men, and I put no film over *their* eyes. *They* will see how beautiful my birds are, and they will know that they are more beautiful alive than dead . . . And to make it still more certain, see yonder on that hill sits the Goddess of Pity . . . Have no fear, then, for until the Goddess of Pity falls asleep my birds are safe.' 'But *may* she not fall asleep?' said Truth. But Dame Nature had hurried away with her scissors, and was out of hearing.

As soon as she was gone, there crept out of a dark cave, where he had been hiding, an ugly little mannikin . . . All that people saw when they looked at him was a suit of clothes, and this suit of clothes was so well made and so fashionable, and fitted him so well, that they always thought the ugly demon inside it was just what he ought to be . . . he knew that when once the Goddess of Pity was asleep he might do whatever he liked . . . He took a pinch of the hot powder which was labelled 'Vanity,' and blew it upon the heads of all the women . . . Then from the other little bottle, which was labelled 'Apathy,' the demon took a pinch of the cold powder and blew it on the women's hearts, and as soon as it fell on them they became frozen, so that all the pity that had been in them before was frozen, too . . .

So, now, what happened after the wicked little demon had behaved in this wicked way? Why, the women whose hearts he had frozen began to kill the poor, beautiful birds, those birds that Dame Nature loved so, and had taken such pains to keep alive. I do not mean that they killed them themselves with their own hands. No, they did not do that, for they had not enough time to go to the countries where the beautiful birds lived, which were often a long way off as well as being very unhealthy. You see they were wanted at home, and so to have gone away from home into unhealthy countries to kill birds would have been *selfish*, and one should never be that. So instead of killing them themselves the women sent men to kill them for them, for *they* could be spared much better, and if they should not come back they would not be nearly so much missed. And the women said to the men, 'Kill the birds and tear off their wings, their tails, their bright breasts and heads to sew into our hats or onto the sleeves and collars of our gowns and mantles' . . . Everywhere the earth was stained with their blood, and the air thick with floating feathers that had been torn from their poor, wounded bodies. It was full, too, of their frightened cries, and of the wails of their starving young ones for the parents who were dead and could not feed them any more.[1] For it is just at the time when the birds lay their eggs and rear their young ones that their plumage is most beautiful – most *exquisitely* beautiful . . . So the birds were killed, and the lovely, painted feathers that had lighted up whole forests or made a country beautiful, were pressed close together into dark ugly boxes – or things like boxes – called 'crates' (large it is true, but not *quite* so large as a forest or a country), and then brought over the seas in ships to dark, ugly houses, where they were taken out and flung in a great heap on the floor. Soon they were sewn into hats which were set out in the windows of milliners' shops for the women with the frozen hearts to buy . . . There they stand, looking and looking, ravenous, hungry – you would almost say they were – longing to buy them, even though they have new ones of the same sort on their head. Ah, if they could see those birds as they looked when they were shot, before they were dressed and cleaned and made to look so smart and fashionable! If they could see them with the blood-stains upon them, the wet, warm drops running down over the bright breasts – perhaps onto the little ones underneath them – the poor, broken wings dragging over the ground and trying to rise into the air, through which they had once flown so easily, the flapping, the struggling! . . . it would be the same, just the same, if all those bright feathers in every one of the hats had been stripped, not from the birds' but from *angels'* wings. Those who could wear the one could wear the other, and if angels were to come down here I should not wonder if angel-hats were to get to be quite the fashion. Only first, of course, angels would *have* to come down here. I do not think they are so *very* likely to . . .

Then is there no way of saving them both, the poor birds and the poor women? Yes, there is a way, and it is you – the children – who are to find it out. Listen. It is so simple. All you have to do is to ask these women (these *poor* women) *not* to wear the hats that have feathers, that have birds' lives in them, and they will not do so any more. They will listen to you. There is nobody else they would listen to, but they will to you – the children . . . Throw, each one of you, your arms round your mother's neck, kiss her and ask her not to kill the birds, not to wear the hats that make the birds be killed. And if you do that and really mean what you say, if you are really sorry for the birds and have real tears in your eyes (or at least in your hearts), then your mother will do as you have asked her, for you will have pressed that spot, that soft spot, that spot that even the wicked little demon, try as he might, could not freeze, could not make hard.

Editorial Endnote

1 It was notorious that egrets were shot in the breeding season when they developed the sought-after 'nuptial plumes', and the fledglings starved after the parent birds had been killed. See, for example, W.H. Hudson, *Osprey; Or Egrets and Aigrettes* (Society for the Protection of Birds, leaflet no. 3, 1896). 'Ospreys' was the familiar but misleading name given to egret feathers in millinery.

Editorial Headnote

69. Society For The Protection Of Birds, *Birds and their Protection. A Lecture* (1895)

The Society for the Protection of Birds, soon to become the *Royal* Society for the Protection of Birds (RSPB), is famous for its campaign against the mass slaughter of tropical birds, the feathers of which were used to decorate ladies' hats and other items of dress. However, from an early date the SPB also worked to protect native British bird species. While careful to keep on the right side of the powerful field sports lobby, the Society sought to end the activities of trappers serving the trade in caged birds (see Chapters 63 and 63.1 of the present work), and also discouraged the casual shooting of rare visitants for collections of stuffed specimens. It was necessary to 'abandon the gun for the field-glass' – to become a bird watcher rather than a bird destroyer.

The SPB aided the implementation and enforcement of county laws protecting various birds in the nesting season. *Inter alia* they organised lectures and published pamphlets which appealed to the aesthetic sensibilities of the public, as a means of gaining support for such measures. From 1895 onwards, according to the SPB's annual reports, an average of sixty illustrated lectures were delivered every year by volunteers across the country, to both adult and child audiences. W.H. Hudson, a leading figure in the SPB, himself sometimes gave talks to children. Copies of W. Kennedy's specimen lecture, which could be borrowed from the SPB along with the costly lantern slides that illustrated it, used a great range of artistic imagery to evoke the beauties of live birds in their natural element – so different from the artifices of taxidermy. The SPB was confident that these visual presentations 'form one of the most valuable means for the education of public opinion and the formation of a strong popular feeling on Bird Protection'.[1] The lecture combined ornithological information with references to uplifting works of literature. Like the chosen art works, these classics lent moral and cultural authority to the cause.

In the following extracts, the subjects of some of the slides that were projected to illustrate particular sections of Kennedy's text (pp. 22–3) have been indicated, in conjunction with the passages in question. Others are then just listed without the accompanying text (from pp. 5–47), simply to exemplify the wide range of visual genres, historical references, and scientific fields that was brought into play. The eclecticism of this set of several hundred images (largely chosen and assembled by Mrs. Margaretta Lemon, the SPB Secretary) reveals the changing artistic tastes of the *fin de siècle*. Now photographs and Japanese drawings of birds in flight could sometimes seem more attractive and truer to life than the elaborate coloured lithographs which had illustrated ornithological folios of the high Victorian era. An impression of *movement* and *freedom* became all-important, but it is sometimes unclear whether 'from life' indicates a sketch or a photograph.

Editorial Endnote

1 The development of the lecture programme and slide collection was often discussed in the SPB's reports: e.g. *Fifth Annual Report* for 1895, p. 5; *Seventh Annual Report* for 1897, p. 5; *Eighth Annual Report* for 1898, p. 7; *Ninth Annual Report* for 1899, p. 11.

69

BIRDS AND THEIR PROTECTION. A LECTURE

Society for the Protection of Birds

Source: Society for the Protection of Birds, *Birds and Their Protection. A Lecture*, 'compiled by W. Kennedy, Assistant-Master, Haileybury College. Published by Request' (Hertford: printed by Stephen Austin and Sons, 1895).

The slides will be found unusually numerous for the lecture. They are, indeed, meant to present a moving panorama of bird-life, rather than a series of pictures for separate and detailed consideration. It is well to warn the operator and the audience of this beforehand . . . It is, perhaps, unnecessary to say that gas or electricity is much superior to an oil-lamp for showing slides – especially those that are coloured.

Personally, I much prefer a simple lantern, with a 'double carrier,' by which one picture takes the place of the last instantaneously, to a double lantern and the somewhat childish device of 'dissolving views.'[1]

These slides, with the others now in the possession of the Society, form a series of unequalled excellence and beauty. Those made from Mr. Lodge's drawings, and a few others, can now be procured by the public from Messrs. Newton, 3, Fleet Street, but the majority, including those done by Lord Lilford's permission from his 'British Birds,' are the exclusive property of the Society.[2] The latter are made, when coloured, at a cost of 10s each, and lecturers are begged to exercise special care in their handling and packing. It is hoped, too, that lecturers will not omit to send the Secretary a contribution to the lantern-fund, that we may complete the series and defray the heavy expenses that we have been put to . . .

Rough sketch of a Bird (Japanese)

'The bird,' says Ruskin, 'is little more than a drift of the air brought into form by plumes; the air is in all its quills, it breathes through its whole frame and flesh, and glows with air in its flying, like a blown flame: it rests upon the air, subdues it, surpasses it, out-races it; – *is* the air, conscious of itself, conquering itself, ruling itself'[3] . . .

Lark soaring

The covering of a bird's skin – the plumage – is essentially the same as hair, scales, and nails, modified into a most beautiful form. Nothing could well exceed

DOI: 10.4324/9781003107835-94

the compactness, lightness, and strength of this clothing. It is also a perfect non-conductor, retaining the internal heat of the body, and no less protecting it from the rays of a tropical sun, thus enabling birds to support with impunity great extremes of temperature.

Kestrel hovering

What shall I say of their powers of flight – opening the feathers as they raise the wing that they may meet the least resistance from the air, and closing them as they strike that they may oppose the greatest resistance to it; soaring, as the larks do, by facing the wind and slanting upwards like a kite (the place of the string being taken by the momentum of the bird); poising themselves motionless with outspread wings, like a kestrel, by adapting themselves almost imperceptibly to every faintest variation in the breeze; or hovering, again, like the tiny humming-birds [Loddigesia, Hudson's 'Naturalist in La Plata.'][4] by a lightning vibration of the wings, so rapid that nothing can be seen but a blur; wheeling and turning from dawn to dusk, like the swifts and swallows, who seem to solve the problem of eternal motion; or, like the albatross, with wings twelve feet across, sailing majestically over the sea for days together – their power of flight, I say, is a mystery that baffled Solomon long ago, and that I, at any rate, am by no means competent to explain.

Woman wearing aigrette[5]
Great White Heron (Lord Lilford)
The small Egret (Lord Lilford), coloured.[6]
Flamingoes (from life)
Dead Heron: G.F. Watts (by permission)[7]
Unmounted Bird of Paradise plumes
Spotted Flycatcher sitting: side view (from life)
Feeding the Sacred Ibis in the Halls of Karnak: E.J. Poynter (by permission)[8]
St. Francis preaching to the birds: Mrs. Jameson's 'Monastic Orders' (by permission)[9]
Swallow after fly: Howard Saunders, 'Manual of British Birds' (by permission)[10]
Swallows flying (Japanese)
Oyster-catchers; Ringed Plover; Little Stint; Curlew (Lodge)[11]
A large order: Du Maurier (by permission)[12]
A bird of prey: Linley Sambourne (by permission)[13]
Hesperornis, Pterodactyls, Archaeopteryx (fossil) Archaeopteryx (restored)
Birds (black) flying (Japanese)
Robin and young: 'Homes without Hands'
Bird with petal in mouth (Japanese)
Puffins and Rabbits: 'Homes without Hands'[14]
Cuckoo ejecting small birds[15]
Swallows in rain: Phil Robinson's 'Birds of the Wave and Woodland' (by permission)[16]

Great Bird of Paradise: 'Royal Natural History' (by permission)[17]
Motmot: Wood's 'Natural History' (by permission)[18]
Gardener Bower-bird: 'Darwin and after Darwin' – Romanes (by permission)[19]
The Keeper's Gibbet: Harting's 'Ornithology of Shakespeare'[20]
Vole or Field-mouse: Bell's 'British Quadrupeds' (by permission)[21]
Common Mice (snap-shot)
Sparrows in snow (snap-shot)
Large bird (Japanese), threatening
Lark (Japanese)
Ruff: 'Lost British Birds' (W.H. Hudson)[22]
Starling (collector's idea) – a stuffed bird
Starling (Nature's idea) (Lodge)
Spotted Flycatcher sitting (from life)

Editorial Endnotes

1 A 'double carrier' on a magic lantern or projector was a horizontal sliding frame with two apertures for lantern slides, which could be slotted in and shown successively. 'Dissolving views' – images which gradually changed in their colours or light effects – were achieved by a 'biunial' magic lantern: two matching images were aligned and one faded as the other appeared. Evidently SPB lecturers preferred the speed and simplicity of the double carrier, which allowed a long sequence of images to be projected as the lecturer spoke.

2 George Edward Lodge was an ornithological illustrator who, together with Archibald Thorburn and others, produced the coloured lithographic drawings for Lord Lilford's seven-volume *Coloured Figures of the Birds of the British Islands* (London: R.H. Porter, 1885–97).

3 John Ruskin, *The Queen of the Air: Being a Study of the Greek Myths of Cloud and Storm* (London: Smith, Elder, 1869), 'Athena Keramitis' (Athena in the Earth), para. 65, pp. 79–80.

4 W.H. Hudson, *The Naturalist in La Plata* (London: Chapman and Hall, 1892), ch. XVI, 'Humming-birds', pp. 205–20.

5 This must have been a fashion plate or a cartoon of a woman wearing feathers, shown to the audience as an object of criticism.

6 The heron and egret will have been plates taken from Lilford's *Coloured Figures* (see n. 2), their staid descriptive style contrasting with the action studies in the Japanese prints.

7 The artist George Frederic Watts was a supporter of the Society for the Protection of Birds: see Diana Donald, *Women Against Cruelty: Protection of Animals in Nineteenth-century Britain*, 2nd ed. (Manchester: Manchester University Press, 2020), pp. 266–8. The *Dead Heron* or *Wounded Heron*, apparently a victim of hawking, is portrayed in Watts's oil painting of 1837 in the Watts Gallery, Compton.

8 Edward John Poynter's *Feeding the Sacred Ibis* of 1871 is an imagined scene of ancient Egypt. It reminded the lecture audience that the ibis had then been sacred to Thoth, the god of wisdom, and was never persecuted.

9 There were numerous editions of Anna Jameson's *Legends of the Monastic Orders, as Represented in the Fine Arts*. Many were illustrated with a wood engraving of Giotto's fresco at Assisi, showing St Francis preaching to the birds. The accompanying text recorded the legend that the saint had rescued and cherished some doves which had been snared and were on their way to slaughter in the market.

10 Howard Saunders, *An Illustrated Manual of British Birds* (London: Gurney and Jackson, 1889), wood engraving on p. 155. The wood blocks were inherited by the publisher from the last edition of Yarrell's *British Birds*.

11 It is not clear whether these were lithographs by George Edward Lodge or photographs by Reginald Badham Lodge.

12 'A Large Order' was the title of a cartoon by George du Maurier in *Punch*, 14 October 1893. A stout lady visits a shop selling feather trimmings. The proprietor asks: 'What can we get for you, Madam?' and she replies 'Wings!'.

13 Linley Sambourne's cartoon with this title in *Punch*, 14 May 1892, showed a feathered woman with claw feet like a raptor or harpy hovering over her prey – water birds. The caption explains the slaughter of egrets etc. that was taking place at the instigation of the fashion trade. Robin W. Doughty, *Feather Fashions and Bird Preservation: A Study in Nature Protection* (Berkeley, Los Angeles, London: University of California Press, 1975), p. 97. Donald, *Women Against Cruelty*, pp. 263–4.

14 Revd J.G. Wood's *Homes Without Hands* (London: Longmans, Green, 1865) includes (p. 62) a wood-engraved illustration of puffins and rabbits, disputing ownership of a burrow. The 'Robin and young' must have been from a similar source.

15 Presumably the cuckoo image was derived, directly or indirectly, from Jemima Blackburn's drawing (see Chapter 13.1 of the present work).

16 Phil [Philip Stewart] Robinson, *Birds of the Wave and Woodland* (London: Isbister, 1894), p. 43, engraving of swallows flying in rain, signed by Charles Whymper.

17 Richard Lydekker (ed.), *The Royal Natural History*, 6 vols. (London: Frederick Warne, 1894–5), vol. 3, p. 334, engraving showing the Great Bird of Paradise displaying.

18 Revd John George Wood, *The Illustrated Natural History*, 2 vols. (London: Routledge, Warne and Routledge, 1862) vol. 2, *Birds*, p. 156, showing two motmots.

19 George Romanes, *Darwin and After Darwin: An Exposition of the Darwinian Theory and a Discussion of Post-Darwinian Questions. 1: The Darwinian Theory* (London: Longmans, Green, 1892), p. 382, fig. 121, 'The Gardener Bower-bird, from Gould's *Birds of New Guinea*'.

20 James Edmund Harting, *The Ornithology of Shakespeare* (London: John Van Voorst, 1871), p. 82: birds of prey etc. killed by the gamekeeper and strung up from a tree.

21 Thomas Bell, *A History of British Quadrupeds*, 2nd ed. (London: John Van Voorst, 1874), p. 323, engraving of 'Common Field-Vole'.

22 W.H. Hudson, *Lost British Birds*, with 15 drawings by A.D. McCormick (Society for the Protection of Birds leaflet no. 14, 1894), p. 27.

Figure 16 Henry Stacy Marks, decorative panel of birds (crowned crane, cockatoo, and scarlet ibis), 1878–80, one of a series painted for the Duke of Westminster's Eaton Hall, oil on canvas. (Private collection/Bridgeman Images)

Editorial Headnote

70. Henry Stacy Marks, *Pen and Pencil Sketches* (1894)

When Henry Stacy Marks turned to animal painting, his approach differed greatly from that of the Edwin Landseer school. Rather than evoking the violence of nature, he depicted birds with humour, fantasy, and decorative appeal. Here he describes the panels commissioned by the Duke of Westminster for one of the ornate drawing rooms at Eaton Hall, the Duke's seat in Cheshire, which had been designed in the Gothic style by Alfred Waterhouse.[1] Marks groups together birds of many different species, continents, and climes in a manner which recalls, perhaps deliberately, the mélanges in sixteenth- and seventeenth-century depictions of the Garden of Eden or in early zoological illustrations (see Figure 16). They create a harmony of varied forms and colours, and the effect is sustained by the continuous background of the panels – a depiction of a flowery lawn and a garden wall, beyond which trees are glimpsed, in a manner that recalls some of the ancient Roman wall paintings at Pompeii. The charm of these compositions contrasts strongly with the qualities of the bold six-foot charcoal sketches which the Duke commissioned from Joseph Wolf for another room at Eaton Hall, depicting the wildlife of the Scottish island of Handa.[2]

Editorial Endnotes

1 The Victorian rooms at Eaton Hall have been demolished, but the bird panels by Marks survive.

2 A.H. Palmer, *The Life of Joseph Wolf, Animal Painter* (London and New York: Longmans, Green, 1895), p. 151.

70

PEN AND PENCIL SKETCHES

Henry Stacy Marks

Source: Henry Stacy Marks, *Pen and Pencil Sketches*, 2 vols. (London; Chatto and Windus, 1894), vol.1, pp. 217–19.

. . . Meanwhile, I had received from and executed for the Duke another commission. It was one the carrying out of which gave me more pleasure and enjoyment than any that I ever had. In November 1877 I was painting some tiny panels of heads of birds for my old fellow-student William Burges.[1] The Duke happened to call to see how the 'Pilgrims' were progressing, and seemed very interested with these birds' heads, looking at them again and again.[2] At length he said, 'How would a room of birds look?' I replied, I thought it would have a very decorative effect, when he gave me to understand I might carry out his idea. When next I was at Eaton, the Duke, Waterhouse, and I went over the hall together, selected a room (one of the smaller drawing-rooms) and decided on the number (twelve) and position of the panels. It was arranged that these should be in groups of three. As I wished to include birds of all shapes and sizes, of different climes and conditions, from the Indian adjutant to the humble English wagtail, the cockatoo from Australia, the macaw from South America, the African crane, and the European stork, I imagined them in a fairy garden, an ornithological Walhalla, where no bird quarrels with another, but is content with the climate, conditions, and surroundings of its present abode – an abode where food is always present without the trouble of seeking for it, into which bands of yelling school-children are not permitted to enter, those terrors of the actual 'Zoo;' where pinioning is forbidden, and wing-hacking unknown.

Before the birds settled down in their permanent home at Eaton, they were exhibited at Agnew's Gallery in Bond Street in May 1880. The little show brought me kind and congratulatory letters (among others) from the President,[3] Sir J.E. Millais,[4] and Briton Riviere,[5] and had the honour of supplying the text for a leader in the *Times*.

Never has any work of mine been so well cared for or shown to such advantage. The frames of the pictures are richly carved and gilt; the walls covered with a warm but delicately tinted grey plush or velvet, which relieves the darks and gives

DOI: 10.4324/9781003107835-95

value to the lights of the painting. I believe Miss Jekyll of Henley-on-Thames is the lady to whom I am indebted for this arrangement.[6]

Editorial Endnotes

1 William Burges was an architect and designer who often ornamented his 'Gothic' furniture with little decorative paintings. It is likely that Marks's 'tiny heads of birds' were panels of this kind.
2 Marks was painting a frieze of Chaucer's Canterbury pilgrims for one of the rooms at Eaton Hall.
3 Marks must be referring to the president of the Royal Academy, then Frederic Leighton.
4 John Everett Millais was originally one of the Pre-Raphaelites, working, like Marks, in an idiom characterised by strong colour and natural detail.
5 For Briton Riviere, see Chapters 52–4 of the present work.
6 Gertrude Jekyll, better known as a horticulturist, designed decorative schemes for the interiors at Eaton Hall.

Editorial Headnote

70.1 Anon., 'Decorative Art: Makart and Marks', *Times* (1880)

This was the *Times* leading article alluded to by Marks in *Pen and Pencil Sketches*.

70.1

DECORATIVE ART

Makart and Marks

Anon., Times

Source: Anon., 'Decorative art: Makart and Marks', *Times* (10 May 1880), p. 5.

The painter's attention has of late been so little turned to decoration that artists and patrons may be almost said to have practically lost sight of such an application of the art . . . Mr. Marks is one of the few members of the Academy who has a turn and a capability for decorative work. He has already executed a series of wall-pictures of excellent effect in the country house of a great Northern captain of industry. He has now painted a series of 12 panels of birds for the Duke of Westminster, to be placed in the ante-drawing room at Eaton-hall, Cheshire. The subjects are not arranged according to climate and *habitat*, but rather with a studied disregard of actual conditions. Thus we see a sober penguin looking curiously up at a group of flamingoes, with a robin in the same frame, evidently illustrating the extremes of contrast in shape and size. So the gorgeous blue and scarlet macaw of South America foregathers in Mr. Marks's panels with the stately but sober-clad African Stanley[1] and Demoiselle cranes, while the sulphur-crested cockatoo and warbling grass-paraquet of the Australian ranges are combined with the pelicans of the Nile and the Scamander.[2] There is the same force of comical contrast between the brisk and tiny long-tailed tit and the ponderous, heavy-headed adjutants, as the opposite extremes of bird-form and colour meet in the grotesque and bright but heavily-beaked toucan, and the slender, sober-clad, high-stilted, tip-tilted godwit. The same principles of arbitrary arrangement sometimes reign in all the 12 panels, governed by principles of humour, chromatic effect, or laws of composition, the two latter, of course, reigning everywhere, but sometimes with one sometimes with the other uppermost. Mr. Marks is especially happy in his treatment of the waders, the flamingoes, various cranes and storks, and the heavy-bodied delicately roseate pelicans. His painting is eminently careful and conscientious as ever – too clear and precise indeed, to please the taste of those in whose judgment the picturesque is an essential element of the pictorial, and no colour acceptable unless it be broken.

But the clearness, exactness, and brightness of Mr. Marks's work make it eminently adapted to decoration. It bears the painter's distinctive stamp of latent humour; and

DOI: 10.4324/9781003107835-96

for exactness it would satisfy Dr. Sclater or Mr. Wolf himself.[3] We are not surprised to hear that the Duke's example is being widely followed, and that Mr. Marks has been plied with commissions for decorations of the same kind.

Editorial Endnotes

1 The Stanley Crane is also known as the Blue Crane.
2 The Scamander was a legendary river.
3 Philip Lutley Sclater was secretary of the Zoological Society of London: he would have checked Joseph Wolf's illustrations of animals for scientific accuracy when they were destined for the ZSL's publications.

Editorial Headnote

71. Correspondence Between Henry Stacy Marks and John Hancock (1875)

There was a friendship between Henry Stacy Marks and the naturalist and taxidermist John Hancock, and part of their correspondence survives. Marks's letter here reveals both the interplay and the tension between natural science and artistic representation of birds in the nineteenth century. In letter 0466 (6 March 1875) Marks had mentioned his preoccupation with 'the decorative designs for work I have to do for the Duke of Westminster' (see Chapters 70 and 70.1 of the present work).

71

CORRESPONDENCE WITH JOHN HANCOCK

Henry Stacy Marks

Source: Correspondence between Henry Stacy Marks and John Hancock, 1875. Hancock archive, Newcastle.

15 Hamilton Terrace, St. John's Wood, NW Nov. 21 1875

My dear Mr. Hancock

Many thanks for your Catalogue of the Birds of the North.[1] It arrived yesterday morning and I shall value it very much not only for the useful knowledge it conveys but also for the loving reverence for Nature which is shown in every page. It is far different from the usual scientific view of birds which we simple minded painters find so hard to get interested in – it is the result of the study of one who has watched these beautiful creatures and studied them keenly – who has as it were, penetrated into the birds' nature and recognised that he has a heart and feelings – and not of one who has only looked at the bird from outside and seen nothing more than a creature with a certain number of primaries secondaries and a greater or less number of cervical . . . [illegible word].[2] I have read the 'Introduction' carefully and quite go with your diatribes on the game preserver and the game keeper[3] – the account of the excursion to Prestwick Car [sic] is very graphic and interesting and that is a humorous touch about your friend who always thought your birds 'stiff in the legs'.[4] You 'had' him rather neatly.

My photographer tells me he forwarded to you yesterday a set of the 'Vaughan Decorations' and I told him also to forward you some copies of a series of decorations I am doing for Mr. Gibbs one of the directors of the Bank of England – consisting of Penguins – Pelicans – Night Heron – Bateleur Eagles and Common Herons.[5] I hope you will accept them with my best regards and deal leniently with them from a critical point of view. I claim only to have given the character of the birds and you will doubtless find in them a hundred errors anatomical and otherwise. – I should be glad however to receive your criticisms on them for future guidance. Life is too short to study all things and it has ever been one of my great regrets that I never had that natural education that the country affords. You will I know, whatever faults you see look on them as the work of a fellow artist who had

DOI: 10.4324/9781003107835-97

done his best, according to his lights to show the wondrous beauty and quaintness of some of God's creatures. Besides these there are a panel of Crested Cranes and one of ordinary Storks, not yet finished . . .

With kind regards, believe me,

Faithfully yours,
H. Stacy Marks

Newcastle on Tyne 26th Nov. 1875

My Dear Mr Marks,

I am in receipt of your kind letter – We should be delighted to meet you at the Gardens, & we shall not leave them until the dusk. In case you come, we will be in front of the Lion's cages from 3 to half past . . .

Your beautiful Photos are here all safe . . . I am very much pleased to possess such interesting copies of your works.

The birds are excellent. In my opinion they are more like live birds than any I have seen in Artistic Works. I have had them set up before me ever since they came to hand. My sister desires me to say she is much pleased with them but those from Vaughan set of the seasons she is delighted with.

So good by for the present, & on Wednesday next if all be well I hope to have the pleasure of seeing you and to make the acquaintance of your family.

Yours very truly
John Hancock

Editorial Endnotes

1 John Hancock, *A Catalogue of the Birds of Northumberland and Durham* (*Natural History Transactions of Northumberland and Durham*, 1873, vol. vi), published in book form (London: Williams and Norgate, 1874).
2 Primary and secondary wing feathers.
3 Hancock himself shot birds, including rarities, for sport and for scientific study and taxidermy. Nevertheless he deplored the cruel and mindless wholesale destruction of raptors and other predatory animals by gamekeepers (*Catalogue*, pp. xviii–xxi).
4 Hancock wrote that one of his friends always criticised his stuffed peregrine falcons as looking too stiff in the legs. In response, Hancock brought a live bird into the workroom. Being hooded, it sat perfectly still, and when Hancock's friend came in, he made the usual criticism, thinking it was another stuffed specimen (pp. 12–13).
5 Henry Hucks Gibbs, a Bank of England Director who later became first Baron Aldenham, was restoring Aldenham House in Hertfordshire in the 1870s, and it seems likely that Marks's bird panels were destined for a drawing room there. Neither this commission nor the 'Vaughan Decorations' seems to be mentioned in *Pen and Pencil Sketches*. The Vaughans were friends of Marks, and it appears from Hancock's letter that this was a set of panels picturing birds or nature in general through the seasons.

Figure 17 Sir Rutherford Alcock, *Art and Art Industries in Japan* (London: Virtue, 1878), frontispiece, colour woodcut of a night scene – a shore with flying birds. (Harvard College Library/Hathitrust)

Editorial Headnote

72. Sir Rutherford Alcock, *Art and Art Industries in Japan* (1878)

Alcock had been British Consul-General in Japan and had organised the assemblage of Japanese art works (including some from his own collection) shown at the International Exhibition in London in 1862. This display was a powerful influence on the rise of *japonaiserie* in Britain. A lecture 'On Japanese art' given by John Leighton at the Royal Institution in 1863 already celebrated Alcock's role in bringing it to the attention of western aesthetes.[1] By the 1880s and 1890s there was a large literature on Japanese art and design (notably William Anderson's scholarly history, *The Pictorial Arts of Japan* of 1886), and fierce competition to acquire examples of the decorative arts. Japanese woodcuts representing birds and other animal motifs were acquired by the South Kensington Museum, later re-named the Victoria and Albert Museum. Alcock's own series of articles on 'Japanese art' appeared in the *Art Journal* through 1875–7, forming the basis for his book. He pondered the Japanese artists' love of 'variety', meaning not simply a wide range of subjects drawn directly from nature, but also a sense of movement and fluidity, and the avoidance of axial symmetry in composition. Later he tried to distil the qualities which differentiated Japanese artists' visions of nature and their pictorial conventions from those found in European art.

Editorial Endnote

1 John Leighton, *On Japanese Art: A Discourse delivered at the Royal Institution of Great Britain, May 1 1863* (privately printed, 1863). The lecture was summarised in *Journal of the Society of Arts* 11:557 (24 July 1863), pp. 596–9. In general, Leighton appraised Japanese art through comparisons – favourable or unfavourable – with European art traditions. However, he already noted the 'wonderful precision' of Japanese artists' studies of birds in flight, and the blend of verisimilitude and fantasy in their animal studies generally.

72

ART AND ART INDUSTRIES IN JAPAN

Sir Rutherford Alcock

Source: Sir Rutherford Alcock, *Art and Art Industries in Japan* (London: Virtue, 1878), pp. 34–5, 87–8, 241–3.

[pp. 34–5]

I think it will be seen that the true secret of the unrivalled success of the Japanese in those branches of Art in which they have most excelled, is to be found more especially in their loving and patient study of all the *processes* in Nature – in other words, the methods by which the *greatest variety* as well as beauty is secured. They have gone to the ornamental part of Nature's works – to the combination of forms and colours observable in plants, flowers, and leaves, in the painting of butterflies' wings, the skins of animals, the plumage of birds, and markings of shells – for their models. In a word, to all that constitutes the glory and the beauty of the visible world, and ministers with unfailing success and lavish bounty to the sense of beauty and harmony. Hogarth was quite right in asserting that the principles are in Nature by which we are guided in determining what is truly beautiful or graceful and excellent in Art.[1] The Japanese went, therefore, to the fountain-head in going to Nature, and there reverently watching and studying the processes by which such infinite variety and beauty are unceasingly evolved, they obtained the power of following in the same lines. It was natural that in profound sympathy with Nature and admiration of all her works, in which beauty and variety are the leading and characteristic features, they should contract a corresponding aversion to sameness, and any appearance of uniformity or regularity, which was nowhere to be found in Nature.

[pp. 87–8]

In a question of originality of conception, and power of rendering pictorially a weird and mystic subject by a poetic and purely ideal mode of treatment, the illustration facing the title-page leaves nothing to be desired, and would not be easily matched among the best efforts of European Art.[2] It is a moonlight scene, with the moon large and full in a dimly coloured sky, across the broad disc of which a flight of strange-looking birds are shadowed with outspread wings coming from afar, as the perspective admirably renders; while others, all in black, of strange presence, are scattered over the picture, some on a branch, others in the air, and on a shore which seems to look into endless space . . .

DOI: 10.4324/9781003107835-98

[pp. 241–3]

The pictorial side of Art is in a comparatively undeveloped state among the Japanese[3] . . . . Yet each time that I find myself giving expression to this denial of their pictorial power, I have a misgiving that it is only the enunciation of an imperfect truth, and without much qualification I may be doing the Japanese a great wrong. I have just returned from a visit to the studio of a Royal Academician to view a picture which I doubt not will be among the most admired of the works at the exhibition of this year. The subject is taken from Oriental life, replete with human interest, and with all the accessories of an Eastern interior . . . Careful drawing, artistic composition, and all the technical excellence of a perfect mastery of material, and the knowledge of every principle of Art practised from the days of Cimabue and Giotto were there, to enhance the interest and impress the imagination. While yet under the spell of a masterpiece of modern painting, a casual reference to the Japanese brought forth from a recess of the studio a long roll, which the artist attached to his easel for view, covering his own picture in the act, to show a recent purchase of a Japanese drawing picked up at one of the Art sales in London, where week by week some of the treasures of the world, both old and new, are redistributed among the fortunate few who have the taste to appreciate, and the wealth to purchase, the creations of genius and artistic power. The design when unrolled presented as striking a picture as can well be imagined. It was a great flight and descent of storks. From above, coming from afar, was seen in graduated perspective a cloud of birds, as if there had been a call from the uttermost ends of the earth for all the species to appear; while below as vast an assemblage had already reached the ground, in every possible variety of form and attitude. Those in the foreground were of considerable size, and dashed in with the hand of a master. There was no colour to aid, it was all in black and white, but the effect of the whole was marvellous. It seized upon the imagination, recalling the vision of the Apostle in the Revelation, where 'all the fowls that fly in the midst of heaven' are summoned to the supper at the opening of the seals – or the Day of Judgment, as Michael Angelo has painted it![4] So well had the artist with his simple materials given the effect of multitudinous flight and assemblage, the one in the air and the other on earth, each answering to the other, that the mind was filled with a sense of something supernatural and weird. And yet every part was so true to Nature that each bird of the flight seemed instinct with life. By a few masterly touches and sweeps of the pencil the rush of the descending flock was vividly presented, and the 'sound of their wings was as the sound of chariots of many horses running to battle.'[5] As the roll disappeared and the picture beneath was again brought in view, the contrast was great, but I felt the Japanese artist, had he been there to look upon and admire it as I did, might, like Correggio when he first stood before a masterpiece of Raphael, have exclaimed with perfect truth, '*Anch' Io son pittore!*'[6]

It is this intense sympathy with Nature which gives the Japanese artist his graphic power, and the hold he establishes on the imagination, by a suggestiveness which rarely defines, but leaves to the spectator the business of interpretation by a kindred poetic feeling and imaginative faculty.

Editorial Endnotes

1 In his book *The Analysis of Beauty* (1753), William Hogarth related 'grace' and 'beauty' to a sense of variety, inspired by the free, sinuous S-curves found in nature. His argument had been construed as an attack on the classical aesthetics of order, regularity, and generalisation underpinning the European academic tradition. Alcock, in his first *Art Journal* article (vol. 37, April 1875, pp. 101–5), quoted Hogarth's ideas extensively.

2 This frontispiece (see our Figure 17) is a bold woodcut printed in two colours only. The moon appears as a large white disc against the blue night sky, with the dark forms of flying birds silhouetted against it.

3 By the 'pictorial side of Art', Alcock means the kind of composition that characterised European painting 'from the days of Cimabue and Giotto' onwards, i.e., since the beginnings of the Renaissance. It involved the creation of a perspectival picture-space contained within a frame. Alcock here hints at the incongruity between such academic conventions of western art and the eastern subject chosen by his unnamed artist. Such realistic scenes of oriental life had been popularised by artists such as John Frederick Lewis.

4 Michelangelo's scene of the *Last Judgment* was on the altar wall of the Sistine Chapel in the Vatican, Rome.

5 Book of Revelation, 9:9.

6 According to legend, the sixteenth-century artist Correggio, standing before a work by his revered predecessor Raphael, exclaimed 'I too am a painter!'

Editorial Headnote

73. William Michael Rossetti, 'Japanese Woodcuts', *Fine Art, Chiefly Contemporary* (1867)

This article had been first published in *The Reader* 2 (July–Dec. 1863). As we have seen in his critique of Edwin Landseer (Chapter 38), W.M. Rossetti was unsympathetic towards the hyperrealism of much contemporary animal painting in Britain – the tendency to portray individual animals in physical detail, and to anthropomorphise their traits. He found an antithesis in the 'perfect refinement, ease, spirit, and fancy' of Japanese art. On the evidence of this article, he was especially fascinated by the illustrations of sagas or legends, where warrior heroes fight with mythic monsters.[1] The stories and their significance were unintelligible to him (he could not read the Japanese text), but this mystery only heightened the suggestiveness of the images. Their imaginative power and sense of the creatures' strangeness and autonomy differed strikingly from the representations of animals in European art, where subjection to the will of human beings, whether as pets or prey, was generally implied.

Editorial Endnote

1 There are examples of this genre in the woodcuts of Utagawa Kuniyoshi, but Rossetti does not name an artist.

73

JAPANESE WOODCUTS

William Michael Rossetti

Source: William Michael Rossetti, 'Japanese woodcuts' in *Fine Art, Chiefly Contemporary: Notices Reprinted, with Revisions* (London and Cambridge: Macmillan, 1867), pp. 363–87, quoting pp. 363–8, 375–80, 385.

[pp. 363–8]

The high state of development which the fine and decorative arts have attained in Japan has come upon most English people as a surprise . . . Nevertheless, it assuredly belongs in various respects to the greatest order of art practised in our day in any country of the world. It has a daringness of conception, an almost fiercely tenacious grasp of its subjects, a majesty of designing power and sweep of line, and a clenching hold upon the imagination, such as no Michael Angelo, Tintoret, or Dürer[1] among us, if we only had them, could afford, or would be in the least minded, to despise . . . The excellence of Japanese woodcuts – for it is especially of woodcuts that we are speaking – is, as far as we have noticed, constant . . . In these, as in other examples of Japanese art, the animal-designing is most consummate, though one often cannot defend such points as the anatomical structure and markings of the quadrupeds. On the other hand, – for such points as the action of birds, their quaint turns of head or lithe deviations of neck; the decorative and at the same time naturalistic treatment of plumage; the shooting, gliding, and patterning, of fishes; the winding of serpents, whose length is to be reckoned by yards of stealthy vertebra-crunching motion, – we incline to say that the Japanese reach higher in point of perceptive knowledge, and instant magic of the realizing hand, than any phase or period of European art: and the same praise, with the necessary deduction, must be understood to apply also even to the treatment of the larger animals . . .

It is to an uncoloured example in our third class, of romantic or legendary histories, – on the whole, perhaps, the finest example we have seen, – that we devote the remainder of our article . . . The impression which the series leaves upon us is that of some popular heroic legend of ancient time: the deeds of some Japanese Theseus or Roland embalmed in the popular heart and memory . . .

No. 2 . . . Here we find an enormous saurian monster or dragon, resembling, and as grotesque as, those which are characteristic of the Chinese fancy, but more conceivable and more terrible. His head tends towards the mammalian character, beset with an array of spiky prickles, two of which curve boldly from above the nostrils, like a cat's whisker-hairs. The splayed vertebrae are grimly distinct along an unending spine; two monstrous tridental claws are visible: the lacertine tail curves round again to the level of the forehead. From one of the claws floats on the air a patterned mantle, whereon rests a little boy with childish confidence . . .
[pp. 375–80]

No. 15. Here we find another monster-beast, even more curious and execrable than the one in No. 2. The designer evidently shares in the Japanese national turn for concocting such miscreations, and does with his pencil what artists of a lower grade in his country do by the actual apposition of the hairs of a cat on the body of a fish, the claws of a hawk on the joints of a lobster, or so on. We almost think the designer must have had some such pseudo *lusus naturae* to copy from,[2] so actual and cohesive is his abortion; it even looks (to the unscientific eye) as if it might be a real form of animal life revealed by the microscope. It is much more a spider than anything else; eight-legged, shaggily bristled all over, clawed not unlike the legs of a crab, striated down the back like a hyæna or a tabby cat, and furnished with monstrous globes of eyes in triple the proportion of those of a dragon-fly. The wretch seems to have made itself a sort of spider-web (though the indication of this is not so clear as to be free from doubt) in the clefts of the crags, and hangs head downward therefrom, the size of a buffalo. Praise be to the inventor, its bloated career is coming to an end: the hero, warily planted opposite against a bluff, is dealing the *coup-de-grâce* with a pike. The thrust looks mortal, and one hopes it is so . . .

No. 20. This represents, as far as we can make it out, a sea-monster lashing the waves, and overturning two men out of a boat; the boat itself, however, is nowhere visible. The monster before us does not yield to either of his predecessors in strangeness and power, but he is much less repulsive; indeed, not repulsive at all, though terrible from his size (at least as big as an elephant) and from his reckless exercise of strength. The head is not greatly unlike a lion's – something between that and a walrus's; the claws cat-like; the tail equine; the body covered all over with a sort of fleece, which clots into starry tufts, studding the whole gigantic surface like so many half-displayed sea-anemones peopling a sea-pool. With the ferocity of vehement suddenness he plunges forward, lashing about him; the sea-surface clangs, and splinters into enormous tress-like arcs and curves . . . Monster and figures stand out upon a ground of solid black, with a rounded upper contour distinctly defined; whether here representing night, or the blackness of the inner sea, where the monster reigns, and the men may just drown, we cannot say for certain – not unlikely the latter, which would account for our not seeing any trace of a boat . . .

[p. 385]

No. 30. The hero has been squatting or kneeling on the broad steps of a building, perhaps a temple. He starts to his feet, and wields his sword-bladed pike at the apparition of a (doubtless supernatural) bird resembling a gannet, whose wings and head, with a profound and portentous eye, stand out in vivid whiteness upon a black ground, symbolizing night. The visionary suddenness of the event is perfectly expressed; and its strangeness enhanced by the peculiarity of leaving the whole middle plane of the picture blank, the upper part of the bird being given relieved upon the black, but no lower part at all, nor other distinct termination of the apparition, after the black has ceased. This is, properly speaking, the last design of our series . . .

Editorial Endnotes

1 Michelangelo, Tintoretto, and Dürer were all famed sixteenth-century European artists.
2 A 'lusus naturae' or 'sport of nature' is an abnormal or freakish form of a species, occurring spontaneously.

Editorial Headnote

74. George Ashdown Audsley, *The Ornamental Arts of Japan* (1882–1885)

The impression of dynamic movement in Japanese representations of animals struck many western observers, including the artist and architect Audsley. As Rossetti had shown, these animals often seemed to have a magic power that made them come alive, in a manner that was quite alien to European traditions: in Japanese art, zoology merged with myth and fantasy. These qualities especially appealed to Audsley, and he found them in the Japanese decorative arts as much as in paintings and prints – a point that was not lost on Victorian designers. In Japanese culture, unlike the European, arts such as embroidery and lacquer work apparently enjoyed equal prestige with painting and had a similar imaginative scope and finesse.

The publication date on the title page of Audsley's work is 1882, but the preface is dated 1885: it may have been issued in parts, and then as a collected edition.

74

THE ORNAMENTAL ARTS OF JAPAN

George Ashdown Audsley

Source: George Ashdown Audsley, *The Ornamental Arts of Japan* (London: Sampson, Low, Marston, Searle and Rivington, 1882–5), 'Section first' pp. 2–4, and 'Section second', pp. 5–7.

[Section 1, pp. 2–4]

With all its beauties and all its shortcomings, we cannot glance over the wide domain of Japanese art more or less connected with the skill of the draughtsman, without being struck by the loving appreciation of nature it displays. Everywhere are happy ideas, quaint conceits, and lovely objects. . . . As we have said elsewhere, 'the Japanese artist is indeed an ardent student of nature; he watches her silent operations with keen perception, and notes her changes of mood and costume with loving eyes, until each detail of her marvellous handiwork, and each expression of her changeful face, becomes imprinted on his mind, to be transferred to every work he sets his hands to do'. . . . As examples of clever animal drawing we may point to the tiger which forms the tailpiece of our Introduction; and to the [wood]cut of two horses on page 2. No one can help being struck with the talent displayed in the latter; and the graphic way in which the graceful actions of the horses are rendered by a few impulsive brush strokes. Legends exist which probably had their origin in the skill evinced by certain early artists in the representation of horses. Two of these legends are thus given by Mr. W. Anderson: – 'Every child in Japan has heard of Kanawoka's horse, painted on a screen in Ninnaji temple near Kiōto: a strange picture, which so far exceeded the limits of mere imitative art, that in the hours of darkness it would quit its frame and gallop wildly through the cultivated land around, till angry peasants, recognising in the matchless form of the mysterious depredator the Kanawoka steed, and finding full confirmation in the damning evidence of the mud that yet clung to its shapely hoofs after its return to pictorial existence, ruthlessly blotted out the eyes of the masterpiece; and thenceforth the nocturnal excursions ceased. A rival horse in the Imperial treasury, a creation of the same brush, was wont to devour the Lespedeza flowers, till by a happy inspiration it was tethered to its panel by a painted rope' . . .

DOI: 10.4324/9781003107835-100

[Section 2, pp. 5–7]

During the latter part of the eighteenth century, the embroidery of *fukusa* attained the highest possible excellence.[1] These dainty squares of the richest silk were made the recipients of the popular artists' many happy thoughts. . . . The designs commonly met with on *fukusa* consist of birds in all positions, fishes, insects, trees, bamboos, flowers, figures, landscapes, buildings, sea scenes with ships, rocks, &c. . . . In those embroidered with birds are found cranes standing or flying; falcons at rest upon their perches, or in full pursuit of or engaged in killing their quarry; ducks and geese swimming, standing or flying; hens feeding with their chickens; cocks perched upon drums; peacocks with their tails displayed; and the *hōwō*,[2] flying, resplendent in its celestial colouring, and gorgeous with its magnificent tail plumage. The fish most commonly embroidered on *fukusa* is the native *koi* or carp. This the Japanese artists never fail to represent with wonderful spirit, swimming or swerving in the water or dashing up a waterfall. Among the most remarkable specimens of Japanese art known to us, are two representations of this fish swimming in still water. One is in the form of a black lacquer panel, on which the carp is depicted in dusted gold, as if indistinctly visible through the water. The wonderful rendering of this picture, and the artistic excellence both of conception and execution which it displays, are beyond the powers of description. . . . When embroidered, the carp is usually of fine twisted gold thread, carefully laid over cording or some raised ground-work, so as to accentuate the scales and give an effective relief to the head and other parts. When represented swimming, it seldom appears straight: one of the most favourite positions is that of a sudden swerve, as shown in the accompanying illustration from a design by HOKUSAI,[3] very probably intended by him for a *fukusa*. One can readily realise the beautiful decorative effect of such a design, with the fishes rendered in raised gold, or in their natural colours flashed with gold, upon a ground of water-blue satin, and amidst glistening green algae.

Editorial Endnotes

1 *Fukusa* were embroidered silk squares, traditionally used as coverings for gifts.
2 The howo was a fabulous bird, used as an imperial emblem.
3 Hokusai is now of course better known for his coloured wood engravings, representative of the popular art of nineteenth-century Japan.

Editorial Headnote

75. W. Crane and L. Day, 'Animals in Pattern Design', *Art Journal* (1901)

This debate between designers Walter Crane and Lewis Day reflects the earnestness with which the principles of decorative design were being discussed at the *fin de siècle*. Both these designers were associated with the Arts and Crafts movement and rejected the naturalism of High Victorian ornamentation of textiles, wallpapers, etc., with its pictorial treatment of motifs such as flowers and birds. Instead, they sought to attain harmonious two-dimensional pattern qualities in their designs through the stylisation or 'formalisation' of natural motifs. Yet the collections of the South Kensington Museum (now the Victoria & Albert Museum), which included Persian textiles and other Asian artefacts, suggested that lively representations of animals *could* be incorporated into designs, without any loss of abstract beauties of line and form.

75

ANIMALS IN PATTERN DESIGN

A Friendly Dispute Between Walter Crane and Lewis F. Day[1]

Walter Crane and Lewis Day

Source: Walter Crane and Lewis Day, 'Animals in pattern design: a friendly dispute between Walter Crane and Lewis F. Day', *Art Journal*, new series (1901), pp. 212.

L.F.D. – Human and animal forms are, as often as not, a disturbing influence in repeated pattern. Why use them there?

W.C. – For three reasons. Because their forms give me certain lines and masses decoratively valuable, and not obtainable by other means. They also give life and movement in ornament. By the use of such forms, also, symbolic meaning may be expressed (or concealed), fanciful allegory or playful ideas – in short they make ornament more interesting and amusing.

L.F.D. – When the end is repeated pattern, it is not best reached by such means. The recurring animal life may, very likely, have too much movement for repose. Don't you find ornament amusing enough in itself?

W.C. – You may easily have too much of a good thing; but in designing a repeating pattern one consciously designs for the repeated effect, and arranges one's units accordingly. Ornament may be amusing enough, or may bore one. But why say 'ornament in itself,' as if the introduction of animals and figures made it not ornament?

L.F.D. – I don't allow that movement is such a good thing when it is repeated over and over again. I like a pattern to be steady. The figures and animals which really make ornament have usually been reduced to something so remote from life and movement as to be no longer animate.

W.C. – Please don't suppose I wish to encourage tipsy patterns. A pattern, whatever movement it contains or expresses, must, of course, have equilibrium . . . Beautiful designs can be made of very few simple and quite abstract units. Decoration is like music somewhat. It is a question of what instrument you will play. You may play on one string or many. It depends on your aim. As to animals made inanimate in ornament I can't agree. What about the lions and tigers on a Persian carpet?

DOI: 10.4324/9781003107835-101

L.F.D. – I can't endure them.

W.C. – If you can't endure them, I am afraid there's little more to be said; but I should like to ask if you can't endure the birds and animals in Egyptian hieroglyphics, or the brush-worked animal borders on early Greek pots, or Chinese dragons, or Sicilian silks, or Heraldry – largely *the* ornament of the Middle Ages – or Italian Renaissance Arabesques?

L.F.D. – Oh, there's plenty to be said. As to 'choice of units,' that depends. The conditions of repeated pattern limit it, and exclude, as I think, lions and tigers crawling about the floor, where you are as likely as not to see them upside down, a view of the creatures undesirable in proportion as the nature in them is not subdued. Nature is not very lively in the archaic Greek and Mediæval and Renaissance ornament you instance. As to Heraldry and Egyptian hieroglyphics, they are not repeated pattern but symbolism: ornament is in their case a secondary consideration.

W.C. – I think you would find it difficult to separate ornament and symbolism. In their earlier forms they are identical . . . We find heraldic details, mainly animals used as ornamental units, and repeated all over a background to figures (for example, in Mediæval paintings and brasses), with a rich and splendid decorative effect not to be obtained by other means. I quite agree that choice of units in ornament must be governed by conditions of material and use.

L.F.D. – Given a meaning to express (as in Heraldry), by all means let it be expressed with every regard to ornamental considerations. We are agreed there. My objection is only to animals *repeated*; they lend themselves, I say, to pattern (and that is our point) about in proportion as the nature in them is sacrificed. It seems to me that the conditions of pattern design mostly rule out of court animal and human forms.

W.C. – That is as much as to say that whatsoever is introduced into repeating pattern requires treatment; but you might say that of all art. Do not all forms require treatment, floral as well as animal? Animals and figures are more difficult to treat, of course. Much depends upon what you mean by nature. Some people think shaded flowers on a wall-paper or cretonne 'more natural'.

L.F.D. – I am not one of those people. Animals seem so difficult to treat that it is the rarest thing to find them taking quite their place in pattern. I have not definitely determined why – perhaps because they are too individual to bear constant repetition? Eliminate the individuality, make a mere type or symbol of a creature, and, I grant you, it becomes more amenable. To me the repetition of a living thing lessens my interest in it. It may even end in boring me more than sheer geometry would do. If it is to be repeated, it should be with a difference; and that, you know, is mostly impossible.

W.C. – It comes to what the designer himself is fond of, or what his critics like, or dislike, as the case may be . . . However, I really do not see that the introduction of animal forms in pattern design is a question of reason.

It must be one of feeling, preference, and treatment, like all artistic questions . . .

L.F.D. – The animals in Persian carpets are not recurring units of the pattern. The animals I can endure in repetition are treated with *such* rigorous convention as hardly to count for living things. There is too much of the menagerie about your Persian lions and tigers for me. If you would admit (which I am afraid you won't) the rigour of convention which would satisfy me, I daresay I could make friends with your pets, and so we could embrace.

W.C. – The Persian animals and birds I had in mind *are* recurring units in one of the finest carpets in South Kensington Museum, and no 'menagerie' about them (see illustration). Art is, after all, not argument, but depends upon demonstration . . .

L.F.D. – Noah's Ark it often is! But whether from Noah's Ark or the Zoo, I don't want animals on my carpet.

Editorial Endnote

1 This dialogue between Crane and Day was later reprinted in an edited form and with a new title, 'The living interest in ornament', in *Moot Points: Friendly Disputes on Art and Industry between Walter Crane and Lewis F. Day* (London: B.T. Batsford, 1903), pp. 86–94.

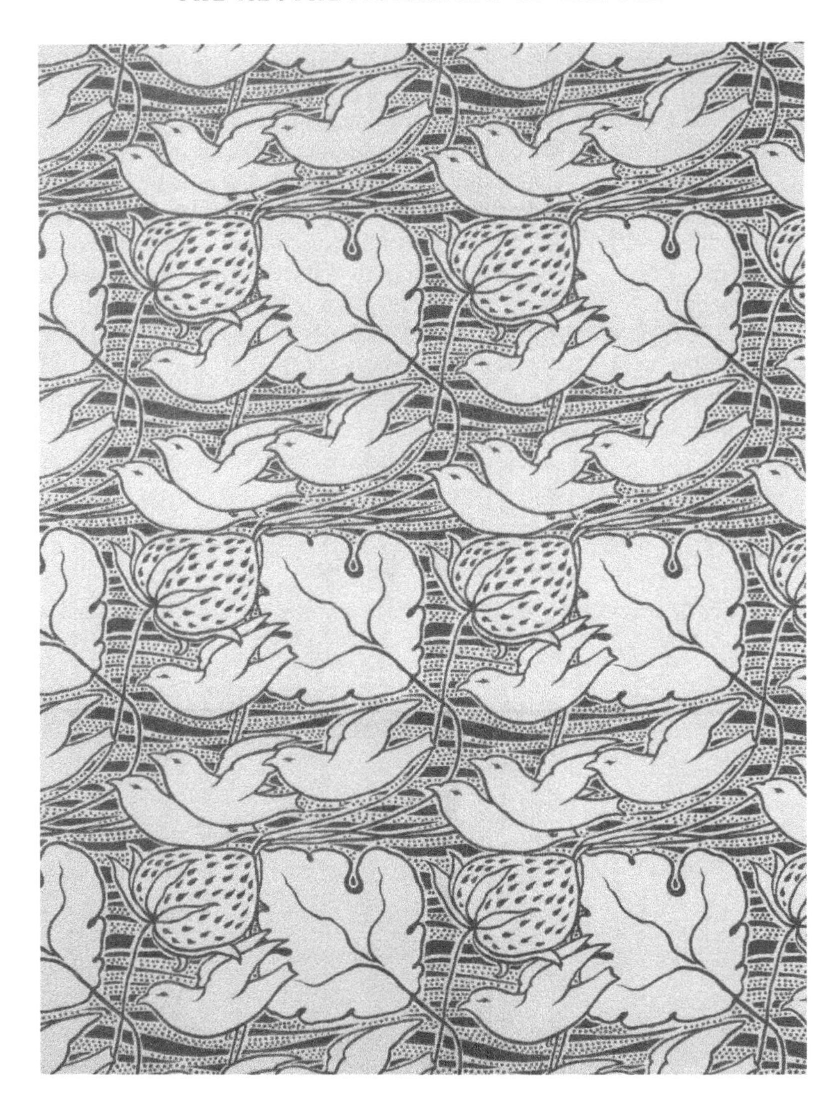

Figure 18 Charles F. Annesley Voysey, cotton furnishing fabric with a design of flying birds and strawberries, 1897–8, manufactured by Newman, Smith, and Newman, London. (V&A Images)

Editorial Headnote

76. Voysey, 'The Aims and Conditions of the Modern Decorator', *Journal of Decorative Art* (1895)

Charles Voysey, an architect and designer, belonged to the same Arts and Crafts circles as Lewis Day (see Chapter 75 of the present work) but differed from him sharply over the suitability of animal representations in repeating patterns.[1] In this lecture he explained his own approach to the use of stylised bird motifs in two-dimensional designs (see Figure 18). The commercial decorators in his audience clearly felt that Voysey was unrealistic and high-handed in his suggestion that the tastes of clients could be questioned or reformed in the ways he suggests. He was actually fighting on two fronts, rejecting both the wider public's taste for pictorialism in design and the objections of Arts and Crafts purists like Day to *any* animal motifs in wallpapers or fabrics.[2]

Editorial Endnotes

1 I am most grateful to Catherine Sidwell, who introduced me to both these sources for Voysey's views on the use of animal motifs. The subject of her PhD thesis was 'Representations of birds in culture, society and decorative designs for the domestic interior 1851–1914, with special reference to the work of C.F.A. Voysey' (Kingston University, 2023). On Voysey's work in general, see Karen Livingstone with Max Donnelly and Linda Parry, *C.F.A. Voysey, Arts and Crafts Designer* (London: V&A Publishing, 2016).

2 *The Studio: An Illustrated Magazine of Fine and Applied Art* 28 (1903), pp. 182–3, in an anonymous review of 'The Arts and Crafts Exhibition at the New Gallery: Third Notice' directly compared the products of Day and Voysey, 'those two so opposite designers'. Voysey's fluent 'art of filling a flat space without covering it', as in 'Japanese work', was contrasted with Day's much denser designs. See also an 'Interview' with Voysey in *Studio* I (15 September 1893), pp. 231–6.

76

THE AIMS AND CONDITIONS OF THE MODERN DECORATOR

Charles Francis Annesley Voysey

Source: 'The Aims and Conditions of the Modern Decorator. Lecture delivered in the Art Gallery, Mosley Street, Manchester, February 15th, 1895, by Charles F. Annesley Voysey, Architect, under the auspices of the Association of Master Plasterers and Painters of Manchester and Salford', *Journal of Decorative Art* 15 (April 1895), pp. 82–90, quoting pp. 86, 88.

[p. 86]

The realistic treatment of birds has very properly been denounced as a painful spectacle when plastered round angles, or cut in half by cornices. But can it not be justly argued that when conventionally treated the bird is merely a flat symbol, and if repeated quickly, the mutilation is scarcely felt? And again, what reason can be assigned for grieving over a bisected symbol of a bird, more than over a bisected symbol of a flower? No doubt strong popular prejudices generally have some foundation in fact, and it may be, there is some justification for the cruel boycotting of the sweetest, most suggestive, interesting, and telling forms of decoration. Perhaps, when the public have given up telegraphing the rise and fall of railway shares, there will be left a little more sympathy for the poetic and imaginative senses, and our playful delight in bird life and strong joyful colour will not meet with so much indifference and disdain. At present it is idle to look among the many for the appreciation of pleasures enjoyed only by the few.

The multitude associate bird-life with the shooting season and bread sauce. But what real delight in bird-life – what belief in individual existence of bird spirits is there? Surely, it is most uncommon to find among men and women any signs of keen interest in animal life; for do not their own pleasures depend less and less on simple Nature, and more and more on Eiffel Towers, Infant Prodigies, and Mahatmas? In countless ways the decorator is hemmed in and hampered by the *Vox populi* . . .

[p. 88]

An additional reason for aiming at flatness in wall-coverings is to be found in the fact that any attempt at realism provokes comparison with nature, which is distressing in proportion to the beholder's appreciation of the subtle beauties of real life; whereas, in conventional ornament, the life of the designer is brought in, and should form a very living and additional attraction . . .

DOI: 10.4324/9781003107835-102

Editorial Headnote

76.1. Voysey, 'Ideas in Things', in Davison (ed.), *The Arts Connected With Building* (1909)

Here Voysey enlarged on his love of natural forms, with a sideswipe at the very different relationship with the living world that was suggested by the stuffed animal trophies in grand houses. He addressed an imaginary architect who might be designing a house for Voysey himself.

76.1

IDEAS IN THINGS

Charles Francis Annesley Voysey

Source: Charles Francis Annesley Voysey, 'Ideas in things', two lectures in T. Raffles Davison (ed.), *The Arts Connected with Building: Lectures on Craftsmanship and Design delivered at Carpenters Hall, London Wall, for the Worshipful Company of Carpenters* (London: B.T. Batsford, 1909), pp. 134–6.

[p. 134]

My station in life must determine your indulgence in the rendering of ideas most fit and harmonious. You will not hang around my hall the dead heads of wild beasts, unless you think me a bloodthirsty murderer, vain of my killing powers; and even then your better natures would check your encouragement of my vice . . .

[pp. 135–6]

The use of animal life is dependent on our spiritual activity. If we are thoroughly materialistic, we prefer fruit and flowers in our wall-papers and fabrics, and feel hurt by the mutilation of birds or animals when cut round furniture or upholstered on to seats.[1] But if the rendering of animals in our decoration is so conventional that we feel only that the spirit of the beast is recorded, no pain is felt. The martlet in heraldry never pained any one, but a very realistic bird with all its feathers carefully drawn and its legs cut off would pain us at once, the dominant impression or idea being, a very material bird injured, mutilated and maimed. While, in the case of the martlet, the illustration is of the bird spirit; it is a generic bird, not any particular species. And our thought is kept in the region of spiritual rather than material realities. It would be well if this distinction could be understood and appreciated more generally, because there is a vast amount of prejudice against the introduction of animal forms in our decoration which is entirely due to our materialistic attitude of mind. Materialism has been the cradle of realism in art. The life of animals might be made a source of stimulating joy to our own lives. We all feel a sense of pleasure when the wild birds sing, and the idea of their lovemaking and aspiring and growing more good and useful every day is delightful, and ought to be recorded in our everyday articles of use, as well as in our natural history books. What is it that makes us all delight in Shakespeare's

DOI: 10.4324/9781003107835-103

work? Is it not his own spiritual delight in spiritual ideas: in life, in thoughts and feelings, rather than in things?

Editorial Endnote

1 By 'materialistic' Voysey means understanding things only in a literal way, as real physical objects: a mentality exemplified by Dickens's Mr. Gradgrind in *Hard Times*, who wanted 'nothing but Facts'. However, the significance of this trait shades into the wider, pejorative meaning of 'materialistic', which Voysey clearly associates with the *nouveaux riches* social classes.

Part IV

NATURAL SCIENCE AND THE LAY PUBLIC

Education, Museology, Spectacle, Entertainment

INTRODUCTION

In early nineteenth-century Britain, the acquisition of scientific knowledge about animals mainly depended on reference to works by recognised authorities of the past, notably Linnaeus and the Comte de Buffon. The British Museum and some university museums held collections of bones, skins, and stuffed specimens which were made available for study by serious researchers (Chapter 83), but there were few academic or curatorial posts specifically devoted to the field of zoology. Observations of the workings of nature were, however, shared between amateur naturalists and collectors through personal correspondence or publication in journals. Gilbert White's letters to Thomas Pennant and Daines Barrington, published as *The Natural History of Selborne* in 1789, are the most famous and remarkable example of this genre, but there were many enthusiasts who swapped specimens or met in local societies to discuss mutual interests.

By the end of the nineteenth century, all had changed. The dramatic expansion of the British empire brought thousands of live animals and zoological specimens to the home country (see the General Introduction). They could now be studied at first hand, notably through the opening of the London Zoo (Chapter 89) and of the Natural History Museum (Chapters 86–7), together with the creation of many public aquaria (Chapters 90–1). The Darwinian revolution in thought had an impact that spread far beyond natural science itself; and, through the great numbers of newspapers and journals which were by then in circulation, the public became conversant with the issues that Darwinism raised. Popular works on zoology, many by Revd John George Wood (Chapters 94–5), were profusely illustrated and catered to the new interest in animal life in the wild. Rather than showing each animal as an isolated figure, as in traditional works on natural history, artists now grouped them in imaginary settings, representing their actions and habitats – with taxidermy following a similar trajectory in the development of dioramas (Chapters 35, 65, 87, 94). Revd Wood also brought his books to life

DOI: 10.4324/9781003107835-104

by lecture tours in which he drew animals with seeming spontaneity on a large screen, to the surprise and delight of the audience (Chapter 95). Ultimately the development of photography, the magic lantern, and then cinematography superseded artwork, and public presentations of natural life entered a new era (Chapters 20–7, 81, 96–7).

At the same time, a concern to improve educational standards in the population at large led to the passing of the Museums Act in 1845, the Public Libraries Acts in 1850 and 1855, and the Education Acts of 1870 onwards. The government's Department of Science and Art, established in 1853 in the wake of the Great Exhibition of 1851, was dedicated to the improvement of teaching of science and of visual design and technical drawing, bringing these fields of study together wherever possible.[1] Using the profits of the 1851 exhibition, the Department of Science and Art collaborated with architects and curators in the design and building of the Natural History Museum and the South Kensington Museum (later renamed the Victoria & Albert Museum). These two huge state institutions, erected side by side in South Kensington, suggested to the onlooker the equal importance and indeed the complementarity of natural sciences and artistic cultures, with a strong emphasis on education in both cases. Objects in the collections of the V&A were then acquired primarily to provide models of good design for the visual training of students.[2] They included many artefacts from Asian cultures, such as Persian carpets and Japanese prints, which revealed, among other things, the decorative possibilities of animal motifs (see Chapters 72–6). At the regional level, the new city museums attracted gifts and legacies from local collectors, many of them comprising either art works or natural history specimens. These two categories of objects partly determine the character of the displays in such museums to this day: they often form complementary groupings in adjacent wings of the museum building (for example, at Birmingham, Derby, and Bolton), sometimes in conjunction with the local public library.

Meanwhile, as science education was introduced at the school and college levels, Thomas Huxley and his circle sought to promote new methods of teaching, based on the idea of participatory 'object lessons' that developed children's interests and faculties (Chapters 79–80). Pupils were encouraged to make their own drawings of animal subjects – an exercise that was also fostered at this time by the school competitions of the [Royal] Society for the Protection of Birds.[3] Victorian natural history classes in schools are often assumed to have involved merely rote learning of basic facts, but actually the concept of 'object lessons' allowed children to handle and analyse plant and animal specimens, even to bring their own live creatures to the classroom. In Cara Bray's storybook for children, *Paul Bradley, A Village Tale, Inculcating Kindness to Animals*, a school lesson on the bone structure of vertebrates is enlivened by the presence of 'Paul's own cat, which he had reared from a kitten' and brought to the school as 'a capital illustration' of a mammal's anatomy – albeit a rather uncooperative one.[4] Educators evidently believed that familiarising children with animal life would engender a more humane attitude towards wild birds and domestic pets, so that the imparting of scientific knowledge went hand in hand with the civilising process.

Natural history museums were a key element in the education of the public, but their curators faced a double challenge. They needed to think of ways in which their collections could illuminate the now widely accepted theory of evolution. At the same time, they needed to cater to a socially diverse range of museum visitors. Those who sought to educate the general public in natural science could not assume a prior knowledge of – or indeed an interest in – the finer points of taxonomy and scientific theory. Entertainment had to be part of the experience of visits to museums, zoos, and public aquaria, and entertainment in turn depended on *visualisation* of animals, whether in live exhibits, pictures, or tableaux of life in the wild. Even Professor William Abbott Herdman, who pressed for a complete reorganisation of museum displays, in order to promote an understanding of evolutionary phylogeny, thought that there could be a 'magnificent addition' to the purely didactic exhibits, 'without any loss of scientific value'. It would take the form of a series of 'picturesque' dioramas, as suggested by the popular natural history writer mentioned earlier, Revd Wood. They would show 'the animals of the various regions . . . with the appropriate surroundings of plant-life and scenery, so as to illustrate their habits and actions' in an attractive way.[5]

Such thoughtful and progressive museology had developed only slowly through the century. The naturalist William MacGillivray, who was curator of the university museum at Edinburgh, toured museums belonging to various other universities and learned bodies across Britain in 1833 on a factfinding mission (Chapter 83). He was dismayed by the sight of overcrowded cases, bungled taxidermy, poor and disordered specimens, dust and decay, and a general lack of proper labelling or beauty of effect. For MacGillivray – himself a sensitive artist when drawing birds and other creatures[6] – scientific cogency and aesthetics went hand in hand. His successors as curators of natural science collections instituted many reforms, always with an emphasis on elucidation and visual appeal, such as to hold the attention of uninstructed visitors. The beautiful glass models of marine invertebrates produced by the Blaschka firm[7]; pictures, charts, and photographs; models of animals that were ideally both accurate and pleasing – their construction perhaps involving a partnership with local art schools: all these things would make a museum visit a delight and a learning process rather than an ordeal. When William Flower took over from Richard Owen as director of the new Natural History Museum in South Kensington in the 1880s (Chapter 87), he insisted on the need to separate the research functions and facilities of the museum (requiring full access to the reserve collections), from its public displays. The latter were to be highly selective and carefully composed, more akin to an art gallery than to a cluttered scientific institution of the traditional kind. High-quality taxidermy groups in pictorial dioramas – a modest version of what Wood and Herdman had in mind – would demonstrate concealing coloration, evidence of evolutionary changes, and other facets of Darwin's ideas (see Figure 19): education of the public in the new science was all-important.

Instruction in zoology was always furthered by the thrill of *seeing* at first hand animals that were unfamiliar, exotic, playful, extraordinary, or frighteningly bloodthirsty.[8] Examples ranged from the stuffed giraffe in Bullock's museum (Chapter 82) to the life-size model dinosaurs at the Crystal Palace (Chapter 88 and Figure 20); from the elephants and the first live hippopotamus at London Zoo, to the crocodile at Jamrach's shop being fed under duress (Chapter 92). The whole *mis en scène* of these spectacles was designed to thrill visitors by the experience of proximity to wild creatures but also to raise thoughts of the power, glory, wealth, and scientific advances of the British nation. According to Richard Owen, the Natural History Museum, with its grand scale, ornate architecture, and rich collections, was to be a 'material symbol' of 'the greatest commercial and colonizing empire in the world'.[9] The magnificence of the great metropolitan museums and of the rebuilt Crystal Palace on its hilltop; the no less palatial architecture of the seaside aquaria (Chapters 90–1); even the splendours of the London theatres where the first nature films were shown (Chapters 96–7): all projected an imperial concept that made animals as well as tribal peoples subject to the will of European man. However, this was an impression that could, it seems, prompt compunction and mental discomfort in visitors as well as pride: live animals communicated in their own bodily languages the pains of imprisonment.[10]

Notes

1 Harry Butterworth, 'The Science and Art Department, 1853–1900' (PhD diss., University of Sheffield, 1968).
2 Paul Barlow and Shelagh Wilson, 'Consuming empire? The South Kensington Museum and its spectacles', in Paul Barlow and Colin Trodd (eds.), *Governing Cultures: Art Institutions in Victorian London* (Aldershot: Ashgate, 2000).
3 Diana Donald, *Women Against Cruelty: Protection of Animals in Nineteenth-century Britain*, 2nd ed. (Manchester: Manchester University Press, 2021), pp. 271–3.
4 Mrs. Charles Bray (Caroline or Cara Bray), *Paul Bradley. A Village Tale, Inculcating Kindness to Animals* (London: S.W. Partridge, undated [c.1876]), pp. 58–62.
5 Herdman's lecture to the Liverpool Literary and Philosophical Society on 'An Ideal Natural History Museum' (1887) was reprinted in Thomas Greenwood's *Museums and Art Galleries* (London: Simpkin, Marshall, 1888), pp. 179–95. For Revd Wood's ideas on museum dioramas, see Chapter 94 of the present work.
6 Robert Ralph, *William MacGillivray: Creatures of Air, Land and Sea* (London: Merrell Holberton and the Natural History Museum, 1999).
7 On the Blaschka models, see Chapters 17 and 84.
8 Helen Cowie, *Exhibiting Animals in Nineteenth-century Britain: Empathy, Education, Entertainment* (Basingstoke: Palgrave Macmillan, 2014).
9 J.B. Bullen, 'Alfred Waterhouse's Romanesque "Temple of Nature": the Natural History Museum, London', *Architectural History*, 49 (2006), pp. 257–85, on p. 278.
10 Diana Donald, '"Captives from mountain and forest": zoos and the imperial project', in *Picturing Animals in Britain, 1750–1850* (New Haven, CT, and London: Yale University Press, 2007), pp. 161–97.

Editorial Headnote

77. Maria Edgeworth and Richard Lovell Edgeworth, *Practical Education* (1798)

The Edgeworths' approach to the education of children of both sexes seems, to the present-day reader, remarkably modern. They emphasise the importance of developing children's curiosity about the natural world, their powers of accurate observation, imagination, creativity, and pleasure in drawing and experimentation. Cabinets for collections of natural objects and simple microscopes were, they thought, better presents to give to children than elaborate toys (vol. 1, p. 30). Furthermore, careful study of live animals would rid children of foolish prejudices about the supposed ugliness or noxiousness of some species. All these recommendations were based on the wide experience of the authors (father and daughter) in teaching the many children in the Edgeworth household. Engravings of animals in books were a potential means of gaining knowledge and understanding, but they found that those then available to children had many shortcomings.

77

PRACTICAL EDUCATION

Maria Edgeworth and Richard Lovell Edgeworth

Source: Maria Edgeworth and Richard Lovell Edgeworth, *Practical Education*, 2 vols. in one (London: J. Johnson, 1798), vol. 1, 'Toys', pp. 12–13, and 'Sympathy and Sensibility', p. 283.

[pp. 12–13]

Children soon judge tolerably well of proportion in drawing, where they have been used to see the objects which are represented: but we often give them prints of objects, and of animals especially, which they have never seen, and in which no sort of proportion is observed. The common prints of animals must give children false ideas. The mouse and the elephant are nearly of the same size, and the crocodile and whale fill the same space in the page.[1] Painters, who put figures of men amongst their buildings, give the idea of the proportionate height immediately to the eye: this is, perhaps, the best scale we can adopt; in every print for children this should be attended to. Some idea of the relative sizes of the animals they see represented would then be given, and the imagination would not be filled with chimeras.

After having been accustomed to examine prints, and to trace their resemblance to real objects, children will probably wish to try their own powers of imitation. At this moment no toy, which we could invent for them, would give them half so much pleasure as a pencil. If we do not put a pencil into their hands before they are able to do any thing with it, but make random marks all over a sheet of paper, it will long continue a real amusement and occupation. No matter how rude their first attempts at imitation may be; if the attention of children be occupied, our point is gained. Girls have generally one advantage at this age over boys, in the exclusive possession of the scissors: how many camels, and elephants with amazing trunks, are cut out by the industrious scissors of a busy, and therefore happy little girl, during a winter evening, which passes so heavily, and appears so immeasurably long, to the idle.

[p. 283]

Children should not be taught to confine their benevolence to those animals which are thought beautiful; the fear and disgust which we express at the sight of certain unfortunate animals, whom we are pleased to call ugly and shocking, are observed by children, and these associations lead to cruelty. If we do not prejudice our pupils by foolish exclamations, if they do not from sympathy catch our absurd

DOI: 10.4324/9781003107835-105

antipathies, their benevolence towards the animal world will not be illiberally confined to favourite lapdogs, and singing birds. From association most people think that frogs are ugly animals. L –, a boy between five and six years old, once begged his mother to come out to look at a *beautiful* animal which he had just found; she was rather surprised to find that this beautiful creature was a frog.

Editorial Endnote

1 The Edgeworths were probably thinking of Thomas Boreman's popular *A Description of Three Hundred Animals*, which was first published in 1730 and went through numerous editions down to the nineteenth century, or perhaps of *The Natural History of Beasts* of 1793, attributed to Stephen Jones. In both works the plates showed a mélange of animals, zoologically unrelated, some mythic, all badly drawn, and with no attention to relative scale. For example, on one page of the tenth edition of Boreman (1769) 'The Lynx' was paired with 'A Cameleon', and they appear as roughly the same size. See Harriet Ritvo, 'Learning from animals: natural history for children in the eighteenth and nineteenth centuries', *Children's Literature*, 13 (1985), pp. 72–93.

Editorial Headnote

77.1 Sarah Stickney, *The Mothers of England* (1843)

The author, better known by her married name, Sarah Stickney Ellis, wrote a series of conduct books for women, reflecting a conservative 'separate spheres' context of ideas. She was, however, very interested in the practice of the visual arts (cf. Chapter 62), being herself an amateur artist, and was also a passionate advocate of kindness to animals.[1] Following in Maria Edgeworth's footsteps, she here urges the importance of teaching young people to observe and draw accurately from nature, rather than copying conventional picturesque motifs. Mothers of middle-class families should make themselves familiar with 'the habits of animals . . . natural philosophy in general', so that they could instruct their offspring (p. 76).

Editorial Endnote

1 Diana Donald, *Women Against Cruelty: Protection of Animals in Nineteenth-Century Britain*, 2nd ed. (Manchester: Manchester University Press, 2020), pp. 151–7.

77.1

THE MOTHERS OF ENGLAND

Their Influence and Responsibility

Anon. [Sarah Stickney]

Source: Anon. [Sarah Stickney], *The Mothers of England, Their Influence and Responsibility* (London: Fisher, Son at the Caxton Press, 1843), pp. 79–82.

[p. 79]

Although a comparison is generally allowed betwixt painting and music, as sources of gratification adapted to a high degree of taste and feeling, yet, in their actual utility, they bear but little relation to each other . . . My business is chiefly to show that there may be great utility in a kind of drawing, which is little calculated to excite the admiration of an evening party; and it would be an unspeakable advantage to all mothers, in conveying lively and correct ideas to the minds of their children, if they were themselves proficients in the art of sketching from nature . . .

[pp. 81–2]

The results to which my ambition for the rising generation points, would consist in habits of observation, clear perceptions of form and outline, so as to have the fac-simile of every well-known object impressed without confusion upon the mind; in quickness of imitation, and facility of touch in delineating all visible objects, so as to represent them truly to others . . . but, above all, and here the subject assumes its most important character, for sketching with promptness and precision all specimens in natural history, as well as almost every other branch of juvenile study, so as at once to strike the eye, and impress the memory of youth – to amuse the fancy, and improve the understanding at the same time.

We all know that even the rudest drawing of a rat, a mouse, or a donkey, with accompanying lively descriptions of some of their peculiar habits, has power to fascinate a group of children on a winter's evening, almost beyond any other resource; and if with greater ease the mother could make these designs at once more spirited, and exactly true to life; if also she could add an illustration of some favourite anecdote, by placing different figures together, or allowing the children to choose how they shall be placed, she would find herself in possession of a means of instruction, almost as refreshing to herself, as delightful and invigorating to the young minds whose education is committed to her care.

DOI: 10.4324/9781003107835-106

Editorial Headnote

78. Thomas Coglan Horsfall, *The Study of Beauty, and Art in Large Towns* (1883)

Horsfall was a friend and disciple of Ruskin, and 'The Study of Beauty', a lecture delivered at the Manchester Field Naturalists' Society (undated), emphasised their shared belief that there was a close connection between appreciation of the beauties of the natural world and personal morality. Working people would live more religious, upright, and productive lives if they were enabled to gain a knowledge of nature and art – at present they were shockingly ignorant about both. Economic considerations as well as ethics were involved here: the Headmaster of the Manchester School of Art reported that the prevailing ignorance of workpeople about the appearance of birds, insects, etc. had prevented their 'gaining that skill in design which is so necessary for success in many kinds of manufacture' (pp. 25–6). Horsfall's second lecture, 'Art in Large Towns' (pp. 33–47), read at the 1882 Nottingham Congress of the National Association for the Promotion of Social Science, spelt out how the education of working people in natural history and aesthetics could be accomplished. He had furthered this aim by setting up an Art Museum Committee in Manchester in 1877, and, after a period of temporary operation at Queen's Park, a museum was established in Ancoats, then an industrial zone of the city, in 1886.[1]

Editorial Endnote

1 On Horsfall's pioneering role in establishing a free art gallery for the benefit of working people, followed by similar enterprises elsewhere: Shelagh Wilson, '"The highest art for the lowest people": the Whitechapel and other philanthropic art galleries, 1877–1901', in Paul Barlow and Colin Trodd (eds.), *Governing Cultures: Art Institutions in Victorian London* (Aldershot: Ashgate, 2000), pp. 172–86.

78

THE STUDY OF BEAUTY, AND ART IN LARGE TOWNS

Thomas Coglan Horsfall

Source: Thomas Coglan Horsfall, *The Study of Beauty, and Art in Large Towns: two papers . . . with an introduction by John Ruskin* (London: Macmillan, 1883). 'Art in large towns', pp. 33–47.

[pp. 35–7]

A very large proportion of the children who live in large towns never, or very rarely, see anything in or near their homes which is beautiful. They have no chance of becoming familiar with birds and flowers, trees and grass, and ferns. But most even of the children who live farthest away from the country see such things occasionally, and as it is chiefly on holidays that they see them, many of them, no doubt, have pleasant associations with the mass of half noticed, indistinctly remembered things which their eyes fall on in the country and in town parks.

If sensibility to beauty is to be common in town-people, the slight acquaintance with beautiful things thus gained must be increased by the help of art. Believing this to be so, the Committee of the Manchester Art Museum intend to offer to the School Boards, and to other managers of elementary day-schools and Sunday schools, in Manchester and Salford, small loan collections of pictures, of casts, of pottery, and of textile fabrics, to be placed on the walls of the schools.[1] Each thing in the collections will be provided with a clearly printed explanation, and, when this is possible, with a description of the process by which it is made.[2] Each collection will include some good coloured pictures of common wild and garden flowers, ferns, grasses, forest trees, common birds, moths, and butterflies, and some pictures, – engravings, photographs, and even chromo-lithographs, – of such pretty places as town children see when they are taken out of town . . . We hope to make arrangements for facilitating the purchase by children or their parents of pictures and other works of art, like those contained in the school collections, and in those collections in the Art Museum which I shall refer to later. Other labels give the title and price of the cheapest books which contain accounts, both interesting and trustworthy, of the things represented in the pictures. For example, our pictures of birds have labels giving the titles, the prices, and the publishers' names of good cheap editions of White's 'Selborne' and of Johns's 'British Birds in their Haunts,'[3] and our pictures of wild flowers and common garden flowers

DOI: 10.4324/9781003107835-107

have labels giving the price and title of Hulme's 'Familiar Wild Flowers' and 'Familiar Garden Flowers.'[4] As we wish our pictures not only to foster love of the beauty of nature but also to excite interest in, and love of, the beauty of art, and to give knowledge of artistic treatment and of art methods and processes, we propose to place side by side a few examples of the representations given by different arts of the same objects, and to call attention to the differences and resemblances of the effects attained by the different methods. For example, we shall place a copy of the coloured plates of birds from Gould's British Birds, which have lithographed outlines, and are coloured by hand, side by side with woodcuts of the same birds from Bewick and from Yarrell, and by means of a label we shall call attention to such points as the mode in which local colour is represented in black and white, and shall invite comparison of the coloured plates and woodcuts with carefully made water-colour drawings of the same birds contained in the Art Museum.[5] Another label accompanying these sets of pictures tells the children that clear descriptions of the processes of wood-cutting, lithography, etching, &c., and all the appliances used in these processes, are to be seen in the Art Museum. We are obliged to use some chromo-lithographs, as it is necessary to give some idea of the colour of the things represented, but they are always accompanied by an explanation of the defects inseparable from the process of colour-printing, and by a reference to good pictures in the museum of the same objects . . .

[pp. 38–9]

It is obvious that the pictures of flowers, trees, birds, &c., which are placed in schools, if they are to be useful, must be both true to nature and beautiful; and as there are many schools, and each school needs many pictures, it is equally obvious that the pictures must not be very costly. We have had no difficulty in obtaining coloured pictures of wild flowers, common and garden flowers, butterflies and moths. Many of the plates in Mr. Hulme's books on Wild and Garden Flowers are good enough for our purpose, and cost only a few pence each. The same may be said of Mr. Morris's books on Moths and Butterflies.[6] But we find that no good coloured pictures of common English trees can be obtained at present, and that good coloured plates of birds cannot be obtained at prices which we can afford to pay. The publishers of the late Mr. Gould's book on British Birds, for instance, charge 7s. 6d. for each plate . . . Mr. H.E. Dresser, the author of the important work 'The Birds of Europe,' which contains beautiful plates, has most generously offered us the use of all the original drawings made for him of those English birds which are represented in his book, and has offered also to have these and other drawings lithographed and coloured by hand for us at cost price by the trained staff employed by him.[7] We desire to accept his offer, but as we need pictures of fifty or sixty English birds, and the set, about 250, of copies of each bird would cost us many pounds, the work is much too costly to be undertaken by a committee which has innumerable uses for its funds. As we believe that the work is of great importance, and as 250 copies of each bird are more than we need, we proposed to the Science and Art Department that it should either have copies made, and provide us with those which we need at cost price, or else make us a grant towards the cost of the work if we get it done on condition that we undertake to sell superfluous copies to other towns at cost price. But the Department, while admitting the importance of the proposed work, replies that it has not the power to take either of the two courses which we have suggested . . . I venture to urge that this Section recommend that the Council request the Science and Art Department to seek to acquire the power of preparing and of selling at cost price to persons or societies interested in public education representations of trees, birds, and other beautiful natural objects, good in respect both of fidelity to nature and of artistic quality.[8]

If this course be not taken, or if it be taken in vain, then I would suggest that the committees of schools of art, or of other bodies interested in the diffusion of knowledge and love of beauty, associate themselves with the Committee of the Manchester Art Museum in the preparation of such representations. Our Committee has already a considerable collection of excellent water-colour drawings of English wild flowers and common wild birds, and would gladly place them at the service of an association, if one be formed, or of the Science and Art Department . . . We intend to have a series of pictures of all the most beautiful places near the town . . . the wild flowers, birds, and butterflies found near it . . . It is those workpeople who care for botany or ornithology whom we find most interested in our pictures, because the pictures of flowers, or birds, which they examine for the sake of their subjects, make the whole collection interesting to them . . .

[pp. 46–7]

If a belief in the greatness and goodness of the Maker of the world is to be felt, – and it is of the essence of healthy religion, – the greatness and beauty of His works must be felt in those years of childhood in which mind and feeling form life-long habits, and it is only by help of art that the influence of the beauty of the world can be made to reach the feelings and thoughts of town children. The means which are necessary for giving them a strong sense of beauty are also necessary for enabling them to have healthy religious feeling.

Editorial Endnotes

1 Horsfall's plan was implemented and sets of pictures were loaned to local schools. 'Thomas Coglan Horsfall and Manchester Art Museum and University Settlement', https://infed.org/mobi/thomas-coglan-horsfall-and-manchester-art-museum-and-university-settlement/ accessed December 2022. This project was comparable to the loan of scientific specimens to schools, as practised by (for example) Liverpool City Council. Cf. 'Circulating museum collections for schools and other educational purposes', *Thirty-fifth Annual Report of the Committee of the Free Public Library, Museum, and Walker Art Gallery, of the City of Liverpool* (1887–8), p. 19.

2 Horsfall evidently felt that the understanding of graphic techniques and of textile production had vocational value for working-class children. He expands on this point later in his volume, in explaining the differing effects rendered by the various printmaking media.

3 The reference is to Gilbert White's *Natural History of Selborne* (1789) and Charles Alexander Johns's *British Birds in Their Haunts* (1862). Both books had a religious frame of reference and were often-reprinted classics.

4 These were attractively illustrated works by Frederick Edward Hulme.

5 Horsfall thought that children should be invited to compare the varying effects that were possible in natural history illustration, depending on the choice of graphic medium. Thomas Bewick's *General History of Quadrupeds* and *History of British Birds* (see Chapters 5 and 6 of the present work), together with William Yarrell's very popular *History of British Birds*, exemplified the black-and-white linear treatment characteristic of wood engraving, where hatched lines suggested tone. John Gould's books, in contrast, had lithographed illustrations which were expensively hand-coloured, achieving much more delicate and accurate effects than commercial chromolithography. However, Horsfall also intended to demonstrate that *all* graphic media had shortcomings when compared with original watercolours of birds etc.

6 Revd Francis Orpen Morris, *A History of British Butterflies* (1853) and *A Natural History of British Moths* (1871). Both works went through several editions.

7 Henry Eeles Dresser's *History of the Birds of Europe* was published by the author in eight volumes between 1871 and 1882. Dresser also showed his interest in natural history education by taking on the editorship of the Royal Society for the Protection of Birds' series of booklets on various bird species, published in the 1890s.

8 The Department of Science and Art had been set up in the 1850s, in the wake of the Great Exhibition, to foster education in the sciences, technical drawing, and art and design more broadly: see the introduction to Part IV of the present work.

Editorial Headnote

79. Anon., 'Science Teaching in London Board Schools', *Nature* (1879)

This report throws light on Thomas Huxley's pioneering role in fostering science education in schools, especially in pressing for a systematic syllabus and maximum use of 'object lessons', which would encourage children to learn directly from visual examination of specimens. Such object lessons indeed became the norm, backed up by illustrations and diagrams drawn by the teacher on the blackboard[1] and by wall charts with pictorial representations of animal species. Huxley chaired the science committee of the School Board for London, and his efforts, described in this extract, were encouraged by another intimate friend of Darwin, Sir John Lubbock.

Editorial Endnote

1 Caitlin Donahue Wylie, 'Teaching nature study on the blackboard in late nineteenth- and early twentieth-century England', *Archives of Natural History* 39:1 (2012), pp. 59–76. Wylie points out (p. 66) that Huxley himself drew freehand on a blackboard when lecturing: he would even partly rub out and alter his drawing of a particular animal to demonstrate dramatically the process of evolution. For the wider frame of reference, exemplified by natural history teaching in North America and Australia, see Dorothy Kass, 'The nature study idea: framing nature for children in early twentieth century schools', in Hannes Bergthaller and Peter Mortensen (eds.), *Framing the Environmental Humanities* (Leiden: Brill, 2018), pp. 221–37.

79

SCIENCE TEACHING IN LONDON BOARD SCHOOLS

Anon., Nature

Source: Anon., 'Science Teaching in London Board Schools', *Nature* 20:501 (5 June 1879), pp. 117–18.

The Committee, of which Prof. Huxley was the chairman, determined that there must be given, in infant schools, 'object lessons of a simple character, with some such exercise of the hands and eyes as is given in the Kindergarten system'; and in boys' and girls' schools, 'systematised object lessons embracing in the six school years a course of elementary instruction in physical science, and serving as an introduction to the science examinations which are conducted by the Science and Art Department.' The time-tables of all the schools under the Board are made to conform to these requirements; the walls of the class-rooms are hung with illustrations in natural history and other diagrams; and in many of the schools boxes of objects are also to be found . . .

In the animal group children should be led to compare and classify the different animals, and to notice the chief differences and resemblances between the leading divisions of the animal kingdom. The children should also have explained to them the preparation, qualities, and uses of animal substances employed in the arts, such as leather, silk, wool, and horn . . .

The foundations of a 'knowledge of common things,' as Dr. Lyon Playfair[1] happily called it, will thus be well laid; and the children of the London schools will at an early age acquire the habit of correct observation – no mean advantage whatever may be their future occupation in life. This additional course of instruction will not occupy more than about two hours a week, and will involve scarcely any extra expense, while it will sharpen the wits of the children and freshen their minds for more literary studies.

Editorial Endnote

1 Lyon Playfair was a Liberal Member of Parliament with a special interest in the sciences and in technical education.

DOI: 10.4324/9781003107835-108

Editorial Headnote

80. Anon., 'The St. George-in-the-East Nature Study Museum', *School Nature Study* (1906)

School Nature Study was the journal of the School Nature Study Union, a body which was founded in 1903 in the East End of London to introduce children from the city slums to living nature and to inculcate thereby greater kindness to animals.[1] The founder was Miss Kate Hall, F.L.S., then Curator of the Stepney Borough Museum at Whitechapel Library; she was supported by Revd Claude Hinscliff, Curate of St George-in-the-East.[2] The SNSU quickly gained enthusiastic support from prominent scientists, local educationalists and civic leaders. Its first president, in post for seven years, was the Liberal MP Sir George Kekewich, who was at various times secretary to the Government's Science and Art Department and to the Board of Education. He was also, perhaps significantly, a prominent anti-vivisectionist. Members of the museum staff aimed to assist local schools in the teaching of natural history, which had been a curriculum requirement since 1900. In particular, they guided the children in direct observation and sketching of live creatures in the collection, noting developmental changes over time. The *Teachers' Times* had reported in January 1904 that gifts of specimens to the museum would be welcome, together with teachers' contributions to 'the *lantern slide department* by sending photographs of their taking and illustrative of school Nature study work (snapshots on Rambles)'.[3] Such 'School Rambles' into the countryside were an important aspect of the SNSU's work with children. Its official motto, inscribed on many of the pamphlets on zoology, was 'To see and admire; not harm or destroy'.

Editorial Endnotes

1 The archive of the SNSU, which was later renamed the School Natural Science Society, is preserved in Leeds University Library. E.W. Jenkins and B.J. Swinnerton, 'The School Nature Study Union, 1903–94', *History of Education* 25:2 (1996), pp. 181–98.

2 M.R.N. Holmer, 'The first years of the School Nature Study Union 1903–1908', *School Nature Study* 47:186 (January 1952), pp. 2–4. David Elliston Allen, *The Naturalist in Britain: A Social History* (Harmondsworth: Penguin, 1978), pp. 203–4. Allen's charges of 'soggy idealism' and 'sentimentalism' in bodies like the SNSU are belied by the seriousness of surviving publications such as Miss Hall's *Handbook to the Vivaria and Fresh Water Aquaria in the Nature Study Branch of the Borough Museum . . . Cable Street, East* (London, Metropolitan Borough of Stepney, 1904) and by the thoughtfulness of its educational methods.

3 Anon., unpaginated manuscript copy in the archive of the School Nature Study Union from *Teachers' Times*, n.s. 2:27 (1 January 1904).

80

THE ST. GEORGE-IN-THE-EAST NATURE STUDY MUSEUM

Anon., School Nature Study

Source: Anon., 'The St. George-in-the-East Nature Study Museum', *School Nature Study* 1 (1906), pp. 5–7.

[p. 5]

The Borough Councillor's Point of View, *By Stanley B. Atkinson, M.A., M.B., B.Sc., J.P., Chairman of the Stepney Public Libraries and Museums Committee.*

In the centre of one of the blackest spots of the sociologist's magpie map of London, at St. George-in-the-East, is a large recreation ground and garden; formerly two adjacent cemeteries made this open space. Until a few years back, the only brick building therein was the parish mortuary, which had become unused and thus disused, having passed into the hands of the Works Committee of the Stepney Borough Council. An anonymous benefactor, prompted by the vigilant Borough Curator, offered to renovate this dead-house into a Museum for Nature Study . . . the rooms were thereupon heated and fitted with electric light and motive power for aërating the aquaria. Later, the flower beds surrounding the Nature Study Museum were handed over for cultivation to the Curator. The Managers and Head Teachers of the local public elementary schools were interested in the objects of the new venture; classes were organised for systematic instruction and observation, and the study of bionomics. Several friends of the scheme presented specimens of animal and plant life. There is a small lecture hall with an electric lantern, shelves with fresh water aquaria, vivaria including ants' nests, and an observation bee hive; in a smaller room are salt water aquaria, and the record of regular meteorological entries . . .

To the onlooker it is at once evident that there is considerable keenness among the privileged scholars, and in many cases among the teachers who accompany them: this little Temple of Nature, in the least romantic and most commercial centre of the metropolis, has stimulated interest in the Nature Study movement alike among the Borough Councillors, the general public, and the local schools.

[pp. 6–7]

The Teacher's Point of View, *By Miss M. Brooks, Headmistress, Myrdle Street L.C.C. Higher Grade School.*

The Nature Study Branch of the Stepney Borough Museum stands in one of those quiet green backwaters still to be found just off the busy thoroughfares of East

DOI: 10.4324/9781003107835-109

London . . . The Museum is a small one-storied building, which has happily been diverted from its original use, and which now contains treasures such as can rarely be found elsewhere in London. Here, arranged on shelves round the walls, are tanks large and small, miniature seas and ponds, in which the water is constantly freshened by means of an air pump cunningly worked by electricity. In these different tanks, sea and fresh water plants – gorgeous anemones or delicate green filmy plants – live and thrive, and many small water beings find their home. Here, also in suitable cases, are many living specimens of the insect and reptile world – salamanders and lizards, toads and frogs, snakes harmless and harmful, worms and ants, and that greatest joy of children and grown-ups alike, an observatory hive of bees.

The Museum is open to the general public daily at stated times, and many strangers visit it. But it is mainly of use to its intimate friends, the teachers and children of the neighbourhood, who come to it and to its kind Curator for inspiration and help in one of the most fascinating and important of all school subjects – Nature Study – alas! so difficult to study at first hand in London.

Miss Hall, to whose indefatigable effort the Museum owes its being, wrote not long after its first formation:-

'. . . Primarily I hope to make a Nature Museum which shall be a source of joy for us in East London if only a small one. I hope teachers will use it themselves, and bring their pupils to see it. I hope for small bodies of scholars from neighbouring schools to come once or twice a week, and make notes and sketches, following the changes which occur in any particular specimen or group they may choose to study. I know it is the desire of the Stepney Borough Council that the Museum should give pleasure to their fellow-citizens, and be of valuable service to elementary education.'

. . . Here the unspoilt child, with its natural instincts of intense curiosity, habit of observation and keen love of question, guided by wise suggestion, may learn much for itself, and is stimulated to acquire habits and interests which may be retained through life . . .

The seasonal scheme of Nature Study is prepared by the teachers of the school, and is submitted to Miss Hall, who makes suggestions as to its improvement. The scheme is type-written by her, and at the same time a parallel column of the illustrative material which will be available at the Museum Lessons is added. School lessons are given each week, according to the syllabus, with the best material that can be procured. A Museum lesson is given once a month, when most of the time is devoted to observation, drawing, and a talk of the utility of the various forms studied . . . I am sure, too, that a demonstration in the Museum as to the methods of constructing simple apparatus, and on those points which make for the well being of plants and animals, would be most helpful to those teachers anxious to have a thriving school aquarium of their own.

Parties of students in training, both at school and college, have visited the Museum with much benefit, and teachers in the country when introduced to it learn much. But the children's appreciation I venture to think is the most important testimony to its use, and their point of view I give in the form of extracts taken at random from a chance set of composition papers – by children of different ages.

'We can learn a great deal at the Museum. We see how lizards change their skins, how fishes breathe, and how frogs do all sorts of things. We also learn how birds live. The bees can be seen making their honey, how snails crawl out of their shells, how worms live, and how the queen bee is different from her subjects. The queen bee can be seen to be different by her body, which is long and pointed. It is also very interesting to watch the sea anemones moving and eating. The moth is seen as a chrysalis, and ants are seen at work. The fishes are most interesting to me, and they swallow the water when they breathe.' . . .

'We learn how to look after the worms, and how to regard Nature as one of ourselves.'

'We learn to draw them as we see them.'

'When I go there I learn many things only by looking at them. I learn for instance, when I look at the bee that it is a wonderful and busy insect.'

'I am always delighted when I hear that I am going to the Nature Study Museum, because I think it is a very beautiful place to visit, and the best place to learn about Nature.' . . .

'In summer, the lady if she can catch birds, or find dead birds, stuffs them and puts them in the Museum for the winter.'

'The reasons why we like these, are because we need not talk about insects and animals without seeing, but when we learn all about them we can see it with our own eyes. In this way we can learn very quickly, because we do not have to wait for somebody to tell us all about them but we just watch them.

'I am glad that I go there, for I have never a chance of seeing these animals elsewhere.'

'I like to go there because everything is real Nature except the birds, which were real birds.'

Editorial Headnote

80.1. Kate M. Hall, 'The Smallest Museum', *Museums Journal* (1901–2)

In her paper, Kate Hall, a librarian and founder of the School Nature Study Union, emphasised that the museum she had created in the East End of London occupied only one room and that the table-cases of fragile specimens had to be pushed aside to make room for chairs when lectures took place. Gifts of specimens from private collectors and loans of art works or scientific objects from the government's Department of Science and Art conditioned the scope of the classes that could be offered to local schools. Nevertheless, Miss Hall explained, 'I do think it is of the greatest importance in an elementary museum in a district like ours that the objects should be as attractive as possible, without forgetting the educational work they have to do' (p. 39).[1]

Editorial Endnote

1 Miss Hall's work was also referenced on p. 35 and pp. 234–5 of this volume of the *Museums Journal*, with glowing praise for her educational methods. Kate Hill, *Women and Museums, 1850–1914: Modernity and the Gendering of Knowledge* (Manchester: Manchester University Press, 2018), pp. 22–5, 37–8, 200, 206.

80.1

THE SMALLEST MUSEUM

Kate M. Hall

Source: Kate M. Hall, 'The Smallest Museum', paper read at the Edinburgh conference of the Museums Association in 1901, *The Museums Journal* 1 (July 1901–June 1902), pp. 38–45.

The method of using the objects is left to the teachers' discretion. As a rule the children are asked to make remarks. The remarks are then criticised and enlarged upon by the teacher, and when the child has got some definite idea in his head he puts it in his note book or makes a sketch.[1]

Personally, I can do very little beyond supplying the best material I have at hand for other people to use. My own aim is always not to give a child facts, but to entangle him or her in an interest and love for living things, which, I believe, will be a source of ample, rational, and healthy occupation for leisure hours, and a continuous solace and delight throughout life. In addition to the moral effect of such an interest, I also believe that it tends to broaden the mind and open the eyes to the needs of progress.

I cannot claim to be teaching children biological science, or any other kind of science, though I do think it of the first importance that the facts children do get hold of should be correct.

As far as possible we endeavour to connect living specimens with the dead ones in the cases, that they may not think the study of natural history a study of dead things only. There are fresh specimens of wild flowers, aquaria of common fish, snails, tadpoles, &c., and breeding cages for moths and butterflies . . .

Our temporary exhibitions of flowers, fungi, and living bees always prove attractive, especially the last, which appeared to the auditor such an unnecessary thing for a museum to do, that he was on the point of surcharging the item for the hire of the observatory hive, when the account was first submitted to him. Nevertheless, the bees are not only very attractive to the general public, but the demonstrations are so much sought after by the schools, that I invariably find myself voiceless after a four days' exhibition of the observatory hive. (pp. 42–3).

Editorial Endnote

1 The emphasis on developing a child's powers of observation and readiness to record the life of nature in sketches was shared with the Royal Society for the Protection of Birds, as was the use of slides in lectures (compare Chapter 69 of the present work). Diana Donald, *Women Against Cruelty: Protection of Animals in Nineteenth-century Britain*, 2nd ed. (Manchester: Manchester University Press, 2020), pp. 271–3.

DOI: 10.4324/9781003107835-110

Editorial Headnote

81. Samuel Highley, 'The application of photography to the magic lantern', *Journal Of The Society Of Arts* (1863)

Highley, a microscope maker and photographer, pioneered the use of the magic lantern for projecting scientific images in lectures to varied audiences. This paper, explaining his ideas and methods, was delivered at a meeting of the Society of Arts on 14 January 1863. It demonstrates the blend of serious research and commercialism, education and entertainment, and science and art, which underpinned the development of photographic lantern slides. The Honourable and Reverend Samuel Best chaired the meeting and responded to the lecture, expressing his appreciation of Highley's work.

81

THE APPLICATION OF PHOTOGRAPHY TO THE MAGIC LANTERN, EDUCATIONALLY CONSIDERED

Samuel Highley

Source: Samuel Highley, 'The application of photography to the magic lantern, educationally considered', *Journal of the Society of Arts* 11:530 (16 January 1863), pp. 141–7.

[pp. 141–3]

It may seem strange (to some presumptuous) that anyone should wish a body like the Society of Arts to give an evening's consideration to that reminiscence of the nursery, the Galanty Show,[1] to that toy of our boyhood, the Magic Lantern. Many scientific phenomena, when first discovered, either from their remarkability or beauty, have excited much interest in the popular mind, but have only been regarded by it as pleasing toys, till in the course of time their practical value has been discovered, and they have been ranked in the list of applied sciences.

Such was the globe of water, magnifying in distorted form the fly or flower, till in the hands of science it sprang into that exquisite refinement of optical knowledge, 'the Microscope,' that discoverer of hidden worlds and life, and the seat or form of disease within the inmost walls of the human frame . . . In Microscopy, Natural History, Physiological, and Pathological research, what an invaluable agent does Photography prove; for Nature here depicts herself with her own pencil, and, possibly, ere long from her own palette, *and in this resides* one of its greatest values, for *truthfulness* is insured, and our studies are delineated with a faithful and unbiassed hand; with what minuteness of detail, the photographs I shall exhibit will bear witness.

I trust that I shall be able to prove this evening, to many who may not previously have given attention to the subject, that the Magic Lantern is likewise, with attention, destined to become an instrument of great Educational value. We are most of us aware that Natural History designs have been produced by the ordinary Magic Lantern colourist, and many such subjects, even produced with care, have made us exclaim with Polonius that the representations have been, – 'very like a whale.'[2] Undoubtedly many subjects painted for the lantern are really artistic productions;

but can the best artist for one moment pretend to cope with Dame Nature in her artistic moods? Can any artist (even a pre-Raphaelite)[3] for one moment hope to introduce the amount of detail she, with her undulating brushes of light, fixes upon the film which her assistant the chemist, has prepared for her? For it must be borne in mind, that while the Artist delights in *broad effects*, the Naturalist regards *detail* as a *sine qua non*, their aims being different; and it must be patent to every one, that while the painted views we have long been accustomed to meet every requirement, where mere amusement is concerned, photographic transparencies on glass will be the great means by which the Magic Lantern will be rendered subservient to the purposes of instruction . . .

I have long been impressed with the conviction that the lecturer on Botany, Zoology, Microscopy, Geology, Astronomy, and even on Pathology would welcome as a boon truthful transcripts of nature that could be packed in a small space, and then shown on a scale to arrest attention in the student. This idea is actuated by no showman's feeling; for all persons who have had any experience in scientific educational matters know the value of appealing to the eye. Book knowledge, or that experience gained even from the most graphic descriptions, is of little value to the student who would become a true naturalist. He must see – if possible, handle – the objects of his study. The next best thing to this is to be familiar with the most accurate delineations of the forms he wishes to become acquainted with; and here photography offers her aid, and the magic lantern popularises her efforts . . .

And now to the means by which we accomplish our purpose. In the first place, the negatives may be those of the usual character; but, if taken expressly for the lantern, it should be borne in mind that the pictures should be included within circles. Whenever it is possible the negatives should be taken from nature, animate or inanimate; but there are many cases where this is impossible, and when a diagrammatic treatment of the subject is desirable. This specially holds good with many Oceanic forms of life; for, when out of a sufficient bulk of their native element, they collapse and look anything but 'from the life.'

Again, from the rarity of the subject desired, it may be necessary to resort to engravings; but no expense should be spared to procure them from the works of the best authorities, and in such a style of execution as is to be found in the works of Ray and Palæontographical Societies.[4] If artistic, the negatives should always be taken from the originals, so that the characteristic touch of the artist may be ensured . . .

But photographic magic-lantern views, even when not in use, may be made available for educational purposes; for I would suggest that, if they represent Natural History subjects, instead of stowing them away in boxes, they should be placed in the open cases of museums, &c., beside allied objects, care being taken that they are fixed at such an angle that light should be reflected through them, by aid of a piece of white paper placed behind the transparency – or by mounting the views in long frames backed with fine ground glass, they might serve as appropriate borders to the windows of a scientific institution . . .

[p. 147]

In conclusion, I would say that every Exploring Expedition should be accompanied by its official photographer; that every National Museum, Observatory, and Hospital should have its appointed operator; and then the hoped-for time may come, when we can, in systemic manner, place the Records of Scientific Travel, the Transcripts of Nature's Treasures, and the History of the Progress of fell Disease, upon the screens of our lecture theatres, the stereographs of our cabinets, and the pages of the books in our libraries . . .

Mr. Highley then exhibited, on a large screen, an extensive series of lantern views of scientific subjects, illustrative of the application of photography to the representation of geological, botanical, zoological, microscopical, astronomical, geographical, ethnological, biographical, and pathological subjects; and afterwards examples of the representations of the artistic works of Kaulbach, Schnorr, and Hogarth[5]; together with groups pf sculpture, as well as some specimens furnished by Mr Charles Jones . . .

The Chairman said . . . he could not thank him too highly for the manner in which he had brought the subject before them, connecting it as he had done immediately with education. The microscopic illustrations exhibited had shown, in a remarkable manner, how the valuable sources of information opened up to us by that instrument might be popularised and rendered available for general instruction . . . he thought they had arrived, happily, at the day when they did not regard education as a mere matter of form. The eye must be entertained, and they might in many ways contribute to education, and enlarge the powers and faculties of the mind without treading merely those old and narrow paths to which education had been hitherto confined.[6]

Editorial Endnotes

1 A 'galanty show' was an entertainment for children: a pantomime in which the shadows of miniature figures were thrown on a wall or screen.

2 Shakespeare, *Hamlet*, act 3, scene 2. Hamlet is making a fool of Polonius.

3 Pre-Raphaelite painters such as Holman Hunt and John Everett Millais introduced a highly detailed kind of realism into art in the 1850s.

4 Highley may have been thinking of the fine intaglio engravings in Darwin's volumes on the *Cirripedia* (1851–4), which had been funded by the Ray Society and the Palæontographical Society (see Introduction to Part I of the present work).

5 Wilhelm von Kaulbach, Julius Schnorr von Carolsfeld, and William Hogarth. The common denominator of these artists was a crowded figural style, rich in detail. The slides were probably made from engravings rather than original paintings.

6 Highley again promoted the educational advantages of the achromatic magic lantern for projecting photographic transparencies of scientific specimens when he addressed a BAAS gathering in 1864 with a presentation 'On the Application of Photography and the Magic Lantern to Class Demonstrations in Microscopic Science and Natural History. By SAMUEL HIGHLEY, F.G.S., F.C.S., &c.', noted in *Report of the Thirty-fourth Meeting of the British Association for the Advancement of Science, held at Bath in September 1864* (London: John Murray, 1865); 'Notes and Abstracts of Miscellaneous Communications to the Sections', p. 98.

Editorial Headnote

82. Anon., *A Companion to Mr. Bullock's London Museum and Pantherion* (1812)

Bullock's London Museum inaugurated the rise of natural history museums in nineteenth-century London. His 'natural curiosities' were taxidermy specimens of many species of animals from across the world – birds, reptiles, and large mammals – their bodies often being obtained from private menageries. In the museum they were picturesquely grouped against appropriate scenic backdrops and amid artificial rocks etc., in an anticipation of the dioramas which appeared later in the century. These zoological exhibits were interspersed with collections of ancient and tribal artefacts, miscellaneous models, pictures, and objects of historical interest – all goods which the knowledgeable Bullock had acquired on his travels and now offered for sale. The scope of his holdings reflects the early growth of the British Empire, and the corresponding expansion of zoological knowledge: a stuffed giraffe was then a complete novelty. Bullock's prime intention was to *entertain* the fashionable public, and he certainly succeeded in this. His emphasis on dramatic spectacle stands in contrast to the mindset evident in the university museums described by ornithologist William MacGillivray (see Chapter 83 of the present work), where researchers' access to carefully identified animal skeletons and skins was all-important. Bullock's 1812 catalogue of his collection of animal specimens (one of many versions of the publication, successively produced as the collections grew from 1810 onwards), also made for exciting reading: in the case of the 'Cincerous Eagle' (evidently the White-tailed Eagle), he gives a blow-by-blow account of how live specimens were obtained from a cliff edge. Such narratives set a precedent for those found in later nineteenth-century popular books on natural history.

82

A COMPANION TO MR. BULLOCK'S LONDON MUSEUM AND PANTHERION[1]

Anon.

Source: Anon., *A Companion to Mr. Bullock's London Museum and Pantherion; containing a Brief Description of Upwards of Fifteen Thousand Natural and Foreign Curiosities, Antiquities, and Productions of the Fine Arts, Collected during Seventeen Years of arduous Research, and at an Expense of Thirty Thousand Pounds; And now open for Public Inspection in the Egyptian Temple, just erected for its Reception, in Piccadilly, London, opposite the end of Bond-Street; by Wm. Bullock*, 12th ed., 'printed for the proprietor,' 1812 (but the 'Address' is dated 28 March 1813), pp. iii–v, 18, 21–3, 97–8, 123–5.

[pp. iii–v]

ADDRESS. Mr. BULLOCK respectfully begs leave to solicit the attention and patronage of the Nobility, Gentry, and the Public, to an Establishment for *the advancement of the Science of Natural History*, which in magnitude and expense, he presumes, is unparalleled, as the work of an individual.

The very flattering and general approbation which honoured the Exhibition of his MUSEUM, on its opening in a temporary situation in London, was a convincing proof that his future efforts for the extension and improvement of the Collection would be duly appreciated. His exertions to obtain articles of rarity and interest, have, therefore been unceasing. In most departments, the subjects have been doubled in number; the specimens are choice, in the highest possible preservation, and are arranged according to the Linnæan system. They consist of upwards of Fifteen Thousand species of Quadrupeds, Birds, Reptiles, Fishes, Insects, Shells, Corals, &c. &c. collected during twenty years of unwearied application, and at an expense exceeding thirty thousand pounds.

In adapting the Edifice which Mr. BULLOCK has just completed for the present collection, by displaying it advantageously for the Study of the Naturalist, the Instruction of the Curious, and the Amusement of those who are delighted in viewing the Beauties of Nature, or the Curiosities of Art, he has endeavoured to render it worthy of the British Metropolis, whilst he has also provided the means for enlargement, as future additions shall accumulate.

One department of the Museum (the Pantherion) completed with much labour and great expence, is entirely novel, and presents a scene altogether grand and

DOI: 10.4324/9781003107835-112

interesting. Various animals, as the lofty Giraffa, the Lion, the Elephant, the Rhinoceros, &c. are exhibited as ranging in their native wilds and forests; whilst exact Models, both in figure and colour, of the rarest and most luxuriant Plants from every clime, give all the appearance of reality; the whole being assisted with a panoramic effect of distance and appropriate scenery, affording a beautiful illustration of the luxuriance of a torrid clime.

The Museums of France have been enriched with the spoils of nearly the whole Continent, and the Gallery of the Louvre contains more treasure in Painting and Sculpture than perhaps will ever again be amassed in one Collection. But though her active and persevering Ruler, desirous of making his capital the centre of every attraction, has contributed to the Museum Naturale, every specimen of Natural History which in the present state of the Continent could be procured, our unrivalled Navy, and the extension of our Colonies throughout the habitable world, present such advantages to this country, that the writer feels confident, that if his exertions are seconded by the Public as they have hitherto been, he will very shortly be enabled to make a Collection of Natural History far surpassing any thing of the kind at present in existence; and he pledges himself to exert his utmost power in accomplishing this important work[2] . . .

[p. 18]
NATURAL HISTORY. BIRDS (CLASS AVIS)
Almighty Being!
Cause and support of all things, can I view
These objects of my wonder; can I feel
These fine sensations, and not think of thee?

This Ornithological department of the Museum contains probably a greater number of species than is to be found in any other collection: they are in the highest possible state of preservation, and arranged in their respective families, according to the Linnæan Classification, in a manner that has met the approbation of the scientific naturalist as well as the general visitor; as combining the whole of the Birds of one genus together, and exhibiting them in the order they stand in the *Systema Naturæ*, in such a way as convey an idea of their haunts and mode of life.[3]

The landscapes at the back of each case are intended to show the description of country in which the respective birds are generally found . . .

[pp. 21–3]

Cincerous Eagle, (Falco Albicilla) *with its young*. This is somewhat less than the Golden Eagle, the colour is also much lighter, and the bill straighter and larger than in any of the other species; it inhabits the northern parts of Europe and America. The young ones were taken on the 10th of June, 1812, when about three weeks old, from their aerie on the tremendous cliff called the West Craigs, in the Isle of Hoy, (one of the Orkneys) the towering rocks of which rise to the perpendicular height of 1200 feet from the sea. About one-third of the way down this awful abyss a slender pointed rock projected from the cliff, like the pinnacle of a gothic building; on the extremity of this is a hollow, scarcely of sufficient size for the purpose these birds had fixed on as a place of security for rearing their young; the situation was such as almost to defy the power of man to molest their habitation; yet with the assistance of a short slender rope, made of twisted hogs' bristles, did the well-known adventurous climber, or Rocksman, 'Woolley Tomson,' traverse the face of this frightful precipice, and for a trifling remuneration brought up the young birds.

After a fatiguing scramble up the sides of the mountains, we arrived at a place from whence we could see the aerie beneath, the distance was so great that the young Eagles appeared no larger than pigeons; after placing us in a secure situation on a projecting ledge of the rock, that commanded a view of the scene of action, Tomson left us, carrying his rope in his hand, and disappeared for upwards of half an hour; when, to our great joy, we discovered him creeping on his hands and knees up the spiry fragment, on which lay the unfledged Eaglets . . . the slender point of the rock on which he knelt was at least 800 feet above the surges of the Atlantic, which with unbroken violence were foaming beneath him. Yet he deliberately took from his pocket a cord, and tying the wings of the young birds, who made some resistance with their bills and talons, he put them into a basket, and began to descend . . . The old birds were in sight during the transaction, and made no attempt to defend their young: but soaring about a quarter of a mile above, occasionally uttered a short shrill scream, very different from their usual barking noise. Had they attempted a rescue, the situation of the climber would have been extremely dangerous, as the slightest deviation or false step would have precipitated him into eternity . . .

[pp. 97–8]

A COMPANION TO THE PANTHERION. *NATURAL HISTORY.* QUADRUPEDS

These are thy glorious works, Parent of Good! . . .
Thou sitt'st above those heavens
To us invisible, or dimly seen
In these thy lowest works; yet these declare
Thy goodness beyond thought, and power divine. MILTON

THE PANTHERION is an exhibition of Natural History, on a plan entirely novel, intended to display the whole of the known Quadrupeds, in a manner that will convey a more perfect idea of their haunts and mode of life than has hitherto been done, keeping them at the same time in their classic arrangement, and preserving them from the injury of dust and air: it occupies an extensive apartment, nearly forty feet high, erected for the purpose. The visitor is introduced through a basaltic cavern (of the same kind as the Giant's Causeway, or Fingall's Cave, in the Isle of Staffa) into an Indian hut, situated in a Tropical Forest, in which are displayed most of the Quadrupeds described by naturalists, with correct models from nature, or the best authorities, of the trees and other vegetable productions of the torrid climes, remarkable for the richness or beauty of their fruit, or the singularity of their foliage; the whole assisted by an appropriate panoramic effect of distance, which makes the illusion produced so strong, that the surprised visitor finds himself suddenly transported from a crowded metropolis to the depth of an Indian forest, every part of which is occupied by its various savage inhabitants.

The Linnæan arrangement of Quadrupeds commences at the first opening on the left-hand of the entrance, where, dispersed on rocks and the branches of a large Orange-tree, are about sixty species of the genus Simia; consisting of Apes, Baboons, and Monkeys. It is difficult to determine the species of many of them, and others are not yet described by any Naturalist . . .

[pp. 123–5]

The Camelopardalis, or Giraffa. (Camelopardalis Giraffa). Which is by far the tallest of all known quadrupeds, measuring the extraordinary height of seventeen feet three inches from the hoof of the fore foot to the top of the head, whilst (so disproportionate is the form) that the body scarcely exceeds that of a horse. Till lately the existence of so wonderful an animal was doubted by many European Naturalists, who ranked it amongst the fabulous monsters of antiquity.

This specimen was lately killed at a considerable distance, in the interior of the Cape of Good Hope, by the Rev. Mr. Edwards, an African missionary, when travelling in that country under the patronage of Lord Caledon, then Governor of the Cape.[4] It is represented as an harmless timid animal, living in small herds of six or seven together, in the plains that border on Caffraria: they are so extremely shy and wary, that it is with the greatest difficulty they can be approached: they feed on the fruit of the wild apricot, and on the tender branches of several species of Mimosa. This specimen, which is a full grown male, and very rich in colour, is allowed to be the finest ever brought to Europe, and is in the most perfect preservation.

Such is the excessive rarity of this singular animal, that from the decline of the Roman Empire till the middle of the eighteenth century its existence was deemed extremely problematical, if not in the highest degree chimerical . . . The narratives of succeeding travellers, who felt little inclination to observe, or whose opportunities of observation were limited and few, only tended to increase this perplexity, already too intricate, and by their dark ambiguous details, equally opposite and vague, to confirm the previous supposition of its fabulous and imaginary origin.

That this conjecture should have been strengthened by a perusal of the several relations of our travellers and naturalists, ought not to excite surprise, when we remember we are told, by one, that the length of its fore-legs is double that of those behind – by another, that this disparity does not exist – by a third, that such is their astonishing height, that a man mounted on horseback may with ease pass beneath its body – and by a fourth, that in point of magnitude, it does not exceed the size of a small horse.

From such a contrariety of evidence, the veracity of the traveller became disputed, and the credulity of the naturalist an object of derision. The whole was rejected as a fictitious invention – was classed with the crude abortions of Pliny's fervid imagination[5]; and such was the influence of this variety of testimony, that though Captain Carteret had given a distinct account of a Giraffa killed at the Cape of Good Hope in the year 1769, Mr. Pennant still refused to yield his assent, till convinced by personal inspection of a skin preserved in the University of Leyden.[6] The cloud of uncertainty, however, which has so long hovered over the real form of this beautiful and extraordinary animal, has of late years been dissipated by the minute descriptions of Gordon, Vaillant, and Sparrmann.[7] From them we have learned its size, its proportions, and peculiarities, with an accuracy and fidelity both laudable and decisive.

Editorial Endnotes

1 A different selection of extracts from the *Companion,* focusing more on the human artefacts that were exhibited, is given in Jonah Siegel (ed.), *The Emergence of the Modern Museum: An Anthology of Nineteenth-century Sources* (Oxford and New York: Oxford University Press, 2008), pp. 15–25. See also Richard D. Altick, *The Shows of London* (Cambridge, MA, and London: Belknap Press of Harvard University Press, 1978), pp. 235–7, and Carla Yanni, *Nature's Museums: Victorian Science and the Architecture of Display* (Baltimore: Johns Hopkins University Press, 1999), pp. 25–8.

2 Bullock here refers to Napoleon Bonaparte's military expeditions, through which many new animal specimens came to the Muséum National d'Histoire Naturelle in Paris – a parallel to the plundering of art works from Italy and other countries for the collections of the Louvre. Bullock claims that his own collecting activities – drawing on the resources of the British navy and colonial settlers – will rival those of the French government.

3 Linnaeus's *Systema Naturae* was then the preferred method of taxonomic classification.

4 Du Pré Alexander, 2nd Earl of Caledon, became Governor of the Cape in 1806. His 'patronage' of Edwards is an early example of the collaboration between colonial officials, big game hunters, professional animal collectors, and zoos or museums in Britain which characterises the imperial age.

5 Pliny the Elder's *Natural History*, written in the first century CE, contains many mythic elements.

6 Captain Philip Carteret, a British naval officer, acquired a drawing of a giraffe and took it to England in 1769: his information was published by the Royal Society. G. Mitchell, 'The origins of the scientific study and classification of giraffes', *Transactions of the Royal Society of South Africa* 64:1 (2009), pp. 1–13. Thomas Pennant was a leading writer on natural history and a correspondent of Gilbert White.

7 Robert Jacob Gordon, François Le Vaillant, and Anders Sparrmann all explored southern Africa in the 1770s–1780s. On Le Vaillant, see Chapter 89, note 15 of the present work.

Editorial Headnote

83. William Macgillivray, *A Memorial Tribute to William Macgillivray* (1901)

This work was undertaken on the initiative of a namesake of MacGillivray and compiled by him as an 'appreciative sketch' of the great ornithologist's career. Besides his achievements as a naturalist and author (among other things, he assisted Audubon with the text that accompanied the plates of the *Birds of America*),[1] MacGillivray produced his own accurate and beautiful watercolour drawings of birds and other creatures.[2] He was also a museum curator who pioneered new and improved methods of organising zoological collections. In 1833, while holding the post of conservator at the Museum of the Edinburgh College of Surgeons, he went on a fact-finding tour of scientific museums in Britain to appraise current approaches to the conservation, labelling, and public exhibition of specimens. His manuscript notes, first published in this *Memorial Tribute*, provide a caustic account of what he found, revealing the disorganised state of museum collections before the great improvements made in the second half of the nineteenth century. The majority of museum displays had neither the educative value nor the aesthetic appeal that MacGillivray sought: 'science and taste must go together in museums'.

His tour began in Glasgow, at the College Museum, and extended to Liverpool, Dublin, and London.

Editorial Endnotes

1 John James Audubon, *Ornithological Biography, or an Account of the Habits of the Birds of the United States of America* (Edinburgh: Adam Black, 1831). MacGillivray's assistance with both 'scientific details' and literary style is acknowledged only on p. xviii of Audubon's 'Introductory Address'.

2 Robert Ralph, *William MacGillivray: Creatures of Air, Land and Sea* (London: Merrell Holberton and the Natural History Museum, 1999).

83

A MEMORIAL TRIBUTE TO WILLIAM MCGILLIVRAY

McGillivray's Tour of Museums

Source: William MacGillivray, *A Memorial Tribute to William MacGillivray, M.A., LL.D, Ornithologist* (Edinburgh: privately printed, 1901), pp. 85–7, 89–94, 102–4.

[pp. 85–7]

At twelve I at length obtained admission to the College Museum.

In the front room are several stuffed skins of quadrupeds: a camelopard[1] of rather small size, a zebra, a hyena, several species of deer and antelope, a lion and lioness, etc., most of them very ill-prepared, and in bad attitudes, with clumsy ununiform pedestals. They are, however, kept very clean, and have in general been good specimens. There are four recesses in the wall, filled with foreign birds and insects, ill-prepared and whimsically disposed.

In the room to the right are coins, medals, snakes, quadrupeds, all without order.

A collection of British birds, very clean and neat, but generally in bad attitudes. The beaks of two eagles were actually polished and varnished, and the legs and bills in general were painted, usually of tints unlike those of the parts in their natural state. The legs of birds ought never to be painted for obvious reasons . . .

The whole Museum is more disposed for show than use, and the most egregious want of method is perceptible in all the rooms – I mean scientific method; for the articles are well disposed for effect and the whole place has a rich and finished look, the furniture and materials being good, and in sufficient quantity . . .

Dr. Hannay could not meet me at the Andersonian Institution, but sent a young gentleman, whom I found exceedingly obliging and polite, and who introduced me to Mr.Scoular who is a keen zoologist.[2] The collection there is contained in a large circular dome-roofed apartment, well lighted, and having a gallery. It consists of fragments of everything under the moon: – rocks, minerals, skeletons, fossils, skulls, stuffed quadrupeds, birds and fishes, reptiles in spirits, coins, antique pottery, plaster casts, human crania, skeletons of mammalia, etc.

The skeletons are horrible. There is one of a small elephant out of all proportion – all the rest are bad. All the birds and quadrupeds and fishes are ill-stuffed – yea, every one of them – at least I did not see one that was good. They are ill-arranged too. The people here may have science, for anything that I know to the contrary,

DOI: 10.4324/9781003107835-113

but they have no taste, no, not a particle. A dome is not a good place for a museum. Galleries are better. Nothing can be got to fill up the central space, unless one should erect a pyramid of elephants, megatheria, giraffes, and crocodiles.

[pp. 89–94]

On Saturday I visited various parts of Liverpool . . . So I went to the Royal Institution, where I met with Dr. Murray and his brother, the former being engaged in delivering a course of lectures on geology. These gentlemen, with great kindness, showed me the Museum, which is contained in a singularly ill-disposed suite of apartments. The disposition, however, is worse as to effect than as to the distribution of the articles. There is an extensive collection of rocks and minerals, generally pretty good, the former deficient in character and uniformity. They are placed in square trays or boxes and are arranged in glazed tables, but they are by no means neatly disposed. The fossils are numerous and generally good. Quadrupeds, ill-stuffed – birds, wretched. There is not one specimen in a characteristic attitude, but they are pretty numerous. A painting by Audubon of the wild turkey, good. A portrait of Doctor Traill, not more like than it should be. Ancient paintings from Roscoe's collection[3]; cast of antique statues; Ognia and Elgin marbles.

I am of opinion that the College of Surgeons of Edinburgh ought by all means to obtain casts of the Apollo Belvidere, Diana, Venus de Medicis, and a few others as specimens of the perfect form of the human body.[4] There are a few Florentine wax casts; a considerable collection of skeletons and skulls of mammalia and birds, fine corals, shells, etc. This, as usual, is an omnium gatherum museum. I say decidedly that everything is ill-arranged, the cases ill-constructed, the ticketing bad . . .

I arrived in Dublin about twelve, and . . . proceeded . . . to the College of Surgeons, where I found Dr. Houston, Conservator of the Museum.[5]

The building is splendid, and has a fine situation in St. Stephen's Green.

The hall is a fine room, with an arched roof, of an oblong form.

The hall of the Museum is about ninety feet long and forty-five feet broad – that is by estimate. It is lighted solely from the roof, and has a gallery all round. The space below the gallery, which is too broad, is very dark. The skeletons are arranged in glass boxes or cases, on the floor, and on shelves, under the gallery, the central part of the floor being unoccupied save by a miserable glazed table, containing skulls and calculi. There is a considerable number of skeletons, but almost all most uningeniously articulated, and in the most preposterous attitudes. About six are excellent, however, viz. a horse, an alpaca, a nylghau, a lion, and one or two more skeletons of grampus, good. In this department almost everything is in the most wretched disorder.

Fine skeleton of boa and pike; a few tolerable corals; three very fine human skeletons – male and female European and male negro.

The preparations are on the whole pretty well put up; but there is a most decided want of taste in the distribution of the articles, which, however, are placed in good order as to their nature – but science and taste must go together in museums.

It is a fine light room; but for a museum decidedly inferior to that of the Edinburgh College – excepting in respect of light.

Things in general *very dirty*. Dr. Houston scolding his assistant – but in fact the place is not yet arranged.

Fine fossil horns and bones of the Irish elk among rubbish, in a lumber room!

Dr. Houston says the members of the Edinburgh College of Surgeons are continually praising their museum, but for his part he leaves to strangers the praise which the Dublin Museum deserves. All I could say in its praise I said, namely that the apartment is light and elegant . . .

At two I visited Dr. Evanson, who drove me out in his car, along with a friend, to the Phoenix Park, the Zoological Gardens, and a limestone quarry about four miles out of town.[6] The gardens are of considerable extent and in a good position . . . They are laid out with much less taste than the Liverpool animals, and contain a smaller number of species. The collection, however, is good, and infinitely superior to a museum of five times the number. These collections will in time teach zoological painters the characteristic attitudes of animals, of which Audubon and myself are the only persons who have succeeded in attempting to afford an idea, in so far as regards birds. As to stuffed animals, they are altogether, entirely, and wholly absurd. I have not seen ten quadrupeds nor five hundred birds that were even tolerable. It is a difficult task to put up a skeleton of a quadruped, and still more to stuff the skin of one . . .

[pp. 102–4]

I proceeded towards Bristol, where I ascended a stage-coach bound for London . . . Soon after I went to the British Museum[7] . . . Montagu's collection of British birds, which is fine on account of its extent, but does not contain ten well-stuffed specimens. When are we to see some improvement in this art? . . . The pervading style of Montagu's birds is distortion. There is not, so far as I have observed, one faultless specimen among them. Good collection of eggs. Montagu's shells in glazed tables – pretty good, and fine, but not extraordinary . . .

Two rows of tables – glazed, with minerals – very splendid and beautifully arranged, although not yet properly named. They are laid on cotton, which covers a board, having a raised black margin. Now, it is pleasant to look at such an arrangement, although there are persons who care very little about the matter, and who would as readily put on their coat with the back before, provided it lay easily . . .

Comparatively few of the articles in the Museum are yet named. The shells are generally placed on disproportionately large cards, and might with advantage be made to occupy less than half the space.

Editorial Endnotes

1 A giraffe.

2 This was John Scouler, his name misspelt by MacGillivray or by the editor. Scouler was Professor of Geology, Natural History, and Mineralogy at Anderson's College in Glasgow between 1829 and 1834.

3 The Liverpool Royal Institution had been established in 1814 by (among others) William Roscoe and Thomas Stewart Traill. Both had assisted Audubon and promoted his

work when he visited Liverpool. Roscoe's 'ancient paintings' must have included the important early Italian works he owned, such as Simone Martini's *Christ Discovered in the Temple* (now in the Walker Art Gallery, Liverpool), which evidently shared space with the zoological exhibits.

4 The Apollo Belvedere (misspelt 'Belvidere') and the Medici Venus were among the most famous ancient classical statues, which MacGillivray here treats as paradigms of human physical perfection, almost in a medical spirit.

5 John Houston was a distinguished doctor of medicine.

6 Dr. Richard Evanson was a physician and lecturer on medicine in Dublin.

7 The British Museum in Bloomsbury then still housed the natural history collections, which were notoriously short of display space.

Editorial Headnote

84. Louis Compton Miall, 'Museums', *Nature* (1877)

Miall was curator of the museum of the Leeds Philosophical and Literary Society from 1871 to 1892. In the forty-odd years since ornithologist William MacGillivray had written his highly critical account of the standards of conservation, taxidermy, and display in natural history museums, great progress had been made. Amid all the debate over the principles of museology, Miall provided practical advice, based on his own experience at Leeds and his appraisal of the needs of ordinary local visitors to museums. *Visual* aids to understanding were all-important.

84

MUSEUMS

Louis Compton Miall

Source: Louis Compton Miall, 'Museums', *Nature* 16:409 (30 August 1877), p. 360.

Fossils are usually kept loose; in the larger collections they are mounted on tablets of wood or glass covered with paper . . . Fossils glued to pasteboard with coaguline are perfectly fast; we range them in wall-cases upon shelves sloped to forty-five degrees, and never meet with accidents.

In our geological wall-cases I have introduced above the level of the eye a range of boards, nearly upright, but sloping slightly forwards at the top, upon which maps, sections, photographs, and descriptive notices can be pinned. In a palæontological collection this space is useful for drawings of restored animals.

It is much to be desired that the dealers would procure a better choice of zoological models in glass and porcelain. Reuss' foraminifera are still useful, though antiquated; Blaschka, of Dresden, keeps no stock, though he has supplied many of our museums with useful models in glass made from drawings.[1] We want artistic and accurate coloured models of mollusca, hydrozoa, &c., far beyond the present supply.

Stuffed animals, especially stuffed mammalia, are the plague of a curator. I do not refer especially to their liability to moths (insects of all kinds can be kept down by placing saucers of carbolic acid in the cases) but to their grotesque deformity, their unnatural attitudes, and their proneness to contract in unexpected places. A model in plaster or clay, strengthened internally by wires would last for ever, and the skin would stretch over it readily enough when moist. Real skill in modelling is required here, and we have not yet been able to command it. The Schools of Art may in time help us over the difficulty. A well-modelled animal can never be very cheap, but if increased costliness should render set-up quadrupeds comparatively scarce, zoology need not suffer on that account.

Public museums should contain far more than they now do the elementary explanations necessary for the right understanding of the objects exhibited. A text-book illustrated by specimens instead of wood-cuts should be our aim, at least where the wants of the public are more concerned than the wants of special students. I should propose to relegate nine-tenths of our existing collections to cabinets were it not that things out of sight in cabinets are so liable to suffer from neglect. At present we aim at too much, introduce too many departments into

DOI: 10.4324/9781003107835-114

a small museum, show too many obscure and uninstructive objects, and spoil everything by over-crowding.

Personally, I do not hold that local collections should be everything in a provincial museum. We have to consider the wants of residents as well as of passing strangers, and what the residents interested in natural history require is a general collection of typical specimens which will teach them something of the elements of their science. It is very easy to make imposing collections of land and freshwater shells, butterflies, and so forth, which a naturalist passing that way praises because they contain here and there a choice thing, but which either teaches nothing to the uneducated visitor, or else teaches him the very undesirable lesson that the best thing he can do is to make a similar collection for himself. We have had more than enough of unintelligent collecting and unintelligent records of occurrence. Our provincial museums should tell the public that to know something of the structure of animals and plants is better than to know many species.

Editorial Endnote

1 It was difficult to find ways of displaying microscopic, aquatic, or highly perishable life forms to museum visitors. August Emanuel Ritter von Reuss had devised models of foraminifera (single-celled micro-organisms with shells). The Blaschka firm produced glass models of marine creatures (see Chapter 17, note 1 of the present work).

Editorial Headnote

85. Henry Acland and John Ruskin, *The Oxford Museum* (1893), 'On the Irish Workmen'

This museum, built in the 1850s, provided space under one roof for all the university's then-existing science departments, as well as for its collections of scientific objects. The zoological specimens had previously been scattered across Oxford. The 'Gothic' design of this iron and glass building was the brainchild of the architect Benjamin Woodward and of Acland's friend John Ruskin, who gave £300 towards the carving of the stone decorations on the museum façade.[1] A history of the project published in 1909 explained the ideas behind it: 'their plan was that the decoration should portray or typify that very natural history for the study of which the building was intended . . . a complete series of Fauna and Flora, the examples being as far as possible British'.[2]

In accordance with Ruskin's ideals, inspired by his study of medieval buildings, these motifs were to be designed by the sculptors or 'workmen' themselves and based on direct observations of nature. However, there was an evident tension between this ideal of spontaneous creativity on the part of the executants, and their actual status as artisan-class employees directed and disciplined by a delegacy of the university authorities. In this late edition of his book *The Oxford Museum*, Acland gives an amusing (but probably embroidered) account of the trials and tribulations of the O'Sheas – the family of Irish sculptors tasked with carrying out Ruskin's programme for the decoration of the building.[3] The university's alleged veto on the carving of monkeys would have reflected the religious sensitivities of the period following the publication of Darwin's *On the Origin of Species* in 1859. It was in this very building that the famous debate over Darwin's theories took place in 1860, involving a bitter exchange between Thomas Huxley and Samuel Wilberforce, Bishop of Oxford – the latter trying to ridicule the notion that humans had simian ancestors.

Editorial Endnotes

1 Eve Blau, *Ruskinian Gothic: The Architecture of Deane and Woodward, 1845–1861* (Princeton, NJ: Princeton University Press, 1982), pp. 48–81. Trevor Garnham, *Oxford Museum: Deane and Woodward* (London: Phaidon Press, 1992, 2010). Carla Yanni, *Nature's Museums: Victorian Science and the Architecture of Display* (Baltimore: Johns Hopkins University Press, 1999), pp. 62–90. John Holmes, *Temple of Science: The Pre-Raphaelites and Oxford University Museum of Natural History* (Oxford: Bodleian Library and Oxford University Museum of Natural History, 2020), p. 63. In 'Science and the language of natural history museum architecture: problems of interpretation', *Museum and Society* 17:3 (2019), pp. 342–61, Holmes had compared the Oxford

Museum to Waterhouse's 'Romanesque' Natural History Museum in London, in their interpretations of natural theology.

2 Horace Middleton Vernon and K. Dorothea Ewart Vernon, *A History of the Oxford Museum* (Oxford: Clarendon Press, 1909), p. 77.

3 Blair J. Gilbert, 'Puncturing an Oxford myth: the truth about the 'infamous' O'Sheas and the Oxford University Museum', *Oxoniensia* 74 (2009), pp. 87–112.

85

THE OXFORD MUSEUM . . . 1859, 'ON THE IRISH WORKMEN'

Henry Acland and John Ruskin

Source: Henry Acland and John Ruskin, *The Oxford Museum, from original edition, 1859. With additions in 1893* (London and Orpington: George Allen, 1893). Notes, II. 'On the Irish Workmen', pp. 106–9.

It had been intended from the first that all decoration should illustrate the Kosmos, as religious histories or allusions for the most part are represented in ecclesiastical edifices. The workmen generally made the designs for places and objects appointed to them by the Architect.

The upper windows in the Front were to illustrate some part of the Fauna and Flora of our planet; the windows on the South of the Front the vertebrate classes – Man, Quadrumana, Carnivora.

The second window was first begun by order of the Architect, but, probably, not by that of the Delegates, it being long vacation.

O'Shea rushed into my house one afternoon, and – in a state of wild excitement – related as follows.

'The Master of the University,' cried he, 'found me on my scaffold just now.' 'What are you at?' says he. 'Monkeys,' says I. 'Come down directly,' says he; 'you shall not destroy the property of the University.' 'I work as Mr. Woodward orders me.' 'Come down directly,' says he; 'come down.'[1]

'What shall I do?' said O'Shea to me. 'I don't know; Mr. Woodward told you monkeys, the Master tells you no monkeys. I don't know what you are to do.' He instantly rushed out as he came, without another word.

The next day I went to see what had happened. O'Shea was hammering furiously at the window. 'What are you at?' said I. 'Cats,' says he. 'The Master came along, and says, 'You are doing monkeys when I told you not.' 'To-day its cats,' says I. The Master was terrified and went away.'[2]

It is quite intelligible that this old century proceeding peculiar to Gothic and Irish art was puzzling to Mr. Fergusson's regulated mind. It did not however so end; Shea was dismissed. I went to wish him good-bye with mixed and perplexed feelings.

I found Shea on a single ladder in the porch, wielding heavy blows such as one imagines the genius of Michael Angelo might have struck when he was first blocking out the design of some immortal work. 'What are you doing, Shea?

DOI: 10.4324/9781003107835-115

I thought you were gone, and Mr. Woodward has given no design for the long moulding in the hard green stone.'

Striking on still, Shea shouted,

'Parrhots and Owwls!

'Parrhots and Owwls!

Members of Convocation!'

There they were, blocked out alternately.

What could I do? 'Well,' I said meditatively, 'Shea, you must knock their heads off.'

'Never,' says he.

'Directly,' said I.

Their heads went. Their bodies, not yet evolved, remain to testify to the humour, the force, the woes, the troubles, in the character and art of our Irish brethren – much to love, much to direct, much to lament.

Editorial Endnotes

1 There is, in fact, a sketch by James O'Shea that apparently shows monkeys as decoration of the carved arch above a window on the facade of the building: Holmes, *Temple of Science*, p. 65. Moreover, Blau in *Ruskinian Gothic*, p. 73, cites a letter of 1859 from James O'Shea to Acland, in which he writes: 'I would not desire better sport than putting monkeys, cats, dogs, rabbits, and hares, and so on in different attitudes on those jambs'.

2 The 'Master' was Revd Frederick Plumptre, Master of University College, who was on the delegacy overseeing the construction of the museum building. This 'cat window' was on the upper level of the façade and is illustrated in Holmes, *Temple of Science*, p. 66.

Editorial Headnote

85.1. James Fergusson, *History of the Modern Styles of Architecture* (1873)

As Acland mentioned in the previous passage, the architectural historian James Fergusson, who was hostile to the revival of a 'Gothic' style for buildings with a modern purpose, passed a withering judgement on the Oxford University Museum and its animal carvings. The following appraisal of it comes from his *History of the Modern Styles of Architecture*, which had been first published in 1862.

85.1

HISTORY OF THE MODERN STYLES OF ARCHITECTURE

James Fergusson

Source: James Fergusson, *History of the Modern Styles of Architecture*, 2nd ed., 4 vols. (London: John Murray, 1873), vol. 4, pp. 374–5.

The third building chosen to illustrate the downward progress of the art is the New Museum at Oxford. This was designed to be Gothic in conception, Gothic in detail, and Gothic in finish. Nothing was to betray the hated and hateful nineteenth century, to the cultivation of whose sciences it was to be dedicated . . . It is to be hoped that no stuffed specimen of the modern genus Felis will be introduced into the museum, or we may lose the illusion to be gained from contemplating the long-backed specimens of the Mediæval species which crawl round the windows of the Library in such strangely pre-historic attitudes. The one really good point in the whole design is the range of pillars with their capitals which surround the inner court; but they are good precisely because they are not Gothic. The shafts are simply cylinders of British marbles; the capitals adorned with representations of plants and animals, as like nature as the material and the skill of the artist would admit of, and as unlike the Gothic cats of the facade as two representations of the same class of objects can well be made.[1]

Editorial Endnote

1 Both the 'cat window' on the exterior of the building and the capitals of the columns in the court were, however, carved by the O'Sheas.

DOI: 10.4324/9781003107835-116

Editorial Headnote

86. Edward Ingress Bell, 'The new Natural History Museum', *Magazine of Art* (1881)

Edward Ingress Bell was himself an architect who contributed to the design of many grand public buildings; his commissions included the main façade of the Victoria and Albert Museum, built alongside the Natural History Museum in South Kensington. In contrast to Fergusson, with his distaste for medievalism in buildings that served a modern function, Ingress Bell responded sympathetically to the blend of 'Romanesque' architecture and imaginative animal forms in Alfred Waterhouse's design for the frontage of the Natural History Museum, built in the 1870s.[1] The terracotta sculptures expressed the purpose of the museum, as conceived by its first director, Richard Owen. They were to present the varied beauties of nature and the divinely ordained hierarchy of species, culminating in a figure of Adam on the skyline, as the being nearest to God. Yet this vision, inspired by natural theology, was already being replaced by Darwin's unsettling notions.[2]

Editorial Endnotes

1 Carla Yanni, *Nature's Museums: Victorian Science and the Architecture of Display* (Baltimore: Johns Hopkins University Press, 1999), pp. 111–46. Mark Girouard, *Alfred Waterhouse and the Natural History Museum*, 2nd ed. (London: Natural History Museum, 1999). J.B. Bullen, 'Alfred Waterhouse's Romanesque "Temple of Nature": The Natural History Museum, London', *Architectural History* 49 (2006), pp. 257–85.

2 Bullen in particular analyses the genesis of Waterhouse's design and its relation to Owen's religious views, with citations of the extensive previous literature on the building. Waterhouse's drawings for the figurative decorations of the building are preserved in the Museum's library.

86

THE NEW NATURAL HISTORY MUSEUM – 1

Edward Ingress Bell

Source: Edward Ingress Bell, 'The new Natural History Museum – I', *Magazine of Art* 4 (1881), pp. 358–62.

[pp. 360–1]

The picturesqueness of the *ensemble*, as seen from either approach, every one who is sensible of such charms will admit. There is a nobility about the building which cannot fail to strike every educated observer . . . the receding planes and deepening shades of the concentric lines of enriched archivolts over windows and doors, the accentuation of leading lines and features by varied and appropriate imagery, and the combination of delicacy with breadth of treatment throughout, show a master's hand.

It would perhaps be thought a little fanciful if one attempted to trace in the form and disposition of the building the distinctive features of the various subdivisions of the organic kingdom; it would be easily done, and would not be a whit more fanciful than the theories applied all round to the examples of the past. We have in the general plan of the structure that bilateral symmetry which is characteristic of the Vertebrata, and other types, such as the Annulosa, the Annuloida, are not unrepresented.

Leaving this part of the inquiry for the amusement of posterity, and descending to a detailed examination of the exterior, the eye is first arrested by a series of boldly-designed animal forms *en silhouette* along the lines of metal crestings; these give at once a clue to the objects of the building. Lower down, along the lines of parapet and surmounting the vertical pilasters, are conventionalised animal forms – vigorous, statuesque, and characteristic. Lower still, in panels under each window, are reptile and other allied forms modelled in high relief. In the archivolts the squirrel, the lizard, and the newt twine themselves through the reticulations of the floral enrichments; monkeys 'squeak and gibber' at the spectator from the recesses of the floral friezes; birds alight on the apex of each smaller gable, they sing on every spray, and hide in the bosky umbrage of the capitals.[1] Not the least beautiful of the many beauties in which this work abounds are those symmetrical arrangements of shell-forms, geometrically disposed and forming the sunk pateræ in the pilaster panels, or points of sparkling light and shade in the voussoirs of the arches. The whole of the scheme of ornamentation was worked out by Mr. Waterhouse – Professor Owen giving him assistance in pointing out the sources from which the various animal and other forms might be best studied.

DOI: 10.4324/9781003107835-117

The purpose and end of the building is disclosed by its design, which says, as plain as a whisper in the ear, that this can be no other than a Museum of Natural History. Glancing upwards over the whole field of its varied and orderly scheme of enrichment, the eye rests upon the consummation of the whole in the figure which terminates appropriately the highest gable. There, standing erect, is seen 'the quintessence of nature,' with outstretched arms and upward gaze directed towards a still higher Power.

The facade is an open book, whereon are recorded, in a language which all can read and understand, the inexhaustible beauty and wonder of this world in which we live, showing 'how high progressive life can go, around how wide, how deep extend below,'[2] and chastening and elevating the mind which contemplates it.

Editorial Endnotes

1 Ingress Bell's description somewhat exaggerates the impression of inexhaustible variety in the animal forms on the façade. Many motifs are repeated, taking advantage of the replicability of terracotta mouldings.

2 Bell here quotes Alexander Pope's *Essay on Man* (1733–4), epistle 1, part viii, lines 235–6: a reflection on 'the great chain of being' in nature, here confirmed by the figure of Adam on the skyline of the museum.

Figure 19 'Northern animals in summer dress' and 'Northern animals in winter dress'. Dateable to soon after 1900. Habitat groups in the hall of the Natural History Museum, London, displaying seasonal changes in coloration: NHM archive photographs 860–1. (Natural History Museum Library, London)

Editorial Headnote

87. William Flower, 'Address by Professor Flower . . . President', *Report of the Fifty-Ninth Meeting of the British Association for the Advancement of Science* (1890)

William Flower was director of the British Museum: Natural History, now known as the Natural History Museum.[1] Its scientific collections had formerly shared space with human artefacts going back to the ancient world in the British Museum in Bloomsbury. However, from the 1880s onwards, they were separately accommodated in the grand building designed by Waterhouse in South Kensington (see Chapter 86), giving scope for a new approach to their management and their presentation to the public. For Flower, this severance of natural objects from the products of human cultures had both advantages and drawbacks. On the downside, he feared it could be used to justify the introduction of further divisions between areas of knowledge, to the detriment of scientific understanding. He deplored the rigid separation of particular fields of natural science which occurred as a result of the proprietorial attitudes of his own departmental heads at South Kensington. What was needed, he thought, was a more open-ended approach to scientific study, encompassing the implications of Darwin's evolutionary theories. Flower noted, moreover, that the recently founded Museums Association was already seeking to promote an extensive 'interchange of ideas' among curators working in many different fields of museology. But while wishing to promote connections between disciplines, Flower – like many writers of the time – insisted that scientific museums had two distinct clienteles, with differing needs. Researchers required unfettered access to the whole range of the reserve collections, but the lay public wanted to see displays that were both visually attractive and informative, and therefore necessarily selective.

As president of the BAAS for 1889, Flower addressed members at their annual meeting, held that year in Newcastle, and used the opportunity to expound his reforming views on museum organisation and display. He confessed to being a stranger to Newcastle, but his chosen theme was one for which the new museum there provided unexpected inspiration.

Editorial Endnote

1 Richard Lydekker, *Sir William Flower* (London: J.M. Dent and New York: E.P. Dutton, 1906), pp. 57–77. William T. Stearn in *The Natural History Museum at South Kensington: A History of the Museum, 1753–1980* (London: Natural History Museum, 1998), pp. 67–76, explains Flower's aims and difficulties as director.

87

REPORT OF THE FIFTY-NINTH MEETING OF THE BRITISH ASSOCIATION FOR THE ADVANCEMENT OF SCIENCE . . . SEPTEMBER 1889

Professor W.H. Flower's Address

Source: William Flower, 'Address by Professor W.H. Flower, . . . President', in *Report of the Fifty-ninth Meeting of the British Association for the Advancement of Science, held at Newcastle-upon-Tyne in September 1889* (London: John Murray, 1890), pp. 3–24.

[pp. 7–10]

The various methods by which the mind of man has been able to reproduce the forms of natural objects or to give expression to the images created by his own fancy . . . depend altogether on museums for their preservation, for our knowledge of their condition and history in the past, and for the lessons which they can convey for the future . . . But I must pass them by in order to dwell more in detail upon those which specially concern the advancement of the subjects which come under the notice of this Association – museums devoted to the so-called 'natural history' sciences, although much which will be said of them will doubtless be more or less applicable to museums in general . . . The happy introduction and general acceptance of the word 'biology,' notwithstanding the objections raised to its etymological signification, have reunited the study of organisms distinguished by the possession of the living principle, and practically eliminated the now vague and indefinite term 'natural history' from scientific terminology. As, however, it is certain to maintain its hold in popular language, I would venture to suggest the desirability of restoring it to its original and really definite signification, contrasting it with the history of man and of his works, and of the changes which have been wrought in the universe by his intervention.

It was in this sense that, when the rapid growth of the miscellaneous collections in the British Museum at Bloomsbury . . . was thought to render a division necessary, the line of severance was effected at the junction of what was natural and what was artificial; the former, including the products of what are commonly called 'natural' forces, unaffected by man's handiwork, or the impress of his mind. The departments which took cognisance of these were termed the

DOI: 10.4324/9781003107835-118

'Natural History Departments,' and the new building to which they were removed the 'Natural History Museum' . . . That there are many inconveniences attending wide local disjunctions of the collections containing subjects so distinct yet so nearly allied as physical and psychical anthropology must be fully admitted, but these could only have been overcome by embracing in one grand institution the various national collections illustrating the different branches of science and art, placed in such order and juxtaposition that their mutual relations might be apparent, and the resources of each might be brought to bear upon the elucidation of all the others – an ideal institution, such as the world has not yet seen, but into which the old British Museum might at one time have been developed . . .

Though the experimental sciences and those which deal with the laws which govern the universe, rather than with the materials of which it is composed, have not hitherto greatly called forth the collector's instinct, or depended upon museums for their illustration, yet the great advantages of collections of the various instruments by means of which these sciences are pursued, and of examples of the methods by which they are taught, are yearly becoming more manifest. Museums of scientific apparatus now form portions of every well-equipped educational establishment, and under the auspices of the Science and Art Department at South Kensington a national collection illustrating those branches of natural history science which have escaped recognition in the British Museum is assuming a magnitude and importance which brings the question of properly housing and displaying it urgently to the front[1] . . .

[pp. 13–17]

I believe that the main cause of what may be fairly termed the failure of the majority of museums – especially museums of natural history – to perform the functions that might be legitimately expected of them is that they nearly always confound together the two distinct objects which they may fulfil, and by attempting to combine both in the same exhibition practically accomplish neither.

In accordance with which of those two objects, which may be briefly called *research* and *instruction*, is the main end of the museum, so should the whole be primarily arranged; . . . If the whole of the specimens really required for enlarging the boundaries of zoological or botanical science were to be displayed in such a manner that each one could be distinctly seen by any visitor sauntering through the public galleries of a museum, the vastness and expense of the institution would be out of all proportion to its utility; the specimens themselves would be quite inaccessible to the examination of all those capable of deriving instruction from them, and, owing to the injurious effects of continued exposure to light upon the greater number of preserved natural objects, would ultimately lose a large part of their permanent value . . .

On the other hand, in a collection arranged for the instruction of the general visitor, the conditions under which the specimens are kept should be totally different. In the first place, their numbers must be strictly limited, according to the nature of the subject to be illustrated and the space available. None must be placed too high or too low for ready examination. There must be no crowding of specimens one behind the other, every one being perfectly and distinctly seen, and with a clear space around it.[2] Imagine a picture-gallery with half the pictures on the walls partially or entirely concealed by others hung in front of them; the idea seems preposterous, and yet this is the approved arrangement of specimens in most public museums. If an object is worth putting into a gallery at all it is worth such a position as will enable it to be seen. Every specimen exhibited should be good of its kind, and all available skill and care should be spent upon its preservation and rendering it capable of teaching the lesson it is intended to convey. And here I cannot refrain from saying a word upon the sadly neglected art of taxidermy, which continues to fill the cases of most of our museums with wretched and repulsive caricatures of mammals and birds, out of all natural proportions, shrunken here and bloated there, and in attitudes absolutely impossible for the creature to have assumed while alive. Happily there may be seen occasionally, especially where amateurs of artistic taste and good knowledge of natural history have devoted themselves to the subject, examples enough – and you are fortunate in possessing them in Newcastle[3] – to show that an animal can be converted after death, by a proper application of taxidermy, into a real life-like representation of the original, perfect in form, proportions, and attitude, and almost, if not quite, as valuable for conveying information on these points as the living creature itself. The fact is that taxidermy is an art resembling that of the painter or rather the sculptor; it requires natural genius as well as great cultivation, and it can never be permanently improved until we have abandoned the present conventional low standard and low payment for 'bird-stuffing,' which is utterly inadequate to induce any man of capacity to devote himself to it as a profession . . .

The ideal public museums of the future will, however, require far more exhibition space than has hitherto been allowed; for though the number of specimens shown may be fewer than is often thought necessary now, each will require more room if the conditions above described are carried out, and especially if it is thought desirable to show it in such a manner as to enable the visitor to realise something of the wonderful complexity of the adaptations which bring each species into harmonious relation with its surrounding conditions. Artistic reproductions of natural environments, illustrations of protective resemblances, or of special modes of life, all require much room for their display. This method of exhibition, wherever faithfully carried out, is, however, proving both instructive and attractive, and will doubtless be greatly extended.[4]

Guide-books and catalogues are useful adjuncts, as being adapted to convey fuller information than labels, and as they can be taken away for study during the intervals of visits to the museum, but they can never supersede the use of labels. Anyone who is in the habit of visiting picture-galleries where the names of the artists and the subject are affixed to the frame, and others in which the information has in each case to be sought by reference to a catalogue, must appreciate the vast superiority in comfort and time-saving of the former plan.

Acting upon such principles as these, every public gallery of a museum, whether the splendid saloon of a national institution or the humble room containing the local collection of a village club, can be made a centre of instruction, and will offer interests and attractions which will be looked for in vain in the majority of such institutions at the present time.

Editorial Endnotes

1 In illustration of Flower's remarks, see, for example, the *Board of Education Catalogue of the Science Collections for Teaching and Research in the South Kensington Museum, 7 (Department of Science and Art)* (London: printed by Eyre and Spottiswoode for H.M. Stationery Office, 1891). This includes many items useful in teaching the natural sciences through visual demonstration, such as specimens of shells and insects, plaster and glass models of invertebrates, and zoological diagrams by Joseph Wolf and other leading artists.

2 While Flower was able to put his new ideas into effect in the entrance hall of the Natural History Museum (see Figure 19), it is evident that the departmental heads, who enjoyed a large degree of autonomy, did not always follow suit. A contemporary engraving of the 'Mammal Section' in the Museum shows some dramatised groups of apes, but there are also wall cases of taxidermy specimens stacked up in five tiers, reaching almost to the ceiling. Thomas Greenwood, *Museums and Art Galleries* (London: Simpkin, Marshall, 1888), p. 236.

3 Flower is referring here to John Hancock's taxidermy mounts in the museum in Newcastle, which he had studied at length on a preparatory, reconnoitering visit to the city and greatly admired. The 'Central or Hancock Bird Room' in the museum (now renamed the Great North Museum: Hancock) contained some 1,300 of his taxidermy specimens of British birds, often representing both sexes and all the seasonal variations in plumage; they had been donated by Hancock himself. Flower's enthusiastic response to them was reported back to Hancock by the museum trustees: Joseph Wright (Keeper of the Museum), letter to John Hancock, 18 July 1889, Hancock archive, University of Newcastle, NEWHM:1996.H67: letter 0855.

4 The displays in the hall of the Natural History Museum included many such habitat groups, illustrations of concealing coloration in animals etc. Flower's own description, from a *Guide* published in 1893, is reprinted in Jonah Siegel (ed.), *The Emergence of the Modern Museum: An Anthology of Nineteenth-century Sources* (Oxford: Oxford University Press, 2008), pp. 239–43.

Figure 20 View of the Crystal Palace at Sydenham, foregrounding the full-scale models of dinosaurs designed by Benjamin Waterhouse Hawkins, coloured 'Baxter print', undated. (Wellcome Trust/Wikimedia Commons)

Editorial Headnote

88. Anon. [Andrew Wynter], 'The new Crystal Palace at Sydenham', *Fraser's Magazine* (1853)

After the closing of the Great Exhibition of 1851, it was decided to rebuild Joseph Paxton's great iron and glass pavilion on a hilltop in Sydenham, and to use it for purposes of popular education and entertainment. Andrew Wynter, a physician and journalist, in an obviously promotional article, describes the architectural marvels of the rebuilt and significantly enlarged Crystal Palace, 'raising a palace to the people' . . . 'clothed with all the beauties of nature and art'.[1] Inside the Palace there were tableaux which showed the relationships between human cultures and their specific natural environments: models of tribal peoples seem to have been combined with taxidermy animals and painted scenes. Representations of animals also featured in some full-scale replicas of the buildings and sculptures of ancient Mediterranean and Middle Eastern countries.

The whole programme of art works at the Crystal Palace was based on the notion of cultural, social, and technological progress in human history, reaching its apogee in Victorian Britain. However, this process could also be tracked downwards or backwards to primitive chaos. At the foot of the hillside, landscaped and laid out as terraced gardens by Paxton with a 'grand system of waterworks', the visitor was to be confronted with a simulacrum of 'the antediluvian world . . . the commencement of that history of the creation, the last and most modern phases of which' were on view at the top of the hill in the Palace (see Figure 20). Here Wynter describes the nature of the dinosaurs' primitive world that was evoked by the models, although they were still incomplete when he wrote.

Editorial Endnote

1 Wynter's article, together with that by Lady Eastlake (Chapter 88.1 of the present work), is referenced by Verity Hunt in '"A present from the Crystal Palace": Souvenirs of Sydenham, miniature views and material memory', in Kate Nichols and Sarah Victoria Turner (eds.), *After 1851: The Material and Visual Cultures of the Crystal Palace at Sydenham* (Manchester: Manchester University Press, 2017), pp. 24–30.

88

THE NEW CRYSTAL PALACE AT SYDENHAM

Anon. [Andrew Wynter], Fraser's Magazine

Source: Anon. [Andrew Wynter], 'The new Crystal Palace at Sydenham', *Fraser's Magazine* 48:288 (December 1853), pp. 607–22, on pp. 617–20.

These broad divisions of the flora of the globe will be again sub-divided, so as to indicate the particular vegetation of different countries, and grouped together in each division will be specimens of the race of men, animals, birds, fishes, and insects, which properly belong to them. And these are not to be, like museum specimens, placed 'all in a row,' but in the very attitudes they assume whilst in a state of nature. Thus, in the Indian group we may have the Hindoo weaving beneath the shadow of a banyan-tree, whilst the branches are alive with gorgeous-coloured birds, and the furtive tiger may be seen slinking through the jungle. In the desert region, the Arab will, perhaps, recline under the date-tree, his mare tethered by the well, and near at hand the dead camel preyed upon by the jackal and the vulture will complete the picture. The Australian savage will sleep on his opossum rug, whilst the kangaroo looks fearfully on. In this manner, natural history will be presented to the multitude in a series of pictures, which can never fade from their minds, and thus will be carried out to its full extent Lancaster's system of instruction.[1] Some people may smile at this attempt to teach men by a method introduced for the use of the youthful intellect. But experience teaches us that the intellect of the ignorant man is but the intellect of a child, and that he is most impressed by images which appeal directly to his senses. And how much may even the cultivated mind learn from a walk through this splendid educational gallery? . . . If it is objected that the specimens of animals, birds, and reptiles may only represent natural history, read by the glasses of some ignorant stuffer or maker of preparations, the directors may with pride appeal to the names of Edward Forbes, Waterhouse, and Gould – names that naturalists hold in respect[2]; and those who are not naturalists, may remember the remarkable specimens of stuffed birds and animals in the transept of the old building – may remember the hawk whose very wings seemed to flutter and whose foot seemed more rigidly to extend itself as his bloody bill tore up the fibres of his carrion – may remember the still life fight between the heron and the falcon, where the deadly strife seemed

DOI: 10.4324/9781003107835-119

to be going on beneath the eyes of the spectators – in such a spirit and by such artists these specimens will be prepared.[3] But how are the fish, the reptiles, the crustaceæ, and the zoophytes to be shown? asks a third caviller. Those who have gazed with mingled wonder and delight at the glass vivarium, in the Regent's-park Zoological-gardens[4] – who have seen the strange fish lying still beneath his native stone, and watched, not without a shudder, the sea-worm drive his spiral way in search of food, and the hundred arms of the zoophyte playing around to seize its prey – those who by this singular contrivance have had brought to their leisurely view the very bottom of the insatiable deep, and have seen here realized in miniature the sights of Schiller's diver, will understand how art can collect together the combinations of nature in her most hidden recesses.[5] . . .

Here he will find himself surrounded with animal, vegetable, and mineral forms, such as he has never seen before . . . the spectator will be startled by sights of gigantic creatures, belonging by form, neither to beasts of the field, birds of the air, fish of the sea, nor to creeping things of the earth, but partaking of the characteristic forms of all. Models of gigantic size, but not greater than the life, will appear, as handed down to us embedded in the blue lias; stone puzzles from the pre-Adamite, or indeed the prefloral age which science has at last unriddled. Among these the plesiosaurus will stretch its swan-like neck, as though it were pursuing its prey along the surface of the water, as of old; specimens of crustaceæ, such as no longer exist, will hang upon the rocks, and the curious stone-lily will hold its solid chalice up to the sky like a tulip flower transformed to stone. A little further on the geological book will disclose a still later page in the history of the globe. Here the slimy mud, exposed to the retreating waters by the action of the sun, will have become dry land, and a profusion of vegetable life will be seen clothing its undulating surface. Vast palm trees will arise on every hand, and the food and temperature being now prepared for the advent of animal life – the huge megatherium and mastodon, monsters of sixty feet in length, built up exactly as they lived in the old world, will be shown bursting through the rank vegetation as easily as an elephant finds its way through a reed-bank[6] . . .

Well may the poor cockney, who has rarely strolled further than his own street, feel bewildered when he finds himself of a sudden transported to this strange spot, where the land looks like something he has seen in a nightmare, and the animals like the strange creatures in the wizard scene of *Der Freischutz*.[7] After doubting his senses for awhile, he will, perhaps, look upon the whole affair as a hoax, and many will be found doubtless to put the question, – How can any one ask us to believe, in representations of the earth as it appeared, ere yet a living thing inhabited it, or to put faith in the representations of huge beasts and reptiles which lived or crawled the earth long before man came upon the scene? Yet there can be little doubt that these restorations will be pretty nearly as like the truth, as the restorations of the Assyrian architecture. Science knows that certain forms must arise from the action of certain elements upon each other, and thus the chaotic epoch will be capable of being pretty correctly generalized. For the rest, nature has left us fragments enough of her early rude sketches to enable us to fill up and clothe them in all their details . . .

Here then, indeed, might all men read 'sermons in stones' without fear that they are looking upon mere chimeras of the brain. A Cuvier from a tooth and a hoof could as faithfully build up the fearful bulk of the Mastodon as a sculptor could replace the self-indicated limb of some expressive torso.[8]

Editorial Endnotes

1 Joseph Lancaster's system of education involved the deployment of the more advanced pupils as 'monitors' to teach their peers. Wynter seems to mean that these visual displays played a similar educative role.

2 Edward Forbes, Frederick George Waterhouse, and John Gould were all noted naturalists.

3 This is a reference to John Hancock's taxidermy groups shown in the Great Exhibition (see Chapters 32–33 of the present work). In a letter of 10 December 1853, addressed 'To the editors of Fraser's Magazine' via its publisher, John William Parker, Hancock strongly objected to the implication that he had been involved in any way in the design of the taxidermy groups permanently installed in the new Crystal Palace. (John Hancock correspondence, Natural History Society of Northumbria Archive, Great North Museum Hancock, Newcastle upon Tyne, letter 0601).

4 An aquarium designed and stocked by Philip Henry Gosse had just been opened at the London Zoo – the first of its kind. The Crystal Palace itself added an aquarium to its range of attractions in 1871.

5 Friedrich von Schiller's 'The Diver' was among his *Poems of Tragedy*.

6 The prehistoric monsters, created by Waterhouse Hawkins, were more fully described by Samuel Phillips (ed. F.K.J. Shenton), in his *Guide to the Crystal Palace and its Park and Gardens* (Sydenham: Crystal Palace Library, 1860), pp. 165–9. See also James Secord, 'Monsters at the Crystal Palace', in Soraya de Chadarevian and Nick Hopwood (eds.); *Models: The Third Dimension of Science* (Stanford, CA: Stanford University Press, 2004), pp. 138–69; and Mark P. Witton and Ellinor Michel, *The Art and Science of the Crystal Palace Dinosaurs* (Marlborough: Crowood Press, 2022).

7 Weber's opera *Der Freischütz* involves black magic, threatening the hero and his beloved. Fear of the reconstructed monsters is discussed by Melanie Keene in 'Dinosaurs Don't Die: the Crystal Place monsters in children's literature, 1854–2001', in Nichols and Turner (eds.), *After 1851*, pp. 159–78.

8 The zoologist Georges-Frédéric Cuvier specialised in animal osteology and palaeontology.

Editorial Headnote

88.1 Anon. [Lady Elizabeth Eastlake], 'The Crystal Palace', *Quarterly Review* (1855)

While praising the intention of the Crystal Palace's owners to educate the general public in art and science, Lady Eastlake, herself an art critic and frequent contributor to *Quarterly Review*, was sceptical about some of the results and gave a much less flattering description of the natural history displays than that offered by Wynter.

88.1

THE CRYSTAL PALACE

Anon. [Lady Elizabeth Eastlake], Quarterly Review

Source: Anon. [Lady Elizabeth Eastlake], 'The Crystal Palace', *Quarterly Review* 96:192 (1855), pp. 303–54.

[p. 344–5].

We have lingered long among the different phases of this world's civilization, each sufficiently illustrated by those arts and manufactures – their products as well as exponents – to inform our eyes and imaginations with their prevailing character; but we have only to turn to the south end of the building to see how inadequate is the same plan when applied to Nature, and how far from successful here. It is especially when compared with Art that Nature's grand characteristic, abundance, becomes manifest.

> 'Art lives on Nature's alms; is weak and poor:
> Nature herself has unexhausted store.'

There is something, therefore, ludicrously disproportioned between the highflown descriptions of the natural history department given in the handbooks, and the comparatively parsimonious and miscellaneous display of stuffed animals and stunted rockeries which meet the eye. Judging from the classifications of different countries here announced as combining the advantages and supplying the deficiencies, in point of geology and botany, of the British Museum and the Kew Gardens, the very least the public are led to expect is as complete a separation between the different quarters of the globe, with their vegetable and animal kingdoms, to say nothing of climates, as between the periods of Nineveh and Nuremburg[1] – the more so as Nature is as much more rigorous than Art in her laws of distinctness, as she is more exacting in her standards of profusion. Directed, therefore, upon paper, to 'proceed rapidly amid European types,' 'to pass southward through the North African provinces of Egypt and Barbary, when we shall find ourselves in unavoidable proximity with the tropical countries of Asia,' the visitor prepares to traverse a region abounding in the more familiar objects of nature, and that done, to lose himself, in fancy at least, first in the Desert, and next in the Jungle. Far, however, from the smallest scope being allowed for such a vision, he suddenly feels himself, as Cassius said of Julius Cæsar, 'bestriding the narrow world before

DOI: 10.4324/9781003107835-120

him, like a Colossus.'[2] The Arctic Regions and the Torrid Zone are scanned in the same glance, and instead of realising the slightest separation between the Old and the New Worlds, he will find it difficult to place himself in any position where he is not in unavoidable proximity with both sides of the Atlantic at once. Setting aside, however, these pretensions, – which indeed would be a harder task to fulfil than all the Company have yet undertaken, and for which, with the ample grounds awaiting us without, there was the less need – there is much that is new, welcome, and interesting in the groups of animals, and in the cases of stuffed birds, marine plants, and live fishes here gathered together.

Editorial Endnotes

1 Lady Eastlake refers here to the Crystal Palace's series of displays, reconstructing the visual effect of the world's great artistic cultures from ancient to modern times.
2 Shakespeare, *Julius Cœsar*, act 1, scene 2.

ELEPHANT IN HIS BATH. (*See p.* 44.)
From the "Mirror," Sept. 6, 1828.

GIRAFFES. (*See p.* 63.)
From the "Saturday Magazine," Sept. 3, 1836.

PLATE 12.

Figure 21 'Elephant in his bath' (1828) and 'Giraffes' (1836), illustrations in journals of those years, reproduced in Henry Scherren, *The Zoological Society of London* (London: Cassell, 1905), plate 12. (Biodiversity Heritage Library)

Editorial Headnote

89. Anon. [William Broderip]. 'The Zoological Gardens – Regent's Park', *Quarterly Review* (1836)

This article was ostensibly a review of various publications of the Zoological Society of London – the *Proceedings*, *Transactions*, and a *List of the Animals in the Gardens of the Zoological Society*.[1] However, naturalist William Broderip was primarily concerned not with the zoo's record-keeping or scientific research, but rather with the *spectacle* it offered to visitors: the novel experience of seeing at close quarters the exotic wild animals it contained (see Figure 21). These encounters prompted thoughts on the psychology of human–animal relations in the nineteenth century and how it differed from that of past times. By structuring the article as a 'promenade' around the gardens, Broderip was able to register his own developing and shifting impressions. The narrative is larded with literary tropes and quotations which, as so often in zoological texts of the time, were unconsciously deployed to distance modern European humans from the 'uncouth' and 'clumsy' beasts on display – and from the native peoples of the countries whence these animals had come. Yet there is also an increasing pathos and moral uncertainty in these descriptions of them. The animals prompted reflections on the power and extent of the British Empire; but their imprisonment, and often their failing health, were painful to see.

Editorial Endnote

1 The most detailed history of the zoo's early years is Takashi Ito, *London Zoo and the Victorians 1828–1859* (London: The Royal Historical Society and the Boydell Press, 2014). Ito identifies Broderip as the writer of this article and comments on his consciously literary style (pp. 74–5).

89

THE ZOOLOGICAL GARDENS – REGENT'S PARK

Anon. [William Broderip], Quarterly Review

Source: Anon. [William Broderip], 'The Zoological Gardens – Regent's Park', *Quarterly Review* 56:112 (June 1836), pp. 309–32.

[p. 310]

Who can walk through the spacious garden of the Zoological Society of London, 'tastefully laid out and well kept' – who can view 'the immense collection of animals of all kinds, from the elephant and the rhinoceros to rats and mice' – without agreeing with Von Raumer, that 'it is only in the neighbourhood of such a city as London that such an establishment could be maintained by voluntary subscriptions and contributions?'[1]

And there is yet another thought that may arise in the mind of the visitor. His memory may carry him back to another great nation – the masters of the world – who exhibited hundreds of the rarest animals, where we have only units to show; but for what a different purpose! The conquered provinces were ransacked; herds of lions, thousands of wild beasts were presented to the gaze of the people, and

> 'Butcher'd to make a Roman holiday.'

Titus, who finished the amphitheatre which his father began, stained the arena with the blood of five thousand beasts at its dedication, while upwards of one hundred thousand Romans looked down upon the slaughter.[2] Trajan, at the conclusion of the Dacian war, gratified the popular thirst for blood by the destruction of ten thousand[3] . . . But enough of these bloody scenes –

> 'My soul turn from them, turn we to survey
> Where rougher climes a nobler race display:'[4]

where enormous wealth is expended, not as it was by the son-in-law of Sylla, but in applying the arts to the comforts and innocent enjoyments of life, in advancing science, and in spreading information among the people . . .

DOI: 10.4324/9781003107835-121

[pp. 313–16]

But the Garden. – As we walk along the terrace commanding one of the finest suburban views to be anywhere seen, let us pause for a moment while 'the sweet south' is wafted over the flowery bank musical with bees, whose hum is mingled with the distant roar of the great city. Look at the richness and beauty of the scene . . . if Nash had never done anything beyond laying out St. James's Park and the picturesque ground before us, he would, in our opinion, have atoned for a multitude of sins.[5]

We must not, however, forget the bears. There they are, with their uncouth gestures and clumsy activity, living together amicably enough, save when an occasional growl proclaims a difference of opinion, arising from the monopoly by some crafty aspirant more ambitious than his neighbours of the head of the pole – a monopoly the more irritating, inasmuch as that elevation generally leads to the acquisition of the good things in the power of a generous public to bestow . . . We have heard some complain that the grisly bear in the den below has no pole to climb; but if he had one he would not climb, if all tales be true, for that accomplishment, it is asserted, leaves him with his early youth. The gigantic species here confined has been known in its native wilds to kill and drag away a full grown bison bull, weighing upwards of a thousand pounds . . .

But we must bend our steps to the eagle-house, and we confess we never pass it by without a pang. Eagles, læmmergyers, condors, *creatures of the element*, born to soar over Alps and Andes, in helpless, hopeless imprisonment. Observe the upward glance of that golden eagle – aye, look upon the glorious orb – it shines wooingly: how impossible is it to annihilate hope! – he spreads his ample wings, springs towards the fountain of light, strikes the netting, and flaps heavily down: – 'Lasciate ogni Speranza, voi ch'entrate.'[6] We know not what their worships would say or do to us if we were to work our wicked will; but we never see these unfortunates without an indescribable longing to break their bonds, and let the whole bevy of these

> 'Souls made of fire and children of the sun'[7]

wander free.

What a collection it is! what a proof that our commerce is pushed to the ends of the earth! Look at the localities; look at that condor, the child of fable but a few years since, and then remember that Sir Francis Head saw a Cornish miner wrestling with one on the Andes.[8] There too is the wedge-tailed eagle of New Holland, one of whose brethren is said to have made a swoop at Flinders, the able and gallant navigator, now at rest from his labours, mistaking, we suppose, the captain, in his solitary walks, for a kangaroo[9] . . .

[pp. 320–5]

We are now in the north garden, and not suffering either squirrels, ostriches, wapitis, elks, or zebras to detain us, we hurry on to the elephants' paddock. These are Asiatics. The twenty elephants which Julius Cæsar opposed to five hundred men on foot for the gratification of the Roman ladies and gentlemen were, in all probability, African, as well as the twenty that Pompey, at the dedication of the temple of Venus Victrix, exposed to the javelins of a host of Getulians; but the people were not yet hardened in blood, and, on this last occasion, the gallantry of the elephants in charging to the rescue of a wounded companion, their general sagacity, and the agony which was pourtrayed in their looks and gestures, so affected the stern Romans, that the whole amphitheatre rose and insisted, with curses against the consul, that the fight should cease[10] . . .

The strong, we had almost said, the sentimental attachments of which the huge creature is capable have been remarked in all ages. Who does not remember the fond beast recorded by Ælian, and alluded to in Athenæus, whose very existence seemed wrapped up in the child that it loved? Never would it eat unless its favourite was present; and, when the innocent slept, the affectionate monster employed itself in driving away the flies from the pillow.[11] We could come nearer home and relate multitudes of instances which have occurred even in our own times in verification of the ancient stories of the amiable, docile, and grateful disposition of the animal; and we might also add, of its tenacity in treasuring up a wrong till the proper moment for vengeance arrived. But we must be brief. Before, however, we quit the subject, we shall be pardoned, we trust, for giving an anecdote or two of Chuny, of Exeter Change memory – poor Chuny, who was obedient even in death, for amid the shower of balls that struck him, he knelt down, – even in his mortal agony he knelt down at the well-known command of his keeper, – to present a more vulnerable point to his murderers[12] . . .

Few contrasts are greater than that between these heavy masses of flesh and bone, and the light, the elegant giraffes, with their sleek, rich, dappled coats, towering swan-like necks, lofty heads, and large brilliant eyes, worthy of Juno herself, and full of a noble expression, such as Edwin Landseer alone could give. The sweep of their vision is most extensive; for they can see before them, below them, and behind them, without turning the head. What an idea does it convey of the power of modification, when we recollect that the number of neck-bones in the elephant and in the giraffe are exactly similar![13] Can we wonder at the emotion with which Le Vaillant saw the first traces of a giraffe, or at the ecstasy – was it not mingled with pity – with which he was possessed when the first lay extended at his feet? He had before him an animal whose very existence was at that time questioned and treated by many as a fable.[14] What a magnificent spectacle must it be to see a herd of these splendid creatures (and we know those who have seen them by forties and fifties at a time) browsing on the mimosas with their long flexible tongues so beautifully adapted for the purpose . . .

[pp. 329–32]

'The forest monarch's roar' reminds us that the great repository and the dogs are still unvisited; but we must return through the tunnel and view the finest collection of parrots ever assembled. Open your eyes and shut your ears – was there ever such an assemblage of rainbow colours – was there ever such a distracting din! We should have thought it indescribable, had not Aristophanes in a chorus of 'the Birds' hit it off to a nicety . . . Mark that elegant parrakeet with its pure golden plumage. It is a variety of *Palæornis torquatus*[15] which is placed beside it. Observe it on the hand of its favourite keeper, expressing its fondness by a thousand winning ways. It is formed to be the *deliciæ* of some beauty. Its delicate shape and hue would well grace her fair hand, and the murmuring caresses of its coral beak would be better lavished on her sweet lip than our worthy friend's bristly chin . . .

Now to the palace of the monkeys, ever active, prying, and mischievous. Those of about the same size engaged in a scuffling fight for a nut – the larger tyrannizing over the smaller – some swinging by their tails – others by their hands – all busy, all chattering, except that silent little group in the corner, looking on with philosophic melancholy, but still unable to repress a sigh at their own nutless condition; they have so often had their nuts, when fortune has thrown them perchance in their way, abstracted by the strong hand, with a cuff and a bite in lieu of them, that they have at last retired from the scramble, hopeless, and resigned. If any visitor be disposed to refresh their spirits, let him tender his snuff-box, and keep off the *stronger boys* with his cane.

But who can look at apes when 'monkey green' is crowded with England's richest beauty. Here is every variety of clear complexion – *ce beau sang*, as we once heard an impassioned Frenchman ejaculate in his admiration at the scene, with such an emphasis on the *beau*, as none but a Frenchman can give . . . We, being sober and cautious Tories, must tear ourselves away from these 'breathing roses,' and proceed to the flower garden; for a very pretty flower-garden it is . . . A flower border to the southward of the great walk would be also an improvement. But it is very beautiful as it is, and we can hardly account for the jaundiced eye with which some – they are not many – look upon everything belonging to the Society . . . We should remember that it is the gale of fashion, more fickle than any 'i' the shipman's card', that has hitherto borne the Society so prosperously along: if it become adverse, all will go to wreck; and we do hope that the fellows will cordially co-operate to sustain, in its present commanding position, one of the first establishments in Europe; an establishment which has done more for zoology in England, during the few years of its existence, than had been effected in a century before. With correspondents in every part of the world, sending home rare animals and interesting papers, the Zoological Society may fearlessly say, with her geological and geographical sisters,

> 'Quæ regio in terris nostri non plena laboris.'[16]

Already the provinces exhibit the influence of the parent society. To say nothing of 'The Surrey,' one of the prettiest lounges in the neighbourhood of London,[17] and surpassingly rich in *carnivora*, the societies of Liverpool, Dublin, and Bristol have all sprung up. The more the better. These are the recreations worthy of a reflecting people, and the more widely they are disseminated, the wiser and the more civilized will the people become. No observer can look upon the endless variety of forms presented in such establishments, without being struck with the wonderful adaptation of mean to an end manifested in each; and the deeper he goes into the science, the more will he be obliged to confess that all are 'fearfully and wonderfully made.'

Editorial Endnotes

1 Friedrich Ludwig Georg von Raumer, trans. Sarah Austin [and H.E. Lloyd], *England in 1835: being a Series of Letters Written to Friends in Germany, during a Residence in London and Excursions into the Provinces*, 3 vols. (London: John Murray, 1836), vol. 1, p. 103.
2 Titus celebrated the completion of the Colosseum in ancient Rome, c. 80 CE, by this mass slaughter of captive animals.
3 The Emperor Trajan defeated the Dacians in the early second century CE.
4 A free quotation from Oliver Goldsmith's poem 'The Traveller', in fact describing the Swiss people, not the English.
5 The architect John Nash, together with James and Decimus Burton, had designed and laid out Regent's Park, in which the zoo is situated.
6 'Abandon all hope, ye who enter'. Dante, *Inferno*, canto 3.
7 A quotation from a speech by Zanga in Edward Young's play *The Revenge: A Tragedy* (1721), act 5, scene 2.
8 Captain Francis B. Head, *Rough Notes Taken during Some Rapid Journeys across the Pampas and among the Andes*, 2nd ed. (London: John Murray, 1826), pp. 211–3.
9 The Wedge-tailed Eagle, *Aquila fucosa*, an Australian species.
10 The story comes from Pliny, *Natural History*, book VIII, chapter 7, and other ancient sources.
11 Aelian, *On the Characteristics of Animals*, book XI, 14.
12 Chuny, usually spelled Chunee, was an elephant in the menagerie at Exeter Change in London, killed by his keepers in 1826 when he became violent and unmanageable in his miserably small enclosure. Richard D. Altick, *The Shows of London* (Cambridge, MA, and London: Belknap Press of Harvard University Press, 1978), pp. 310–3. Diana Donald, *Picturing Animals in Britain 1750–1850* (New Haven, CT, and London: Yale University Press, 2007), pp. 171–3. Helen Cowie, *Exhibiting Animals in Nineteenth-century Britain: Empathy, Education, Entertainment* (Basingstoke: Palgrave Macmillan, 2014), pp. 16, 174.
13 This reference to the 'power of modification' already hints at the possibility of evolution of species.
14 The explorations of François Le Vaillant were recorded in *Voyage de Monsieur Le Vaillant dans l'Intérieur de l'Afrique Dans les Années 1780 . . . 1785* (Paris: Le Roy, 1790), pp. 393–9, with engraved illustrations, p. viii.
15 The Rose-ringed Paroquet.
16 The Loeb Classical Library translates this passage from Virgil's *Aeneid*, book I, in context to mean: 'Is there any place, Achates, any land on earth not full of our sorrow?'
17 The Surrey Zoological Gardens were in Newington, in the suburbs of London.

Figure 22 Interior of the Brighton Aquarium, wood engraving from the front page of *The Illustrated London News* 61:1718 (10 August 1872). (Bridgeman Images)

Editorial Headnote

90. W. Saville Kent, 'The Brighton Aquarium', *Nature* (1873)

This impressive aquarium on a fashionable stretch of Brighton's seafront had recently been opened to the public, setting a trend that was followed in other seaside resorts. William Saville Kent was the Brighton Aquarium's first curator, but he had just handed in his resignation: he was dissatisfied with the existing system for oxygenating and replenishing the water in the tanks, which the owners declined to replace. However, at a deeper level, the aquarium's managers confronted the difficulty of reconciling the requirements of serious zoological researchers with the need to entertain paying visitors. The grand Romanesque architecture, lavish ornamentation, and picturesque grounds of the building were intended to attract wealthy holidaymakers and residents of Brighton (see Figure 22). As the *Illustrated London News*'s writer remarked, the aquarium would promote 'the popular study of an interesting branch of zoology' and 'supply the seaside loungers with constant means of rational entertainment'.[1] The massive scale of the tanks provided an unprecedented spectacle of living marine creatures, anticipating the 'immersion' effects of later zoos and aquaria and glorifying the progress of natural science. However, the scale and elaboration of the building, the complexity of its hydraulics, and the costs of its stocking and maintenance proved in the end to be financially ruinous.

Editorial Endnote

1 Anon., 'The Brighton Aquarium', *Illustrated London News* 61:1718 (10 August 1872), pp. 121, 123. This article was written before the tanks had been filled, but it described the rich polychrome effect of marbles, terracotta, mosaics, stained glass, patterned tiles, and figurative carvings in the building. One of the tanks was 'over 100ft. in length, and capable of accommodating the largest-sized whale, or, if need be, the famous sea-serpent itself'.

90

THE BRIGHTON AQUARIUM

W. Saville Kent

Source: W. Saville Kent, 'The Brighton Aquarium', *Nature* 8 (23 October 1873), pp. 531–2.

In accordance with an intention entertained previous to resigning the tenure of my office as Curator to the Brighton Aquarium, I propose to give a brief outline of the plan of construction and general system of arrangements obtaining in that institution.

The Brighton Aquarium, while emulated by several buildings of a similar nature, in different parts of the kingdom and on the Continent, still holds its own in being on a scale of magnitude hitherto unsurpassed, more than one of its tanks, in illustration of this, being of sufficient size to accommodate the evolutions of porpoises and other small Cetaceæ. The architect and originator of the undertaking, Mr. Edward Birch,[1] well known as the engineer of the new pier at Hastings, entertained the idea of constructing this Aquarium as long ago as the year 1866 when visiting the one on a small scale then existing at Boulogne; Brighton was selected as a site on account of its proximity to the sea-coast and its great popularity as a place of resort. The works were commenced in the autumn of the year 1869, but owing to various interruptions the building was not formally thrown open to the public until August 1872, the ceremony taking place during the week in which the members of the British Association honoured Brighton as their place of meeting.[2]

The area occupied by the Brighton Aquarium averages 715 feet in length by 100 feet in width, running east and west along the shore line between the sea and the Marine Parade; the principal entrance is at the west end facing the eastern angle of the Royal Albion Hotel. The building internally is divided into two corridors separated from one another by a fernery and considerable interspace. The approach to the first or Western corridor is gained through a spacious entrance-hall supplied with reading-tables, and containing between the pillars which support the roof portable receptacles of sea-water for the display of small marine specimens that would be lost to sight in the larger tanks.

The tanks for ordinary exhibition commence with No. 1 on the left side of the western corridor . . . The smallest of these tanks measures 11 feet long by 10 feet broad, and is capable of holding some 4,000 gallons of water, while the largest, No. 6, in the western corridor, and the subject of the accompanying engraving, presents

DOI: 10.4324/9781003107835-122

a total frontage, including the two angles of 130 feet, with a greatest width of 30 feet, and contains no less than 110,000 gallons. Every gradation of size occurs between these two extremes, the depth of the water in all ranging from 5 to 6 feet. Supplementary to the foregoing, a series of half-a-dozen shallow octagonal table-tanks occupies a portion of the interspace between the two corridors, these being especially adapted for the exhibition of animals such as starfish, anemones, and others seen to best advantage when viewed perpendicularly through the water. Flanking one side of this same interspace are several ponds fenced off for the reception of seals and other amphibious mammalia and larger Reptilia, while at its further or eastern extremity artistic rock-work runs to a height of 40 feet, thickly planted with choice ferns and suitable exotic plants, and broken in its course by a picturesque waterfall and stream. Tanks 12 to 17 in the eastern corridor . . . are set apart for the exclusive exhibition of fresh-water fish . . . The bulk of water thus utilised in the fresh and sea-water tanks collectively amounts to 500,000 gallons . . .

The style of architecture dominant throughout the building is Italian and highly ornate, the arched roof of the corridors being groined and constructed of variegated bricks, supported on columns of Bath stone, polished serpentine marble, and Aberdeen granite; the capital of each column is elaborately carved in some appropriate marine device, while the floor in correspondence is laid out in acrostic tiles. The divisions constituting the fronts of the tanks are composed each of three sheets of plate glass, each plate having a thickness of one inch, and measuring six feet high by three feet wide, separated from one another and supported centrally by upright massive iron mullions . . . Among other conspicuous structural features of the aquarium demanding notice are the huge masses of rock entering into the composition of the tanks and fernery. Part of these are composed of porous tufa brought from Derbyshire, while the remaining and greater portion presents the appearance at first sight of old Red Sandstone of the Devonian epoch. This latter, however, is entirely artificial, being built up of smaller nondescript fragments, faced with cement and coloured sand, though so true to Nature have the boulders been fashioned and stratigraphically arranged, that more than one eminent geologist has been deceived by their aspect, and it is difficult in looking into the larger tanks to get rid of the impression that some of the miniature picturesque coves characteristic of the Devonshire coast have been transported bodily to Brighton.

Editorial Endnotes

1 Saville Kent has mistaken Birch's first name, which was Eugenius, not Edward. Birch, an architect and engineer, designed many piers. The one at Hastings had been opened in the summer of 1872.

2 A report on 'The British Association meeting at Brighton' in *Nature* 6 (15 August 1872), p. 305, indicated, however, that the aquarium was then still partly unfinished.

Editorial Headnote

91. William Chambers, 'The Brighton Aquarium', *Chambers's Journal* (1873)

Chambers, co-publisher of the *Journal*, was well-informed about the natural sciences. Here he gives his impressions of the aquarium, especially of the novel sensory experiences it offered. While in Brighton, he could visit it 'day after day', making it 'a lounge for study and amusement'.

91

THE BRIGHTON AQUARIUM

William Chambers

Source: William Chambers, 'The Brighton Aquarium', *Chambers's Journal of Popular Literature, Science, and Art*, Series 4, No. 504 (23 August 1873), pp. 529–32.

[pp. 529–31]

Some years ago there set in a fashion of keeping, by way of parlour ornament, a fanciful crystal tank, replenished with sea-water, in which were placed anemones, hermit crabs, and other curious little creatures, collected from the rocks and sands of the sea-shore.[1] A tank of this kind, called an aquarium, was in fact a cage, only instead of wires there was glass, instead of pet birds there were animals moving about in water, whose appearance and habits could be studied with leisure almost at the fireside. So, apparently, began a taste, which at length led to the establishment and maintenance of those marine aquaria on a great scale for public gratification, such as that at the Crystal Palace, the *Jardin des Plantes*, Paris, Boulogne, Havre, and Hamburg, all more or less serving a useful purpose in spreading a love for an interesting branch of natural history . . .

From the open court, we step into a large entrance-hall, lighted like other parts by the roof, and devoted to purposes of a reading-room, a stall for the sale of photographs, and a species of orchestra for a band of music, which keeps playing at intervals. At one end is an apartment laid out as a Restaurant. Along the sides of the hall are several stands with round glass vases with water, in which, as a sort of beginning to the business of our visit, we are indulged with a view of some interesting small animals, the most curious and beautiful of all being a group of *hippocampi*, or sea-horses. Though we are anxious to hurry through the vestibule, these creatures do not fail to rivet attention for a few minutes. We looked at them at every successive visit. Their pretty head, shaped exactly like that of a horse (or a knight at chess), their glancing eyes, and their long tapering and speckled body twisted round the stalk of a water-plant, from which they look placidly around, are a singular freak of nature . . . Satisfied with this part of the exhibition, we move towards the interior galleries, or we might almost call them subterranean corridors, for the light to them comes from the surface of the water-tanks ranged along the sides. Into these galleries, visitors are left to wander at pleasure. You roam about as you list, picking up such information as you can from what addresses itself to the eye. At the side of each tank is an inscription indicating the names of

DOI: 10.4324/9781003107835-123

the animals. Excepting this amount of information, there was nothing to instruct visitors, which we could not but regret, for without intelligent explanation, an establishment of this kind becomes little better than a toy. Apparent deficiencies in this respect are now in some degree remedied. Since the time of our visit, a hand-book to the aquarium has been issued, and people are no longer left in doubt concerning a thousand interesting particulars.[2]

Entering the long dim corridor, we are at once ushered into the presence of the animals in their respective watery cells. Like a row of shop-windows of plate-glass, the tanks invite curiosity, one after the other. The depth of the water in each tank may be from five to six feet, with a frontage of generally ten feet, and a fully greater length from front to back. The sides and ends of the tanks are constructed to resemble rock-work. The rough blocks of stone have, we believe, been brought from Derbyshire, and being disposed in ledges and recesses, provision is alike made for vegetable submarine growth, and to furnish recesses for the resort of the animals seeking a temporary solitude. Already, in some of the tanks, vegetation has made some progress. Over the bottom of the tanks, which is about thirty inches from the ground, there is thickly spread that kind of yellowish pebbly shingle found on the adjacent beach . . .

The first tank on the left introduces us to an acquaintance with corals, sea-anemones, sea-cucumbers, and tube-worms. We have before us some of the most interesting zoophytes – things growing and budding on rocks, half-vegetable, half-animal; some of them with sprawling tentacula, as if seeking to grapple and devour anything which unwarily comes within the compass of their sensitive feelers. The anemones of a pinkish colour are a pretty kind of animal flowers. There they flourish as peacefully on the edge of some projecting bit of rock-work within a few inches of us, as if they were in the depths of the sea . . .

[p. 532]

This is our first collection, on a large scale, of animals which dwell in water, and a visit to it has the quality of novelty. In roaming through the establishment, with so much animal vivacity close at hand – sometimes within only two or three inches from our face – we are not less struck with the singular silence which prevails, than with the vast variety of forms of existence that are presented to our observation.

It cannot be doubted, that under careful and critical inspection, the collection will solve a multiplicity of questions as regards marine and river animals, about which naturalists have hitherto been considerably at a loss, and legislation at fault. Hence, its service to science and social economics, as well as its more general use in imparting popular instruction and amusement to old and young of both sexes. Patiently surveying the respective tanks and their inmates, we are wholesomely reminded of the prodigious wealth of Creative Energy, in close adaptation to conditions and circumstances. In pious wonder and admiration, we bow down before the infinite and beneficent Power of the Almighty.

Editorial Endnotes

1 This fashion had been largely created by Philip Gosse's publications of the 1850s (see Chapters 56–7 of the present work), and there were many popular guides to the management of domestic aquaria, such as John Ellor Taylor's *The Aquarium: Its Inhabitants, Structure and Management* of 1876.

2 Chambers is perhaps referring to the anonymous *Life Beneath the Waves, & a Description of the Brighton Aquarium* (London: Tinsley brothers, 1871).

Editorial Headnote

92. Anon., 'Jamrach's', *Strand Magazine* (1891)

The Jamrach family's business was situated in the port area of east London. They bought exotic live animals at the dockside from the crews of incoming ships and displayed them for sale alongside miscellaneous ancient or eastern *objets d'art.*[1] Jamrach's customers included travelling showmen but also many wealthy owners of private menageries and even the prestigious Zoological Society of London.[2] While the hectic and motley assemblage of unfamiliar and often dangerous beasts in his shop was a product of the far-flung British Empire, its presentation harked back to the menageries of earlier times. The public force-feeding of a crocodile even evoked circus performances. The bizarre array of oriental weapons and ornaments helped to confer an atmosphere of strangeness, profusion, and exoticism on the captive animals. It also recalled the heterogeneity of earlier museum displays that combined stuffed animals with man-made objects. Presumably anyone could enter the shop and enjoy such exciting visual spectacles, whereas the Zoological Gardens in Regent's Park were generally accessible only to the better-off.

Editorial Endnotes

1 On Jamrach: Helen Cowie, *Exhibiting Animals in Nineteenth-Century Britain: Empathy, Education, Entertainment* (Basingstoke: Palgrave Macmillan, 2014), pp. 84–5, 89–90, 99–100, 166, 168. Cowie, *Victims of Fashion: Animal Commodities in Victorian Britain* (Cambridge and New York: Cambridge University Press, 2022), pp. 200, 214–16, 237.

2 Eleanor Larsson in '"On Deposit": animal acquisition at the Zoological Society of London, 1870–1910', *Archives of Natural History* 48:1 (2021), pp. 1–21, shows how Charles Jamrach worked closely with the Zoological Society of London. He deposited animals in the Zoological Gardens on loan, thus compensating for the high level of mortality of animals in the zoo, and simultaneously displaying his stock to potential buyers.

92

JAMRACH'S

Anon., The Strand Magazine

Source: Anon., 'Jamrach's', *The Strand Magazine* 1 (Jan.–June 1891), pp. 429–36.

[pp. 429–31]

The shop we are about to visit – perhaps quite the most remarkable in London – stands in a remarkable street, Ratcliff-highway . . . In a street like this, every shop is, more or less, an extraordinary one; but no stranger would expect to find in one of them the largest and most varied collection of arms, curiosities, and works of savage and civilised art brought together for trade purposes in the world, and this side by side with a stock of lions, tigers, panthers, elephants, alligators, monkeys, or parrots. Such a shop, however, will be the most interesting object of contemplation to the stray wayfarer through St. George's-street, and this is the shop famed throughout the world as Jamrach's. Everybody, of course, knows Jamrach's by name, and perhaps most know it to be situated somewhere in the waterside neighbourhood of the East-end; but few consider it anything more than an emporium from which the travelling menageries are supplied with stock. This, of course, it is, but it is something besides; and, altogether, one of the most curious and instructive spots which the seeker after the quaint and out-of-the-way may visit is Jamrach's . . .

The first window we reach might be passed as that of an ordinary bird-fancier's, were the attention not attracted by the unusually neat, clean, and roomy appearance of the cages displayed, and the uncommon shapes and colours of the birds that inhabit them. The next window is more catching to the eye. Furious Japanese figures, squatting Hindoo gods, strange and beautiful marine shells, and curious pottery bring the pedestrian to a stand, and arouse a desire to explore within. All this outside, however, gives small promise of the strange things to be seen and learnt behind the scenes. Returning to the door by the aviary window, we enter, and find ourselves in a bright, clean room, eighteen or twenty feet square, properly warmed by a stove placed in the centre. The walls, from floor to ceiling, are fitted with strong and commodious wire cages, in which birds of wonderful voice and hue and monkeys of grotesque lineament yell, whistle, shriek, and chatter. Great and gorgeous parrots of rare species flutter and scream, and blinking owls screw their heads aside as we pass. But the cause in chief of all this commotion is the presence of an attendant in shirt-sleeves, who, carrying with him a basket, is distributing therefrom certain eatables much coveted hereabout. Beaked heads are thrust between bars, and many a long, brown arm reaches downward and forward from the monkey cages, in perilous proximity to the eager beaks. In a special cage, standing out from the rest, a beautiful black and white lemur sits and stretches his neck to be fondled as the attendant passes, but shyly hides his face when we strangers approach him[1] . . . Mr Jamrach takes us into a small, dusty back room quaint in its shape and quaint in its contents. Arms of every kind which is not an ordinary kind stand in corners, hang on walls, and litter the floors; great two-handed swords of mediæval date and of uncompromisingly English aspect stand amid heaps of Maori clubs, African spears, and Malay kreeses; on the floor lies, open, a deal box filled with rough sheets of tortoise-shell, and upon the walls hang several pictures and bas-reliefs . . .

Then Mr. Jamrach shows us wonderful and gorgeous marine shells, of extreme value and rarity, and some of a species which he originally introduced to men of science, in consequence of which it now bears an appalling Latin name ending with *jamrachus* . . . here we stand amid the most bewildering multitude of bric-a-brac and quaint valuables ever jumbled together: fantastic gods and goddesses, strange arms and armour, wonderful carvings in ivory, and priceless gems of old Japanese pottery. Merely to enumerate in the baldest way a tenth part of these things would fill this paper, and briefly to describe a hundredth part would fill the magazine . . . We have come to St. George's-street expecting to see nothing but a zoological warehouse, and all this is a surprise. That such a store as we now see were hidden away in Shadwell would have seemed highly improbable, and indeed we are told that very few people are aware of its existence. 'The museums know us, however, 'says Mr. Jamrach the younger, 'and many of their chief treasures have come from this place.' Among the few curious visitors who have found their way to Jamrach's there has been the Prince of Wales, who stayed long, and left much surprised and pleased at all he had seen. The late Frank Buckland, too, whose whole-souled passion for natural history took him to this establishment day after day, often for all day, could rarely resist the fascination of the museum, even while his beloved animals growled in the adjacent lairs.[2] The Jamrachs do not push the sale of this bric-a-brac, and seem to love to keep the strange things about them. Their trade is in animals, and their dealings in arms and curiosities form almost a hobby . . . A natural love of the quaint and beautiful first led Mr. Jamrach to buy carvings and shells from the seafaring men who brought him his birds and monkeys, so that these men soon were led to regard his warehouse as the regulation place of disposal for any new or old thing from across the seas; and so sprang up this overflowing museum . . .

[pp. 433–5]

There are many things bought at the sale of the effects of the late king of Oude . . . Among the old King's treasures in this place are seven small figures, of a dancing bear, a buck antelope, a gladiator, a satyr riding a furious bull, another riding a camel, an armed man on a rhinoceros, and a monkey mounted on a goat, respectively. Each of these little figures is built up of innumerable smaller figures of beasts, birds, and fishes, fighting and preying upon each other, not one speck of the whole surface belonging to the main representation, while, nevertheless, the whole produces the figure complete with its every joint, muscle, sinew, and feature. And so we pass, by innumerable sacred masks, pashas' tails and alligators' skulls, toward the other and main department of this remarkable warehouse – that devoted to natural history.

We cross Britten's-court, where we observe a van with a small crowd of boys collected about it. A crane is swung out from a high floor, and from the end of the dependent chain hangs a wooden case or cage, violently agitated by the movements of the active inhabitant. He is a black panther, the most savage sort of beast with which Mr. Jamrach has to deal, and, as this one feels himself gradually rising through the air, his surprise and alarm manifest themselves in an outburst strongly reminding the spectator of Mark Twain's blown-up cat 'a-snorting, and a-clawing, and a-reaching for things like all possessed.'[3] He arrives at his appointed floor at last, however, and as the cage is swung in, the blazing eyes and gleaming teeth turn from our side toward the attendant who receives him.

The wide doors on the ground floor are swung open, and we enter a large apartment fitted with strong iron-barred cages on all sides. This is the lowest of three floors, similarly fitted, in which is carried on a trade in living creatures which is known from one end of the earth to the other. Jamrach's is *the* market for wild animals from all the world over, and whatever a menagerie-keeper or a zoological collection may want, from an elephant to an Angora cat, can be had in response to an order sent here. Whatever animal a man may have to sell, here he may sell it, providing that it be in good and healthy condition . . .

And so, with many an anecdote of his own and his father's experiences in their peculiar business from Mr. Jamrach the younger, we go upstairs and wander among the stock. This, of course, is ever varying in quantity and species, but has always some interesting feature. We are introduced to a solemn monkey, who salaams gravely three times, and then waits to be asked to shake hands, which he does with great ceremony. We see porcupines, black swans and antelopes, and we hear, at the peril of never hearing anything afterwards, the noisy cranes. There is a Sumatra civet cat, with a small, fox-like head, and a magnificent tail; he is not cordial, and snaps an awkward-looking row of sharp teeth at us. Just behind his little cage is a large one, which contains a fine, tall guanaco or wild llama. The docile-looking creature moves to and fro behind the bars, keeping his eye on us, and pursing his mouth the while. Suddenly Mr. Jamrach says, 'Look out, he's going to spit!' and we all duck in different directions with great celerity – only just in time. The intelligent quadruped has conceived a prejudice against the shape of somebody's hat, or the colour of somebody's tie, and expresses it by spitting, with much force and precision, at the offender's face.

A large increase in the general chatter and growl around us announces the approach of an attendant with food. The emus and cassowaries stretch their long necks as far between the bars as possible, and the pelicans and cranes yell agonisingly. A large black panther throws himself against the bars of his cage, and gives voice unrestrainedly. In contrast to these, the domestic cat of the establishment follows the man's heels, with much tender purring and a sharp eye to any stray morsel. There are other cats here in cages – cats too valuable to be allowed to run loose – magnificent Angoras and Carthusians, who rub their heads against the wires, and, as we approach, extend their paws in an appeal to be noticed and petted.

We are promised an interesting feeding sight downstairs, and we descend to the ground floor. Among the more risky speculations of the commercial naturalist are the alligator and the crocodile. They will sulk and go into a decline on the least provocation or without any provocation at all, and, being expensive to begin with, often prove awkward losses. They almost invariably sulk at first, we are told, and refusing to take food, would be likely to get into a bad way unless cured; and the curing of a crocodile's sulks is a surprising thing to see. We find, on reaching the ground floor, poor crocodilus laid by the heels and perfectly helpless, lashed immovably to iron rings and posts. His head is ignominiously sat upon by a sturdy man in shirt-sleeves, who presently pokes the end of a crowbar among the big teeth, and forcibly prizes the mouth open into that position of comprehensive smile so familiar to the readers of children's natural history books. Then another man kneels before the unfortunate reptile and feeds him. That is to say, he takes a lump of meat weighing five or ten pounds or so, and dexterously pitches it into the æsophagus, afterwards firmly and decisively ramming it home with a long pole. This is the dinner of all naughty, sulky crocodiles, and, after having it served in this fashion four or five times, the victim gives up sulking as a bad job . . . Whereupon he reforms and becomes a respectable crocodile, taking regular meals, and is in time promoted to the Zoological Gardens, or a respectable menagerie.

Editorial Endnotes

1 Lemurs are native to Madagascar: several species such as the Indri and the Ruffed Lemur have black and white markings.
2 For Frank Buckland, see also Chapter 48 of the present work.
3 Mark Twain's story, 'Dick Baker's cat', about a cat accidentally shot into the air by explosives at a quartz mine, comes from his *Roughing It* (Hartford, CT: American Publishing Co., 1872), ch. 61.

Editorial Headnote

93. George and Edward Dalziel, *The Brothers Dalziel* (1901)

The authors were members of the large Dalziel family firm of wood engravers. Their book reveals the complexity of the process by which wood-engraved illustrations were produced for multi-volume works of popular zoology in the Victorian era, such as Revd Wood's *Illustrated Natural History* and *Homes Without Hands*. Such books were often issued in parts, and the many draughtsmen and engravers employed to illustrate them had to keep up with the author on the production line, working against deadlines, while also maintaining some consistency in style. Wood was difficult to please: mindful of his readers' expectations, he wanted the illustrations to picture the *life* and vital spirit of the animals, not just their anatomy (see Figure 23). However, artists had to contend with the difficulty that often little was known about the animals' behaviour in the wild. Indeed, Wood's illustrators were often drawing from poorly preserved specimens, or even from earlier drawings and models, rather than from the living creatures themselves.

93

THE BROTHERS DALZIEL

A Record of Fifty Years' Work in Conjunction with Many of the Most Distinguished Artists of the Period 1840–1890

George and Edward Dalziel

Source: George and Edward Dalziel, *The Brothers Dalziel: A Record of Fifty Years' Work in Conjunction with Many of the Most Distinguished Artists of the Period 1840–1890* (London: Methuen, 1901), pp. 266–70.

A most important and comprehensive work which Messrs. Routledge entrusted to us was the production of the pictures for the 'Illustrated Natural History,' by the Rev. J.G. Wood. They were, of course, to be under the superintendence of the author, who was at that time Chaplain of St. Bartholomew's Hospital.[1] During the publication of the book, which was issued in monthly parts, and extended over a period of nearly four years, it was our custom to go there and see him every Monday morning, accompanied generally by Mr. George Routledge, to receive new lists of subjects, to report progress of those in hand, and to discuss the matter generally. From there we went on to the printing office of Richard Clay & Sons, who were printing the work under our supervision.

Among the many distinguished artists engaged we would first mention William Harvey . . . He did not, however, make many drawings, from the fact that J.G. Wood thought them too mannered and conventional: the same objection was held by the author to Harrison Weir. Although this clever artist contributed considerably to certain sections of the book, J.G. Wood summed up his drawings in a few words: 'Always picturesque, but never correct'.[2]

Joseph Wolf, a German by birth, made a large number of drawings for the work, and gave the author every satisfaction. By many it is held that his birds are more correct than those by any other draughtsman; certainly his perfect manipulation gives them a beauty that cannot be excelled. There can be no doubt that his contributions are by far the best: take his lions, tigers, or his groups of monkeys and of birds – all denoting the artist of high culture. He was appointed Special Artist to the Zoological Society, and worked very much at their Gardens in Regent's Park and also at their Museum.[3]

DOI: 10.4324/9781003107835-125

While we were preparing the first sheets for the press, a very fine specimen of the gorilla, preserved in spirits, most opportunely arrived at the Zoological Gardens, one of the first, we were informed, that had ever reached this country.[4] Permission was obtained for Mr. Wolf to be present at the opening of the barrel which contained the defunct animal, so that he might have a better opportunity of making notes for his guidance in doing the drawing, one of the best in the entire book, than the indifferently stuffed specimen in the Museum afforded him. Wolf afterwards remarked that opening the barrel and lifting the animal out of the spirits was extremely interesting, but the effluvia was sufficient to poison a regiment of soldiers.

Editorial Endnotes

1 For Wood's career, combining clerical duties and church music with authorship of popular works on natural history and illustrated lectures, see the biography by his son, Revd Theodore Wood, *The Rev. J.G. Wood: His Life and Work* (London, Paris, New York, and Melbourne: Cassell, 1890).

2 William Harvey had been trained as an illustrator by Thomas Bewick in the years 1810–17, and his style might have seemed old-fashioned by 1860. Wood's criticism of Harrison Weir, who was expert in lively animal illustration, is more surprising.

3 For Wolf, see also Chapters 19 and 43 of the present work.

4 This specimen arrived in 1858 and was mounted by Abraham Bartlett, the Zoological Society's superintendent, for its museum collection. Wilfred Blunt, *The Ark in the Park: The Zoo in the Nineteenth Century* (London: Book Club Associates, 1976), pp. 136–7.

Figure 23 Revd John George Wood, *The Illustrated Natural History* (London: Routledge, Warne and Routledge, undated, c.1859–60), vol. 1, 'Mammalia', illustration of 'Hyænas Quarrelling Over Their Prey', wood engraving by Dalziel, probably from a drawing by Joseph Wolf or Harrison Weir. (Biodiversity Heritage Library)

Editorial Headnote

93.1 Revd John George Wood, *The Illustrated Natural History* (C.1859–60)

There were numerous editions of this popular *Illustrated Natural History*, many undated: the earliest seems to have appeared in 1853. The edition featured here ran to two volumes, respectively on 'Mammals' and 'Birds', the former undated, the latter dated 1862. Wood's remarks show the challenge he set to his illustrators: to combine anatomical accuracy with an impression of a creature's 'animating spirit', and thus appeal to young or uninstructed readers.

93.1

THE ILLUSTRATED NATURAL HISTORY, MAMMALIA (PREFACE)

Revd John George Wood

Source: Revd John George Wood, *The Illustrated Natural History, with new designs . . . by Wolf, Zwecker, Weir, Coleman, Harvey, etc., etc., engraved by the Brothers Dalziel*, 2 vols. (London: Routledge, Warne and Routledge): vol. 1 [c.1859–60]), 'Mammalia', Preface, pp. vi–vii.

The true object of Zoology is not, as some appear to fancy, to arrange, to number, and to ticket animals in a formal inventory, but to make the study an inquiry into the Life-nature, and not only an investigation of the lifeless organism. I must not, however, be understood to disparage the outward form, thing of clay though it be. For what wondrous clay it is, and how marvellous the continuous miracle by which the dust of earth is transmuted into the glowing colours and graceful forms which we most imperfectly endeavour to preserve after the soul has departed therefrom. It is a great thing to be acquainted with the material framework of any creature, but it is a far greater to know something of the principle which gave animation to that structure . . . The lion, for example, is not predacious because it possesses fangs, talons, strength, and activity; on the contrary, it possesses these qualities because its inmost nature is predacious, and it needs these appliances to enable it to carry out the innate principle of its being; so that the truest description of the lion is that which treats of the animating spirit, and not only of the outward form. In accordance with this principle, it has been my endeavour to make the work rather anecdotal and vital than merely anatomical and scientific . . . What can an artist learn even of the outward form of Man, if he lives only in the dissecting room, and studies the human frame merely through the medium of scalpel and scissors? . . . The zoologist will never comprehend the nature of any creature by the most careful investigation of its interior structure or the closest inspection of its stuffed skin, for the material structure tells little of the vital nature, and the stuffed skin is but the lay figure stiffly fitted with its own cast coat . . . the minutest atom of animated life which God has enfranchised with an individual existence, forms, though independent in itself, an integral and necessary portion of His ever-changing yet eternal organic universe.

DOI: 10.4324/9781003107835-126

Editorial Headnote

93.2. Anon., 'Homes Without Hands', Review, *Times* (1865)

The idea that animals, directly guided by God, had often forestalled humans in their inventions was a popular theme in the nineteenth century.[1] In *Homes Without Hands. Being a Description of the Habitations of Animals Classed According to the Principle of Their Construction* (London: Longmans, Green, 1865), Revd John George Wood had described the various protective structures or dwellings that animals create for themselves – often of great artistry. The reviewer discusses and quotes, with eager interest, some of Wood's accounts of the designing and building activities of various species, from insects to mammals, giving special attention to unusual phenomena. He concludes his full-page review of the book with further praise of Wood's approach.

Editorial Endnote

1 For example, Charles Williams's *Art in Nature and Science Anticipated* (London: Frederick Westley and A.H. Davis, 1832).

93.2

'HOMES WITHOUT HANDS' REVIEW

Anon., Times

Source: Anon., 'Homes without Hands', *Times*, 25 September 1865, p. 12.

The Rev. J. G. Wood seems to possess the gift – much cultivated, though but rarely attained – of translating the labours of the scientific into the language of every-day life. The scientific man proper scorns to condescend to the crowd; he invents a nomenclature at which the ordinary mind recoils as a dog recoils from a hedgehog. The zoologist is, perhaps, from the very nature of his subject, less open to this charge than others of his class, for the reason that he must deal with natural objects of which all of us have some knowledge; but even he is apt to lock up his knowledge in technical language, the key to which but few of us have time to find. Let us be thankful, then, at meeting with one who is clever enough to perceive that we are, all of us, children in the matter of natural wonders. Surrounded as we are by domesticated animals, so few of which show any inclination to provide themselves with habitations of any kind, we little dream of the wonderful variety of houses built without hands which exist among the lower animals . . .

With this extract we must close Mr. Wood's singularly interesting volume. It does not pretend to much original research or observation; indeed, it treats of the wonderful instincts of animals spread over the entire globe. It cannot, therefore, be anything but a compilation; but it is done with so much skill that in all probability it will put many a now little known work on zoology into circulation, which otherwise would have been confined to the comparatively confined class of naturalists. The profuse illustrations with which the work is furnished add an additional charm to this wonder book. In natural history we are but children of a larger growth, and the curious woodcuts which meet us at every page will open wide other eyes than those of our little ones. Mr. Wood is continually referring us to the British Museum[1] for specimens of some of the more singular examples of homes without hands. The Government have supplemented the floral world at Kew with a museum of natural curiosities cognate to the living collection. What a gain it would be to a zoological garden to possess such a collection of natural objects as that stowed away in the National Museum, where they are rarely seen, and where they take up so much room that could be better occupied!

DOI: 10.4324/9781003107835-127

Editorial Endnote

1 The British Museum in Bloomsbury then still housed the nation's natural history collections, which were very short of display space.

Editorial Headnote

94. Revd J.G. Wood, 'The Dullness of Museums', *The Nineteenth Century* (1887)

In this article Wood stressed the fact that a majority of people, especially in the working classes, were still ignorant about even the elementary aspects of zoological science, and therefore they were bored by museum visiting. In contrast, all zoo visitors were fascinated by the sight of the live animals being fed – a display of natural behaviour that was exciting and immediately comprehensible. Wood therefore suggested that natural history museums, too, should present the world of nature *visually*, through dioramas. While he stressed the need for close primary study of the features of animals and their habitats, his evocations of life in the wild were in truth largely based on sportsmen's narratives and existing genres of visual imagery, including Edwin Landseer's paintings and the illustrations to his own natural history books.[1] Some inspiration must have come from Rowland Ward's taxidermy groups (his more ambitious exhibition pieces – see Chapter 35 of the present work), but Wood's ideas also foreshadowed the development of large, dramatic dioramas in American museums, such as Carl Akeley's for the American Museum of Natural History.[2]

Editorial Endnotes

1 Wood visualised a group showing a fierce struggle between a lion and a horned gemsbok, and then a follow-up scene showing the skeletons of them both, still fatally entangled. This scenario recalls Landseer's *Night* and *Morning* of 1853, depicting a fateful encounter between rival stags.

2 Karen Wonders, *Habitat Dioramas: Illusions of Wilderness in Museums of Natural History* (*Acta Universitatis Upsaliensis Figura Nova Series 25* (Uppsala: published thesis, 1993).

94

THE DULLNESS OF MUSEUMS

Revd John George Wood

Source: Revd J.G. Wood, 'The Dullness of Museums', *The Nineteenth Century* 21:121 (March–June 1887), pp. 384–96.

[p. 385]

Now this apparently unimportant proceeding[1] gives a clue to the construction and organisation of museums which will attract the general public, and after attracting the people, will arouse their attention, and excite and retain their interest. The creatures which are exhibited in a museum which will be acceptable to the public must be represented as doing something, not as staring straight in front of them . . . Not only must the creatures be represented in action, but they must be shown as acting their natural life. Thus it is that people are soon tired of seeing the elephants and camels acting as beasts of burden,[2] but they are never tired of seeing the animals feed . . .

[pp. 390–3]

A very old Utopian dream of mine is a Natural History Museum for the public which would attract them and give them an interest in animal life . . . Had I the good fortune to live in Utopia, I would construct a museum especially adapted to the despised Tom, Dick and Harry, which should amuse them, should be of such a nature as to compel them to take an interest in the subject, and perchance to transform them into the Thomas H. Huxleys, Richard Owens, and P. Henry Gosses of the next generation[3] . . . In the first place, such museums should be pre-eminently attractive. They should essentially deal with zoology in its true sense – i.e. the science of life – and not with necrology, or the science of death, as is too often the case . . . I suggest then, on behalf of Tom, Dick and Harry, that their museum of zoology should consist not of isolated animals, but of groups, some large and some small, but all representing actual episodes in the life history of the animals exhibited. Neither scenery, trees, nor herbage should be conventional or evolved out of the inner consciousness of the maker. They should be truthfully copied from the many photographs or trustworthy sketches which are at our command. As far as possible, each group should be the reproduction of some scene which has actually been witnessed and described by travellers. Let us, for example, take a few African scenes as described by hunters such as Gordon Cumming, Anderson, Baldwin, and others.[4]

DOI: 10.4324/9781003107835-128

Nothing could give a more vivid idea of animal life in South Africa, and of the country, than the mixed herds so often seen and admired by sportsmen. There would be giraffes, zebras, or quaggas, ostriches, and gnus, all mingled together, the gnus performing the extraordinary prancings, gyrations, and tail-whirling wherewith they are accustomed to beguile the time. Some of the ostriches would be feeding, others resting in the quaint attitude common to all their kind, while others would be represented as running at full speed, with outstretched wings.

Care should be taken that each attitude should be studied from the living bird in actual action, as nothing is more common than for taxidermists to set up animals in attitudes which they could not possibly assume in life. There should be mimosa trees, on the leaves of which one of the giraffes should be browsing, coiling its long and flexible tongue round the twigs, and drawing them downwards within reach of its mouth. On the branches of the mimosa might be one of the enormous nests of the social grosbeak, together with specimens of the birds, some on the wing, others entering and leaving their nests, and others again bringing strips of grass wherewith to add to the compound nest.[5] Some skulls of springboks and gnus should be lying about the ground, as actually seen by travellers, thus giving a good idea of the wealth of animal life produced by the country.

In all the large groups there should be a background representing faithfully a local landscape, actual objects being merged gradually into the pictorial representation in the way which has of late years proved so effectual in the various panoramas representing the siege of Paris, the battle of Tel el Kebir, and similar scenes. In the present case a landscape should be selected which includes the Table Mountains, which are so characteristic a feature in South Africa . . .

[p. 395]

Many such subjects might be described, but I have only mentioned a few as examples of the life-groups which I would place in my Utopian museum. Attached to the building which contains them I would have a type-series of the vertebrates, so that in going through the galleries the visitors would recognise the creatures which they had seen grouped, and would realise the relationship in which they stood to other animals.

This, however, is not all. Putting aside the absolute ignorance with which we have to deal, we must remember that the faculty of observation is almost in abeyance in many individuals, while that of generalisation has never been developed. To each group, therefore, a placard should be attached, stating that it would be explained at a certain hour, and that the lecturer would remain for the purpose of answering questions. Such a course would attract thousands who otherwise would not set foot inside a museum.

Editorial Endnotes

1 Wood is referring here to feeding time at the London Zoo.
2 He means the elephants and camels giving children rides in the zoo.

3 Thomas Huxley, Richard Owen, and Philip Henry Gosse were all famous natural scientists.
4 For these big game hunters, see Part II of the present work (Introduction and Chapters 28–30).
5 Social grosbeaks of southern Africa built huge communal nests from grasses, sometimes in mimosa trees.

Editorial Headnote

95. Revd Theodore Wood, *The Rev. J.G. Wood* (1890)

As we have seen, John George Wood was a highly successful writer of popular zoological works, and from 1879 onwards he capitalised on his literary fame by giving public lectures on animal topics to large audiences across Britain and the United States.[1] While these events conveyed some scientific information to his listeners, they were essentially spectacles of performative and artistic bravura. Wood sketched animals freehand on a scale large enough to be seen and appreciated by a whole audience.

Before the introduction of the magic lantern, lecturers on scientific topics, including Wood himself, had always needed to make (or to commission) large-scale drawings and diagrams to explain their subjects, as Gideon Mantell did in the 1830s when introducing his audiences to the appearance – and the scale – of dinosaurs.[2] However, the ability to draw 'lightning sketches' freehand had also become a popular music-hall or party entertainment, for which the cartoonists Phil May and Harry Furniss were especially famous. Theodore Wood, who had accompanied and assisted his father on many of his arduous lecture-tours, explains the techniques which were involved in each theatric performance, and the effect they created.

Editorial Endnotes

1 Richard Whittington-Egan in *The Natural History Man: A Life of the Reverend J.G. Wood* (Great Malvern: Cappella Archive, 2014), pp. 105–20, emphasises the wide social range of Wood's audiences. His shows could be varied in scope and intellectual level and were thus rendered 'popular with all classes', with a special syllabus for schools.

2 See, for example, the report on one of Mantell's lectures to a Brighton audience in the *Brighton Gazette*, 27 October 1836.

95

THE REV. J.G. WOOD
His Life and Work

Revd Theodore Wood

Source: Revd Theodore Wood, *The Rev. J.G. Wood: His Life and Work* (London, Paris, New York, Melbourne: Cassell, 1890), pp. 136–7, 146–60.

[pp. 136–7]

My father had soon discovered, not only that he possessed an almost unique talent for what may be best denominated 'descriptive freehand drawing,' but that audiences were far more interested and pleased by even a rough-and-ready extempore sketch than by the most carefully prepared and elaborate diagrams. He had used the ordinary black drawing-boards for the Brixton lectures, and had found them to answer his purpose fairly well in a comparatively small room. But now, with the prospect before him of lecturing in large buildings, before audiences of perhaps twelve or fourteen hundred, he clearly saw that something on a larger scale must be provided, if the effect of his drawings was not to be entirely lost. Now what was this 'something' to be? . . . after much thought, and a long discussion with one of the engineers employed by the Crystal Palace Company, the difficulty was overcome. An iron framework of great strength, some seven feet in height by eight in width, was constructed in such a manner as to stand firmly erect when braced up by two strong stays . . .

[pp. 146–60]

Although the large portable blackboard which my father had had specially made for these lectures had proved satisfactory in many ways, he soon discovered that, like all experiments, it was open to a great deal of improvement. It was far too heavy . . . Then again, in spite of its quite unusual dimensions, the board was far too small! My father had taken to drawing whales and other sea-monsters upon a large scale, and found that a board only eight feet long did not afford him space enough for a sketch of sufficient magnitude; while, even with drawings of lesser size, the available space became so rapidly filled that the constant use of the sponge and towel was necessary. And, thirdly, he wanted a more yielding, more elastic surface. He had now taken to drawing with pastils of many colours – some manufactured specially for himself – instead of with the plain white chalks as at first. The board did not 'take' these colours well; and the pastils, moreover, were

DOI: 10.4324/9781003107835-129

for the most part so soft that the pressure against the unyielding wood crumbled them into fragments, so that they could not be used with any degree of certainty. So the big blackboard was doomed.

But what was to be substituted for it? Mr. Waterhouse Hawkins, who about this time had been lecturing at the Crystal Palace,[1] had employed a large sheet of black canvas, loosely stretched by means of guy-ropes; but this did not at all fall in with my father's fastidious requirements . . . He soon saw that the canvas must be stretched on a wooden frame . . . and this, after a few alterations and improvements had been made, proved perfectly satisfactory, and afforded a clear surface of eleven feet by five feet six inches; so that a drawing made thereupon was clearly visible in every part of the largest hall . . .

And even if nothing in the way of repairs or improvements happened to be necessary, still almost my father's first proceeding upon reaching home was to put up one of his frames in a large lumber-room, either for the purpose of fitting a new canvas, in readiness for future necessities, or else that he might practice some of his drawings. For all those wonderful sketches, produced so rapidly before the eyes of the audience, and seemingly without a moment's consideration, were the outcome of long and careful prior preparation. First he used to make a tracing, if possible, of the object he wished to draw from some thoroughly trustworthy wood-cut. Then he would copy this two or three times upon a slate, which hung by a chord from his table, always attempting to do so with the fewest possible lines, and, as he frequently used to say, 'making every line tell its own story.' Then having contrived this to his own satisfaction, he would make a very careful sketch *in colour* upon the back of one of the small paper strips which contained his brief lecture-notes. And finally, chalks in hand, he would go off to his frame and practice that drawing diligently, until he could execute it accurately without hesitation and without a mistake.

No doubt these coloured sketches contributed more than all else to the invariable success of the lectures. Every drawing elicited a round of applause, and the newspapers always commented admiringly upon the great artistic power which could produce such a result with such simple means, and apparently with such perfect ease. In the words of Dr. Oliver Wendell Holmes, who was present at one of his lectures upon 'Pond and Stream' during his first American tour and who afterwards wrote to him a letter of warm admiration:-

'I looked as well as listened, and saw the stickleback and his little aquatic neighbours grow up on the black canvas from a mere outline to perfect creatures, resplendent in their many-coloured uniforms. The lecture had much that was agreeable, but the coloured chalk improvisation was fascinating to the old and young alike, and was – as it deserved to be – heartily applauded' . . .

I may perhaps also be permitted to quote the following from the *Altrincham and Bowdon Guardian* of October 8th, 1881:-

'Mr. Wood's method of lecturing is, we believe, unique. It consists in producing upon a black canvas screen drawings of the objects to be described. These are drawn in the presence of the audience. They are not mere diagrams, but finished pictures in colours of great beauty. These, as they literally started into life under the lecturer's artistic touch, elicited very marked approbation from the audience. One picture especially showed the very highest skill. A particular species of the hydrozoa had to be described, which, from the transparency of its substance and the near approach of its refractive power to that of water, can scarcely be distinguished from the element in which it swims. It requires a practised eye and close attention to see it at all. Mr. Wood drew it on the screen as one would gradually come to distinguish its parts; here a flash of light and there a filament; here a red, and there a blue tint, till the creature ultimately took shape and stood forth in all its beauty of iridescent colours and gracefulness of form' . . .

Of course, all this artistic skill was the outcome, not merely of much careful practice at home, but also of many experiments and failures with chalks of various descriptions . . . By degrees, he added considerably to the number of different shades which he employed, and in his boxes I find three shades of red, three of blue, two of green, three of yellow, an ochre, a brown, and a neutral tint, all of which have clearly been used upon several occasions.

These he used with wonderful discrimination and judgment, seeming to know by a kind of instinct just how and where to apply the colours so that they might produce the desired result at a distance . . . In the later years of his sketch-lectures he was very particular about light, and would have neither gas nor lamp anywhere near the screen itself, save in the form of footlights some six or seven feet in front . . . For, in order that the drawings should show out to the best advantage, it was necessary that the light should come from *below*. If it proceeded from above it merely dazzled the eyes of the audience when reflected back from the screen, and prevented them from seeing the sketches at all, while side-lights were almost equally unsatisfactory, and so were tabooed also. But light from below brought out the full effect of the colours, and showed them out in bold relief with the dull black of the canvas; and if there were no other light in the hall at all, the result was even more satisfactory still.[2]

Of course some of his sketches were more striking and remarkable than others. One of his best was that of two ants fighting, in which jaws, limbs, and antennæ were hopelessly interlocked, and yet the individuality of each insect was clearly preserved. There was a drawing of the spermaceti whale, too, in which the spine came first, and then was followed by some of the other bones and internal organs, while, finally, a line was quickly run round these and the whale seemed to be complete, with every part in due proportion. And the drawing of the male stickleback in all the glories of his courting array always elicited a special round of applause. The odd thing was, that no line was ever rubbed out, no alteration ever made. The sketches were hastily executed, but were always perfectly exact in every particular. No measurements seemed to be taken, and yet the proportions were invariably correct. Of course there was a great deal of art in this, although it did not appear – *ars est celare artem*[3] – and any one who thinks otherwise has only to try to reproduce the drawings, even with the small coloured sketches to guide him, to find out his mistake.

Editorial Endnotes

1 The artist and sculptor Benjamin Waterhouse Hawkins had designed the models of prehistoric monsters at the Crystal Palace (see Chapter 88 of the present work). He also gave popular lectures on palaeontology to large audiences, boldly sketching his illustrations on a blackboard or other black surface as he spoke. R. Fallon, 'The illustrated natural history lectures of Benjamin Waterhouse Hawkins given in Britain, 1850s-1880s', *Archives of Natural History* 50:2 (2023), pp. 347–69.

2 C.D. Wylie, 'Teaching nature study on the blackboard in late nineteenth- and early twentieth-century England', *Archives of Natural History* 39:1 (April 2012), pp. 59–76, on p. 66.

3 'The true art consists in concealing art'.

Editorial Headnote

96. Anon., 'Microphotography and the bioscope', *Manchester Guardian* (1903)

By the early years of the twentieth century it had become possible to project microphotographic films of minute, often aquatic animals or animal organs onto a screen for showing to large audiences in London West End theatres and music halls. Their popular success surprised commentators of the day and put paid to conventional use of large drawings to illustrate public lectures, like those of Revd Wood, described earlier. This article of 1903 in a Manchester newspaper explains the process and its effect on a popular audience.

96

MICROPHOTOGRAPHY AND THE BIOSCOPE

Anon., Manchester Guardian

Source: Anon., 'Microphotography and the bioscope', *Manchester Guardian*, 15 August 1903, p. 7.

The bioscope takes pictures at an ordinary rate of 18 per second, which allows of an exposure of one-thirty-second of a second for each picture. Now one can understand that in these days of sensitive films such an exposure is ample for an ordinary subject, such as a Coronation procession or a Delhi Durbar.[1] But a microphotograph, one would think, would require a much longer exposure. Yet by employing very sensitive films Mr. Urban, of Rupert-street, Piccadilly, London, has succeeded in producing photographs of living objects on the stage of the microscope, and exceedingly interesting they are. The initial magnification on to the film, writes a London representative of the 'Manchester Guardian,' is in some cases 1,000 diameters, although the exposure of each picture is only one-thirtieth of a second. Consider a moment what a diminution in light is implied in a magnification of 1,000 diameters. It means that the light has only one-millionth of the intensity that it has on the stage of the microscope. Yet we were shown photographs – living pictures of the larva of the May-fly, the circulation of blood in the frog's foot, the rotation of the protoplasm in a vegetable cell, and various other subjects which can in general only be observed by a skilled observer with a high-class microscope. The illumination employed seemed in most cases to be dark-ground illumination – that is, the centre beam of the light impinging on the stage of the microscope was cut out by an opaque disk placed below the condenser.

The most striking photograph, however, was one of a fresh-water hydra. This animal, which is always a fearsome-looking beast when seen under the microscope, looked positively dangerous when magnified on the screen to a size of some three feet across. He or she was surrounded by a swarm of infusoria and rotifers, and the general effect was most awe-inspiring. It is positively necessary to remind oneself that the real thing is too small to be seen by any but the sharpest unaided eye, and that the host of infusoria surrounding it and flying about in all directions are in actual life quite invisible.

DOI: 10.4324/9781003107835-130

Editorial Endnote

1 Edward VII's coronation in 1902 was not filmed directly. Méliès's film of the event was a reconstruction, produced by Charles Urban, who was also involved in the production of this film of microscopic organisms. The Delhi Durbar of 1903 was filmed directly but very briefly and incompletely.

Editorial Headnote

97. Anon. ['Cosmos'], 'Jottings', *British Journal of Photography* (1903)

The reviewer recognises the great potential of the new medium of moving film, both for scientific instruction and entertainment.

97

JOTTINGS

Anon. ['Cosmos'], British Journal of Photography

Source: Anon. ['Cosmos'], 'Jottings', *British Journal of Photography* 50:2260 (28 August 1903), p. 686.

I cordially congratulate my friend Mr. F. Martin Duncan, the worthy son of an eminent father,[1] on the fine reception which is accorded by Press and public to the series of micro-animatographs of the lower organisms recently presented at that popular place of amusement, the Alhambra Palace of Varieties, Leicester Square, London . . .

Before me as I write is an eight-paged catalogue of the studies in microscopy and animal and insect life, numbering over fifty, which Mr. Duncan and his co-adjutors have produced by means of micro-photography: that is, by the substitution of the microscope for the photographic lens in taking animated photographs of small objects. The series is appropriately classified as the 'Unseen World.' I am a little in doubt as to whether such subjects will permanently appeal to the tastes of the joyous and debonaire habitués of your modern music hall, but I have no qualms as to their enlisting and holding the deep attention of that large and growing intellectual class which seeks in its hours of recreation a combination of entertainment and instruction now less readily obtainable than in the days of the old Polytechnic, the Panopticon, and other mid-Victorian institutions[2] . . . It seems curious that we should have had to wait no less than six years before scientific animatography could be brought before the eyes of the general public. One often hears the remark that animated photographs have killed lantern slides. The process, however, has been a slow one and is not yet complete. It will not be until photographs of motion displace in the lecture room and entertainment hall the inadequate still representation of movement, which your lantern transparency obviously is.

It is in this direction, I think, that the splendid scientific work of Mr. Duncan will find its true acceptance and appreciation. Not all of us like music-halls . . . Moreover, popular scenes and events exhibited secondhand have long lost their attraction for me. But I would go miles to see moving representations of the vast, the illimitable, the glorious world of nature; nature, that is, as your true naturalist knows it, and I believe my feeling is shared by myriads of nature lovers throughout the world, members of literary, philosophical, and cognate societies. It is to

DOI: 10.4324/9781003107835-131

these that I think Mr. F.M. Duncan's work will strongly appeal. There are two other achievements which photography has yet to place before us in practical perfection, namely, animated photographs in colour, and stereoscopic photographs on the screen. When shall my cup of happiness be filled?

Editorial Endnotes

1 Francis Martin Duncan was a microscopist and photographer who created nature films for Urban's firm and wrote many popular books on natural history. His *First Steps in Photo-Micrography: A Handbook for Novices* was published in 1902. His father was the paleontologist and naturalist Peter Martin Duncan.

2 The Royal Polytechnic Institution in Regent's Street, London, staged exhibitions and held lectures 'for the advancement of the Arts and Practical Science'. The Royal Panopticon of Science and Art in Leicester Square had similar aims.

Editorial Headnote

97.1. Anon., 'Scientific Photography at the Music Halls', *British Journal of Photography* (1903)

This reviewer was also startled to find that lay audiences were receptive to the 'life histories' of minute creatures, revealed by moving film.

97.1

SCIENTIFIC PHOTOGRAPHY AT THE MUSIC HALLS

Anon., British Journal of Photography

Source: Anon., 'Scientific Photography at the Music Halls', *British Journal of Photography* 50:2262 (11 September 1903), p. 722.

If anyone, twenty years ago, say, had prophesied that a lantern exhibition of scientific photographic slides would be a musical hall 'turn,' and that of all such places in the world that home of the ballet, the Alhambra, would set the lead, his vaticination would have been received by a smile of derision. Yet – and whether the explanation be the better general education in scientific matters of the man in the street, or the inherent marvellousness of the show itself, we are unable to say – the fact remains that the microbioscope has been exhibited at the Alhambra, and instead of an interesting study of the motions of the highest expression of organised life – man, or woman – as displayed in the accustomed terpsichorean feats peculiar to the habitués of that hall,[1] the audience is attracted by the life history of some of the lower forms of minute life in functional activity, as shown in that wonderful instrument the microscope on an immensely magnified scale, sufficiently so as to be visible to a large audience. We can only express the hope that this may but be the beginning of a successful career for it on the music hall stage.

Editorial Endnote

1 The Alhambra normally staged dance shows.

DOI: 10.4324/9781003107835-132

FLYING ACROSS THE WIND.
BLACK-HEADED GULLS (WINTER PLUMAGE).

Figure 24 Oliver G. Pike, photograph of Black-headed Gulls from his book *Woodland, Field and Shore: Wild Nature Depicted with Pen and Camera* (London: Religious Tract Society, 1901), chapter 18, 'Nature on the Kent Coast'. (Biodiversity Heritage Library)

Editorial Headnote

97.2. Anon., 'Palace Theatre', *Times* (1907)

By this time, filming of animals in their natural habitats had become possible, and its techniques were developed by Oliver Gregory Pike. He was an early wildlife photographer like the Kearton brothers and G.M. Levick, specialising in birds (see Chapters 24–7 of the present work), and he graduated to filming in the early 1900s, becoming very successful and popular in this field. His action studies in still photographs like the study of flying gulls (Figure 24) underpinned this development.

97.2

PALACE THEATRE

Anon., Times

Source: Anon., 'Palace Theatre', *Times*, 30 August 1907, p. 10.

At the Palace Theatre yesterday afternoon there was a private view of a new bioscopic entertainment which is to be included in the programme of that house next week. The 'animated pictures' are illustrative of wild bird life, and have been taken by Mr. Oliver G. Pike and Mr. H. Armytage Sanders[1] in circumstances of no small difficulty, as some of the scenes exhibited testify. The camera has been adventurously taken over cliffs, where, hanging from ropes in the air between earth and water, its manipulators have surprised the sea birds in their lonely fastnesses, and shown us, as it were, their private and not always harmonious domestic life. Seldom at sea or seaside can such a near view of these wild birds be obtained as will now be had at the Palace Theatre with leisure enough to study the features and peculiarities of kittiwake, gannet, cormorant, puffin, and others. Not only an adventurous spirit, but no little patience and skill and special mechanical appliances have been necessary to obtain these representations. Mr. Pike yesterday explained that the construction of a camera which would work silently was one of the initial difficulties; but he and his colleague should be well rewarded by the results achieved and the warm interest displayed by the experimental audience.

Editorial Endnote

1 Henry Armytage Sanders subsequently became a war photographer.

DOI: 10.4324/9781003107835-133

INDEX

Note: Numbers in *italics* indicate a figure.

Milton Keynes UK
Ingram Content Group UK Ltd.
UKHW031328071224
451979UK00004B/27